D0984348

Tomboys

Tomboys

A Literary and Cultural History

MICHELLE ANN ABATE

TEMPLE UNIVERSITY PRESS
Philadelphia

Michelle Ann Abate is an Assistant Professor of English at Hollins University.

TEMPLE UNIVERSITY PRESS
1601 North Broad Street
Philadelphia PA 19122
www.temple.edu/tempress

⊛ The paper used in this publication meets the requirements of the American National Standard for Information Sciences—Permanence of Paper for Printed Library Materials, ANSI Z39.48-1992

Library of Congress Cataloging-in-Publication Data

Abate, Michelle Ann, 1975–
    Tomboys : a literary and cultural history / Michelle Ann Abate.
        p. cm.
    Includes bibliographical references and index.
    ISBN-13: 978-1-59213-722-0 (alk. paper)
    ISBN-10: 1-59213-722-9 (alk. paper)
    1. American fiction—19th century—History and criticism.   2. American fiction—20th century—History and criticism.   3. Sex role in literature.
4. Girls in literature.   5. Women in literature.   6. Sex role—United States—History.   7. Girls in motion pictures.   8. Women in motion pictures.
9. Sex role in motion pictures.   I. Title.
    PS374.S46A23 2008
    813'.3093522—dc22
    2007050234

090908P

Contents

Photographs follow page 144

Acknowledgments

Tomboys have been variously viewed as icons of feminist defiance, symbols of juvenile delinquency, and precursors of sexual deviance. These classifications have proved especially resonant, for the process of conceptualizing and completing this project routinely involved a wide range of defiant, delinquent and even deviant behavior, from the gender delinquency of my own tomboy childhood to my deviant absence at various social gatherings because I was busy researching and writing these pages. To all of those who have spent years living with, apologizing for and especially nurturing my various forms of aberrance, I send my love and gratitude.

To my partner and co-conspirator, Rachel MacKnight, I owe special thanks. Your boundless patience, kind criticism and thoughtful understanding provided the gentlest sounding board as I struggled to articulate these ideas. For your humor, intelligence, love and companionship, you will always be my first and best honorary tomboy.

I am indebted to many readers, colleagues and friends who have helped shape and sharpen these ideas along the way. First of all, to my committee at the City University of New York Graduate Center—David S. Reynolds, Wayne Koestenbaum and Marc Dolan—under whose direction this project began as my doctoral dissertation: the knowledge part of these Acknowledgments comes from each of you.

I would also like to thank Hollins University for its support of my project, as well as my colleagues there; I feel very fortunate to be in the company of such talented teachers and skilled scholars. I want to extend special gratitude to University librarians Joan Ruelle, Amanda Hurst, Renée McBride and Maryke Barber, who skillfully tracked down countless references and whose good cheer brightened many long days spent in front of my computer. I am also grateful to Lisa Marie O'Quinn for her skill and patience while photographing many of the tomboy objects and artifacts presented in this manuscript. Likewise, I am deeply appreciative of Emily Faye Jewett, whose diligence researching and obtaining copyright permissions for the use of these items, some obscure and decades old, saved me many headaches and hassles.

I wish to offer special thanks to several people who provided invaluable help with specific chapters: Pauline Kaldas, Kenneth Kidd and Rhonda Brock-Servais for their insightful readings of the Introduction; Kenneth Kidd, Katherine Capshaw Smith and several anonymous readers at the *Children's Literature Association Quarterly* for their engaged analysis of an article version of Chapter One; Anne K. Phillips and Christine Doyle, along with two anonymous reviewers for the Alcott-themed issue of *Children's Literature*, who provided many helpful comments on a journal essay about Chapter Two; Cheryl Fish for her wise and important feedback on Chapter Three; Rachel Adams for her wonderfully valuable comments about Chapter Seven; Eric Tribunella, who provided excellent pinpoint critiques of some of the material in Chapter Nine; Philip Nel, whose wisdom and encouragement came at a crucial point in the final stages of revision; and Mick Gusinde-Duffy along with the anonymous readers at Temple University Press, who offered support as well as many valuable suggestions about the manuscript.

Finally, to my grandmothers: Lorraine B. Hunt, who has looked forward to the publication of this book with great excitement and anticipation, and Emma Violet Schwelle (*1912–2000*), for whom this volume unfortunately comes too late. Through the brave examples of your lives, you have been my first and best teachers of delinquency. Thank you for your continued love, guidance and encouragement. You have shaped my life in more ways than you will ever know, and I dedicate these pages to you both.

Introduction: From Antebellum Hoyden to Millennial Girl Power

The Unwritten History (and Hidden History) of Tomboyism in the United States

In the second chapter of *Women and Economics*, Charlotte Perkins Gilman argued, "The most normal girl is the 'tom-boy'—whose numbers increase among us in these wiser days,—a healthy young creature, who is human through and through; not feminine till it is time to be" (29). By the time Gilman penned her famous meditation on gender and capitalism in 1898, tomboyism as both a cultural phenomenon and literary convention had become ubiquitous in the United States. As historian Frances Cogan has illustrated, an alternative and more physically active code of conduct emerged for women during the mid-nineteenth century. Dubbing this phenomenon "Real Womanhood," she argued, "This popular ideal advocated intelligence, physical fitness and health, self-sufficiency, economic self-reliance, and careful marriage . . ." (Cogan 4). Echoing these sentiments, Martha Banta has asserted that these behaviors helped establish a new paradigm of behavior for the American girl by the dawn of the twentieth century: the vigorous, athletic and even muscular "Outdoors Pal."

As tomboys emerged in American culture during the nineteenth century, they also became a fixture in its literature. Joining the ranks of literary icons like the "fallen woman" or the male "rake," boisterous female figures appeared in popular narratives like Elizabeth Stuart Phelps' *Gypsy Breynton* (1866) and Susan Coolidge's *What Katy Did* (1872). Most famous among these was Jo March from Louisa May Alcott's 1868 classic *Little Women*. The appeal of this topsy-turvy tomboy propelled *Little Women* to instant success upon its release and has helped it remain a favorite among young girls today.

As the nineteenth century turned into the twentieth, America's interest in and production of tomboys did not abate. Changes in the nation's social, political and even economic climate, in fact, facilitated the expansion of this figure. By the end of the First World War, women were voting, engaging in such formerly masculine activities as smoking and drinking, and even asserting their right to participate in the "male" world of work. Compared with young women only a generation before them, the entire sex had been "tomboy-ified."

As the number of tomboys increased in the early twentieth century, so did the variety of media in which these figures could be found. From the earliest days of commercial motion pictures in the United States, for instance, the tomboy appeared as a distinct screen persona. Films such as Wilfrid North's *Miss Tomboy and Freckles* (1914), Carl Harbaugh's *The Tomboy* (1921) and Edward Ludwig's *Some Tomboy* (1924) featured young women who engaged in such tomboyish actions as playing sports and climbing trees. Similarly, by the 1930s, gender-bending female figures were well-established on the stage, in productions like Charles George's musical *My Tomboy Girl* (1936), as well as in the recording studio, via tunes such as Red Norvo's hit song "Tomboy" (1934).

The outbreak of the Second World War and its accompanying transformation to female gender roles inspired a wave of films that featured gender-bending adult as well as adolescent figures, including George Stevens's *Woman of the Year* (1942), Henry Hathaway's *Home in Indiana* (1944) and Clarence Brown's *National Velvet* (1945). This phenomenon continued into to the postwar era, as tomboyism surfaced in an array of new and often unexpected cultural venues. In the late 1950s, for example, the *Li'l Tomboy* comic book series was launched and a tomboy-themed girlie magazine, humorously titled *International Tomboy: Around the World in 80 Dames*, appeared. During the 1960s, these items were joined by Ezell Helen Ingle's *Snips and Snails: Twelve Piano Solos for Boys and Tomboys*, along with various flavors of carbonated "Tomboy" soda from the Tom Joyce Company in Indianapolis, Indiana. By the end of this decade, tomboyism had become so prominent and pervasive that the mini-book *Kansas Tomboy*—which was a brief biography of aviatrix Amelia Earhart—was featured as a prize in boxes of Cracker Jack.

With the rise of second-wave feminism during the 1970s and early 1980s, gender-bending female figures became even more ubiquitous. The period saw the release of an array of feature-length films like Peter Bogdanovich's *Paper Moon* (1973), Michael Ritchie's *The Bad News Bears* (1976) and Norman Tokar's *Candleshoe* (1978) that each featured a tomboy character. Finally, during the 1990s, the rise of LGBTQ movement and the advent of queer theory gave tomboyism a new gendered look and cultural life. An array of lesbian-themed novels and films, including Fannie Flagg's best-selling book *Fried Green Tomatoes at the Whistle Stop Café* (1987) and Maria Maggenti's movie *The Incredibly True Adventure of Two Girls in Love* (1995), teemed with tomboyish characters.

In spite of both the long history and the strong presence of tomboyism in the United States, comparatively little work has been done on the subject. To date, no full-length study of the issue from a literary, cultural or psychological perspective has been published. Scholars seeking information about tomboys, in fact, will find no listing for the topic in the Library of Congress or, perhaps more shockingly, either *The Oxford Companion to Women's Writing* or *The Cambridge Guide to Children's Books in English*. In addition, seminal works on the history of women's gender roles and sexual identities omit tomboyism from their discussions. In *Disorderly Conduct*, for instance, Carroll Smith-Rosenberg discusses the emergence of the New Woman without mentioning her adolescent antecedent, the tomboy. Likewise, Lillian Faderman in *Surpassing the Love of Men* discusses the crystallization of lesbian identity during the early twentieth century without addressing the role that nineteenth-century tomboyism played in this process.

This book offers a long-overdue corrective to this trend. The chapters that follow present the beginnings of a literary and cultural history of tomboyism in the United States. Starting with the figure of the hoyden in the mid-nineteenth century and ending with the emergence of the "Girl Power" movement on the eve of millennium, I uncover the origins of tomboyism, chart its trajectory, and trace the literary and cultural transformations the concept has undergone in the United States. Opening with a discussion of when this code of conduct first made its appearance in the nation's literature and culture, I explore the root of the term "tomboy" and also outline the social, political and even economic circumstances that precipitated the idea's emergence at this particular point in history. Then, in each of the following nine chapters, I focus on a key literary or cinematic work to examine how alterations to women's gender roles, changing cultural conceptions of girlhood and shifts in national childrearing practices influenced the development of tomboyism. During this discussion, I address the eras in which this code of conduct was hailed as a sign of lively girlhood and a precursor to a life as a vigorous and vibrant adult woman; conversely, I explore the historical periods when tomboyism was reviled as a perversion of the physical and psychological traits of femininity and even a menacing index of proto-lesbianism. The final few chapters contemplate the current status of tomboyism in light of the impact of second-wave feminism, the LGBTQ movement and queer theory. Given that young women now commonly participate in many of the same activities as young men, I probe the form, or forms, that tomboyism takes today. Throughout each stage of this process, I expose unknown aspects of a cultural concept and literary phenomenon with which many may think they are already familiar. Indeed, tomboyism is commonly considered a monolithic phenomenon—with individuals making frequent reference to "the tomboy" as if this figure were both singular and static—but I demonstrate how it is an unstable and dynamic one, changing with the political, social and economic events of its historical era.

While *Tomboys* strives to unveil the previously uncharted literary and cultural history of tomboyism in the United States, it has a second and equally important goal: to expose the hidden history of this code of conduct as a racialized construct. During an era in which the health of middle- and upper-class young white women had become imperiled from equating femininity with frailty, tomboyism emerged as an antidote. Calling for sensible clothing, physical exercise and a wholesome diet, this code of conduct was designed to improve the strength and stamina of the nation's future wives and mothers and, by extension, the offspring that they produced. In this way, tomboyism was more than simply a new childrearing practice or gender expression for the nation's adolescent girls; it was a eugenic practice or, at least, a means to help ensure white racial supremacy. In living this lifestyle, tomboys disrupted the rigid dichotomy separating "good" and "bad" female conduct that Lynne Vallone and other critics have identified as a defining feature of Anglo-American girlhood.[1] From their inception, tomboys demonstrated how unruly female behavior that was formerly seen as socially "bad" could be racially good.

In a compelling paradox, however, this code of conduct that was intended to strengthen white women and, by extension, the white race was consistently yoked with various forms of nonwhiteness. Authors repeatedly described ostensibly Caucasian tomboys with "brown" skin tones and "dark" physical features. Jo March in Louisa May Alcott's *Little Women*, for instance, possesses a "brown" complexion and a "dark mane" of chestnut hair. In addition, because of the proclivity for tomboys to engage in rambunctious outdoor play, writers often linked them with such racially charged traits as being "wild" and "uncivilized." Characters throughout E. D. E. N. Southworth's *The Hidden Hand*, for instance, call the tomboyish central figure an "impertinent monkey" and even a "ridiculous little ape" (36) because of her gender-bending ways.

Going far beyond the trope of the dark-haired tomboy and her fair and feminine foil, *Tomboys* probes the possible historical, literary and cultural reasons why these ostensibly Caucasian figures are, to echo the title of a book by Werner Sollors, "neither black nor white yet both." Building on the observation that both syllables of the term "tomboy" evoke common racial pejoratives, I demonstrate how these figures do more than simply exist on

---

1. For more information on this binary, see Lynne Vallone's *Disciplines of Virtue: Girls' Culture in the Eighteenth and Nineteenth Centuries* (New Haven: Yale UP, 1995).

the boundaries between male and female, adult and child, heterosexual and homosexual, masculine and feminine; they also occupy a liminal position between blackness and whiteness. Drawing on such elements as blackface minstrelsy, modernist white fantasies about primitivism, and the racialized language of white feminism, this volume considers the way in which tomboyishness and blackness mutually construct or at least reinforce each other throughout these periods. White tomboys have long had a reputation for climbing trees and throwing softballs; this book demonstrates that they also have a hidden history—to reference Toni Morrison's well-known concept—of "playing in the dark."

Tomboyism as a Concept and a Cultural Phenomenon in the United States

"'You see . . . That's the surprise. I'm a girl. But now I'm a boy too and I can do anything and anything and anything.'" So remarks the bold and beautiful heroine in Ernest Hemingway's posthumously published novel *The Garden of Eden*. Although the gender-bending Catherine utters these remarks in response to cropping her hair, they could serve as the motto for tomboys in U.S. literature and culture. From their inception, tomboyish characters and their accompanying behaviors have been linked with such elements as social surprise, gender duplicity and unlimited possibility.

Although the rise of feminism and the advent of queer theory make tomboyism seem like a relatively contemporary phenomenon, the concept actually originated in the sixteenth century. Interestingly, the term "tomboy" initially referred to rowdy gentlemen courtiers rather than boisterous young women. The first listing in the *Oxford English Dictionary* defines "tomboy" as "A rude, boisterous or forward boy" and gives the following textual example from 1553: "Is all your delite and joy in whiskying and romping abroad like a Tom boy?" (211). Not until several decades later, in the 1570s, did the term shift from characterizing spunky young men to likeminded individuals of the opposite gender. Tomboyism acquired newfound sexual associations and age coordinates when it was applied to boisterous girls instead of boys. As the *Oxford English Dictionary* notes, unlike the innocently playful connotations the term possessed when it referred to an actual boy, a tomboy now began to signify a "bold and immodest woman" (211). Finally, in the late 1590s and early 1600s, the term underwent a third transformation, morphing into its current usage: "a girl who behaves like a spirited or boisterous boy; a wild romping girl; a hoyden" (*OED* 212).

The etymology of the word "tomboy," however, cannot cease with a mere consideration of the gender-bending origins of the term itself. In addition to an awareness of the way in which tomboys began as literal boys, attention must also be paid to the rich and varied meanings of the term "tom," for at least some of the multiplicity inherent in the word "tomboy" can be traced to this loaded prefix. Forming a possible explanation for the historical connection of tomboys with immodest women, one of the most common slang meanings for a "tom" is a prostitute (*OED* 207). However, the prefix has also been used to connote everything from male sexual predators (tom cats) and clowns (tomfools) to lesbians (tommy girls) (*OED* 207–210). As Mary Elliott has pointed out, the cultural richness of the prefix "tom" causes tomboyism to have "more complexity . . . than is commonly supposed" (*Closet* 5). Embedded within its reference to boisterous young women, the term fuses "notions of masculinity, promiscuous sexuality, prostitution, and lesbianism together in various configurations" (*Closet* 5).

While tomboyism as both a concept and a cultural phenomenon may date back to the Renaissance Era in England, it did not become prevalent in the United States until nearly three hundred years later. Adolescent girls and adult women who engaged in behavior that could be characterized as tomboyish, however, certainly existed in American literature and culture prior to this period. From the hearty women who traversed the Atlantic for a new life in the colonies during the sixteenth century to those who moved Westward during the early days of the republic, strong, gender-defiant women have been a longstanding hallmark of the United States. Nevertheless, these individuals neither considered themselves nor were labeled by others as "tomboys." The term, along with its underlying premise that physically active women constituted their own distinct category of identity, is simply absent in writings from early America.

If such bold and daring female figures were called anything, in fact, it was "hoyden," a word which is commonly—although somewhat problematically—seen as a synonym or precursor to "tomboy." First appearing in the late sixteenth century, the term shares a similar etymological history: it also initially referred to rambunctious boys and men rather than girls and women. Indeed, the *Oxford English Dictionary* provides the following definition for "hoyden": "A rude, ignorant, or awkward fellow; a clown, boor" (457). By the late seventeenth century, however, this meaning shifted and the word began referring to like-minded members of the opposite sex: "A rude, or ill-bred girl (or woman): a boisterous noisy girl, a romp" (*OED* 457). Unlike a tomboy, a hoyden was more closely associated with breaching bourgeois mores than female gender roles. As the *OED* notes, a hoyden "calls people by their surnames," is "ungainly in her Behaviour" and is "slatternly ignorant" (457). When the concept of "tomboy" made its debut during the mid-nineteenth century, it supplanted "hoyden." After 1876, in fact, the *OED* includes no new definitions of, or textual referents to, this term.

While "tomboy" may have eclipsed "hoyden," it also expanded on it, for this new code of conduct crystallized around a different set of cultural anxieties and served a vastly different societal purpose. Emerging in the mid-nineteenth century as a product of growing concerns over the deplorable state of health among middle- and upper-class white women, tomboyism was designed as an alternative. Not surprisingly, given this purpose, narratives that were intended for a largely female readership, featured young girls as protagonists and were written by women were among the first to feature tomboys. Louisa May Alcott's *Little Women* (1868), Elizabeth Stuart's Phelps *Gypsy Breynton* series (1866–1867) and Susan Coolidge's *What Katy Did* (1872) form some of the most poignant examples. As tomboyism grew in cultural popularity, gender-bending female figures began to appear in narratives that fell outside of this realm. Soon, tomboys became fixtures in adventure novels about the "Wild West" that were geared for boys. From Prentiss Ingraham's *Crimson Kate, the Girl Trailer* (1881) to Edward Wheeler's Deadwood Dick/Calamity Jane series (1877–1885), a rootin'-tootin' tomboy who roped, rode and 'rangled became a stock character.

Before long, tomboyish figures began to surface in texts that were written for an adult audience. Henry James, with his interest in exploring national social types, for example, depicted tomboyish figures. In his 1878 novel *Watch and Ward*, Hubert Lawrence is dismayed by the gender-bending nature of his cousin's twelve-year-old ward, Nora Lambert. As he candidly tells Roger one evening about the dependent child, "'I can't think of her as a girl . . . she seems to me a boy. She climbs trees, she scales fences, she keeps rabbits, she straddles upon your old mare, bare-backed. I found her this morning wading in the pond up to her knees'" (25).

In light of this increased presence of gender-bending female characters, the late nineteenth and early twentieth centuries are often identified as the heyday of tomboy narratives in the United States. More specifically, both Christian McEwan and Elizabeth Segel have identified the years from the end of the Civil War to the middle of the Depression Era as the "golden era" of literary tomboyism. Commencing with the publication of Elizabeth Stuart Phelps's *Gypsy Breynton* in 1866 and extending to the appearance of Ruth Sawyer's Newbery Award-winning book *Roller Skates* in 1936, this period includes such classic tomboy narratives as Kate Douglas Wiggin's *Rebecca of Sunnybrook Farm* (1903), Carol Ryrie Brink's *Caddie Wood-lawn* (1935) and Laura Ingalls Wilder's *Little House* books (1932–1943).

In spite of the seemingly monolithic classification of "tomboy novel," the representation of this code of conduct can vary greatly. Indeed, as Lynne Yamaguchi and Karen Barber have written, the term "tomboy" may connote "a virtually uniform picture of a girl who—by whatever standards society has dictated—acts like a boy," but how one defines a "transgression into boys' territory" differs for every individual (10). "For some girls, it is in excelling in—or even just playing—sports; for others, it's as simple an act as biking to the creek to catch frogs. Still other girls cross the gender line by preferring math to English, science to history, shop to home ec[onomics]" (Yamaguchi and Barber 10). This detail is especially important when considering tomboys who possess different coordinates of identity: who hail from different historical eras, live in different geographic regions, belong to different racial or ethnic groups or inhabit different socio-economic classes. For instance, wearing bloomers may have been the epitome of tomboyish daring during the nineteenth century, but that is no longer the case today. Similarly, working outside the home is often seen as the apogee of tomboyish independence for wealthy women, but it is a basic fact of life for their working class counterparts. Finally, plowing the fields, baling hay or herding livestock might seem acutely tomboyish for many urban girls, but it constitutes a common chore for those who live on a farm or ranch. Given the way in which the construction of tomboyism is contingent upon a complex constellation of factors, the term has encompassed a wide range of sometimes complementary but often competing traits. Indeed, it is precisely the fluidity inherent within this code of conduct that causes tomboyism to have a rich and multivalent history.

These details notwithstanding, in the years since the term "tomboy" made its debut in U.S. literature and culture, a number of common or defining characteristics have emerged. In many ways, in fact, tomboyism "seems to be so familiar a concept in contemporary North American culture that it needs no definition" (Yamaguchi and Barber 10). The traits most Americans are likely to name as constitutive of this code of conduct include a proclivity for outdoor play (especially athletics), a feisty independent spirit, and a tendency to don masculine clothing and adopt a boyish nickname. By the late twentieth century, such elements had become so culturally codified that a group of psychologists articulated what they called a twelve-point "Tomboy Index." In a 1996 article, Shawn Meghan Burn, A. Kathleen O'Neil, and Shirley Nederend deemed the following behaviors unmistakable indicators of tomboyism: (1) preferring shorts and jeans to dresses; (2) preferring traditional boys' toys (e.g., guns, matchbox cars) over girls' toys (e.g., dolls); (3) resembling a boy in appearance; (4) wishing to be a boy; (5) preferring traditionally boys' activities (e.g., climbing trees, playing army) over traditionally girls' activities (e.g., ballet, playing dress-up); (6) having girl friends that are tomboys; (7) participating in traditionally male sports (e.g., football, baseball, basketball) with boys; (8) engaging in loud or boisterous play with others; (9) preferring to play with boys over girls; (10) using traditionally girls' toys in stereotypically boys' activities (e.g., Barbie driving a Tonka truck); (11) engaging in rough and tumble play; and (12) playing with many different peer groups (e.g., tomboys, non-tomboys, boys) (Burn, O'Neil and Nederend 422).

Although these characteristics may encapsulate the general nature of many tomboys, they are by no means exhaustive. To the twelve-point Index devised by Burns et al., the tendency for tomboys to form close relationships with effeminate male characters could be added. More often than not, a tomboy's closest friend is a "sissy" boy rather than another tough girl. Countless tomboy narratives—written by men and women, featuring both masculine and feminine tomboys and intended for both child and adult audiences—contain this dyad, including Scout and Dill in Harper Lee's *To Kill a Mockingbird* (1960), Tommy Shirley and Jay Harper in Willa Cather's "Tommy, the Unsentimental" (1896) and Frankie Addams and her cousin John Henry West in Carson McCullers' *The Member of the Wedding* (1946).[2]

While such an intimate relationship between members of the opposite sex—and especially those who are not blood relatives—would likely arouse suspicion for more feminine girls or masculine boys, the union between a tomboy and a sissy generally poses no threat.[3] Since these figures exist outside of conventional gender roles, their relationship also exists outside of conventional sexual ones. As Lee Zevy notes, contrary to the sexually charged prefix "tom," "Tomboys have always been treated as an asexual entity, a time of cuteness" (186). Foreshadowing contemporary queer interpretations of tomboys as proto-lesbians and sissies as proto-gay men, their friendship does not contain an erotic charge. In addition to destabilizing gender codes, therefore, the tomboy/sissy dyad also disrupts heteronormative ones.

In an interesting but often-overlooked detail, tomboys and sissies may defy the boundaries between heterosexuality and homosexuality, but they often reinforce the ones between masculinity and femininity. Contrary to expectations, these figures frequently police each other's gender transgressions rather than serving as company in which to safely display them. In numerous nineteenth- and twentieth-century narratives, tomboys often help masculinize effeminate boys: they teach their weak counterparts to be adventurous, assert themselves and even fight. By the close of the novel, the previously sissy boy has been transformed by his tomboy friend into a strong and even powerful man. In Louisa May Alcott's *Little Women*, for

---

2. To this list, the following could be added: Becky Sleeper and her brother Teddy in George M. Backer's *Running to Waste: The Story of a Tomboy* (1874), Hellfire Hotchkiss and Thug Carpenter in Mark Twain's "Hellfire Hotchkiss" (written 1897), Charlotte Laborde and Gus Bradley in Kate Chopin's short story "Charlie" (written 1900), Georgiana Isham and a French Baron in Phyllis Duganne and Harriet Gersman's short story "Tomboy!" (1928), Kerry and Mick in Hal Ellson's *Tomboy* (1950), Francie Lou Babcock and Russell Carson in Allyn Allen's *Lone Star Tomboy* (1951) and Gabrielle "Gabby" Lucette and her twin brother Adrian in Barbara Clayton's *Tomboy* (1961).

3. As I will discuss in more detail later, this is only true for pre-pubescent tomboys. Once gender-bending young girls reach puberty, their association with even effeminate males becomes suspect. In Mark Twain's "Hellfire Hotchkiss," for instance, the fifteen-year-old title character's close associations with young men arouse suspicions about her possible promiscuity. As her Aunt Betsy informs her, rumors have started to circulate: "'You always preferred to play with the boys. Well, that's all right, up to a certain limit; but you've gone way beyond the limit. You ought to have stopped long ago—oh, long ago'" (198).

instance, Jo is instrumental in reforming the effete Laurie Laurence into an upstanding citizen, honorable gentleman and good husband for her sister, Amy. Similarly, in Allen Allyn's *Lone Star Tomboy*, Francie Lou Carter tells her effeminate cousin, "'You better stick around me, Russell. I'll show you how to stand up to boys'" (Allen 158). By the end of the novel, the formerly weak boy has become so tough that he has joined a bastion of masculinity: the military academy.

Interestingly, however, this pattern is rarely reversed: sissies hardly ever feminize tomboys. As Mary Elliott has written, "Even when tomboys pair off with reformed male sissies, they are tempered not by these flawed boys but through the historically constant presence of gender and heterosexual pressure" (11). As a result, sissies often drop out of tomboy narratives, becoming "spent characters" who after a certain point "have nothing further to contribute" (Elliott 110).

Coupled with a tomboy's important friendship with a sissy, she is characterized by another key relationship or, rather, the lack thereof: one with her mother. Countless nineteenth- and twentieth-century narratives present tomboy characters who have been orphaned or otherwise lack a maternal influence in their lives. The mothers of Nancy Vawse in Susan Warner's *The Wide, Wide World* (1850), Frankie Addams in Carson McCullers's *The Member of the Wedding* (1946) and "Scout" Finch in Harper Lee's *To Kill a Mockingbird* (1960) passed away when they were young.[4] Meanwhile, the mothers of Capitola Black in E. D. E. N. Southworth's *The Hidden Hand* (1859) and the title character in Kate Douglas Wiggin's *Rebecca of Sunnybrook Farm* (1903) were compelled to give up their daughters or send them away. During the latter half of the twentieth century, rising divorce rates, coupled with increasing numbers of women working outside the home, only added to this phenomenon. Now, the mothers of many tomboys were not physically missing but emotionally absent. Throughout Carson McCullers's *The Heart is a Lonely Hunter* (1940), for instance, twelve-year-old Mick Kelly disappears for hours and her mother—who is distracted by the demands of her large family, numerous boarders and disabled husband who is unable to work—does not even seem to notice: "After breakfast, Mick took the kids out and except for meals they were gone for most of the day. A good deal of the time they just roamed the streets . . . end[ing] up in a place they did not recognize" (McCullers *Heart* 82).

---

4. Once again, this list is far from exhaustive. To it, the following could be added: Nora Lambert in Henry James's *Watch and Ward* (1878), Nan Prince in Sarah Orne Jewett's *A Country Doctor* (1884), Charlotte Laborde in Kate Chopin's "Charlie" (written 1900), Rena Morgan in Amy E. Blanchard's *A Little Tomboy* (1903), Hila "Hi" Dart in Mary E. Mumford's *A Regular Tomboy* (1913), Antoinette "Tony" Porter in Lilian Garis's *Ted and Tony: Two Girls of Today* (1929) and Sarah Brown in Bryan Forbes's film *International Velvet* (1978).

Whether the absence of a mother stems from a physical or psychological source, it is seen as the cause or impetus for tomboyism in many narratives. As Louise Westling has argued, "Without mothers, these female protagonists define themselves most comfortably in masculine terms" (155). Provided with only a male role model in the form of their father, they too become masculine. In Harper Lee's *To Kill a Mockingbird*, for instance, the sister of Atticus Finch frequently makes this insinuation in relation to her tomboyish niece, Scout. In the second part of the novel, in fact, she even comes to live with her brother's family, at least in part so that young Jean Louise will have "some feminine influence" (127).

Motherlessness—and the tomboyism that emerges from it—need not be seen in such pathological ways, however. Akin to other characters who are disconnected from family roots (Mark Twain's Huck Finn and Theodore Dreiser's Sister Carrie come to mind), this phenomenon can be beneficial. In the words of Mary Elliot, "The presence of the orphaned tomboy in the narratives creates an orphaned space in the ideological fabric of the narrative as well, freeing it temporarily from its overarching didactic purpose" (10). Without mothers to indoctrinate them in women's traditional gender roles, they are able to define these elements for themselves.

In spite of the libratory potential and personal benefits of tomboyism, it is not often seen as a lifelong identity. As Sharon O'Brien notes, this code of conduct is most frequently cast as "a very common phase through which little girls would pass on their way to the safe harbor of domestic femininity" ("Tomboyism" 354). Although the nation may value strength, independence and assertiveness in young girls, it does not esteem such qualities in adult women. As a result, within a few decades after the emergence of tomboyism, a new phenomenon was created, commonly dubbed "tomboy taming." Young girls were now expected to slough off tomboyish traits when they reached a specific age or stage of life: usually, the beginning of adolescence or the onset of puberty. In the opening pages of Louisa May Alcott's *Little Women*, for instance, Meg admonishes her tomboyish younger sister: "'You are old enough to leave off boyish tricks and behave better, Josephine. It didn't matter so much when you were a little girl; but now you are so tall, and turn up your hair, you should remember that you are a young lady'" (3). Likewise, in Ruth Langland Holberg's *Tomboy Row* (1952), the father of the title character announces, "'It is high time that a big ten-year-old girl stopped acting like a tomboy'" (34). Finally, in Norma Klein's *Tomboy* (1978), taming is precipitated by the onset of menses. When the central character Antonia "Toe" Henderson thinks about menstruating, she wonders, "How could you be a tomboy at all if you could have a baby?" (34).

As these comments indicate, by far the most compelling reason for young women to abandon tomboyish behavior was pressure to get married and become a mother. Indeed, while tomboy narratives are often seen as critiquing women's traditional gender roles, many eventually capitulate to them. From Jo March's much-lamented marriage to Professor Bhaer to Laura Ingall's union with Almanzo, numerous narratives conclude with the all-too-familiar trope of wedding bells and baby cries.

If a tomboyish character was too young for wedlock or the author did not wish to engage in a conventional marriage plot, another popular method for eliminating gender-bending behavior was a life-threatening illness or injury. Susan Coolidge's *What Katy Did* (1872) largely established the paradigm. In the opening chapters of the novel, twelve-year-old Katy Carr "tore her dress every day, hated sewing, and didn't care a button about being 'good'" (9). But, as Elizabeth Segel notes, the punishment for her gender disobedience "is an injury to her back that keeps her bedridden and in pain for four years" ("Tomboy" 54). Katy's invalidism provides instruction in "'God's School,' the School of Pain, with its lessons of Patience, Cheerfulness, and Making the Best of Things" (Coolidge 54). By the time her injury heals, the young girl has sloughed off her tomboyish independence.

A final common paradigm for tomboy taming, especially in narratives written for children, was the relocation of a gender-bending character to a strict boarding school or the home of urban relatives. In Allyn Allen's *Lone Star Tomboy*, Francie Lou is taken away from the family's ranch and sent to live with relatives in San Antonio, where she quickly discovers that city children behave quite differently: "The girls walked more quietly, talking in much softer voices. And Francie Lou made up her mind to be like them, and not ever to forget and shout and yell like she and [her brother] Grayson did outdoors at the ranch. She did not want the people here to call her a tomboy" (153). Laura Ingalls has a similar experience while attending the town school in the sixth book of the *Little House* series, *The Long Winter* (1940). When the active tomboy leaps up to catch a ball at recess, the other children ridicule her gender inappropriate action. Laura, who was formerly so proud of her strength and agility, now ruminates: "She did not know why she had done such a thing and she was *ashamed, fearful of what these girls might think of her*" [my italics] (78).

The process of taming tomboys, however, is not a universal or inevitable phenomenon. Some gender-bending female characters not only retain their tomboyishness but see it as an important facet of their adult personality. In Miriam Parker Betts's *Tomboy Teacher*, for instance, Nancy Adams asserts that her gender-bending ways make her a better educator: "'I romp with my pupils; and I despise paper work. I can't get it done because I stop to bother about each child, as more than a mere name on a card'" (Betts 47–48). Similarly, in Ruth Langland Holberg's *Tomboy Row* (1952), the parents of the title character, Rowena "Row" Carey, abandon their crusade to feminize their gender-bending daughter once they realize the healthful benefits of her active lifestyle. When Rowena attempts to please her parents by giving up baseball and starting ballet lessons, her physician father is appalled by the slim, pale and frail appearance of these more feminine girls: "'Listen, honey. Maybe you have to play ball and do all the things I have been trying to make you stop doing. Your form of activity is better for you than dancing. I can see now'" (146).

Anxiety about the persistence of childhood tomboyism into adulthood, however, was not limited to concerns over women's future reproductive health or feminine gender identity. The advent of sexology and growing popularity of Freudian theory during the late nineteenth century introduced worries about the sexuality of such girls. Many began to worry that it was only a matter of time until tomboyish figures who were dressing and romping like boys would begin loving and even lusting like them. As a result, tomboyism went from being seen as an effective preparatory stage for marriage and motherhood to a potential breeding ground for lesbianism. Indeed, as Judith Halberstam argues, "There is always the dread possibility . . . that the tomboy will not grow out of her butch stage and will never become a member of the wedding" ("Bondage" 175).

Willa Cather's short story "Tommy, the Unsentimental" (1896) presents one of the earliest but also most vivid illustrations of such fears. Near the middle of the narrative, the title character who looked "scarcely girlish" and "had the lank figure of an active half-grown lad" (473), brings home "a girl she had grown fond of at school, a faint, white, languid bit of a thing, who used violet perfumes and carried a sunshade" (476). Echoing the growing link between tomboyism and lesbianism during this era, a group of men in town remark, "[I]t was a bad sign when a rebellious girl like Tommy took to being sweet and gentle to one of her own sex, the worst sign in the world" (476).

The rise of the LGBTQ movement and the emergence of queer theory during the second half of the twentieth century strengthened this connection. In pulp novels from the 1950s and early 1960s, for instance, any female character who was even remotely tomboyish was also, ultimately, a lesbian. In Vin Packer's *Spring Fire* (1952), for instance, central character Susan Mitchell—who falls in love with her sorority sister soon after arriving at college—is such a talented athlete that some of her classmates characterize her as a "muscle-bound Amazon" who is "built like a barn" (4, 58). Similarly, in Paula Christian's *The Other Side of Desire* (1965), Carrie Anderson—a suburban housewife who becomes involved with another woman—has a penchant for wearing "boy's shirts and slacks" (17). Finally, in Patricia Highsmith's *The Price of Salt* (1952), the sexually aggressive Abby is described as behaving "like a tomboy" when she was young (173).

By the 1990s, the association of tomboyism with lesbianism had become so pervasive that many began to see this code of conduct as a firm indicator of, or at least an adolescent precursor to, homosexuality. An anthology edited by Lynne Yamaguchi and Karen Barber and released by the lesbian press Allyson Books, for instance, bore the suggestive title, *Tomboys!: Tales of Dyke Derring-Do* (1995). Echoing this matter-of-fact association of tomboyism with lesbianism, an array of films were released in the 1990s that featured a lesbian main character who possessed an unmistakably tomboyish identity. Through figures such as Randall "Randy" Dean in Maria Maggenti's film, *The Incredibly True Adventure of Two Girls in Love* (1995), and the tough title character of Rachel Talalay's *Tank Girl* (1995), tomboyism and lesbianism became strongly aligned if not practically synonymous.

Although tomboyism was created in the mid-nineteenth century by white women for white women as a means to bolster and strengthen whiteness, this gradually changed. In the same way that tomboyish young women can be found in nearly every period, genre and phase of U.S. literature and culture, so too can they be located in nearly all of the nation's racial and ethnic groups. As *Completely Queer: The Gay and Lesbian Encyclopedia* asserts, "Tomboy identities cross racial, ethnic, class and regional lines with only slight variation" (Hogan and Hudson 543). In fact, the first full-length novel published by an African American woman, Harriet Wilson's 1859 *Our Nig*, showcases a tomboyish heroine who plays school pranks, daringly walks across rooftops and even cuts her hair short. In addition, Sui Sin Far's collection of Chinese American folktales, *Mrs. Spring Fragrance* (1912), contains several narratives that showcase gender-defiant female characters. In "The Smuggling to Tie Co.," for instance, a young girl dresses as a boy in order to make a border crossing. Similarly, in "Tian Shan's Kindred Spirit," a brave young woman is disguised as a man so she can be smuggled into China. Finally, Zitkala-Sa's *American Indian Stories* (1921) contains several tales that operate along the lines of tomboyishness. Most famous among these perhaps is the appropriately named "A Warrior's Daughter," in which a brave young woman infiltrates an enemy camp to rescue her beloved.

Contemporary writers of color, especially women writers, continue this tradition. Numerous novels released in recent years by African American, Latino/a and Asian American authors contain gender-rebellious female figures that can be placed on the spectrum of tomboyish behavior. Of these, the central characters in Maxine Hong Kingston's *The Woman Warrior* (1975), Jamaica Kincaid's *Annie John* (1982) and Sandra Cisneros's *The House on Mango Street* (1984) are perhaps the most well known. In the same ways that factors such as geographic region, historical time period and socio-economic class impact the construction of this code of conduct, so does racial and ethnic identity. Together with being excluded from prevailing definitions of (white) womanhood by their racial and cultural heritage, these gender-bending female figures are being reared in environments that contain differing conceptions of femininity and masculinity. In

Jamaica Kincaid's well-known narrative "Girl," for instance, the speaker's directives about women's proper conduct include instructions about "how to catch a fish," "how to bully a man," and "how to spit up in the air if you feel like it" (29), activities that would all be considered tomboyish for their Anglo-American counterparts, especially from the middle and upper classes. In this way, nonwhite and especially non-Western gender-bending figures exemplify the way in which tomboyism is culturally situated, culturally specific and—perhaps most importantly—culturally relative.

In recent years, tomboyism has undergone a conceptual crisis and even critical reconfiguration. By the latter decades of the twentieth century, the rise of the second-wave feminist movement and accompanying expansion of women's gender roles caused many to wonder if it was an antiquated category. In Norma Klein's 1978 novel *Tomboy*, for instance, the mother of Antonia "Toe" Henderson argues that the concept of tomboyism assumes "'there's a certain way girls should act and a certain way boys should act. That's so old-fashioned!'" (16). For these reasons, she asserts, "'there's no such thing as a tomboy'" (16). As these comments suggest, the gradual erosion of essentialist views of gender called into question both the contemporary importance and even modern-day relevance of the term "tomboy." Given that it is now routine for girls to wear pants, play sports and have short hair, it would seem that nearly all contemporary young women could be placed on the spectrum of tomboyishness. As Judith Halberstam has observed, "it has become almost commonplace nowadays for at least middle-class parents to point to their frisky girl children and remark proudly upon their tomboy natures" ("Bondage" 159).

Although this "normalization" of tomboyism is a seemingly positive and even beneficial phenomenon, it has had several harmful effects. Rather than helping to remove the taboos associated with gender-defiant behavior, deeming a certain form of tomboyishness more "natural" or "normative" causes alternative forms to face increased stigmatization. When such behavior becomes associated with what Halberstam dubs "preadult female masculinity" ("Bondage" 160), societal tolerance for it changes. The moment that gender rebellious girls insist on wearing only boy's clothes, adopting a boy's identity, or refusing to relinquish their tomboyism at puberty, they are punished and—with the advent of Gender Identity Disorder—even pathologized. In the wake of GID, such girls became subjected not simply to peer ridicule or parental disapproval, but to gender reorientation counseling, aversion therapy and even institutionalization.

In spite of this often negative reconceptualization, tomboyism continues to be both a powerful concept and a pervasive cultural phenomenon in the United States. Although modified by the impact of feminism and the advent of queer theory, tomboys have not disappeared from American literature and culture, and it does not appear that they will do so any time soon. Gender-bending female figures have been the subject of songs by an eclectic collection of musical groups, including The Beach Boys, who recorded a single titled "Hey Little Tomboy" for their 1978 *M.I.U. Album*; Crosby, Stills and Nash, whose "Tomboy" appeared on their 1990 *Live It Up* compilation; and folk singer Tret Fure, whose story song "Tomboy Girl" appeared on her 1999 *Radio Quiet* album with Cris Williamson. As the millennium approached, the popular and material representation of tomboyism became even more diverse. From the debut of Tomboy Red lager beer by a microbrewery in Detroit to the unveiling of the "Pretty Tomboy" online clothing store, this code of conduct was no longer simply a literary trope or form of childrearing. It had become a national brand name, recognizable icon and even marketable commodity.

Coupled with maintaining a strong presence in U.S. culture, tomboyism remains a fixture in its literature as well. Gender-bending female characters continue to be featured in an array of recent children's novels, such as Jerry Spinelli's *Who Put that Hair in my Toothbrush?* (1984), Cynthia Voight's *Jackaroo* (1985) and Pam Muñoz Ryan's *Riding Freedom* (1998). Similarly, the burgeoning field of lesbian-themed literature and film, including such classic literary works as Rita Mae Brown's *Rubyfruit Jungle* (1973) and Fannie Flagg's *Fried Green Tomatoes at the Whistle Stop Café* (1987), along with 1990s cinematic releases like Marita Giovanni's *Bar Girls* (1995) or the Wachowski Brothers' *Bound* (1996), showcase gender-bending young women who can be placed on the spectrum of tomboyishness.

Tomboyism and Shifting Racial Identities

Tomboys are commonly seen as figures who critique women's gender roles, but a closer examination of their presentation in American literature and culture suggests another possibility. Especially in works created by white female authors or intended for a largely white female audience, the ambiguity of the tomboy's gender mirrors the ambiguity of her purported Caucasian identity.

As Richard Dyer has aptly observed, "Race . . . is never not a factor, never not in play" in the United States (1). Although the importance of race may remain a constant in the United States, the same cannot be said for the way in which it is determined or defined. Anne McClintock has written that in the last decades of the nineteenth century alone "the term 'race' was used in shifting and unstable ways, sometimes as synonymous with 'species,' sometimes with 'culture,' sometimes with 'nation,' sometimes to denote biological ethnicity or sub-groups within national groupings" (52). Moreover, Michael Omi and Howard A. Winant have discussed how the classifying criteria for race grew increasingly more complex as the twentieth century progressed. As an ideological concept that is contingent on specific times, places and situations, it has never had a stable definition or universal meaning.

In the same way that the criteria used to determine race has changed over time, so too has the racial status of various demographic groups. Individuals who are classified under a certain racial category in one historical era may find themselves categorized differently during a later period. Although numerous examples of such shifts or what Susan Gubar has termed "racechanges" permeate U.S. history, the most pertinent to the chapters that follow are those that concern Caucasians. Perry Curtis and, more recently, Matthew Jacobson have discussed that groups like the Irish and the Jews, who were commonly designated as racial and ethnic Others, experienced a change in their racial classification and gained Caucasian status.[5]

While building on the fractures, fissures and instabilities within whiteness that are highlighted by racechanges among the Irish and the Jews, this volume is concerned with the opposite phenomenon. Rather than charting the process by which a formerly nonwhite group was able to become white over time, the chapters that follow examine the way in which previously Caucasian individuals became associated with various elements of nonwhiteness. Characterized with "brown" skin tones, associated with "dark" features and affiliated with other nonwhite racial and ethnic minorities, these figures were not only distanced from, but even seemed to have disavowed, their purported racial heritage.

Although what I am calling this "hidden history" of white tomboyism has not been discussed before, it does not constitute the first time that Caucasian figures have been presented in ways that place them in dialogue with nonwhite minority groups. Throughout the nineteenth and twentieth centuries, an array of ostensibly white men and especially women had a contested connection with their purported racial identity. As Sander Gilman has discussed, for instance, Victorian England forged an array of connections between white prostitutes and Sartje Baartman, the so-called Hottentot Venus. Although these figures had radically different racial, national and cultural identities, both were seen as possessing the same primitivistic sexual urges and atavistic genitalia.[6] Anne McClintock has documented a similar event involving white female coal miners during the nineteenth century. Because of their "primitive" association with dirt

---

5. See Perry Curtis's *Apes and Angels: The Irishman in Victorian Caricature* (Washington, D.C.: Smithsonian Institution, 1971) and Matthew Jacobson's *Whiteness of a Different Color: European Immigrants and the Alchemy of Race* (Cambridge, MA: Harvard UP, 1998).

6. In the words of Sander Gilman, with her enlarged buttocks and unique genitalia, "the female Hottentot came to represent the black female *in nuce*, and the [white] prostitute to represent the sexualized [white] woman" ("Bodies" 225). Given that "the anomalies of the prostitute's labia [were] seen as atavistic throwbacks to the Hottentot," a kinship was established whereby the "perception of the prostitute in the late nineteenth century merged with the perception of the black" ("Bodies" 245, 248).

and their "barbaric" participation in mannish labor, these women were thought to have a tenuous link with both whiteness and white womanhood.[7] These examples provide a backdrop against which to consider the racialization of white American tomboys, while they also place this process within a broader historical context. The racialization of white tomboys is far from an anomalous occurrence; it participates in a larger Western phenomenon.

One possible root for the racialization of white tomboyism can be traced to historical origins of this code of conduct itself. From its inception, tomboyism was interested in redefining not only conventional female gender roles but conventional notions of whiteness in the United States. Implicit in the effort of tomboyism to bolster the health of white women was its effort to have adolescent girls and young women embrace new forms of whiteness. As historians such as Lois Banner have noted, fair skin was prized among middle- and upper-class Anglo-American women for generations. Ladies wanted to look not simply white but almost ghost-like in appearance. Those who possessed naturally fair skin assiduously protected it with parasols and long sleeves. Meanwhile, those with tones that were dark or ruddy employed artificial methods to lighten their complexions. From applying talcum powder to taking doses of arsenic, women in Europe and the United States stopped at nothing—even when it involved risking their lives—to obtain this fair shade (Banner 35).

Although whitening the skin ostensibly showcased a bourgeois class position, it could also be seen as showcasing a certain level of racial purity. Together with demonstrating that they did not have to work outdoors, these white women were demonstrating that they lacked any trace of racial mixing. From both a literal and a figurative perspective, they were "Fair Maidens."

Tomboyism radically changed this phenomenon. Adopting a more natural lifestyle and unadulterated appearance, gender-bending young girls not only avoided the use of harmful cosmetics that artificially lightened their skin but also played outdoors. As a result, these figures often had tanned cheeks and ruddy complexions. Even a cursory examination of tomboyish characters reveals the widespread predominance of this phenomenon. Compared to their more fair and feminine counterparts, tomboys were often described as having dark white and even nonwhite features. Beginning with the second book in the *Little House* series, Laura is repeatedly admonished by her sisters and especially her mother for not

---

7. As Anne McClintock has written, "In newspapers, government reports, personal accounts and journals, the pit miners were everywhere represented as a 'race' apart, figured as racial outcasts, historically abandoned, isolated and primitive" (*Imperial* 115). Indeed, "One witness described them as 'weird, swarthy creatures, figures of women, half-clad in men's and half clad in women's attire'" (McClintock *Imperial* 116).

wearing a bonnet and allowing her skin to tan brown. Likewise, in Kate Douglas Wiggin's *Rebecca of Sunnybrook Farm* (1903), the tomboyish title character's face and neck are described as "brown and thin" (6). Finally, in the first scene of Caroline Snedeker's *Downright Dencey* (1927), the heroine is called "Nigger-face!" and a "Portugee girl!" because of her dark complexion (5, 7).

Tomboys redefined acceptable notions of whiteness as they redefined acceptable notions of female behavior for middle- and upper-class white women. After generations of Caucasian women lightening their skin, this new code of conduct was not predicated on the glorification of heightened states of whiteness. Tomboyism demonstrated that young girls could remain within the bounds of upper- and middle-class white womanhood even if they had browned skins and dark features. Frances Cogan has remarked that by the mid-nineteenth century the tanned complexion of a middle- or upper-class white girl did not "call into question the mother's sense of *female propriety*; or of spoiling her by *indulgence*" [italics in original] (39). In an illuminating example of this shift in attitude, physician Dr. Dio Lewis asserted in 1871, "The fragile, pale young woman with a lisp is thought, by many silly people, to be more a *lady*, than another with ruddy cheeks, and vigorous health" [italics in original] (6667). While this increased coloration of course did not transform Caucasian girls into black ones, it did broaden prevailing conceptions of "shades" of whiteness. With their crimson cheeks and ruddy complexions, tomboyish figures possessed what may be characterized as the dark glow of white tomboy health.

In the chapters that follow, I explore the way in which the nonwhiteness of ostensibly white tomboys is not merely "skin deep." In addition to being associated with nonwhite or, at least, dark white skin tones, these gender-bending female figures are connected with an array of stereotypes about racial Otherness in general and blackness in particular. Possessing behavioral tendencies, physical characteristics and narrative roles that place them in dialogue with what Toni Morrison would characterize as "American Africanism," these ostensibly white figures seem to distance themselves from, and often even disavow, their Caucasian identities.

In probing these and other issues, I rely heavily on what Frantz Fanon has characterized as the "epidermal schema" of racial difference. Although an individual's racial heritage is determined by a large constellation of factors—from nationality and economic status to geographic region and historical era—it has often been cast as a biological classification in the West. Indeed, Fanon has written in *Black Skin, White Masks* that "cultural logic presupposed a biological foundation of race visibly evident in physical features such as facial structures, hair color and texture, and skin color" (112). For these reasons, while the precise definition of race may change in the United States, Richard Dyer observes that one element remains constant: "concepts of race are always concepts of the body" (*White* 20).

Because racial traits are written on the body in the form of real (or imagined) facial features, physical characteristics and especially skin coloration, the concept is rooted in corporeality.

Tomboyism is also a distinct bodily identity. Together with being linked to corporeal traits like short hair, it is also predicated on such bodily acts as tree-climbing. Contemplating how the body-based realms of gender and race mutually construct and even reinforce each other, my discussion frequently pivots around questions of embodiment and disembodiment. Especially in light of the original eugenic purpose and hegemonic aim of tomboyism, this project may be primarily concerned with the co-joined bodies of the white tomboy and the nonwhite minority in the United States, but it is also interested in what this phenomenon has to say about the national body politic. Each of the following chapters considers the way in which strengthening the physical health of the nation's middle- and upper-class white women through tomboyism helped to strengthen the racial health of its Anglo-American ruling class.

Methodology and Organization

Even though this book spans nearly 150 years of American literary and cultural history, its discussion about the nonwhiteness associated with purportedly white tomboys operates within an admittedly limited framework. As Lisa Lowe and Philip Deloria, among others have illustrated, the historical periods under consideration were a time of rich racial and ethnic pluralism. Throughout the nineteenth and twentieth centuries, American Indians, Asian Americans and Latina/o Americans constituted an important facet of the nation's demographic composition, and they also played a crucial role in national attitudes about race.

My decision to focus on white tomboys who acquire suggestions of nonwhiteness through their connections with African American signifiers, therefore, is two-fold. In addition to giving the project a more manageable scope, my focus also reflects the era's pre-occupation with the black-white color line. As both Werner Sollors and Siobhan Somerville have asserted, it is difficult to underestimate the cultural anxiety about and accompanying fixation on African Americans in the United States. From the importation of the first African slaves, debates have raged over the place of blacks in white American culture. Various efforts to draw and redraw the distinctions between these groups brought to the forefront the diacritical nature of blackness and whiteness. Examining the way in which white tomboys who wore masculine breeches were able to breach the color line, *Tomboys* joins as well as disjoins this debate. With racialized white tomboys transgressing contemporary conceptions of black/white, male/female and heterosexual/homosexual, these figures occupy an important but often overlooked nexus of race, gender and sexuality.

On the subject of methodology, I want to say a word about my emphasis on literary and cinematic works largely by, about and for middle- and upper-class white women. As mentioned before, tomboyism was created by whites to bolster the health of white women and, by extension, the white race. Thus, this code of conduct made its initial debut and long-standing cultural home in works designed for this demographic group. Given this history, it seems fitting and even somewhat necessary that my discussion be primarily located in works by, or at least for, middle- and upper-class white women. Each chapter seeks to unpack the process by which white female figures constructed libratory narratives for white tomboys that paradoxically drew on racist stereotypes about nonwhite peoples and cultures.

The limited scope of my investigation, however, ought not to imply that female gender rebellion that draws on signifiers of race and ethnicity which exist outside of the black/white divide does not merit attention. The frequency with which adolescent tomboys are characterized as metaphoric "wild Indians" throughout children's literature, for instance, constitutes just one instance of the need for such work. Thus, while my project spotlights a specific type of tomboy character created during a specific historical era, it is my hope that it will open up a larger dialogue about the ways in which white women's gender rebellion is often predicated on forms of racial and ethnic nonwhiteness in the United States.

● ● ●

Having provided this general overview of tomboyism, the following chapters explore it with increased depth, detail and complexity. Chapter One, on E. D. E. N. Southworth's *The Hidden Hand* (1859), explores the moment when national childrearing practices shifted from promoting female invalidism to advocating female athleticism. At the same time, it demonstrates that in addition to the oft-mentioned feminist influence on tomboys, these figures had their root in such burlesque theatrical modes as blackface. Chapter Two, on Louisa May Alcott's *Little Women* (1868), examines how the female gender incivilities precipitated by the Civil War catapulted tomboyism from a fledgling cultural practice into a widespread national phenomenon, while it simultaneously details the way in which the tomboyish civil war over middle- and upper-class white womanhood was not entirely divorced from the national one over black slavery. Chapter Three, on Sarah Orne Jewett's *A Country Doctor* (1884), examines the process by which the tomboy matured into the New Woman and the debates that erupted over extending tomboyish behaviors into adulthood. In doing so, it reveals that much of the social as well as scientific language used to denounce white tomboyish gender difference during the postbellum period was patterned after that which had been used to police black racial difference during the antebellum era.

Chapter Four, on Charlotte Perkins Gilman's *Herland* (1915), examines how lingering fears over the mannish woman and female invert caused tomboys to be reinvented as exercise enthusiasts during the Progressive Era, and the way in which the eugenic benefits of "getting physical" were closely aligned with prevailing white fantasies about the rejuvenative powers of "going primitive." Chapter Five, on Willa Cather's *O Pioneers!* (1913) and *My Antonia* (1918), examines this code of conduct as an agent of acculturation, assimilation and even Americanization for newly arrived immigrants. More specifically, it investigates the process by which formerly nonwhite immigrants were able to become white in the context of the frontier and the role that tomboyism played in this process. Chapter Six, on Victor Fleming's *Hula* (1927), explores the tomboyish roots of the Twenties flapper and how this predominantly white figure was linked with the "wild," "uncivilized" ways of nonwhite tribal peoples.

Chapter Seven, on Carson McCullers's *The Member of the Wedding* (1946), probes the widespread proliferation of, and accompanying paranoia about, tomboyish figures during the Second World War, and the way in which figures like Frankie Addams became a symbol for the era's gendered, raced and sexualized concerns about the crumbling wartime distinctions between normality and abnormality, ordinary and freakishness, moderation and excess. Chapter Eight, on Ann Bannon's *Women in the Shadows* (1959), considers how postwar emphasis on redomestication caused tomboyism to become yoked with a butch form of lesbianism, and how this process participated in the white envy for black culture during the 1950s. Chapter Nine, on Peter Bogdanovich's *Paper Moon* (1973), explores the way in which the rebirth of white feminism during the 1970s and early 1980s catapulted tomboyism from the margins into the mainstream of American culture once again, and the way in which this cinematic forum allowed white tomboys to "fade to black." Finally, the Epilogue addresses how the rise of queer theory, the emergence of whiteness studies and the re-engineering of white feminism during the 1990s precipitated a time of both tomboyish boom and bust.

In the opening pages of *Speech Genres and Other Late Essays*, Mikhail Bakhtin observes, "the most interesting and productive life takes place on the boundaries" (2). Tomboy characters in general and racialized white tomboys in particular participate in this phenomenon. Existing on the boundaries between male/female, black/white, adult/child, heterosexual/homosexual, savage/civilized, different/same and drag/passing, these figures dismantle cultural binaries while they participate in them. Accordingly, this book places itself on the interstices between high and low culture, printed and visual texts as well as narratives written for children and those written for adults to investigate this previously unexplored facet of U.S. literature and culture.

1

The White Tomboy Launches a Gender Backlash

E. D. E. N. Southworth's The Hidden Hand

The mid-nineteenth century was one of the most dynamic times in U.S. social, cultural, and economic life. Between 1840 and 1880, more than 7.5 million immigrants arrived on the nation's shores during what would become the biggest immigration wave in American history; about 1.5 million immigrants arrived in the decade between 1840 and 1850 alone.[1] In addition, both the number and the size of the nation's cities increased rapidly, with the population of urban areas nearly doubling each decade from 1840 to 1860.[2] Finally, the era saw the advent of numerous technological innovations, including the steam locomotive, the telegraph, and the new art of photography. As even these few examples indicate, during the period from the end of the War of 1812 to the outbreak of the Civil War, the United States experienced profound changes.

When historians or cultural critics discuss new developments in antebellum America, however, they rarely include tomboyism. During

1. Data from the *1997 Statistical Yearbook of the Immigration and Naturalization Service*, which is available online from the U.S. Department of Justice, Immigration and Naturalization Service at: www.dhs.gov/xlibrary/assets/statistics/yearbook/1997YB.pdf

2. For the precise numbers, see Series A 57–72, "Population in Urban and Rural Territory, by Size of Place, 1790–1970," in the *Historical Statistics of the United States, Colonial Times to 1970*, Part I, U.S. Dept of Commerce, Bureau of the Census, Washington, D.C.: U.S. Government Printing Office, 1975: p. 12.

the 1840s and 1850s, a constellation of social, economic and political forces precipitated a shift from True Womanhood to tomboyhood for adolescent girls and young women. Although tomboyism is one of the most consistently overlooked elements in American culture, it is an acutely influential one. After its debut, the nation's childrearing practices, the gender expression of its young girls, and the lived experiences of many grown women would never be the same.

This chapter addresses the causes, characteristics and consequences of antebellum tomboyism by focusing on the adolescent character who helped launch this concept in the nation's literature and culture: Capitola Black from E. D. E. N. Southworth's 1859 novel *The Hidden Hand*. A spunky female figure who used slang, spurned patriarchal authority and even cross-dressed, Cap was the wildly popular central character of Southworth's novel. The tomboyish antics of this thirteen-year-old figure made *The Hidden Hand* a best-seller and tomboyism a national phenomenon. From the first serial publication of the novel, enthusiasm for it was immense. Praised by critics and adored by readers, the narrative was reprinted in Robert Bonner's *New York Ledger* in 1868–1869 and again in 1883 before being released in book form in 1888. In spite of these frequent reprints, public demand for the book was never quite satisfied. Susan Coultrap-McQuinn has noted that requests to republish *The Hidden Hand* or make back issues that contained the story more widely available poured into Bonner's office throughout the 1860s and 1870s (52). After Southworth's story had exhausted multiple press runs, the *Ledger* touted it as the "best story the author had ever written" and heralded it as the most popular—and certainly the most lucrative—one that the paper had ever serialized (Boyle 66).

The Hidden Hand was also a cultural phenomenon. As Alfred Habegger notes, at least forty dramatic adaptations of the text were made during Southworth's lifetime ("A Well Hidden Hand" 198). While nearly all of these productions enjoyed extended runs in major cities throughout the United States and Great Britain; one of the most infamous featured seasoned actor and future presidential assassin John Wilkes Booth in the lead male role as the novel's notorious villain, Black Donald. For the duration of its engagement, this dramatic version played to theatrical houses that were standing-room only.[3] As these details indicate, *The Hidden Hand* was truly a crossover phenomenon: both its theatrical viewership and its literary readership encompassed adult and adolescent audiences. Indeed, although the book is not included in Mitzi Myers and U. C. Knoepflmacher's 1997 special edition of *Children's Literature* dedicated to works that possess this

---

3. For more information on this theatrical production in general and John Wilkes Booth's performance of Black Donald in particular, see Regis Louise Boyle's "Mrs. E. D. E. N. Southworth, Novelist," MA thesis, Catholic University, 1939.

"dialogic mix of older and younger voices" (vii), it is such a book in several respects. As Joanne Dobson has noted in her introduction to the recently reissued edition of *The Hidden Hand*, the novel appealed equally to children and adults, men and women as well as Northerners and Southerners. Through the 1859 novel, Southworth satisfied her longstanding artistic desire to "please the multitude" (Dobson Introduction xi).

While antebellum audiences delighted in nearly every facet of *The Hidden Hand*, they had a special affection for its tomboyish protagonist. Admiring her pluck and delighting in her humor, readers wanted to emulate her. Within months after the serial appearance of Southworth's narrative, an array of hats, boots and coats modeled after those worn by the mischievous main character began appearing on clothing store shelves (Hudock 10). Forming what came to be known as the "Capitola look," the items were popular among adolescent girls and young women. Many new mothers even began naming their daughters "Capitola" in honor of their beloved heroine (Boyle 13).

Rather than a gender-specific phenomenon, Cap's popularity once again transcended the nineteenth-century dictum of separate spheres. As Joanne Dobson notes, boats, racehorses, hotels and even a town on the frontier during the era bore the name "Capitola" (xl). Although some owners were undoubtedly trying to capitalize on the character's popularity by aligning their businesses with her, others chose the appellation out of a genuine affection for Southworth's tomboyish figure. In the words of Helen Waite Papashvily, it seemed that everyone—male and female, old and young, urban and rural—"appropriated her magic name" (126). Indicating the extent of the book's fame, Regis Louise Boyle has written that *The Hidden Hand* "was exceeded in popularity only by *Uncle Tom's Cabin*. Meanwhile, Capitola was as famous as Topsy" (13).

Despite the seemingly innocuous entertainment value of Southworth's narrative, *The Hidden Hand* contained a radical social critique. Capitola's ostensibly gender-related tomboyism was also inextricably connected with race. More than simply an alternative childrearing practice or form of gender expression for adolescent girls in antebellum American society, this code of conduct embodied a gender "blacklash" in many ways. In its rebellion against prevailing constructions of adult white womanhood, antebellum tomboyism drew on various aspects of nonwhiteness. A potent combination of proto-feminism, fears over various threats to white racial supremacy, and an underlying loyalty to the white South shaped E. D. E. N. Southworth's fictional presentation of this code of conduct, and, in doing so, revealed its origins as an intensely racialized construct. Although tomboyism emerged in response to the declining state of health in white women throughout America, this author highlighted the way in which it had a particular resonance for those in the South. Subjected to a powerful patriarchy, enfeebled by debilitating fashion trends and threatened by the Northern abolitionist movement, these figures were in an especially perilous position. Even more so than their neighbors on the other side of the Mason-Dixon line, they needed a code of conduct that would empower both their gender and their race. Throughout E. D. E. N. Southworth's *The Hidden Hand*, tomboyism is the means by which this task is accomplished.

From True Womanhood to Tomboyhood: The Birth of the Antebellum Tomboy

As Barbara Welter and Carroll Smith-Rosenberg have each written, middle- and upper-class white women equated femininity with fragility during the early decades of the nineteenth century. Under the auspices of what has come to be known as the Cult of True Womanhood, they considered physical strength, emotional fortitude and constitutional vigor unwomanly. Echoing prevailing medical opinions about the inherently weak nature of women, they prided themselves on being frail and raised their daughters in accordance with these beliefs. Cinching their corsets tightly and instructing them to avoid strenuous exercise, mothers often deemed their female children the most feminine when they were the most ill and languishing.[4] For these reasons, Lynne Vallone has observed, "An almost universal complaint against American girls [in the antebellum era] was that although they were thought to be the prettiest national type (in comparison with the English and Continental girls), they often neglected their beauty through sheer idleness and indolence" (115).

During the mid-nineteenth century, however, this paradigm began to change. The era's increasing economic instability made what Diane Price-Herndl has termed "the vogue of the 'Invalid Woman'" no longer desirable. During a period that predated government regulation of business practices, FDIC protection of bank deposits, and social welfare programs, great fortunes could be made, as well as lost, overnight. In the words of Frances Cogan, "a man and his family could be hiring servants and building a new house one year and barely able, because of bankruptcy, to afford two rooms in a run-down boardinghouse the next" (13).

Since the economic future of the American family was never secure, it became clear that girls from all socio-economic strata needed to learn practical job skills. Displays of ornamental artistry might showcase feminine refinement and class sophistication, but—as Cogan has remarked—they would not put food on the table in the event of a financial crisis (14). Instead,

---

4. For more information, see Barbara Welter's *Dimity Convictions: The American Woman in the Nineteenth Century* (Athens: Ohio UP, 1976) and Carroll Smith-Rosenberg's *Disorderly Conduct: Visions of Gender in Victorian America* (New York: A. A. Knopf, 1985).

during such uncertain times, advice books for girls "almost unanimously advocated for training in some marketable skill or trade in the unhappy event that some evil befall the girl and her family" (Vallone 118).

This new mandate for female participation in family financial matters called for an alteration to both current childrearing practices and standards of feminine beauty. Because the time may come when adolescent girls and young women would be called upon to support their families, they could no longer afford to be weak, ill and languishing. Instead of deeming female health, strength and vigor unattractive, society now considered these qualities desirable in the nation's young women. In the words of Lynne Vallone once again, "The physically fit and healthy girl not only enlarged her capacity for work and service, but also enhanced her beauty and chances on the marriage market" (115). Especially in a nation that was still as young as the United States, "For the girls who were to become pillars of their homes, maintaining a healthy body and mind was considered a moral duty" (Vallone 114).

The nation's unstable economic climate was a key component to the emergence of this new code of conduct, but it was certainly not the only one. Of equal importance as the era's declining financial condition was its burgeoning feminist movement. During the 1830s and 1840s, figures such as Elizabeth Cady Stanton and Lucretia Mott began a national movement to eradicate societal practices that disempowered women. At events like the Seneca Falls Convention in 1848, they called attention to everything from the harmful nature of female fashions to laws that denied women basic civil rights.

While the efforts of first-wave feminists are commonly thought limited to issues concerning adult women, they had resonance for female children as well. The overplot to countless domestic novels during the mid-nineteenth century demonstrated that young girls were just as susceptible to patriarchal oppression as grown women. As Nina Baym has shown, the juvenile heroines in bestsellers such as *The Wide, Wide World* (1850) and *The Lamplighter* (1855) experience some of their most profound abuse and neglect at home. They are denied love, attention and even basic life necessities by male relatives, guardians and friends. Given that men often failed to provide for women in real life as in literature, feminists argued that young girls must be prepared to perform these tasks for themselves.

Together with the birth of white feminism and the increasingly unstable economy, the era's turbulent political climate formed a final factor in the antebellum emergence of tomboyism. During the 1840s and 1850s, abolition evolved from an isolated religious faction into a powerful national movement in the United States. While efforts to eradicate slavery raised hopes about finally fulfilling the democratic vision of the Founding Fathers, it simultaneously elicited fears about the entrance of blacks into white American society. Especially in areas where the number of blacks exceeded that of whites, Anglo-Americans feared that maintaining white racial control after emancipation would be difficult and—in some regions—perhaps even impossible.

While tomboyism is not commonly connected with this issue, it had a direct link to it. Changes in the nation's racial and ethnic composition raised fears over the literal and figurative health of Anglo-American girls and young women. The Cult of True Womanhood was interfering with the ability of these middle- and upper-class white figures to be not only productive wives and mothers but, more importantly, reproductive ones. Numerous physicians noted that as a result of eating rich foods, wearing tight corsets and avoiding physical activity, many were unable to conceive children while those who did often gave birth to sickly and even defective infants. Declining birth rates among upper- and middle-class white women, coupled with the declining vitality of the children they did produce, elicited fears about the potential "race suicide" of Anglo-Americans. In 1851, for instance, advice writer T. S. Arthur urged white female readers to understand "the duty that rests on them to preserve their health for the sake of the happiness of others, and the general well-being of society" (105). Between the rapid influx of foreign immigrants from abroad and the potential emancipation of black slaves at home, many feared that whites would soon become a minority in the United States. As Shelley Streeby discusses in a recent book about the era, some experts predicted that this phenomenon was only a generation or two away (42).

Tomboyism offered an antidote to this problem. A new code of female conduct that stressed proper hygiene, daily exercise, comfortable clothing, and wholesome nutrition, it was designed to boost the health of middle- and upper-class white women and, in doing so, better prepare them for the physical and psychological demands of marriage and motherhood. As Sharon O'Brien has written, childrearing manuals asserted that girls who were raised as tomboys "would surely develop the resourcefulness, self-confidence, and, most importantly, the constitutional vibrancy required for motherhood" (352). In this way, while tomboyism is commonly seen as challenging or, at least, standing in opposition to heteronormativity, it was introduced in the 1840s and 1850s as a preparatory stage for it. Young girls embraced this new code of conduct not as a means to transgress their adult roles as wives and mothers but, on the contrary, to train for them.

In light of this societal purpose, tomboyism went beyond simply being an innovation in American childrearing practices or the gender expression among its young girls. It was also a eugenic strategy or, at the very least, one that would help maintain white racial supremacy. With its intention to bolster the physical health of the nation's future wives and mothers, tomboyism was also intended to bolster the racial health of whiteness. During an era when the hegemonic status of Anglo-Americans seemed threatened, it would help ensure that today's young white girls would be sufficiently robust to produce tomorrow's crop of equally robust white citizens and, perhaps more importantly, male leaders.

Literature in general, and narratives that were intended for a largely middle-class female readership and had young girls as protagonists, became a popular means to present the benefits of tomboyism and persuade young girls to adopt it. From the title character in Mary J. Holmes' *'Lena Rivers* (1856) to the unruly Nancy Vawse in Susan Warner's *The Wide, Wide World* (1850), female figures who displayed the tomboyish traits of athleticism, adventurousness and autonomy began to emerge in domestic and sentimental novels by women.

Of the antebellum authors who engaged this new code of conduct, however, E. D. E. N. Southworth stands out. One of the most popular writers during the mid-nineteenth century, she was also one of the earliest proponents of tomboyism. Abandoned by her husband soon after the birth of their second child, the author had first-hand knowledge about the importance for women to be emotionally, physically and intellectually strong and self-sufficient. As a result, throughout her more than fifty published narratives,[5] she called into question codes that required women to be passive, submissive and accepting. In the prefatory comments to her 1849 novel *The Deserted Wife*, for instance, Southworth identifies *"a defective . . . physical education"* as one of the primary causes for failed marriages, sickly children and female unhappiness [italics in original] (24). Arguing that "[a] girl cannot be a useful or a happy wife . . . unless she be a healthy woman," she calls for a "great reform" in female behavior that is in dialogue with tomboyism *(Deserted* 25–26). Rather than allow girls to grow up "drinking hot tea and coffee, eating hot meats and rich gravies and pastries, never bathing, taking little exercise, confined in crowded school-rooms or close house-rooms," she advocates "exercise, cleanliness and temperance" *(Deserted* 27). Asserting that "happiness depends upon a free circulation, unobstructed perspiration, and a good digestion," the author asks mothers to allow their female children "[d]aily exercise by walking, skipping rope, calisthenics, horseback riding . . . fresh air, simple, plain food, comfortable clothing, the disuse of corsets, tight-waisted dresses, [and] tight shoes" *(Deserted* 26, 27). Given this ethos, Southworth's female protagonists defy their categorization in works like *The Deserted Wife* (1849), *The Discarded Daughter* (1852)

---

5. As numerous critics and biographers have noted, it is difficult to determine the precise number of novels that Southworth published during her lifetime given her propensity for reissuing texts under different titles. For instance, the writer's 1855 novel, *The Missing Bride*, was republished in 1874 as *Miriam, The Avenger*. According to Regis Louise Boyle—the author of the only full-length study on Southworth—"her serials amounted to fifty-four as closely as I have been able to ascertain" (146).

and *The Lost Heiress* (1853) (Dobson xii); they adopt the tomboyish attributes of physical strength, intellectual fortitude and emotional perseverance to overcome adversity.[6]

E. D. E. N. Southworth was concerned about the health and vigor of the nation's white women almost as much as she was troubled by the health and vigor of those who hailed from her place of birth: the South. In yet another example of bell hooks' admonition that white opposition to the institution of slavery did not automatically imply support for black social equality, this author held conflicted views on African Americans. Although Southworth serialized her first novel in the *National Anti-Slavery Era*, was friends with leading abolitionists like Harriet Beecher Stowe, and even opened up her home in Washington, D.C. to wounded Union soldiers during the Civil War, her commitment to abolition was not as clear in her professional writings as it was in her personal life. As previous critics have pointed out, many of Southworth's novels draw on racist literary conventions, present blacks in stereotypical ways and glorify—or at least romanticize—the plantation way of life. In the words of Regis Louise Boyle, "Happy slaves are more numerous in her work than unfortunate negroes" (82). With their masters depicted as unequivocally benevolent and their daily lives presented as perpetually carefree, many are unwilling to leave the plantation even after emancipation.[7] For these reasons, Janet Gabler-Hover has offered an ironic recombination of the author's name to characterize her work: "Her monogram—E. D. E. N.—made her a canny or uncanny personification of the Jeffersonian South, which must have struck her as showing the hand of divine intervention. One can only add that having the surname 'Southworth' must have made this writer feel even more ordained to produce a 'worthy' fictional paradigm of a revitalized South" (38).

6. Given the often extensive gap between the serial release of E. D. E. N. Southworth's novels and their publication in book form, critics and biographers often disagree over the chronology of her work. For instance, although Southworth's wildly popular *The Hidden Hand* made its debut in Robert Bonner's *New York Ledger* in 1859, it was not released in book form until nearly thirty years later, in 1888. In light of such discrepancies, I have chosen to use the narrative's initial date of release—whether in serial or book format—as the date of its publication. While this approach diverges from some extant publication histories of Southworth's novels, it provides a more accurate reflection of both the personal composition and public release of her work.

7. Ironically, given the pro-slavery elements of her work, Southworth's passion for storytelling had its roots in African American culture. As Regis Louise Boyle notes, one of the author's favorite pastimes when young "was listening to the negroes in the kitchen tell ghost stories, old legends, and tales of the times when 'Ole Mist'ess was rich and saw lots of grand company'" (4). Throughout her career, Southworth attributed her interest in reading and eventually writing stories to hearing these black-authored tales. In this way, while most critics cite the author's desertion by her husband and need for financial support as the primary impetus for her literary career, an American Africanist catalyst is also possible.

While it is not surprising that Southworth's Southern sympathies influenced the representation of black slaves and white slaveowners in her fiction, the possibility that they informed her construction of Caucasian tomboys is less expected. Throughout her lengthy and prolific career, Southworth penned many tomboyish characters who lived below the Mason-Dixon line: Hagar Churchill in *The Deserted Wife* (1849), Garnet Seabright in *The Discarded Daughter* (1852), Helen Wildman in *Vivia; or, The Secret of Power* (1857), Harriette "Harry" Joy in *The Three Beauties* (1858) and Lionne Delaforet and Kate Kyte in *The Fatal Marriage* (1863). Of these numerous and diverse figures, however, Capitola Black from her 1859 narrative *The Hidden Hand* was by far her most famous. Smuggled from her home in Virginia to the slums of New York after a sinister relative has murdered her father and abducted her mother in a plot to acquire the family fortune, the adolescent character demonstrates the benefits of tomboyism for white women in general and well-to-do Southern ones in particular. Recalling Janet Gabler-Hover's clever reconfiguration of the author's name once again, this code of conduct allows them to engender an Edenic South. At repeated points throughout *The Hidden Hand*, Capitola's tomboyish physical strength, emotional fortitude and intellectual cunning enable her to overcome obstacles that have ruined many female figures before her. Surviving poverty, abandonment and even attempted murder and rape, she is able to regain her status as not simply an upper-class white woman but one who is the heiress to a large Southern plantation. As a result, *The Hidden Hand* demonstrates how, by fortifying one imperiled white woman, tomboyism could help to fortify an equally imperiled white South.

Gender Bending for Racial Building: Tomboyism and The Maintenance of the White Status Quo

From her first appearance in Southworth's novel, Capitola showcases the physical, emotional and—perhaps most importantly—racial benefits of tomboyism. Echoing a trope of nineteenth-century literature as well as many children's classics, the thirteen-year-old girl is penniless, homeless and alone when first introduced to readers. Whisked away at birth to prevent her father's evil brother from murdering her, Cap is unaware of her heritage, and her maternal relatives are, in turn, unaware of her existence. For more than a decade, the mulatto nurse who brought Capitola to New York and has been serving as her guardian has hidden the Virginia heiress. Now, the aged and ailing Nancy Grewell feels that the time has come to finally unveil the girl's existence. Leaving her ward with a stock of food and money, Nancy sets out for the South. Although the elderly woman succeeds in her quest, the trip exhausts her. Within hours of revealing Cap's identity to her maternal uncle, Nancy dies.

Back in New York, Capitola's previously desperate situation has become even more dire. During the months that Nancy has been away, the girl has run out of food and money. Evicted from her tenement home, the would-be heiress is now a homeless street beggar. Harassed each night by lecherous men and forced to sell pieces of her clothing for food, Cap finds herself in both physical want and sexual danger. As she later tells a magistrate about the experience, "'being always exposed, sleeping out-doors, I was often in danger from bad boys and bad men'" (45).

Although Southworth's character faces a situation that has ruined many young white women before her, she does not share their fate. Raised outside the confines of genteel white womanhood in the rough and tumble slums of New York, Cap has been schooled in the tomboyish qualities of street-smarts and savvy rather than the bourgeois Southern traits of sentimentality and submissiveness. Consequently, when hardship hits, the plucky youngster possesses the physical, emotional and intellectual skills to survive.

Blocked from various forms of employment because of her gender, Cap realizes that her life would be much easier if she were male. As a result, rather than wait for a boy to take care of her, Capitola decides to transform herself into a boy so that she may take care of herself. Cutting her hair short and trading her petticoats for a pair of pants, she announces, "'I went into that little back parlor *a girl*, and I came out *a boy*'" [emphasis in original] (46). The ease with which Capitola is able to change from female to male calls into question prevailing beliefs about the biological basis of gender. Appearing more than 150 years before Judith Butler's *Gender Trouble*, the tomboyish character highlights the performative nature of masculinity and femininity. Moreover, her transvestism places her in dialogue with a longstanding tradition of cross-dressed women on the American stage. As historian Elizabeth Reitz Mullenix has written, the breeches performance—in which a woman appeared in men's clothing and a male role— was a theatrical staple for the bulk of the nineteenth century. Unlike the phenomenon of the "Antebellum Actress-as-Boy" (Mullenix 127), Capitola's transvestism is not for the erotic enjoyment of a male audience. Instead of providing a titillating "leg show" (Mullenix 4), her boyish garb serves a more iconoclastic function.

As a young man, Capitola's life is completely different. Freed from harassment and presented with an abundance of employment options, the young girl not only embraces her male persona, but delights in it. As she later asserts, "'the only thing that made me feel sorry, was to see what a fool I had been, not to turn to a boy before, when it was so easy!'" (46). While Capitola's masquerade may be an effective solution to her current woes, it is not a permanent one. When a policeman discovers her false persona one day, he arrests her. Although this event ends Cap's boyish days, it reunites her with her kind if cantankerous maternal relative, Major Ira Warfield. Setting out for New York after learning of his niece's existence, the gentleman—in one of the many coincidences in Southworth's novel—happens to be at the police station when his niece is brought before the magistrate. Paying Cap's fine, Major Warfield brings her back to the South.

Capitola's reunion with a member of her Virginia family, however, does not signal a happily-ever-after ending. Nor does it signal an end to her tomboyish behavior. When Cap's villainous paternal uncle—a man who, reflecting nineteenth-century beliefs about the "dark" nature of villainy, is named Gabriel LeNoir—learns of her existence, he vows to eliminate her: "'Yes! It is that miserable old woman and babe! . . . [I]n every vein of my soul, I repent not having silenced them both forever while they were yet in my power!'" (148). With the help of the town's most notorious criminal, who also bears the suggestive appellation Black Donald, LeNoir makes repeated attempts to abduct and murder his heiress niece. In keeping with the sensational style that made Southworth famous, each of these plots involves an array of thrilling, page-turning events: Gabriel and Black Donald don disguises, leap out from behind bushes, hide under beds, establish secret hideouts, fall through trap doors, live in haunted mansions, and—in one especially hilarious moment—even impersonate a camp minister. Indeed, Capitola is not alone in exploring the performative nature of identity.

In spite of such imaginative and persistent efforts, the duo consistently fails. In each of their attempts, Cap uses her tomboyish physical strength, emotional fortitude and intellectual cunning to foil their plans. Making frequent harangues against sentimentality and submissiveness, she not only insists on protecting herself but consistently demonstrates that she can, in fact, do so. When Black Donald appears at her door dressed as a sailor, for instance, the young girl has the smarts to see through his disguise, the courage to leap on his back, and the strength to hang on for several minutes while various servants frantically chase him around the estate. Likewise, when Gabriel's son Craven accosts her while she is out riding, Capitola employs her cunning to escape. Instead of panicking when she realizes the young villain's lecherous intentions, she uses her intelligence to con him into unsaddling his horse. Feigning interest in sitting and talking with the evil Craven, she convinces him to spread his saddle cloth on the damp ground for a blanket. Once he has done so—and thereby eliminated his ability to pursue her on horseback—the physically fit young woman leaps on her steed and gallops away to safety. "Hearing the shout, the lash and the start of the horses, the baffled villain saw that his game was lost! He had been outwitted by a child! He gnashed his teeth and shook his fist in rage" (Southworth 118). Finally, in the climax of the novel when Black Donald makes one final attempt to abduct and rape her, she not only foils his plan, but captures him in the process. Tricking the dastardly villain into sitting atop the trapdoor in her bedroom, Cap plunges him into a cavernous pit. In an accolade more fitting a nineteenth-century hero than heroine, "Capitola was everywhere lauded for her brave part in the capture of the famous desperado" (393). Black Donald had eluded male authorities for decades, but the tomboyish girl was able to bring him to justice.

The power of Capitola's tomboyism is so great, in fact, that it enables her to rescue other imperiled white female characters. When close friend and confidant Clara Day is threatened with a forced marriage to the lecherous Craven LeNoir near the middle of the narrative, for instance, Capitola uses her tomboyish cunning to foil the plan. Switching places with the frail and frightened girl, Cap waits until Clara has escaped to safety and then unveils the ruse and flees. As the narrator notes, when the tomboyish young girl reveals her true identity, "The priest dropped his book. . . . The two LeNoirs simultaneously sprang forward, astonishment, disappointment and rage contending in their blanched faces" (315).

In keeping with the eugenic purpose of white tomboyism, Capitola's bravery, daring and autonomy do not turn her against either men or marriage. Whereas many latter-day tomboys frequently proclaim that they dislike boys and will never marry, Southworth's gender-bending character makes repeated reference to her intention of getting married in general and being betrothed to childhood friend Herbert Greyson in particular. Upon her arrival in Virginia, Cap remarks to a fortune-teller, "'I haven't the most distant idea of being an old maid'" (272). Similarly, while foiling an attempted forced marriage ceremony, Cap ruminates, "'Well, I declare, this getting married is really awful interesting. If it were not for Herbert Greyson, I'd just let it go right straight on to the end, and see what would happen next'" (315).

If Cap is eager to get married, many men are eager to wed her. Rather than being repulsed by her physical strength or emotional fortitude, they find these qualities attractive. Impressed by her pluck and amazed by her independence, male characters ranging from the admirable Herbert Greyson and Major Warfield to the villainous Craven Le Noir and Black Donald fall in love with her. Craven swoons at the sight of Cap's "flaming cheeks," Black Donald speaks of her complimentarily as a "brick," and the cantankerous Old Hurricane concedes that the capricious young woman is his favorite (161, 349 , 127).

Although Capitola weds Herbert Greyson at the end of the novel, there is no indication that this union signals the end of her tomboyish behaviors. On the contrary, these elements form a crucial component to her personality. If Cap were to abandon her tomboyishness, she would become more like the submissive and sentimental Clara Day, a character whose behavior largely serves as a cautionary tale. As a result, Southworth's tomboyish character maintains her gender-bending elements long after childhood. After all, it is unclear what challenges marriage and motherhood will bring. As the author herself learned all too vividly when her husband abandoned her and she was left to care for two young children alone, this gender-bending female figure may need to draw on her tomboyish elements again one day.

A key component to Capitola's embrace of tomboyism as a lifelong identity, along with its accompanying sexual appeal, is her comparatively normative gender identity. Although tomboyism is now seen as a gender-bending code of conduct that allows "girls to be boys," it began in the 1840s and 1850s as a different way for girls to be girls. Tomboyism was innovative and even radical compared to the Cult of True Womanhood, but it was not seen as androgynous or even mannish; these labels, in fact, would not become associated with it for several decades. Although antebellum tomboys were more rough-and-tumble than their prissy indoor counterparts, they remained firmly grounded in a female identity. As Frances Cogan notes, Real Womanhood, like its cultural descendant tomboyhood, "demanded that one do so as a *woman*, not as an *androgynye* or 'freak'" [author's emphasis] (Cogan 5). Rather than disparaging stereotypically gender-appropriate activities, tomboyish girls relished them.

Even though Capitola is an iconoclastic figure in many ways, she adheres to this paradigm. Commonly touted for her rebellious qualities, this character is actually more gender normative than past or present criticism has been willing to concede.[8] Upon being arrested for cross-dressing, for instance, Cap makes it clear that she donned the male attire out of necessity rather than choice. As she attests, there were a number of reasons which "'finally *drove me* to putting on boy's clothes'" [my emphasis] (45). In constant danger from "bad boys and bad men" and denied access to an array of honest jobs, Cap informs the judge that she saw no other solution than to trade in her petticoats for pants: "'Well, your Honor, . . . when I couldn't get a job of work for love nor money, when my last penny was spent for my last roll—and my last roll was eaten up—and I was dreading the gnawing hunger day by day, and the horrid perils at night, I thought to myself *if I were only a boy*'" [italics in original] (46). Even though Capitola's male persona is an effective solution to her current woes, she does not find it a satisfactory one. Although the young woman's survival is predicated on maintaining a boyish appearance, she is unable to fully relinquish her feminine traits. As she tells the magistrate, "'I forgot and let my hair grow, and instead of cutting it off, just tucked it up under my cap; and so this morning, on the ferry-boat, in a high breeze, the *wind blowed off my cap* and the *policeman blowed on me!*'" [italics in original] (47).

8. For a discussion of Capitola as a cross-gender identified figure, see especially Lynette Carpenter's "Double Talk: The Power and the Glory of Paradox in E. D. E. N. Southworth's *The Hidden Hand*," *Legacy*, 10.1 (1993): 17–30. While Carpenter does concede that Capitola contains some isolated feminine qualities, she nonetheless reads her a powerful symbol of Southworth's interest in undermining women's traditional gender roles.

Although Capitola is disappointed that she has been caught, she is pleased to be able to abandon her boyish appearance. When Ira Warfield takes his ward to a dressmaker's shop after she has been released from police custody, the tomboyish girl cheerfully sheds her gender-bending garb. Gladly removing the newsboy outfit, she is furnished "with a half dozen complete suits of female attire" (50). Unlike the tomboys of many future novels, Cap puts on a dress without complaint. In many ways, in fact, the young woman is relieved by the change. Riding with the Major in her new gender-appropriate attire, "Capitola sat deeply blushing at the recollection of her male attire" (51). In fact, she begs her new guardian to refrain from mentioning her cross-dressing escapade to longtime friend and love interest Herbert Greyson: "'Uncle! Herbert has been at sea three years! He knows nothing of my past misery and destitution, nor of my ever wearing boy's clothes'" (53).

Coupled with adopting feminine dress, Cap also embraces feminine activities. Soon after arriving at Hurricane Hall, Mrs. Condiment begins instructing the young ward in traditional feminine skills and activities. Significantly, the tomboyish figure not only willingly learns such tasks, she excels at them. "A pupil as sharp as Capitola soon mastered her tasks, and found herself each day with many hours of leisure" (109). Cap's feminine nature goes beyond her love of dresses and accompanying aptitude for needlework. Even the young woman's seemingly most daring acts of boyish bravery can be seen in gender-appropriate ways. Her duel with Craven LeNoir forms a poignant example, for Cap calls the villain out only after her male relatives have refused to do so. Repudiated by John Stone and Edwin Percy, she exclaims, "'The men are all dead! if ever any really lived!'" (367). As these comments indicate, Capitola's "manly" bravery is precipitated not by her own inherent mannishness, but by the cowardice of men. By refusing to protect their female dependent, they force her to protect herself. Indeed, as Cap later tells the magistrate about the root or cause for her unusual actions, "'I happen to be without father or brother to protect me from affront, sir, and my uncle is an invalid veteran whom I will not trouble. I am, therefore, under the novel necessity of fighting my own battles'" (370). In doing so, Capitola illustrates the sharp distinction between the morality-based terms "manly" and the biologically rooted "masculine" in nineteenth-century America. As Gail Bederman discusses in a recent book, "manly" referred to "possessing the proper characteristics of a man; independent in spirit or bearing; strong, brave . . . honorable, highminded" (18). In contrast, the term "masculine" was a medico-scientific designation that connoted "the distinguishing characteristics of the male sex among human beings" (Bederman 18). While Capitola demonstrates that she is capable of "manly" behavior in Southworth's text, she also makes clear that her tomboyish conduct does not signal "masculine" biology.

Such distinctions recur later in the narrative. Although Capitola vows to be a "hero" when she arrives at Hurricane Hall (77), she often behaves in ways that are more characteristic of a stereotypical heroine. Cap is tomboyishly rebellious and often even impertinent, but she is also pious, compassionate and forgiving. The character's most oft-cited act of heroism—her capture of Black Donald—forms a vivid example. Akin to the patient and forgiving Victorian woman, Cap gives the notorious villain every chance to repent before plunging him into the pit. First, she adopts a maternal approach, calling him by his first name in her plea to have him abandon his plan and leave her room. As she lovingly tells him, "'I believe that there is good in all, and much good in you'" (391). In a commentary on the ineffectuality of True Womanhood to influence male behavior, these entreaties fail. Hence, Cap engages in another stereotypical act for a Victorian lady: she asks Black Donald to utter a prayer before meeting his doom:

"Say—'Lord have mercy on my soul,' say it Black Donald, say it, I beseech you, she prayed" (393). When he is unwilling to do so for himself, Capitola prays for him: "'May the Lord pity and save Black Donald's soul, if that be yet possible, for the Savior's sake!'" (393). Even after offering this blessing, however, the tomboyish figure still does not drop the villain into the abyss. Still hoping to change him, she pauses and delays. It is only after Donald makes a threatening lunge toward her that Capitola finally releases the trap door.

Rather than rejoicing at the elimination of the heinous villain, Capitola is grief-stricken that she has killed someone. Throwing herself on her bed, she "lay [there], with her face buried in her pillow, the greater portion of the time from two o'clock until day" (393). The next morning, Cap is relieved to hear that Donald has not perished, just been badly injured. In an act that is more characteristic of Victorian heroine than a tomboyish hero once again, she gushes, "'Oh, heaven! he is living! he is living! I have not killed him! . . . for it was a fearful thought that I had been compelled to take a sacred life'" (396). Even more shocking, the formerly unapologetic girl deeply regrets her actions because they will result in another person's imprisonment. "Capitola was everywhere lauded for her brave part in the capture of the famous desperado. But Cap was too sincerely sorry for Black Donald to care for the applause" (399).

Such feelings increase when the villain is tried, convicted and sentenced to death several weeks later. Bursting into tears upon hearing the news, she vows to have his conviction commuted: "'God help you, Donald Bayne, in your great trouble, and I will do all I can to help you in this world. I will go to the Governor myself, and tell him I know you never did any murder'" (466). Although Capitola is convinced that Donald is not a murderer and therefore shouldn't be sentenced to death, no one in the community shares her sentiments and she is forced to abandon the "fruitless enterprise" (468).

Thwarted by conventional methods, Capitola formulates another, more extreme plan that is also extremely feminine: in an effort to reform Black Donald, she decides to help him escape. Giving Donald the tools necessary to break out of prison and the reward money she has been given for his capture, she implores her former seducer to flee the area and become a better person: "'Good-bye! and again,—God redeem you, Donald Bayne!'" (480). Although a seemingly foolish act given the villain's formerly intractable nature, Capitola's efforts prove effectual. Immediately after his release, Donald disbands his group of henchmen, pays for a horse he had previously stolen, and leaves the region to start life anew. In a testament to his changed nature, the once-heinous villain not only writes Capitola a thank-you note for her deed, but even signs it, "Black Donald, Reformed Robber" (484).[9] As this remark indicates, Capitola's tomboyism has allowed her to save her own imperiled white Southern womanhood as well as Black Donald's equally endangered white Southern manhood. The young woman's gender-bending behavior has transformed this formerly villainous figure into a virtuous one.

Capitola Blackface: The Minstrelized Root of White Tomboyism

In a compelling paradox, this code of conduct that was used to empower white adolescent girls like Capitola was connected with various forms of nonwhiteness in *The Hidden Hand*. Although an ostensibly Caucasian character, Southworth's tomboy is associated with elements of blackness or, at least, dark whiteness. Described with "jet black eyelashes," "thick black hair" and "black eyebrows" (33), she is presented as not simply the figurative but literal antithesis to the "Fair Maiden." In light of this description, Capitola is often linked with the villainous Black Donald; the two share a similar physical appearance (dark hair and features), crimson hand (his stained from bloody crimes and hers marred by a birthmark) and names (*Black* Donald and Capitola *Black*). Although the two are

---

9. Another example of Capitola's "feminine tomboyism" can be found in the dueling scene between her and Craven Le Noir. Although Cap is furious with Craven for slandering her character, she cannot bring herself to kill him. Overcome with compassion and pained by her conscience, she replaces the bullets in her gun with split peas. As she explains to the doctor, the night before the duel, "'I wouldn't sleep without praying, and I couldn't pray without giving up my thoughts of fatal vengeance upon Craven Le Noir. So at last I made up my mind to spare his life, and teach him a lesson. The next morning I drew the charges of the revolvers, and re-loaded them with poor powder and dried peas'" (375). Although this ammunition bloodies Craven's face and will leave it scarred, it does not inflict a mortal wound. In an act that recalls stereotypical feminine mercy, Capitola decides to spare the villain's life.

ostensible foils, the murderous villain is in many ways a physical manifestation of her own repressed Otherness. Cap's features are so dark, in fact, that at one point she is sold into slavery with her mulatto nurse on their way to New York. As Nancy Grewell tells Major Warfield, "'And there, master, right afore my own looking eyes, me and the baby was traded off to the captain! It was no use for me to 'splain or 'spostulate! I wan't b'lieved!'" (25). Although a well-timed shipwreck saves them both from enslavement, the white girl occupies—however temporarily—the position of racial Other.

These details may seem to detract from the purportedly Caucasian heritage of Capitola and suggest a racially ambiguous status, but they do not. Because her blackness is metaphoric and not literal, she retains a firm link to whiteness and the socio-economic privilege it affords. Cap may flirt with the fantasy of existing outside mainstream culture, but, as Janet Gabler-Hover has said of other white characters who engage in similar actions, her biology provides her with an important escape hatch. Echoing the condition of white performers in blackface, her racialized association can be removed at any time and her "true" identity reclaimed. Accordingly, when this unruly young character conforms to the expected gender roles for white women—marriage and motherhood—her various forms of darkness fade. Capitola symbolically dilutes her rebellious blackness by marrying a young man named *Greyson*.

In this way, the tomboyism of Southworth's character strengthens not simply her gender but, perhaps more importantly, her race. Recalling the eugenic origins of this new code of female conduct as well as Southworth's own Southern sympathies, the association of this young woman with various forms of nonwhiteness paradoxically reinforces white racial dominance. The gender rebellion of Southworth's tomboyish character may allow her to temporarily play in the dark, but—recalling Toni Morrison's argument about the centrality of blackness in white American culture—this phenomenon is ultimately in the service of whiteness.

Capitola's racialized nature, however, is more than simply "skin deep." In the same way that the young woman's physical features call into question her purported whiteness, so does her gender-bending behavior. The tomboyish girl's antics defy the conventions of white womanhood, and thus they can be seen as defying the conventions of whiteness and even establishing a kinship with blackness. As Hazel Carby, Barbara Christian and Jacqueline Jones have each noted, especially during the nineteenth century, notions of what was "feminine" and "womanly" were contingent on having white skin as well as being of a certain socio-economic status. African American women, because of white racist attitudes about blacks coupled with their financial imperative to work (either in the Southern fields or in the Northern homes of middle- and upper-class white women), were excluded from it. As James Oliver Horton writes,

[T]raditional Western views of acceptable roles for women did not prevent slave women from being used in heavy field work as well as in domestic duties. For them the ideals of feminine delicacy proved no shelter from the punishing lash or the lustful whims of slave masters. They were never too pregnant or too young or too frail to be subject to the harsh demands of an insensitive owner. They shouldered the work load of their race, unable to draw upon the protection generally accorded their sex.[10] (Horton 100)

Such attitudes caused black women to be seen as not only lacking femininity, but also possessing various forms of masculinity. In the words of Barbara Christian, "the black woman was also seen as different from the white woman in her capacity to do man's work" (7). Not coincidentally, one of the most infamous examples of what may be called this "masculinization" of black women occurred one year before the first serial publication of *The Hidden Hand*. In what has become an oft-recounted biographical detail, when black feminist and abolitionist Sojourner Truth was speaking to a crowd in Indiana in 1858, "she bared her breast to prove that she was a woman" (Painter 888). Standing a full six feet tall and possessing a muscular build from years of heavy labor, Truth's gender identity was called into question by her largely white audience.

Although Capitola is an ostensibly Caucasian character, her tomboyish antics illuminate the gendered, classed and especially raced nature of white womanhood. By refusing to conform to the manners and mores of white women through her tomboyish antics, Capitola forges a possible kinship with black women. At various points in *The Hidden Hand*, Major Warfield associates his spunky white ward with both disempowering simian

10. Similar sentiments permeate an array of other books and articles. In *Labor of Love, Labor of Sorrow: Black Women, Work, and the Family from Slavery to the Present*, for instance, Jacqueline Jones provides firsthand accounts of such attitudes. Recording oral histories of slaves and their children, she demonstrates how black women performed an array of labors traditionally gendered male. As one interviewee asserted, "'The women had to split rails all day long, like the men . . . In the winter [they] sawed and cut cord wood just like a man'" (Jones 17–18). Meanwhile, Barbara Christian in *Black Women Novelists: The Development of a Tradition* takes such observations one step further. Rather than seeing white womanhood and black womanhood as oppositional or mutually exclusive entities, she argues that they are mutually constructed. Especially during the antebellum period, middle- and upper-class white women could not have satisfied the requirements of Southern female gentility without the presence of black women: the mammy to do the childcare, the servant to assume the domestic labors and even the Jezebel to perform the sex work. Commenting on the reciprocal nature of white and black womanhood during this era, she asserts, "If the image of the delicate alabaster lady were to retain some semblance of truth, it would be necessary to create the image of another female who was tougher, less sensitive and who could perform with efficiency and grace the duties of motherhood for her mistress and of course for herself. The image of the southern lady, based as it was on a patriarchal myth, demanded another female image, that of the mammy" (Christian 8–9).

qualities and empowering Africanist ones. Calling Cap by such racially charged epithets as an "impertinent monkey," a "ridiculous little ape" and even a "Nubian lion" (36, 123), he maps her transgressions of gender onto transgressions of race.

Coupled with being linked to such generalized forms of blackness, Southworth's Capitola is associated with a particular manifestation of it: minstrelsy. Making its debut in urban theatres in the North during the 1830s and 1840s, when its visual style and comedic methods permeated nearly all facets of American society by the mid-nineteenth century. First published in 1859, *The Hidden Hand* was written and released during the cultural ascendancy of minstrelsy. A recent article by Patricia Okker and Jeffrey R. Williams, in fact, examines the way in which this performance mode formed the basis for the novel's black characters. As they point out, from the physical appearance of Wool to the comic antics of Pitapat, the novel's African American characters are largely drawn from minstrel stereotypes. Together with shaping the presentation of black characters in *The Hidden Hand*, blackface minstrelsy plays an important role in the construction of white tomboy Capitola. Throughout Southworth's narrative, the iconoclastic main character engages in a minstrelized form of gender rebellion. A considerable portion of the young woman's tomboyish actions are modeled after blackface behaviors.

From the moment of her birth, Capitola enters a racially charged, minstrelized world. The young woman is raised in not simply the slums of New York, but the region Eric Lott has identified as the birthplace of blackface: the Bowery. In this rough-and-tumble area, working-class young men—known in vernacular as "b'hoys"—were among the first performers of, and audiences for, minstrelsy. When Capitola trades her petticoats for pants, she can be seen as assuming the persona of not simply an adolescent boy but a Bowery b'hoy in many ways. Referring to Major Warfield as "governor" and his plan to bring her to Virginia as "bully," she employs their slang (36, 49). Likewise, with her success finding an array of lucrative odd jobs, she inculcates their savvy.

Although Major Warfield may take his niece out of the Bowery, he cannot take the Bowery out of her. When Cap returns to Virginia, she brings many facets of the b'hoys with her, and it is these elements that form the basis for her tomboyism. Frustrated with the Major, for instance, Cap makes a gesture that Southworth characterizes "as more expressive than elegant" (118). Similarly, missing the excitement of New York, Capitola repeatedly says that she is "spoiling for a fight" (110). At one point, Ira Warfield becomes so frustrated by the presence of these qualities that he fears his young ward will never "'leave off this Bowery boy talk'" (173).

Together with echoing such generalized traits of the b'hoys, Capitola echoes the minstrel tradition with which these figures were associated. Recalling blackface performers, Major Warfield notes that his niece delights in being "a droll . . . a mimic" (175). In addition, the young woman engages in the malapropisms commonly associated with this performance mode. Confusing the word "pillow" for "pillory" (34), she evokes such popular minstrel characters as Zip Coon. Moreover, as Okker and Williams have noted, such traits typify the novel's minstrel-infused black characters. Throughout *The Hidden Hand*, Wool and Pitapat engage in many similar types of verbal misunderstandings, humorous use of homonyms and nonsense language (see Okker and Williams 134–136).

The various connections between Southworth's gender-bending main character and minstrelsy illuminate blackface as another, previously overlooked, source for this code of female conduct. Although white tomboys and minstrel performers are not commonly studied in tandem with one another, they are twinned figures in many ways. Both are interested in lampooning traditional gender roles, satirizing established codes of sexual conduct and ridiculing conventional manners and mores. In many ways, in fact, many of the qualities that are among this code of conduct's most famous and endearing—such as the tomboy's playfulness and parodic transvestism and her feisty irreverence and jovial good humor—can be traced back to this performance mode.

Blackface minstrelsy also formed an important component to the tomboy's interest in the maintenance of white racial supremacy. In the same way that white blackface performers smeared their faces with burnt cork to buttress rather than blur the distinctions between blackness and whiteness, so too does Capitola Black adopt a minstrelized form of white tomboyism. Whereas this young woman's behavior had previously illuminated the fluidity of gender, it now illuminates the fluidity of race. The character's various links to blackness in general and blackface minstrelsy in particular aver rather than eradicate her whiteness. Recalling the rhetorical strategy of many antebellum feminists who used the language of black slavery to characterize the condition of white womanhood, Cap repeatedly insists that she is not a "cur" or "slave" who will submit to the "gilded slavery" of patriarchal oppression (123–124, 187). In addition to constituting a performative position that Cap can embrace and discard at will, the characterization also negates the very real hardships of slavery and thus contributes to the romanticized view of Southern blacks. As her guardian's harsh treatment of black servants Wool and Pitapat has illustrated, not all slavery is as gilded or benevolent as her description suggests. Moreover, Cap easily gives orders to her uncle's black slaves, and even threatens to whip them if they do not obey. Likewise, Cap frequently belittles her black handmaid Pitapat, calling her a "goose," "blockhead" and even "stupid dolt" (194). By permitting Capitola to defy white patriarchal authority and the confines of "ladylike" behavior, her minstrelized tomboyism allows her to reap the transgressive benefits of "playing in the dark" without jeopardizing her superiority over actual black characters.

This phenomenon extends to include her bourgeois class status as well. From the moment Cap arrives in Virginia, she has no trouble asserting her position as a genteel white woman. Although the tomboyish girl traffics in various forms of blackness and blackface minstrelsy, she adamantly refuses to be treated as anything other than a white Southern aristocrat. Joanne Dobson has noted that even before she meets Major Warfield or becomes aware of her claim to the Le Noir estate, Cap has an inherent sense of class superiority. While living in Rag Alley, for instance, she refuses the menial jobs that Nancy Grewell had performed to support the pair: taking in laundry or doing piece-work. On the contrary, when orphaned by the mulatto nurse, she transforms herself into a boy so that she may assume more respectable forms of labor, some of which are even considered middle-class. As she tells the court magistrate: "'I carried carpet-bags, held horses, put in coal, cleaned sidewalks, blacked gentlemen's boots, and did everything an honest lad could turn his hand to!'" (47). As Patricia Okker and Jeffrey R. Williams have written of this scene, Southworth is "careful to distance her heroine from actual working-class women's culture" (142).

When Capitola returns to Virginia, this characteristic only increases. From the moment the young woman arrives at Hurricane Hall, she immediately purchases a long list of items that belie her sense of entitlement:

> Capitola . . . did not fail to indulge her taste for rich and costly toys, and supplied herself with a large ivory dressing-case, lined with velvet, and furnished with ivory-handled combs and brushes, silver boxes and crystal bottles; a papier mache work-box, with gold thimble, needle-case and perforator and gold-mounted scissors and winders; and an ebony writing-desk, with silver-mounted crystal standishes. . . . (79)

As Joanne Dobson has observed, Cap's keen eye for finery seems instinctual or intuitive; her taste must be a product of her inherent good breeding since it cannot have arisen from her Rag Alley upbringing (xxix). Capitola uses her tomboyism to assert her class status. When her reputation is slandered by the villainous Craven Le Noir, for instance, she mirrors the behavior of upper-class white men by engaging him in a duel. In fact, she asks for the "satisfaction of a *gentleman*" [my emphasis] (367). Compared by the narrator to Pierre Terrail, seigneur de Bayard, a heroic French soldier from the fifteenth century (351), Cap's actions assert her race and class status as much as her gender one. By defending her reputation as a virginal white woman, she is also defending her inclusion in the landed aristocracy of the Southern ruling class.

In this way, while both Eric Lott and David Roediger have emphasized the role that minstrelsy played in engendering white working-class masculinity, *The Hidden Hand* suggests that it shaped the construction of antebellum white tomboys as well. Although this racially charged performance mode and gender-bending code of female conduct are not commonly thought to have much in common, they mix and mingle in Southworth's famous novel. The depiction of Capitola reveals that blackface minstrelsy and white tomboyism did more than simply emerge at similar moments in the nation's history, they performed the same cultural work; both sought to bolster whiteness.

The Capitola Craze: Tomboyism Emerges as a National Phenomenon

The immense literary and cultural regard for *The Hidden Hand* not only catapulted the 1859 narrative into the national spotlight, it did the same for tomboyism. The widespread appeal of Capitola Black and her gender-bending antics transformed this code of conduct from a fledgling cultural practice into a widespread national phenomenon. In the years following the release of *The Hidden Hand*, a growing number of girls began adopting this code of conduct, and a growing number of narratives began depicting tomboys as a main or at least minor character.

As a result, in the decade that followed, what may be termed a "second generation" of tomboy characters appeared in U.S. literature and culture. From the title characters in Susan Coolidge's *What Katy Did* (1872) and Elizabeth Stuart Phelps's *Gypsy Breynton* (1868) to Cassandra Morgeson in Elizabeth Stoddard's *The Morgesons* (1862) and rootin'-tootin' cowgirl Calamity Jane in Edward Wheeler's *Deadwood Dick* dime novels (1877–1897), the 1860s and 1870s witnessed a dramatic increase in both their literary presence and cultural power. Of the numerous gender-bending characters that appeared during these decades, however, Jo March from Louisa May Alcott's *Little Women* (1868) is by far the most famous. Wildly popular in the late nineteenth century, she remains a beloved icon of female gender rebellion to this day.

Interestingly, the second serial reprinting of Southworth's *The Hidden Hand* coincided exactly with the first appearance of this literary tomboy whose popularity would eventually come to eclipse that of Capitola. Although the publication date of *Little Women* is commonly listed as 1868, the text was initially released as two separate volumes, the first of which appeared in October 1868 (and consisted of chapters one through twenty-three), while the second installment was released in April 1869 (and was comprised of the chapters now numbered twenty-four through forty-seven). The historical overlap between Southworth's *The Hidden Hand* and Alcott's *Little Women* was more than simply a literary coincidence. In many ways, Jo March can be read as the heiress to the tomboy throne inaugurated by Capitola. In an often overlooked literary allusion in *Little Women*, Jo makes a veiled reference to the writings of E. D. E. N. Southworth. As the tomboyish figure discusses her literary aspirations with a young man at a lecture one afternoon, he calls attention to an author he considers particularly successful and who has a narrative in the story paper that Jo is reading: "he pointed to the name of Mrs. S. L. A. N. G. Northbury, under the title of the tale" (267). Inspired by both the young man's respect for the author and his assertion that "'she makes a good living out of stories like this'" (267) Jo vows to pen a narrative in this style. Since she ultimately publishes this story under a pseudonym, one could say that it, too, was written by a "hidden hand." In the following chapter, I examine how Louisa May Alcott's topsy-turvy character continues not only Capitola's legacy of white tomboyism, but also its association with various forms of nonwhiteness. *Little Women* reveals how the Civil War necessitated new forms of female gender incivility and, in doing so, demonstrated that the battle over changing notions of white womanhood was not entirely divorced from the one over the abolition of black slavery.

2

The Tomboy Becomes a Cultural Phenomenon

Louisa May Alcott's Little Women

Whereas the antebellum era began to recognize the need for healthy white women who would bear the next generation of robust white leaders, the Civil War period became unequivocally convinced of it. Throughout the North and the South, the outbreak of hostilities and the exodus of thousands of men for the battlefield precipitated a crisis that compelled many adolescent girls and young women to engage in an array of gender-bending behaviors. As Carroll Smith-Rosenberg has noted, "The Civil War, in the name of patriotism and humanitarianism, called hundreds of thousands of women out of their homes" (173). With their husbands, fathers and brothers away, adolescent girls and young women assumed an array of formerly male roles and responsibilities. Although formerly forbidden to own property or hold bank accounts, many were now left in charge of managing their family's financial affairs. Similarly, whereas previously barred from participating in government, some women were now largely responsible for maintaining civic law and order. Finally, while expected to rely on male protection before, scores of wives and mothers were placed in the position of defending their homes from invading troops. As a result, many women who may not have considered themselves gender iconoclasts before the Civil War found themselves engaging in an array of tomboyish actions during it. The large-scale involvement of women during the Civil War, in fact, prompted James McPherson to note that the conflict "affected the female half of the population as profoundly as the male half" (xv).

Given the way in which the outbreak of hostilities disrupted conventional gender roles for middle- and upper-class white women, Catherine Clinton, Judith Fetterley and most recently Elizabeth Young have viewed the Civil War as a rich metaphor about the era in addition to a military conflict during it.[1] As Young points out, "the term 'civil war' encoded a complex set of gender connotations. From 'civus,' of or pertaining to citizens, 'civil' is both a description of a political status and a set of behavioral norms" (11). The disruptions of the literal Civil War can be seen as having precipitated a figurative one in which white women went to battle over notions of gender civility. Working as laundresses, cooks and seamstresses, not to mention spies, scouts and even cross-dressed soldiers for the forces, they waged intentional or unintentional war against traditional notions of female behavior.

The invaluable work that adolescent girls and young women performed during the Civil War had a profound effect on the popularity of tomboyism. Whereas this code of conduct had been a relatively small societal practice during the antebellum era, it morphed into a widespread cultural phenomenon. During the 1860s and 1870s, Americans witnessed the benefits of creating physically strong, intellectually capable and emotionally resilient young women. More than simply helping to ensure white racial supremacy, tomboys could help ensure national unity. In *Divided Houses: Gender and the Civil War*, in fact, Catherine Clinton and Nina Silber make a direct link between the wartime activities of Northern white women and the Union victory (245).

In the wake of such events, tomboyism as both a cultural concept and a literary convention became more powerful and pervasive in the United States. As Alfred Habegger has observed, akin to stock characters such as the "fallen woman" and the male "rake," "The tomboy became a major type in the 1860s" ("Funny" 172). From Gypsy Breynton in Elizabeth Stuart Phelps's series by the same name (1866–1867) to the beloved Katy Carr in Susan Coolidge's *What Katy Did* (1872) and its sequels, spunky female figures increased in number as well as notoriety. Moreover, far from being limited to the portrayal of fictional female characters, tomboyism permeated the lives of factual girls and young women. As Anne Scott MacLeod has written, the memoirs, reminiscences, and autobiographies of adult women who were raised during the 1860s and 1870s are filled

1. See Catherine Clinton's *The Other Civil War: American Women in the Nineteenth Century* (New York: Hill and Wang, 1984); Judith Fetterley's "*Little Women*: Alcott's Civil War," *Feminist Studies*, vol. 5 (1979): 369–383; and Elizabeth Young's *Disarming the Nation: Women's Writing and the American Civil War* (Chicago: U of Chicago, 1999).

with tales of their youthful tomboyish adventures: climbing trees, fishing in horse troughs, playing outdoors, skinning knees, even falling into rain barrels (7). As MacLeod notes, reading these accounts eradicates conceptions the "prim and proper little girls" that are commonly associated with nineteenth-century American life (7).

Of all the gender-bending female figures who made their debut during the 1860s and 1870s, however, Jo March from Louisa May Alcott's *Little Women* (1868) merits special attention. As Elizabeth Janeway aptly notes, this figure is "the tomboy dream come true" (97). More than any other gender-bending female character highlighted in this study, her name is synonymous with tomboyism. Although nearly 150 years have passed since Jo's first appearance, she continues to be seen by critics and readers alike as not simply one example of a rebellious tomboy, but the paradigm for such figures. Writers as diverse as Gertrude Stein, Simone de Beauvoir and Joyce Carol Oates have commented on the influence that Alcott's novel in general and that Jo March in particular had on their development. Likewise, an array of books and articles have paid homage to this iconic tomboyish character. From Christian McEwan's collection of tomboy tales about "high adventure, true grit and real life" called *Jo's Girls*, to Ruth Berman's essay on sex roles in children's literature which bears the emphatic title "No Jo Marches!," her gender iconoclasm is well known even to those who have not read Alcott's text.

Focusing on this popular tomboy character from one of the most famous tomboy novels, this chapter explores the expansion of this gender-bending code of female conduct from a fledgling cultural concept to a widespread national phenomenon and the changes that resulted from its movement into the mainstream. Given the important role that the Civil War played in the popularization of tomboyism, Jo March has long been considered a tomboy icon, but the pages that follow make a case for seeing her as a Civil War one as well. This beloved character was created by an author who was a tomboyish girl when young and a direct participant in the female gender incivilities wrought by the Civil War as an adult. In a journal entry that the future author wrote when she was fifteen years old, for instance, she commented, "I was born with a boys nature & always had more sympathy for & interest in them than in girls" (Alcott *Journals* 79). Frolicking outdoors, getting into scrapes and generally running wild, Alcott consistently rejected True Womanhood in favor of tomboyhood. As the future author would recall later in life, "'No boy could be my friend until I had beaten him in a race, and no girl if she refused to climb trees, leap fences and be a tomboy'" (Alcott *Life* 20).

The outbreak of the Civil War and its accompanying call for women to engage in various gender-bending behaviors provided Alcott with the social justification and even patriotic obligation to act on these desires. As a member of a New England family that had a long-standing commitment to abolition,[2] the future author quickly volunteered for wartime service. In 1862, at the age of thirty, she left her home in Massachusetts to work as a nurse in a Union army hospital near Georgetown. In a journal entry she wrote just before departing, Alcott revealed how her wartime activity allowed her to actualize some of her own tomboyish dreams and desires: "I set forth . . . feeling as if I was the son of the house going off to war" (Alcott *Journals* 110).

Although Alcott served only two months before a bout of typhoid fever forced her to return home, the experience had a profound impact on her life. Permanently damaging her health, it also became the impetus for her career as a writer. Soon after her arrival back in Massachusetts, Alcott began work on a thinly veiled account of her nursing experiences based on the letters that she had written to friends and family. Titled *Hospital Sketches*, the book was first published in 1863 and launched her literary career. Like Alcott's own brief but influential time at the Union hospital, the narrative was filled with accounts about the gender iconoclastic nature of this ostensibly gender normative task. As she revealed, Civil War nurses were frequently required to tap into such stereotypically masculine traits as physical strength, constitutional fortitude and emotional steadfastness. Often working around the clock, they engaged in such "unwomanly" tasks as assisting with amputations and cleaning festering wounds.

Alcott's engagement with the Civil War and the female gender incivilities that it precipitated are commonly thought limited to *Hospital Sketches* and the handful of short stories that appeared in the subsequent edition,[3] but this chapter makes a case for seeing them as an important component to her famous girls' novel *Little Women* as well. In the pages that follow, I argue that the conflict does more than simply provide the historical backdrop for the book; rather, it plays a central role in the construction of its tomboyish main character. From the opening pages of *Little Women*, the gender-bending behavior of Jo March is rooted in her desire to be a Union soldier and join her father in the conflict. Clomping around in army boots and declaring herself "the man of the family" (5), Jo frequently bemoans having to knit socks for the soldiers rather than be one. As she asserts in the opening chapter of *Little Women*, "'I can't get over my

2. For more information on the anti-slavery efforts of Louisa May Alcott and her family, see Sarah Elbert's *Louisa May Alcott on Race, Sex and Slavery* (Boston: Northeastern UP, 1997); Martha Saxton's *Louisa May: A Modern Biography of Louisa May Alcott* (Boston: Houghton Mifflin, 1977); and Madelon Bedell's *The Alcotts: Biography of a Family* (New York: C. N. Potter, 1980).

3. In 1869, Alcott released a second edition of *Hospital Sketches*. Called *Hospital Sketches and Camp and Fireside Stories*, the book contained the author's original account about nurse Tribulation Periwinkle as well as a handful of Civil War-themed short stories that she had published previously. These included the now-famous narratives "M.L.," "My Contraband," and "Nelly's Hospital."

disappointment in not being a boy, and it's worse than ever now, for I'm dying to go and fight with papa, and I can only stay at home and knit like a poky old woman'" (3). At one point, Jo even cites some of the gender-bending labors assumed by wartime women, including the one performed by Alcott herself: "'I wish I could go as a drummer, a *vivan*—what's its name? or a nurse'" (8). While critics have frequently cast Jo as longing to enjoy the freedoms associated with a generic form of middle-class white masculinity, she wishes to partake in a more specific, heroic and politicized version of Northern white male bellicosity.

The Civil War embodies much more than a mere patriotic justification for Jo March's participation in tomboyism; it also serves as a powerful metaphor for her subjective experience of it. Throughout Alcott's text, the tomboyish character engages in an internal conflict or what may be termed "civil war" over her gender role. Unlike Capitola Black, whose gender-bending conduct was generally praised and admired, Jo's is routinely disparaged. She faces constant pressure to abandon her gender-bending habits and become, as the title of the novel suggests, a "little woman." In the opening pages of the text, for instance, Amy wishes that sister would "'stop making a guy of herself'" (3). Likewise, a few moments later, Meg implores after her tomboyish sibling begins to whistle, "'Don't Jo, it's too boyish'" (3). As these comments indicate, the young woman's disregard for stereotypical codes of female civility and her engagement in tomboyish forms of incivility are met with disapproval.

Investigating the famous gender rebellion of Civil War era tomboy Jo March along with the pressure that she feels to abandon it, this chapter explores the innovative but often incendiary characteristics of this code of conduct during the 1860s and 1870s. Although tomboyism experienced heightened popularity in this era, it also became the subject of heightened controversy. A combination of the massive rise in the number of gender-bending female figures, an increase in the professional and economic opportunities for women, and the emergence of a new stage of development called "adolescence" that transformed childhood in general and girlhood in particular sparked a crisis for practitioners like Jo March. Although Alcott's character may be excluded from directly participating in the nation's military conflict, she is fighting a civil war of her own. With her identification as "the man of the family" and desire for a professional writing career, Jo is not engaged in a war between the North and the South but between masculinity and femininity. Moving the Civil War from the background to the forefront of Alcott's narrative, this chapter illustrates that although *Little Women* omits the violent clashes of men at the battlefront, it spotlights the equally turbulent battles waged by tomboyish women on the home front. Building on work by Catherine Clinton, Judith Fetterley and Elizabeth Young, I discuss how *Little Women* chronicles the civil war that is raging within its gender-bending female character over her participation in tomboyism.

Tomboyism Experiences "Growing Pains": The Emergence of Adolescence and the Inauguration of Taming

American political, social and economic life were not the only areas to undergo profound changes during the Civil War era. As historians Philippe Ariès and Peter Hunt have written, so too did its conception of childhood. During the 1860s and 1870s, parents and physicians moved away from dividing the human life span into the two periods of childhood and adulthood, preferring instead to break it into three stages of development. In the years directly following the Civil War, they added an intermediary phase called adolescence, from the Latin verb *adolescere* meaning "to grow up." Encompassing the period from roughly twelve years old to around twenty, adolescence was envisioned as a type of apprenticeship or training ground. Instead of being suddenly catapulted from childhood directly into adulthood, it allowed boys and girls to more slowly slough off their juvenile ways and receive extended instruction in the responsibilities of later life.

The expansion of white tomboyism and the birth of adolescence were closely connected during the Civil War era. In many ways, in fact, this new stage of human development became yoked with this code of female conduct in the literary depiction of girlhood. Nearly all of the narratives that showcased gender-bending female characters during this era presented them as adolescents: Jo March is fifteen years old at the start of *Little Women*, while both Katy Carr from *What Katy Did* and Gypsy Breynton from Phelps's series by the same name are twelve at the beginning of those novels. As a result of this widespread literary depiction of tomboys as adolescents, these books were as much about this new stage of human development as they were about this new code of female conduct.

Although the representation of tomboyish characters as adolescents may seem to indicate a positive connection between this code of female conduct and new stage of human development, the opposite was true in many ways. Whereas tomboyism was seen as a beneficial entity during the antebellum period, increases in the social, economic and professional opportunities for women caused its presence to be more problematic during the Civil War era. Rather than engaging in tomboyish behavior in order to better prepare themselves for the private sphere, many adolescent girls seemed to be doing so to gain entrance into the public one. From assuming responsibility for the family business to leaving home to aid the military forces, they participated in behaviors that were far removed from the feminine institutions of marriage and motherhood.

Alcott's representation of Jo March reflects this shift.[4] Unlike Capitola Black, whose oft-expressed goal was to marry her childhood friend Herbert

---

4. Susan Coolidge's *What Katy Did* encodes these sentiments as well. The tomboyish title character asserts that her greatest wish is not to get married and become a mother but

Greyson, Jo has a different dream. As she repeatedly asserts, her greatest wish is "'to place the name of March upon the roll of fame'" (238). She tells her neighbor Laurie Laurence, in fact, "'I think I shall write books, and get rich and famous; that would suit me, so that is my favorite dream'" (143). Jo does not simply long for a life that contains pursuits outside of marriage and motherhood; she envisions her literary aspirations taking their place. When Laurie predicts that his tomboyish playmate will be the next to get married, she replies, "'Me! don't be alarmed; I'm not one of the agreeable sort. Nobody will want me, and it's a mercy, for there should always be one old maid in a family'" (246). Even the birth of Meg's twins does not change her mind. Although enamored with the infants, Jo informs her sister, "'I don't believe that I shall ever marry; I'm happy as I am, and love my liberty too well to be in any hurry to give it up for any mortal man'" (365).

Closely related to this weakening connection to marriage and motherhood was a weakening connection to femininity. Unlike antebellum tomboys, who may have challenged traditional mores for women but retained a firm link to feminine behaviors and a female identity, their Civil War counterparts were more masculine and male-identified. Although Jo is the main female character in Alcott's girls' novel, she is more like a male one. Not only does Jo dress in masculine attire and adopt boyish habits, but she prefers the masculine version of her name and refers to herself by male pronouns. Indeed, when she befriends Laurie, the two get along so well because Jo "seemed to understand the boy almost as well as if she had been one herself" (Alcott *Little* 54). Rather than expanding the boundaries of acceptable notions of femininity, tomboys during the Civil War era began to co-opt elements of masculinity: they bemoaned being born female and having to participate in feminine activities.[5]

The addition of both a more masculine gender identity and professional ambitions tarnished the otherwise laudatory public perception of tomboyism. Although this code of conduct had the potential to preserve

---

to do something that "would make her famous, so that everybody would hear of her, and want to know her" (Coolidge 10). Together with listing "rowing out in boats or saving people's lives" as means by which she could accomplish this goal, Katy offers another activity that indicates how the gender incivilities precipitated by the Civil War have shaped her desires: "'Or perhaps I shall go and *nurse in the hospital like Miss Nightingale*'" [italics mine] (Coolidge 20).

5. Similar observations could be made about the title characters in *Gypsy Breynton* and *What Katy Did*. Coolidge's Katy Carr "tore her dress every day, hated sewing, and didn't care a button about being called 'good'" (4). Likewise, Phelps' tomboy wishes she were a cloud so that she did "not have anything to do but float round all day in the sunshine—no lessons nor torn dresses nor hateful old sewing to do" (Phelps *Gypsy* 89). Indeed, in a passage that recalls Alcott's description of Jo, Phelps asserts of her tomboyish main character: "Altogether Gypsy seemed like a very pretty, piquant mistake; as if a mischievous boy had somehow stolen the plaid dress, red cheeks, quick wit, and little indescribable graces of a girl, and was playing off a continual joke on the world" (*Gypsy* 51).

national unity, it also had the potential to eradicate traditional American social and family life. Instead of producing feminine wives and mothers—as tomboyism had been intended—it would engender male-identified single women.

In an effort to combat this hazardous potential, another new characteristic was added to this code of conduct during the Civil War era: what would come to be known as "tomboy taming." As its name suggest, this process sought to eradicate—ideally by choice, but if necessary by force—a gender-bending girl's iconoclastic ways and have her adopt more feminine behaviors. This process was imposed at a particular point in the tomboyish girl's development: with the onset of puberty and entrance into the newly created stage of adolescence. As the time when young girls were seen as exceedingly impressionable and thus in need of receiving firm instruction in traditional female roles, adolescence was also the period when tomboyish girls needed to shed their gender-bending ways and adopt more feminine behaviors.

Together with signaling the end of tomboyism as a lifelong mode of behavior, taming became the defining feature of literary representations of this code of conduct during the 1860s and 1870s. In Alcott's girls' novel, for example, Jo abandons her topsy-turvy ways and acquiesces to life as a "little woman." Underscoring the way in which this transformation was connected with age in general and the onset of adolescence in particular, Jo's sister Meg remarks, "'You're old enough to leave off boyish tricks and behave better, Josephine. It didn't matter so much when you were a little girl; but now you are so tall, and turn up your hair, you should remember that you are a young lady'" (3). Although Jo implores later, "'Don't try to make me grow up before my time, Meg; it's hard enough to have you change all of a sudden; let me be a little girl as long as I can'" (394), she cannot stave off the encroachment of womanly constraint upon girlhood freedom any longer. By the end of Alcott's novel, Jo abandons her goal of being a literary spinster for one that is more selfless and feminine: teaching. When one of her sisters asks how this vision compares to her previous dream of becoming a famous author, she responds in a gender-appropriate way: "'the life I wanted then seems selfish and lonely and cold to me now'" (489). Given the way in which the advent of taming changed the fate of rebellious female figures, it also changed the plot of the narratives written about them. Whereas antebellum novels like *The Hidden Hand* sought to persuade young girls to adopt tomboyism, postbellum texts such as *Little Women* were lengthy treatises about why such behaviors should be abandoned.[6]

---

6. Once again, similar observations could be made about *Gypsy Breynton* and *What Katy Did*. In Elizabeth Stuart Phelps's novel, Gypsy is transformed from a "Regular Romp" who has the "ease and fearlessness of a boy" to a "grown-up lady, with long dresses and

Tomboy taming may have been a universal feature of narratives during the 1860s and 1870s, but it was far from a simple one. Attempts to eradicate iconoclastic behavior in tomboyish girls and institute more gender-appropriate conduct sparked a crisis for many of these figures. Permitted to be adventurous and autonomous as young girls, they were required to be submissive and accepting as young women. As a result, in the words of Sharon O'Brien, tomboy taming "introduced a crucial discontinuity between childhood and adolescence which made stress and conflict almost inevitable" ("Tomboyism" 354). Of all the tomboy characters who appeared during the 1860s and 1870s, perhaps none illustrates this internal crisis about the "civil war" over female gender roles better than Jo March. For the bulk of Alcott's narrative, the beloved main character struggles to eliminate her gender-bending ways and behave as an appropriate "little woman." During a conversation with Laurie, for instance, Jo grapples with the gender-appropriate pronoun by which to refer to herself. After hearing numerous admonitions to leave off with her tomboyish ways, she corrects herself mid-sentence. "'I'm a business man—girl, I mean'" (51). Similarly, while playing with Laurie's classmates from school later in the narrative, she "found it very difficult to refrain from imitating the gentlemanly attitudes, phrases and feats which seemed more natural to her than the decorums prescribed for young ladies" (239).

In this way, although the gender incivilities precipitated by the Civil War sparked a surge in tomboyish behaviors, they also ignited a backlash against them. Just as the nation was at war over the civil future of slavery, tomboys were engaged in a war of their own over female gender civility. Fighting not on the battlefront but on the home front, they transformed this era's domestic conflict (a war between the states) into one about domesticity (a war between masculinity and femininity). Exemplifying this link, Jo makes an explicit connection at one point between her internal conflict over gender identity and the external one over national unity. Discussing the struggle to control her emotions and be a proper "little woman," she asserts, "keeping her temper at home was a much harder task than facing a rebel or two down South" (9).

---

hair done up behind" who doesn't "care anything about climbing" (25, 20, 134). From the opening pages of the text, in fact, tomboyism is identified as a problem on which the main character needs to work rather than an asset that she should cultivate. As Gypsy's brother says to his tomboyish sibling, "'you're a diamond decidedly in the rough. . . . You need cutting down and polishing'" (Gypsy 45). Likewise, Katy Carr is scolded by both her teacher and her Aunt Izzie for not "acting like a lady" (35). As discussed in the introduction to this project, when the rambunctious young girl refuses to abandon her tomboyism by choice, she is compelled to by force: a serious injury leaves her bedridden for four years. The long convalescence transforms Katy from an independent, daring and autonomous adolescent tomboy to a passive, submissive and even saintly adult woman.

Topsy and a Topsy-Turvy Tomboy:
Uncle Tom's Cabin in *Little Women*

In a detail that demonstrates the reciprocal nature of this phenomenon, the tomboy's inner civil war over gender was not entirely divorced from the outer one over slavery. Throughout *Little Women*, Jo's struggle with the cultural construction of middle- and upper-class white womanhood becomes a struggle in many ways with the cultural construction of whiteness. In the same way that the gender incivilities of factual white women during the Civil War had a powerful impact on the cultural production of tomboyism, the well-known antics of a fictive black female figure—Topsy from Harriet Beecher Stowe's *Uncle Tom's Cabin*—may have influenced this code of conduct as well. In addition to being one of the most famous characters from the 1852 abolitionist novel, she may have been a source of inspiration for Alcott's beloved Jo March. With Topsy's rambunctious behavior and iconoclastic gender identity, Stowe's rebellious black character plays an important but previously overlooked role in the tomboyish rebellion against not simply female gender roles but, as I will show, the manners and mores of white "little women."

Since the publication of *Little Women* in 1868, Jo March has commonly been seen as Alcott's semi-autobiographical alter ego. The numerous physical, emotional and especially behavioral connections between the author and her fictional creation have been well documented by critics and biographers. Consequently, the primary lens through which Alcott's narrative and its tomboyish main character have been viewed is autobiography.[7] This section pushes such readings one step further by arguing that the novel's tomboyish main character resonates not only with Alcott's own gender identity and childhood experiences, but with her literary influences and readerly tastes. Together with the oft-mentioned autobiographical links between Jo and Alcott, this beloved tomboy possesses another and previously unforeseen textual connection with Topsy from *Uncle Tom's Cabin*.

The influence of Harriet Beecher Stowe's *Uncle Tom's Cabin* on nineteenth-century American literature in general and on writing from the Civil War era in particular is difficult to overestimate. Outselling every book except the Bible, the novel enjoyed unprecedented success and, as Jane Tompkins famously demonstrated, was able to exert extensive cultural power. The sentimental story about the plight of enslaved black characters and the white people with whom they come in contact so intensified the conflict over slavery that many even credited it with being a catalyst for

---

7. For more on the autobiographical nature of *Little Women* in general and Jo March in particular, see especially Madeleine B. Stern's literary biography *Louisa May Alcott* (Norman: University of Oklahoma, 1971).

the Civil War. In what has become an oft-cited anecdote—and one which Elizabeth Young astutely observes also embeds the future title of Alcott's novel—Abraham Lincoln characterized Stowe as the "little woman who made this great war" upon meeting her in 1862.

Like many other Americans during this era, Alcott was a devotee of Stowe's writing. In a journal entry, the future author of *Little Women* identified *Uncle Tom's Cabin* as one of her favorite books (Alcott *Life* 283). Coupled with possessing a professional admiration for the popular abolitionist author, Alcott forged a personal connection with her. Both Sarah Elbert and Elizabeth Ammons have discussed that the two shared mutual friends, publishing connections and even views about writing.[8] More than simply socializing on several occasions, Alcott and Stowe occasionally commented on each other's work.[9]

Stowe's literary influence on Alcott did not end there, for Alcott also clearly had the elder author's most famous novel in mind while penning her own Civil War story. Early in *Little Women*, Marmee advises her daughters who are frustrated by the burdens of wartime hardship to concentrate on the happiness wrought by friends and family rather than lamenting the material pleasures that are beyond their reach. Identifying an apt literary parallel, Jo humorously notes that Marmee has urged them to do "as Old Chloe did in *Uncle Tom*—'Tink ob yer marcies, chillen, tink ob yer marcies'" (45).

While Jo's humorous imitation of Aunt Chloe connects the two novels in the general context of the Civil War, Alcott's tomboy can be placed in dialogue with a specific character from Stowe's text: the mischievous Topsy. In light of Alcott's esteem for Stowe and the ubiquitous nature of *Uncle Tom's Cabin* at the time, this central character from the 1852 abolition novel may have consciously or unconsciously influenced Alcott's construction of Jo March. Indeed, this unruly black character anticipates many of the tomboyish actions and attitudes that would come to characterize *Little Women*'s beloved tomboy. With her hair cropped short to her head and her rebellion against the manners and mores of white womanhood, Topsy embodies a tomboyish figure as much as a comedic one. Even though these

---

8. For more on the shared vision of Stowe and Alcott, see Sarah Elbert's *A Hunger for Home: Louisa May Alcott and* Little Women (Philadelphia: Temple, UP, 1984) and Elizabeth Ammons's *Conflicting Stories: American Women Writers at the Turn into the Twentieth Century* (New York: Oxford UP, 1991).

9. Janet S. Zehr has written that Stowe read a copy of Alcott's 1864 novel *Moods* and "attacked the morality of *Moods* in vague terms in a conversation with Thomas Niles," the editor who later would commission Alcott to pen her famous girls' novel (331). While there is no explicit evidence indicating that Niles relayed this information to Alcott, when she revised *Moods* in the early 1880s, she seems to have had Stowe's remarks about it in mind; in keeping with the elder author's criticism of the book, she excised objectionable passages to make the new version more universally appealing.

two characters may seem like opposites in many ways—one is black, the other white; one has no mother, the other idolizes her mother; one is a Louisiana slave, the other is a New England abolitionist; one delights in being "wicked," the other constantly strives to behave—they possess an array of common traits. From Jo's rebellion against the confines of white women's gender roles and her repeated association with a brown skin tone to her outbursts of anger and her use of the phrase "topsy-turvy" which embeds the name of Stowe's character, the personality traits and even daily behaviors of this well-known white tomboy mirror this equally popular black character. For these reasons, although Jo March has long been seen as a celebrated icon of white tomboyism, the pages that follow suggest that she has much in common with a character who is described in Harriet Beecher Stowe's novel as "one of the blackest of her race" (258). As my discussion will demonstrate, Jo March may be commonly celebrated for her adoption of a Civil War era form of heroic white masculinity, but her behavior is also buttressed by an antebellum vision of unruly black femininity.

From the moment that Topsy first appears in Harriet Beecher Stowe's *Uncle Tom's Cabin*, she stands in sharp opposition to women's gender roles in general and those for middle- and upper-class white figures in particular. As both Hazel Carby and Patricia Hill Collins have written, nineteenth-century America associated whiteness with such traits as civility, decorum and self-control, and blackness with the characteristics of unruliness, impulsiveness and excess. Although *Uncle Tom's Cabin* makes a compelling case for the abolition of slavery, it draws on an abundance of racial stereotypes in its presentation of black characters like Topsy. As her name suggests, the young girl is literally and figuratively topsy-turvy. Nearly every aspect of her physical appearance, personal temperament, and daily behavior inverts the heavily raced and classed notions of what was "womanly" and "feminine" during this era. Rather than possessing long feminine locks, for instance, Topsy has a short and unkempt mane. As the narrator notes, "Her wooly hair was braided in sundry little tails, which stick out in every direction" (259, 258). Likewise, instead of being clothed in demure feminine dress, Topsy's garments are both scant and soiled. As a shocked Miss Ophelia exclaims upon first seeing her, in fact, "'She's dreadfully dirty, and half naked'" (260). Moreover, rather than displaying the feminine traits of spiritual piety and familial respect, Topsy is "heathenish" (258). In what has come to be an oft-quoted passage, Miss Ophelia asks the black youth,

> 'Have you ever heard anything about God, Topsy?'
> The child looked bewildered, but grinned as usual.
> 'Do you know who made you?'
> 'Nobody, as I knows on,' said the child, with a short laugh.

The idea appeared to amuse her considerably, for her eyes twinkled, and she added—

'I 'spect I grow'd. Don't nobody never made me.' (262)

During an era when women were expected to be pious keepers of the faith, Topsy is, as the narrator frequently observes, "goblin-like" (259). The young girl is not merely ignorant about the finer points of catechism, but about the very concept of God and creation; Topsy believes that she is a singular creation that just "grow'd." In a powerful index of this character's association with such traits, the listing for "Topsy" in the *Oxford English Dictionary* indicates that in the years following the publication of *Uncle Tom's Cabin*, the appellation came to be "used allusively as the type of something that seems to have grown of itself without anyone's intention or direction" (261).

Given the way in which Topsy defies many of the manners and mores of white womanhood, Miss Ophelia begins the task of turning this topsy-turvy character—in the words of Louisa May Alcott's girls' novel—into a proper "little woman." Miss Ophelia's first task is to tame Topsy's unruly physical appearance by giving her a bath, haircut and new set of clothes. These efforts prove successful, and Topsy is indeed transformed: "When arrayed at last in a suit of decent and whole clothing, her hair cropped short to her head, Miss Ophelia, with some satisfaction said she looked more Christian-like" (261).

Having "civilized" Topsy's external appearance, Miss Ophelia attempts to do the same with the young girl's internal traits. The New England spinster believes that the education of women ought "to teach them the catechism, sewing, and reading; and to whip them if they told lies" (263). In spite of such overarching aims for Topsy's intellectual and spiritual development, Miss Ophelia commences with a task that is highly gendered: housework. In the words of the novel's narrator, "Miss Ophelia began with Topsy by taking her into her chamber, the first morning, and solemnly commencing a course of instruction in the art and mystery of bed-making" (263). Although the New England spinster gives extensive instruction, the lesson proves a failure. Rather than displaying proper feminine obedience during the tutorial, the mischievous young girl engages in unfeminine disobedience: Topsy uses the tutelage in domestic housework as an opportunity for domestic thievery. "[D]uring the time when the good lady's back was turned, in the zeal of her manipulations, the young disciple had contrived to snatch a pair of gloves and a ribbon, which she had adroitly slipped into her sleeves" (264).

If stealing these items were not sufficiently shocking, Topsy then lies about the theft a few moments later when the ribbon slips out of her sleeve and is spotted by Miss Ophelia. "'Laws! why, that ar's Miss Feely's ribbon, ain't it? How could it get caught in my sleeve'" (264). She persists in her denials both when threatened with whipping and then when a pair of stolen gloves falls from her clothing. When the now-bewildered guardian asks her charge what compelled her to behave in this way, Topsy gives a response that denies any sense of personal agency or Christian principles: "'Cause I's wicked,—I is. I's mighty wicked, any how. I can't help it'" (265).

As the novel progresses, the topsy-turvy young girl continues to turn the manners and mores of white womanhood on their head. The activity that most frequently elicits this response is one that is, once again, highly gendered: needlework. As the narrator notes, "the confinement of sewing was her abomination; so she broke her needles, threw them slyly out of windows, or down in the chinks of the walls; she tangled, broke, and dirtied her thread, or, with a sly movement, would throw a spool away altogether" (269). Topsy's dislike for sewing is matched only by her dislike for domestic labor. Although the young girl quickly masters the method for making her mistress's bed, she requires constant supervision. If the New England mistress does not keep a close eye on her ward, Topsy would do as her name suggests and turn the room "topsy-turvy." The young girl

> would hold a perfect carnival of confusion, for some two or four hours. Instead of making the bed, she would amuse herself with pulling off the pillow-cases, butting her wooly head among the pillows . . . she would climb the posts, and hang head downward from the tops; flourish the sheets and spreads all over the apartment; dress up the bolster in Miss Ophelia's night-clothes, and enact various scenic performances. . . . (270)

As this long list of examples suggests, instead of imposing domestic order, Topsy institutes unruly disorder.

Coupled with engaging in actions that are unladylike, Topsy displays emotions that can be classified in this manner. When she is angry or upset, she does not adhere to notions of feminine civility by displaying patience, forgiveness and understanding. On the contrary, she partakes in uncivil behaviors like anger, vengeance and even malice:

> It was soon discovered that whoever cast an indignity on Topsy was sure to meet with some inconvenient accident shortly thereafter;— either a pair of ear-rings or some cherished trinket would be missing, or an article of dress would be suddenly found ruined, or the person would stumble accidentally into a pail of hot water, or a libation of dirty slop would unaccountably deluge them from above when in full gala dress. (269–270)

In light of the numerous ways in which Topsy rebelled against the mores of white women, it is not surprising that she was often mistaken for a male rather than female character. "George L. Aiken, author of the most influential stage adaptation of the novel, originally conceived of Topsy as a boy, and although the character was scripted as a girl, Topsy was played by a man" (Young 36). As Young goes on to assert: "The cross-gendered casting of Topsy reinforced the racism of the role, for it replicated what Patricia Morton terms the 'defeminizing' assault of slavery, whereby black women were denied access to marriage, children, and other prerogatives of white femininity" (36–37). Recalling the experiences of factual black women like Sojourner Truth who once bared her breast to "prove" that she was female, fictional figures like Topsy were also often seen as mannish.

Jo March emerges from a profoundly different social, economic, geographical, racial and cultural milieu, but she possess an array of uncanny similarities to Stowe's character. Among the most obvious—and in many ways most compelling—is her self-chosen moniker. Given Jo's sharp divergence from the behaviors commonly associated with "little women," she adopts a phrase that encapsulates her rambunctious nature while it embeds the name of Stowe's unruly black character: the tomboyish young girl signs her name "Topsy-Turvy Jo" in Alcott's novel. In the note she pens to her mother, she closes with this autograph (171). After addressing the complicated history and numerous spellings of the term "topsy-turvy," the *Oxford English Dictionary* defines it as "With the top where the bottom should be; in or into an inverted position; upside down, bottom upwards. . . . With the higher where the lower should be; in or into a reversed condition; with inversion of the natural order" (262).

The name of Stowe's character Topsy was, in fact, based on the phrase "topsy-turvy." As a figure who specializes in turning the St. Clare household on its head, the abbreviated version of this common expression announces this figure's character. Because Stowe's novel was the first to use the term "Topsy" as a proper noun, the name is almost exclusively associated with the famed antislavery text. According to the *OED*, the word denotes the "name of a character in Mrs. H. B. Stowe's *Uncle Tom's Cabin*; used allusively as the type of something that seems to have grown of itself without anyone's intention or direction" (261).

The unprecedented success of Stowe's novel not only made characters like Little Eva, Uncle Tom and Topsy household names, it also caused them to morph into other cultural forms. Together with the oft-discussed minstrel shows based on *Uncle Tom's Cabin*, board games and even children's toys were produced. While doll versions of Eliza and Little Eva were the first to appear, a Topsy figure was widely available by the publication of *Little Women*.[10] As Shirley Samuels has written, a toy called the "topsy-turvy doll" emerged in the American South during the nineteenth century

10. *The Collector's Encyclopedia of Dolls*, in fact, reprints advertisements placed by American doll companies throughout the nineteenth and twentieth centuries and contains numerous listings for Topsy dolls as early as 1860. In this way, the ostensibly Caucasian

and is, in fact, still produced today. Rather than presenting a figure who, like Jo March, is topsy-turvy in her gender role, the toy depicted a topsy-turvy racial boundary. "Held one way, the doll appears as a white woman with long skirts. Flipping over her skirts does not reveal her legs, but rather exposes another racial identity: the head of a black woman, whose long skirts now cover the head of a white woman" (Samuels 113).[11] Not surprisingly, some of the first topsy-turvy dolls contained the literal Topsy: the unruly black character occupied one end of the figure while her racial and behavioral antithesis, the angelic white Little Eva, comprised the other. By the 1890s, this particular kind of topsy-turvy doll was known, appropriately, as the Topsy/Eva doll. The existence of this toy underscores Elizabeth Young's comment that these two characters "function as split selves within normative white femininity" (40). Given the numerous physical, psychological and behavioral connections between Jo March and Topsy, Alcott's beloved white tomboy may sign her name "topsy-turvy," but it may be more accurate to characterize her as "Topsy/turvy." With her brown skin tone, penchant for rambunctious behavior, and disheveled personal appearance, she has much in common with Stowe's unruly black character.

Of course, Jo's linguistic connection to Topsy is connected to her behaviorial one. Alcott's character similarly stands in opposition to middle- and upper-class white womanhood. The tomboyish character shakes hands, refers to herself by masculine pronouns, repeatedly declares herself the "man of the family," insists on being called the "son Jo," and "play[s] male parts to her heart's content" in dramatic productions with her three sisters (298, 223, 5, 16). For these reasons, Jo, like Topsy, is often seen as more of a boyish rather than girlish figure. John W. Crowley has argued that while *Little Women* cannot exactly be classified as a "boy-book," its tomboyish central character frustrates efforts to cast it as a "girl-book" (388). Although Jo March is a female figure, she seems more like a male one.

Even though Topsy rebelled against the confines of white women's gender roles, her young age coupled with her status as a slave prevented her from accompanying these outbursts with a critical commentary on the limiting nature of female conduct. Not so with Jo March; this tomboyish figure almost always pairs her gender-bending actions with feminist words. Indeed, Jo's embrace of masculinity largely emerges from her critique of

---

figure's autograph embeds the name of a popular black character, the doll version of which little girls may have been snuggling while they read Alcott's novel.

11. Most contemporary topsy-turvy dolls depict fairy tale heroes and villains rather than racial dyads. Little Red Riding Hood and her foil the "Big Bad" Wolf, for instance, is perhaps the most frequent combination. For additional information on the topsy-turvy doll and its significance in nineteenth-century American culture, see Karen Sanchez-Eppler's *Touching Liberty: Abolition, Feminism, and the Politics of the Body* (Berkeley: University of California, 1993).

femininity. Associating femininity with confinement, submission and restraint, and masculinity with independence, adventure and excitement, Jo seeks to distance herself from the disempowered status of feminine women. As she tells one of her sisters, "'I hate affected, niminy piminy chits'" (3). Akin to Topsy, Jo's frustration alights on the feminine and domestic task of needlework. Given Jo's initial distaste for knitting, one can only imagine the delight she would take in following Topsy's example and throwing her needles and thread "slyly out of windows, or down in the chinks of the walls" (269). In some ways, in fact, the extreme actions of Stowe's black character embody a type of secret fantasy for Alcott's white one.

Jo's resistance to feminine domestic chores is accompanied by an equally strong resistance to feminine forms of self-control and personal decorum. Echoing the tendency of Stowe's unruly black character to "hold a carnival of confusion" (270), Jo tells her sister "'I like to fly about and cut capers'" (24). Although Jo impresses on Laurie the merits of a tidy room and is disturbed by the disorder generated from the week of "Experiments," the topsy-turvy tomboy also enjoys "'having a good romp'" (23). Whether playing outdoors, working at home or attending Mrs. Gardiner's party, disorder and even chaos seem to follow her. When preparing for her "operatic tragedy," for instance, "Jo brought in the wood and set chairs, dropping, overturning, and clattering everything she touched" (7). Likewise, while working on one of her manuscripts, she covers the floor in a sheaf of papers, dabs the ink from the pen on her dress, and then has a clamorous romp with her rat Scrabble (147).

Coupled with reflecting Topsy's behavior, Jo reflects her unkempt physical appearance. Although her hair is neatly combed and her body physically clean, her clothes have a "fly-away look" (4). The topsy-turvy tomboy has ruined her good gown by standing too close to a fireplace. One of her sisters tries to cover up the blemishes, but "'the burn shows horridly'" (23). A few chapters later, this predicament recurs. While racing down a hill with Laurie, Jo loses her hat and hairpins. Although the young woman tried to behave, she simply could not resist the tomboyish urge to run and play (140).

In the same way that Jo has a complicated connection with the conventions of white womanhood, she has a complicated connection with the conventions of whiteness. In a detail that has often been overlooked by critics, Alcott's tomboy is ostensibly Caucasian, but her skin is not characterized as the expected "fair," "pale" or even "white" used to describe her sisters. From the moment the young woman is first introduced to readers, her face, arms and especially hands are repeatedly noted as "brown." In the opening pages of *Little Women*, for instance, the seemingly white young woman is described as "very tall, thin and brown" (4). Coupled with the dark nature of her skin is her equally dark hair. Throughout the novel, she is distinguished by her "dark mane" of chestnut locks (3). The dark white nature of the ostensibly Caucasian Jo March, however, is far from simply "skin deep," for she is associated with racialized scenes and situations. As Elizabeth Keyser has written, Jo's reference to *Uncle Tom's Cabin* in the opening pages of *Little Women* has a racially charged implication: "Rebellious Jo attempts to subvert the sermon with blackface humor but, by alluding to *Uncle Tom's Cabin* in general and her imitation of Aunt Chloe in particular she inadvertently likens the girls and their mother to slaves" (61). Echoing white feminists who repeatedly asserted that they were "fettered" by fashion trends and seen as mere "chattel" in the eyes of the law, Jo uses the rhetoric of black slavery to characterize white womanhood. Stowe's Topsy is a literal slave, but Jo casts herself and her siblings as metaphoric ones.

Of all the various connections between Jo and Topsy, however, perhaps none is more significant than their shared tempers. An integral part of Jo's effort to slough off her tomboyish ways and become a gender-appropriate "little woman" is taming her unladylike displays of anger. Like Topsy, whenever the young woman feels wronged or mistreated, she is overcome by a desire for vengeance: "A quick temper, a sharp tongue, and a restless spirit were always getting her into scrapes" (38). By far the most oft-cited instance of how Jo can get "into a fury" (74) occurs after her sister Amy has destroyed one of her beloved manuscripts. Still smarting from the incident, she allows her sister to go skating on ice she knows is too thin. Laurie is able to rescue Amy before she either freezes or drowns, but the event highlights the potentially lethal consequences of Jo's temper. As she soberly confesses while Amy recovers, "'Mother, if she *should* die, it would be my fault'" [italics in original] (78).

Jo's displays of anger go beyond simply a shared personality trait with Topsy; they form a compelling point of convergence with Jo's dark white coloration, the root of which has its root in Alcott's life. Although the author's father was a staunch advocate for abolition, he held the racist association of dark skin with an equally dark and "primitive" soul. As Sarah Elbert notes, Bronson Alcott "was very blond and had blue eyes and, delightedly tracing his ancestry, persisted in believing that Anglo-Saxon 'races' possessed more spiritually perfect natures, were generally 'harmonious,' and had more lofty intellects than darker-skinned people" (*Introduction* xv). Together with applying these attitudes to various minority groups, he attributed them to members of his own family. Both Louisa May and her mother, Abba, were dark or what they frequently termed "sallow" complexioned. In addition, both young women had spirited, even rebellious, natures.[12] As a result of this

---

12. In the words of Madelon Bedell, "Louisa was a villain. At two years of age, she had not changed one whit from her tempestuous infant self. . . . When remonstrated with, she would throw herself into a vortex of crying and violent activity . . . beating on herself and anyone else who happened to be around" (73).

combination of "dark" behavior and dark skin tone, Bronson frequently referred to Louisa and her mother as "two devils" and even joked that his daughter was "a true-blue May, or rather, a brown" (B. Alcott *Journals* 173). This correlation between brown skin and "bad" behavior not only shaped Louisa's youthful self-image,[13] it appeared in her writing. Characters who can be placed anywhere on the spectrum of villainy—from the dastardly evil to the mildly mischievous—are frequently given a dark hue in her fiction.[14]

In light of Alcott's tendency to connect brown coloring with "bad" behavior, it comes as no surprise that the mischievous Jo March is assigned a nonwhite, or at least dark white, skin tone. Echoing the racist associations of whiteness with civility, decorum and self-control, and blackness with rudeness, wildness and even excess, Jo uses the language of primitivism at various points to describe her outbursts. As she confesses to Marmee, "'It seems as if I could do anything when I'm in a passion; I get so *savage*, I could hurt anyone, and enjoy it'" [my emphasis] (79). These comments place the ostensibly white young woman in dialogue with nineteenth-century stereotypes about the racial Other. Giving further credence to this conjecture, Alcott often read her own brown coloration in racially charged ways. In a letter to a childhood friend, for instance, she remarked that because of her sallow complexion she resembled a "stout mulatto lady" in photographs (Alcott *Letters* 67). Likewise, while serving as a nurse in the Civil War, she noted that her "brown ghost" could be seen walking the ward at night (Alcott *Letters* 142). In this way, while critics commonly presume that a tomboyish personality and a proclivity for writing are the primary traits Alcott bequeathed to her fictional alter ego, an American Africanist identity may also have been one of Jo's inheritances.

13. In an 1855 letter, for instance, the future author compared her father's childhood temperament with that of her own. As she observed, "I know *you* were a serene & placid baby when you began your wise meditations in the quiet little Spindle hill farm house. . . . Fifty six years have passed since then, & that peaceful babys [sic] golden head is silver now. . . . *I* was a crass crying brown baby, bawling at the disagreeable old world where on a dismal November day I found myself" [her emphasis] (Alcott *Letters* 13–14).

14. A rambunctious little girl in her 1873 short story "Cupid and Chow-Chow," for instance, has sparkling black eyes and a "little brown face" (4). The ill-behaved character Tommy from her 1885 children's story "How They Ran Away" has a "brown face" that beams with joy when he is defiant (140). Similarly, a young man who was "full of mischief" in the autobiographical "My Boys" (1871) has grown into "a big, brown man" (10). The nonconformist Rose in her "Water-Lilies" (1887) is presented as a "tall robust girl of seventeen with dark eyes and hair, a fine color of brown cheek and vigor in every movement" (96). Finally, the untamed "firebrand" Dan in Alcott's 1871 sequel to *Little Women* is repeatedly described with a brown face and features (Alcott *Men* 138, 243).

"The Black Image in the White Mind": Topsy's Unruly Black Womanhood as the Tomboyish Dream of White Womanhood

While the links between Jo and Topsy seem to destabilize the racial identity of Alcott's beloved white character, they do not. Instead, this relationship offers further evidence for Janice M. Alberghene's astute observation about the "unconscious privileging of whiteness" in *Little Women* (347). Significantly, this phenomenon occurs not because Jo sloughs off her various associations with Topsy's blackness and reasserts a kinship with whiteness, but because Topsy does. In the same way that Stowe's famous character has a topsy-turvy gender identity that combines masculinity and femininity, so too does she have a topsy-turvy racial one that straddles blackness and whiteness. As numerous critics have noted, the unruly black figure is modeled after minstrel characters. When Augustine St. Clare first sees Topsy, in fact, he characterizes her as a "rather funny specimen in the Jim Crow line" (258). Accordingly, when the young girl is asked to perform, she commences a routine that mirrors countless minstrel shows:

> The black, glassy eyes glittered with a kind of wicked drollery, and the thing struck up, in a clear shrill voice, an odd Negro melody, to which she kept time with her hands and feet, spinning round, clapping her hands, knocking her knees together, in a wild, fantastic sort of time, and producing in her throat all those odd guttural sounds which distinguish the native music of her race. (259)[15]

Given Topsy's connection to minstrelsy, she is, to quote the title of an influential book by George Frederickson, "the black image in the white mind." Rather than an actual black figure, she is a white interpretation of one. Topsy may be described as "one of the blackest of her race," but her character says at least as much about whiteness as it does about blackness. As Elizabeth Young has written, "Topsy constitutes a blackface projection of white femininity, in which inversion is at once utopian fantasy and demonized grotesque" (30). By engaging in behaviors that white women had to resist and even repress, Stowe's black character functions as a type of dream figure. "In a culture that mandated civility for middle-class white women, black women could form a conduit for white women's psychic release and a screen onto which they could project their

---

15. Moreover, after completing this performance, the narrator notes that the black servant possesses a minstrel-like "talent for every species of drollery, grimace, and mimicry—for dancing, tumbling, climbing, singing, whistling, [and] imitating every sound that hit her fancy" (269).

own impulses toward incivility. In *Uncle Tom's Cabin*, Topsy is one such screen, reflecting white womanhood back onto itself" (Young 35). For these reasons, white female readers may have publicly disapproved of Topsy's "incivility," but they may have been privately envious of it; the black young girl engages in behaviors about which they could fantasize, but never indulge.

Given the way in which Stowe's unruly black character offers a critique of white womanhood at least as much as black womanhood, it comes as no surprise that she is paired with a figure who embodies a powerful commentary on gender and race: Augustine St. Clare's daughter, Evangeline. Although Topsy and Little Eva are positioned as racial opposites, they actually occupy different sides of the same gendered, classed and racialized coin: the saintly Little Eva embodies an extreme form of feminine obedience while the devilish Topsy represents the opposite pole of "dark" disobedience.[16]

Jo March, like many white American women of the period, encountered these contrasting poles of white womanhood and struggled to reconcile them. In the same way that Alcott's tomboy and Topsy engage in similar types of tomboyish behaviors, a series of analogous events persuades them to conform to the mores of "little women." Recalling how Topsy's seemingly unfeminine short haircut both feminized and civilized her—making her look, as Miss Ophelia declared, more "Christian-like" (261)—Jo undergoes a similar transformation. To raise money for her mother's trip to nurse her ailing father, she sells her hair. Arriving home late one afternoon, she "took off her bonnet, and a general outcry arose, for all her abundant hair was cut short'" (161). Significantly, the barber was initially disinterested in purchasing Jo's locks until she persuaded him via what she calls "'my topsy-turvy way'" (163).

Like Topsy, Jo's lack of long feminine locks paradoxically brings her closer to womanly codes of conduct. While readers would expect that the tomboyish figure would revel in the masculine haircut, the opposite is true. After going to bed later that evening, Jo weeps over the loss of her long hair (164). When Mr. March returns home several chapters later, he notices the surprising feminization of his short-haired daughter. "'In spite of the curly crop, I don't see the 'son Jo' whom I left a year ago. . . . I see a young lady who pins her collar straight, laces her boots neatly, and neither whistles, talks slang, nor lies on the rug, as she used to do'" (223).

While a short haircut may have inspired more "ladylike" conduct in Jo and Topsy, the influence of a particular person who meets an untimely

---

16. As Elizabeth Young has written, the theatrical history of *Uncle Tom's Cabin* gives further credence to such assertions. In the numerous plays and minstrel versions of the novel, Topsy and Little Eva were often portrayed by actresses who were closely related: mothers and daughters, older and younger sisters, even identical twins.

death solidifies this change. From the moment that Topsy encounters the angelic Little Eva, she is overwhelmed by her goodness and love: "It was the first word of kindness the child had ever heard in her life; and the sweet tone and manner struck her strangely on the wild, rude heart, and a sparkle of something like a tear shone in the keen, round, glittering eye" (267). As Little Eva nears her death, this influence only increases. The angelic young girl implores Topsy to repent her wild ways. "'Oh, Topsy, poor child, I love you!' said Eva, with a sudden burst of feeling. . . . 'I love you, and I want you to be good. . . . I wish you would try to be good, for my sake;—it's only a little while I shall be with you'" (304). Upon hearing Eva's wishes, the black servant vows: "'I will try, I will try; I never did care nothin' about it before'" (305).

Little Eva's goodness also opens Miss Ophelia's heart. The Northern spinster who formerly had a strong aversion to physical contact with the young black girl is now able to literally as well as figuratively embrace her, a phenomenon that further hastens Topsy's conversion. Soon after the pair relocates to New England, in fact, Topsy "rapidly grew in grace and favor with the family and neighborhood. At the age of womanhood, she was, by her own request, baptized, and became a member of the Christian church" (463). By the end of the novel, she "showed so much intelligence, activity, and zeal, and desire to do good in the world" that she began work as "a missionary and has been sent on assignment to Africa" (463). As Elizabeth Young has written of this event, "Topsy has moved from uncivilized heathen to civilizing agent" (46). The formerly "wicked" black "heathen" has become a "good" black woman because she has finally conformed to many of the era's prevailing notions about white women's proper gender role.

Jo abandons her tomboyish behavior through the influence of a similarly angelic figure: her younger sister Beth. Although her blonde-haired sibling Amy resembles Little Eva physically, it is Beth who possesses the character's saintly personality and who inspires her to conduct herself in more ladylike ways. As she tells Laurie, "'Beth is my conscience'" (186). Beth's sickness and eventual death do not signal the end of her influence over Jo. Akin to Little Eva's effect on Topsy, her sway actually increases postmortem. Leaning over her sister's sickbed, Jo confesses, "'I used to think I couldn't let you go; but I'm learning to feel that I don't lose you; that you'll be more to me than ever, and death can't part us, though it seems to'" (418). After Beth's death, the once topsy-turvy tomboy self-consciously tries to emulate her saintly sister. "Jo found herself humming the songs Beth used to hum, imitating Beth's orderly ways, and giving the little touches here and there that kept everything fresh and cozy" (434).

The taming of a Civil War era tomboy through the influence of an invalid forms an ironic inversion of the antebellum origins of this code of conduct: as an antidote to the declining state of white women's health.

Although frail and sickly individuals were presented in negative ways during the antebellum period, both Diane Price-Herndl and Carroll Smith-Rosenberg have shown that the massive casualties suffered by both the Union and Confederate armies precipitated a radical shift in societal views of infirmary. Rather than considering soldiers weak or unmanly because they had been wounded, they were deemed heroic and even angelic. Especially in the North, their injuries were often considered a type of stigmata and their deaths a virtual apotheosis: Jesus had died for humanity's original sin, and these saintly men had died for the nation's sin of slavery.

While the vast majority of individuals killed or wounded during the Civil War were men, this veneration had a ripple effect on attitudes about invalid women. Whereas frail and sickly women were often condemned during the antebellum period, they began to be lauded during the Civil War one. As a consequence, while the invalid still existed in opposition to the tomboy, she was now seen—like Alcott's Beth—as a figure to emulate rather than one from which to rebel. By following the example of this sick but saintly individual, gender-rebellious girls would abandon their unladylike willfulness and learn the feminine traits of humility and especially self-sacrifice.[17]

Akin to Topsy's partial reformation by Little Eva, Jo's transformation is also not complete, for Beth may have tamed her sister's tomboyish personality, but she did not temper her equally tomboyish professional aspirations. This task is accomplished by Professor Frederick Bhaer, who convinces Jo that the blood-and-thunder tales she has been writing corrupt readers in general and children in particular. Ashamed of her participation in this harmful genre—and, arguably, even more ashamed that this work has disappointed Frederick—she "stuffed the whole bundle into her stove, nearly setting the chimney afire with the blaze" (356). This act largely marks the end of her ambitions to be a professional writer and the beginning of her path to becoming a loving wife. Indeed, not long after this event, Jo and Professor Bhaer marry.

---

17. This phenomenon is not limited to Alcott's presentation of Jo and Beth, but permeates the other tomboy novels of the era. In the Gypsy Breynton series, for example, the tomboyish title character is tamed in large part through the influence of her frail and sickly neighbor, Peace Maythorne. Learning patience, selflessness and especially piety from the invalid woman, Gypsy is changed from a rough and tumble tomboy into a selfless surrogate mother. When the young girl dutifully nurses her injured brother at a Union hospital, for example, she draws on memories of the then-deceased Peace Maythorne for help, strength and guidance: "So, with the pictured face of Peace smiling in that silent corner of her heart, she told God all the story,—all that she feared, all that she hoped, all that she thought she could not bear" (Phelps *Sowing* 279). Meanwhile, Susan Coolidge's *What Katy Did* takes this paradigm one step further. The tomboyish title character is tamed not simply by following the positive example of an invalid—Katy's her sick and saintly cousin Helen—but by becoming an invalid herself.

Having tamed or "civilized" her own tomboyish ways, Jo again mimics the actions of Topsy and turns her attention to doing the same for others. With the inheritance from her Aunt March, Jo announces her plan to open a school. Instead of dedicating the institution to the reform of unruly white "little women," Plumfield will be committed, as the title of Alcott's 1871 sequel suggests, to taming unruly white "little men." In a textual detail that is not to be overlooked, Jo employs the phrase "topsy-turvy" to characterize her potential pupils. As she tells Laurie, "'I've a special interest in such young bears, and like to show them that I see the warm, honest, well-meaning boys' hearts, in spite of their clumsy arms and legs, and the topsy-turvy heads'" (483). Having conquered her own "topsy-turvy ways," she can now—like Topsy—help others do the same. In this way, Jo March also becomes a type of missionary. Although she does not travel to the "dark continent" of Africa, she immerses herself in an equally untamed "'wilderness of boys'" (483). Moreover, one of the first pupils that Jo and Professor Bhaer enroll in their school is "a merry little quadroon, who could not be taken in elsewhere, but was welcome to the 'Bhaer-garten'" (486).

This ending does not simply bring Jo into alignment with the antebellum origins of tomboyism as a means to maintain white racial supremacy, it expands on it. The once masculine and professionally ambitious tomboy builds on the original societal purpose for this code of conduct by becoming a dutiful wife and multi-faceted type of mother. Jo serves as an actual mother to the son that she has with Frederick, along with a surrogate one to her male pupils at Plumfield. Indeed, in the final chapter of the novel, Alcott's character goes from being known as "topsy-turvy Jo" to being called "Mother Bhaer." During a period that had just seen its young white male population decimated by a bloody Civil War while, at the same time, witnessing the entrance of blacks into white society, Jo's decision to get married, have a son, and open a school for wayward boys perhaps never seemed more important. The white male children to which Jo will either personally give birth or professionally rear will help ensure that the future status of Anglo-Americans remains that of the dominant, ruling class.[18]

---

18. Once again, Katy Carr and Gypsy Breynton are involved in the same cultural project. During Katy's convalescence, she becomes the caretaker for her widowed father and motherless younger siblings. Likewise, Gypsy is transformed from a rough-and-tumble tomboy into a selfless surrogate mother to her older brother. The young girl who formerly hated to sew now devotes herself to maintaining his college wardrobe (Phelps *Sowing* 94). Then, when Tom joins the army and is wounded in battle, Gypsy serves as his nurse. Upon recovering, Tom returns to college and graduates at the top of his class. As he tells his sister, "'I should not be where I am to-day if it weren't for you'" (Phelps *Sowing* 301). In this way, both Gypsy and Katy may be too young to get married and have children of their own, but they fulfill the hegemonic purpose of tomboyism: each helps raise the next generation of strong white male citizens and even leaders.

From Civil War Nurses to *Fin-de-Siecle* Physicians: The Tomboy Matures into the New Woman

Although Jo March is Alcott's most famous fictional tomboy, she was certainly not her only one. In part because of the success of this topsy-turvy character and in part because of the author's own tomboyish childhood identity, she penned several other gender-bending characters throughout her career. A little girl named Chow-Chow in her 1873 children's story, "Cupid and Chow-Chow," for instance, is a spirited figure who "stood by the pond throwing stones at the swans" (5). Similarly, in her 1880 narrative *Jack and Jill*, the female title character vows, "I won't be told I don't 'dare' by any boy in the world" (4). Finally, the nonconformist young woman Rose in Alcott's narrative "Water-Lilies" (1887) is presented as a "tall robust girl of seventeen with . . . vigor in every movement" (96).

Of all the tomboyish female figures that Alcott created after Jo March, Annie Harding from the 1871 sequel to her famous girls' novel, *Little Men*, is perhaps the most well-known. Given her proclivity for defying traditional notions of proper feminine behavior, the youngster acquires the nickname "Naughty Nan." Although a generation younger than Jo March, this tomboyish figure is in many ways patterned after her. In fact, Jo mentions her strong identification with the ten-year-old child. Reminded of her own tomboyish antics while observing Nan, she tells her husband: "'You see, Fritz, I feel a great sympathy for Nan because I was such a naughty child myself'" (102). In a telling index of shifting societal attitudes about gender-bending female behavior as the nineteenth century progressed, Jo characterizes tomboyism as a mischievous defiance of women's gender roles rather than a beneficial expansion of them.

Whereas topsy-turvy Jo dreamed of becoming a famous author, Nan takes such tomboyish aspirations one step further. Rather than pursuing the largely self-taught and comparatively feminine profession of writing, Nan longs to redefine acceptable occupations for women by attending college and becoming a certified physician. As she announces to her playmates, "'I don't want any house to fuss over. I shall have an office, with lots of bottles and drawers and pestle things in it, and I shall drive around in a horse and chaise and cure sick people'" (226).

More than simply embodying another example of Alcott's lifelong literary interest in tomboyism, Nan represents the next phase of it in the United States. During the *fin-de-siecle*, this code of conduct would evolve from a method of raising adolescent girls to a type of training ground for professional adult women. During the 1880s and 1890s, women gained entrance into formerly all-male institutions of higher education and embarked on careers in an array of traditionally masculine professions. Serving as lawyers, business leaders, and—echoing Nan's desire—doctors, they forged a radically new conception of womanhood for the coming new century.

In the chapter that follows, I examine a spunky female figure who not only has the same first name as Alcott's tomboy in *Little Men*, but the same aspiration of being a physician: Nan Prince from Sarah Orne Jewett's *A Country Doctor* (1884). Personally unwilling and possibly biologically unable to slough off her iconoclastic ways, Jewett's character chooses as tomboyish a path for adult life as for her childhood identity. This shift in both the origins of tomboyism and its cultural function caused a similar shift in public opinion about female gender iconoclasm. In the span of only a few decades, tomboyism went from a beneficial code of conduct that had valiantly helped to preserve the nation, to a gender and sexual perversion that now threatened to destroy it.

3

The Tomboy Matures
Into the New Woman

Sarah Orne Jewett's A Country Doctor

T he anxiety and flux created by the outbreak of the Civil War and the abolition of slavery gave rise to an entirely new way of life for millions of Americans. In the years following the surrender of General Robert E. Lee, both the North and the South saw massive increases in the rate of industrialization, urbanization and commercialization.[1] As Gertrude Stein would later assert, the United States was one of the first modern nations because of the profound transformations wrought by the Civil War.

Coupled with the changes in the nation's socio-economic structure came alterations in women's gender roles. Building on the liberties brought about by the Civil War and the freedoms made possible by

---

1. As Jean Matthews notes, in 1870 there were only fourteen cities in the U.S. that boasted a population of more than 100,000; by 1900 that number had climbed to thirty-eight (8). In addition, the postbellum era saw the birth of the department store and, with it, the transformation of shopping from a mundane errand into a pleasurable and—to paraphrase Thorstein Veblen—conspicuous leisure activity. Finally, with the laying of the golden spike at Promontory, Utah on May 10, 1869, railroads now crisscrossed the nation. For more information on the profound social, economic, political and cultural changes of the late-nineteenth century, as well as their impact on women's gender roles, see Carroll Smith-Rosenberg's *Disorderly Conduct: Visions of Gender in Victorian America* (New York: Oxford, 1985), and Jean V. Matthews *The Rise of the New Woman: The Women's Movement in America, 1875–1930* (Chicago: Ivan R. Dee, 2003).

a consumer society that no longer required women to be confined to the home, the New Woman was born. As her name implied, this figure was not interested in merely challenging conventional roles for women; she sought to invent them anew. As Carroll Smith-Rosenberg has written, with her agitation for the right to vote, entrance into formerly masculine professions and enrollment at formerly all-male universities or the growing number of women's colleges,[2] "The New Woman challenged existing gender relations" and "violated virtually every late-Victorian norm" (246, 252).

Although the presence of characteristics that had previously been associated with adolescent tomboyism in the adult New Woman may seem to indicate an increased acceptance for gender-bending codes of female conduct, the opposite was true in many ways. As the number of independent and assertive young women grew, so did societal fears that the nation was in the midst—as Elizabeth Reitz Mullenix has noted—of a "usurpation by so-called Amazons" (75). Of equal concern as the New Woman's desire to be an economically productive member of society was her refusal to be a biologically reproductive one. With many of these figures either drastically delaying marriage or deciding to forgo it altogether,[3] they elicited anxiety about the declining birth rate among wealthy, well-educated Caucasian women. As a result, the nation's patriarchal powers worried that the New Woman would not only destroy the American social fabric but bring about the "race suicide" of Anglo-Americans.

To prevent such events from occurring, the male medical establishment—fueled by the new field of sexology—launched an assault against the New Woman. Physicians argued that the "weaker sex" did not have the physical strength or intellectual capacity to handle the rigors of higher education or a professional career. Many predicted, in fact, that if young women were permitted to participate in these activities, they would ruin their health in general and reproductive abilities in particular. As Dr. Edward H. Clarke of the Harvard Medical School asserted in *Sex in Education* (1878), women were "destroying their wombs and their childbearing potential by pursuing a course of higher education intended by nature only for the male sex" (63). By engaging in activities that were formerly confined to men, New Women would become more physically and psychologically like them. Scientists predicted that these women would develop large muscles, begin growing beards and become "mannish." In a sentiment that epitomized

2. On the East Coast alone, for instance, Vassar was founded in 1865, Smith and Wellesley in 1875 and Bryn Mawr in 1884. Indicating the steadily increasing rate of women's participation in postsecondary education, Jean Matthews notes, "In 1870 fewer than 1 percent of young Americans went to college, but women already made up 21 percent of those students; by 1890 they were just under 36 percent of a much larger student body" (11).

3. According to Carroll Smith-Rosenberg, "From the 1870s through the 1920s, between 40 and 60 percent of women college graduates did not marry, at a time when only 10 percent of all American women did not" (253).

nineteenth-century medical beliefs, they contended: "motherhood was a woman's natural destiny and those females who thwarted . . . their body's design must expect to suffer" (Smith-Rosenberg and Rosenberg 336).

Sexologists like Havelock Ellis and Richard von Krafft-Ebing went one step further. They argued that if the New Woman was already a gender deviant who worked and studied like a man, it was only a matter of time until she became a sexual deviant who loved and lusted like men as well. In his highly influential *Psychopathia Sexualis* (first released in Germany in 1882 and in the United States in 1886), Krafft-Ebing published a series of case studies about women who possessed a mannish physical appearance and masculine desire for women. These individuals were deemed "inverts" because of the perceived inversion of their gender and sexual identities; the Western concept of female homosexuality was born.

Attacks on female gender iconoclasm were not limited to the adult New Woman; they extended to include her adolescent precursor, the tomboy. Once encouraged as a desirable code of conduct for young girls, tomboyism was now seen as a breeding ground for the mannish and even inverted New Woman. In an 1895 essay, for instance, physician James B. Weir argued that the first sign of this monstrous new figure was the tomboy, "who abandons her dolls and female companions for the marbles and masculine sports of her acquaintances" (822). Similarly, in *Psychopathia Sexualis*, Richard von Krafft-Ebing identified "a bold and tomboyish style" as an adolescent symptom of adult sexual inversion (420). Reflecting one of the most common characteristics of tomboyism, in fact, he argued "the female urning may be chiefly found in the haunt of boys. She is their rival in play" (Krafft-Ebing 399). Although tomboyism had been popularized as a preparatory stage for marriage and motherhood, it was now seen as a dangerous diversion from these institutions. The *fin-de-siecle* marked the beginning of this code of conduct's association with homosexuality and gender dysphoria.

Sarah Orne Jewett had a special connection to social and scientific debates about the maturation of the adolescent tomboy into the adult New Woman. As both past and present critics have pointed out, the writer did more than simply live and work amidst *fin-de-siecle* changes in women's gender and sexual roles, she was a reflection of them. Like many of the other female writers spotlighted in this study, the future author was an avid tomboy as a child. Biographical discussions about Jewett are filled with accounts of the numerous skating, snowshoeing, hiking, rowing, horseback riding and even fishing expeditions in which she participated as a young girl. As Paula Blanchard notes, "Her nickname in letters to one of her teenage friends was 'Dear Boy,' and all her life she was proud that she could row and drive as well as a man" (32).[4] Rather than abandoning such gender-bending

---

4. Jewett's lifelong commitment to such tomboyish activities may necessitate a reconsideration of an oft-quoted remark that the author made in a letter written on her forty-eight

behaviors with her youth, Jewett maintained them throughout adulthood. In the words of Elizabeth Silverthorne, "Sarah's love of the outdoors and of outdoor sports . . . remained true all her life" (41). In what has become an oft-quoted anecdote, in fact, the author engaged in a lively sledding expedition when she was in her early forties. In a letter written directly after the event, Jewett gleefully boasted that she had plunged down the slope *"just like the rest of the boys!"* [italics in original] (Jewett *Letters* 50).

Such displays of tomboyishness permeated Jewett's professional career as well. As Ann Douglas Wood has discussed, while women authors had existed for generations in the United States, Jewett carved out a new niche for them. Disliking the "'Breathings, Sighs, Cameos, Silhouettes' that was in literary vogue" during previous historical eras, she sought to replace this florid, flowery and what she saw as a decidedly "feminine" mode of writing with a more direct, simple and "masculine" style (Wood 5). This new approach "thoroughly changed the image and the function of the woman writer in America" and allowed Jewett to do something of which her female predecessors had only dreamed: gain the respect of the male literary establishment (Wood 5). In the words of Richard Brodhead, "Jewett broke the woman author out of the earlier domestic definition of her work and recreated her as a 'literary' artist in the same sense as her highly respected male contemporaries" (152).

Closely related to Jewett's defiance of gender norms for women was her deviation from sexual ones. Akin to other New Women, she refrained from wedlock throughout her life. However, Jewett did not embrace prevailing nineteenth-century stereotypes about the lonely, isolated spinster; the author formed a "Boston marriage" with society woman and literary patroness Annie Fields.[5] While critics and biographers have debated whether the powerful emotional connection that these women possessed had an erotic component, their relationship nonetheless existed outside the realm of heteronormativity and could thus be viewed through emerging social and scientific discourses about inversion. As Josephine Donovan has persuasively written, Jewett was likely aware of the writings of Richard von Krafft-Ebing, whose *Psychopathia Sexualis* was released in Europe the same year that Jewett and Fields made their first trip to the Continent.

---

birthday: "This is my birthday, and I am always nine years old" (Fields 125). Although this comment is commonly seen as infantalizing, it can be considered more iconoclastic and even empowering when viewed via her childhood tomboyism.

5. As Richard Brodhead has written, "Jewett met Annie Fields in the 1870s, but became more intimate with her during James Fields's final illness; and when Fields died in 1881 Jewett became Annie Fields's companion or second consort" (154). Living and traveling together for more than twenty-five years, the duo's relationship was what Lillian Faderman has termed a "romantic friendship." In the words of F. O. Matthiessen, "The two were together constantly . . . when they were separated, daily letters sped between them, hardly letters, but jotted notes of love" (73).

"'Virtually every literate European household' had a copy" of Krafft-Ebing's book after its appearance, and "Fields had a reading knowledge of German, the language in which it was published" (Donovan "Apples" 26).

While biographers frequently maintain that Jewett viewed her relationship with Fields as admirable rather than abnormal,[6] both seemed cognizant of the era's changing attitude about women's romantic friendships. When Annie Fields was assembling a collection of Jewett's letters in 1911, for instance, she followed the advice of her editor to delete all of the passages in which the two used terms of endearment. As biographer Sarah Way Sherman has aptly observed, this act "in effect censor[ed] her expressions of love for Annie" (80). Similarly, in spite of Jewett's oft-mentioned commitment to "the female world of love and ritual," she also engaged in analogous forms of self-censorship. For example, the author refrained from identifying some of the dedicatees to her 1877 novel, *Deephaven*: "I dedicate this story of out-of-door life and country people to my father and mother . . . and also to all my other friends, whose names I say to myself lovingly, though I do not write them here" (3). Although this remark could be viewed as feminine modesty, the subject matter of the narrative coupled with its strong autobiographical overtones suggests a more subversive impetus. As Judith Fetterley has detailed, *Deephaven* concerns the romantic friendship of two young women whose homosocial interaction at times becomes homoerotic.[7]

Jewett's engagement with *fin-de-siecle* changes in women's gender and sexual roles also permeated her 1884 novel, *A Country Doctor*. Rather than exploring general shifts in female identity, it focused on one that was seen as particularly pernicious: the growing number of female physicians. Together with the numerous newspaper articles, magazine features and editorial cartoons that addressed this controversial phenomenon,[8] fictional narratives emerged as an important medium for debate. In characters such as Caroline

---

6. For an illuminating discussion of such attitudes, see especially Paula Blanchard's *Sarah Orne Jewett: Her World and Her Work* (Reading, MA: Madison-Wesley, 1994) along with Sarah Way Sherman's *Sarah Orne Jewett, An American Persephone* (Hanover: University of New England, 1989).

7. Near the end of the novel, for instance, one of the characters makes references to one of the most well-known lesbian couples in history, "Kate laughingly proposed one evening, as we sat talking by the die and were particularly contented, that we should copy the Ladies of Langollen and remove ourselves from society and its distraction" (135). Moreover, as biographers Sarah Way Sherman, Elizabeth Silverthorne and Paula Blanchard all have pointed out, the relationship between the two female main characters in *Deephaven* is patterned after a romantic friendship that the author shared with childhood friend Kate de C. Birkhead. In light of these details, Judith Fetterley made a case for seeing the 1877 novel as a lesbian text.

8. For more on the New Woman in newspapers, magazines and cartoons in both the United States and Europe, see Angelique Richardson and Chris Willis's *The New Woman in Fiction and Fact: Fin-de-Siecle Feminisms* (London: Palgrave, 2001).

Simmons in Harriet Beecher Stowe's My *Wife and I* (1871), Dr. Cornelia D'Arcy in Lillie Devereux Blake's *Fettered for Life* (1874), Lurida Vincent in Oliver Wendell Holmes's *A Mortal Antipathy* (1885), Dr. Mary Prance in Henry James' *The Bostonians* (1886), Nan in Louisa May Alcott's *Jo's Boys* (1886), and the title characters in William Dean Howells' *Dr. Breen's Practice* (1881) and Elizabeth Stuart Phelps' *Doctor Zay* (1882), the female physician became a recurring feature of many novels.

A *Country Doctor* was created in direct response to these literary debates over women and medicine. As both Valerie Fulton and Malinda Snow have written, Jewett was dissatisfied with the treatment of the issue in novels by her contemporaries, and thus decided to craft her own narrative commentary. The 1884 novel, however, did more than simply embody a professional retort; it also embedded Jewett's strong personal connection to the subject. In what has become an oft-cited biographical detail, the author was the daughter of a country doctor and had once considered becoming a physician herself. Although rheumatoid arthritis—a condition from which Jewett suffered throughout her life—forced her to abandon this plan, she used these experiences as the basis for *A Country Doctor*. Modeling the text's tomboyish main character on herself and Nan's sage guardian after her father, she created a novel that is commonly read as a type of "imaginative autobiography" (Cary *Sarah* 139). As Richard Cary has written, *A Country Doctor* "chronicles the life Jewett would have had if she had chosen to enter medicine" (*Sarah* 138).

Drawing on this novel that Jewett would later identify as the one she liked "best" of all her published narratives (Renza 75), this chapter demonstrates that the *fin-de-siecle* was not simply the next phase in the history of tomboyism, but one of its most turbulent. Due to new theories about its biological roots or origins, changing beliefs about its physical and psychological characteristics, and heightened fears over its social and sexual consequences, this code of conduct was virtually dismantled and constructed anew during the 1880s and 1890s. As my discussion will demonstrate, it would never be the same again. Formerly seen as a beneficial childrearing practice, tomboyism would, in the hands of the *fin-de-siecle* scientists, become cast as a social scourge and even a genetic defect.

Tomboyism Goes from a Societal Asset to Scientific Anomaly: The Benefits of a Voluntary Choice Become the Bane of the Biologically Chosen

Although tomboyism had undergone an array of modifications since its introduction during the 1840s and 1850s, one characteristic had remain constant: it was a voluntarily chosen code of conduct. Girls were not born as tomboys, but rather were made or molded into them. Encouraged to engage in active, outdoor play for the benefit of their present physical health and future reproductive ability, these figures made a conscious choice to participate in this code of conduct.

During the *fin-de-siecle*, attitudes about the root or origins of all forms of human behavior, including tomboyism, began to change. Scientists argued that men and women engaged in certain activities not because of parental instruction or environmental influence, but because of their genes. In the same way that children acquired the physical traits of eye color and facial structure from their parents, they also inherited various behavioral tendencies. It was no coincidence, for instance, that the son of an exceptional athlete also excelled at sports, or that the daughter of a gifted singer similarly possessed a beautiful voice. As Charles Darwin had demonstrated in *The Origin of Species* (1859) and *The Descent of Man* (1871), these traits had been biologically passed down.

Growing belief in the genetic basis for human behavior changed theories about the root of tomboyism. This code of conduct came to be viewed not as a voluntary personal choice, but as an involuntary biological compulsion for some girls. Sarah Orne Jewett was a strong believer in the genetic basis for human behavior. As Richard Cary has observed, "the most potent influence on her sensibility was hereditarian" ("Rubrics" 198). Taking great pride in her ancestry, the author frequently credited genetic qualities rather than cultivated ones for her positive personality traits and exceptional writing talent. Elizabeth Silverthorne has written that Jewett "believed strongly in the indelible print of inherited characteristics, and acknowledged the deep impression on her life and on her writing of the three men whose genes she carried. These patriarchs were her paternal grandfather, her maternal grandfather, and her father—whose influence was the greatest of all three" (19).

Jewett's firm belief in the genetic basis for human behavior permeated her presentation of tomboy Nan Prince in *A Country Doctor*. The young girl is weak and sickly when she first arrives in Oldfields, leading Dr. Leslie to advise Nan's Grandmother—in keeping with the antebellum origins of this code of conduct—to "'let the girl run wild and grow strong'" (173). Tomboyism may initially be externally imposed on Nan, but it perfectly suits her personality. Members of the community would rather see the young girl behave in a more demure manner, but no one is able to quell her tomboyish spirit. Much to Mrs. Thatcher's dismay, she is often "playing in the brook, or scampering over pastures when she should be doing other things" (175).

Such assertions about the biological root of tomboyism did more than simply alter previous views about this code of conduct as a childrearing practice; it also eradicated the institution of tomboy taming. If tomboyism was involuntarily ingrained rather than voluntarily chosen for certain girls, it could neither be picked up nor—in a detail that would have profound social and scientific consequences—sloughed off. In *A Country Doctor*, for instance, Nan's tomboyishness cannot be abandoned with age. Instead, she chooses a path for her adult life that is just as iconoclastic as her childhood behavior: as the title of Jewett's novel suggests, she becomes a country doctor. In keeping with the era's belief in the biological basis for human behavior, Nan's interest in and even ability for doctoring is rooted in genetics. As Jake Dyer remarks in the opening pages of the novel, her father Jack Prince "was the smartest fellow in his class to college" and went on to become "a talented naval surgeon" (163).

Although Dr. Prince died when Nan was just an infant, she has inherited his aptitude for medicine. When Dr. Leslie sets the broken bone of injured neighbor, for instance, the pre-adolescent girl observes with acute interest. Several days later, Nan uses this information to help an injured turkey on her Grandmother's farm. As Mrs. Meeker says of the incident: "'She told how it was the way you'd done to Jim Finch that fell from the hay-rigging and broke his arm over to Jake an' Martin's, haying time'" (187). Upon hearing of this event, the country physician immediately attributes her proclivity for doctoring with genetics: "'Her father was a surgeon in the navy. It is the most amazing thing how people inherit'" (187).

When Nan is placed in the guardianship of Dr. Leslie, her opportunity to act on this inclination increases exponentially. From the moment that the young girl arrives at the physician's abode, she is more interested in his anatomy books than her toys. As Dr. Leslie remarks, "'she sat here all afternoon with one of my old medical dictionaries. I couldn't help looking over her shoulder as I went by, and she was reading about fevers, if you please, as if it were a story-book'" (214). When the country physician is accused of using the little girl to indulge his own whims, he insists that Nan's interest in medicine "'is quite unconscious'" (214). As he explains, "'up to seven or eight or eight years of age children are simply bundles of inheritance'" (212).[9]

Reaffirming the link between adolescent tomboyism and the adult New Woman, Nan's determination to study medicine is renewed by a tomboyish frolic in nature. Feeling uncertain about her future after facing repeated criticism from friends and family members, the young girl "told herself that there was nothing like a good run" (252). Reaching a low-growing cedar, "she sat there, breathing fast and glowing with bright color" (252). While

---

9. The trope of inheritance in *A Country Doctor* is not merely limited to Nan's possession of a tomboyish spirit or genetic talent for doctoring. Together with biological deployments of this concept, the 1884 narrative also contains legal manifestations of it as well. In the opening chapters of the novel, the orphaned young girl is an inheritance herself: bequeathed first to her maternal grandmother and then to Dr. Leslie. Then, at the end of the novel, Nan's status as an inheritance comes full circle when the young woman, who is now a certified physician, inherits Dr. Leslie's medical practice.

enjoying the woods and grasses, Nan gets a renewed zeal for becoming a doctor: "a decision suddenly presented itself to her with a force of reason and necessity the old dream of it had never shown. Why should it not be a reality that she studied medicine? The thought entirely possessed her. . . . [H]er whole heart went out to this work, and she wondered why she had ever lost sight of it" (253).

The *fin-de-siecle* belief in the biological origins of tomboyism not only altered longstanding characteristics like taming, but it simultaneously forged a connection with another common marker of identity which also had its root in biology: race. In the same way that tomboyish girls inherited a certain gender identity, blacks were born with a specific racial one. The next segment of this chapter explores the various links that were forged between social and scientific attitudes about postbellum white tomboyishness and antebellum racial blackness. Whereas the racialization of gender-bending figures had previously been metaphoric, the *fin-de-siecle* made them literal.

Postbellum White New Womanhood and Antebellum Black Free Womanhood: *A Country Doctor* and the Case of the Two Nancy Princes

While the tomboyish New Woman may have embodied an array of innovative traits, many of the condemnations launched against her were neither original nor unique. Instead, they were largely patterned after those from a previous great debate in American society: antebellum discussions about race and the abolishment of black slavery.

As Stephen Jay Gould has written, throughout the 1840s and 1850s, the fields of comparative anatomy, anthropology and human biology made frequent pronouncements about the innate inferiority of blacks to justify their subjugation in American society. Calling attention to their supposed smaller brain capacity, mental inadequacy and even stagnated state of evolutionary development, scientists characterized blacks as either a low human form or a simian species. In 1854, for instance, "E. Hushke, a German anthropologist argued, 'The Negro brain possesses a spinal cord of the type found in children . . . and beyond this, approaches the type of brain found in higher apes'" (quoted in Gould 135). Likewise, in *Types of Mankind* (1854), J. C. Nott and George R. Gliddon concluded, "'The palpable analogies . . . between an inferior type of mankind and a superior type of monkey require no comment'" (quoted in Gould 34). Pronouncements about the stagnated stage of black physical development were coupled with remarks about their arrested intellectual one. Operating under the assumption that a direct correlation—and even causation—existed between physical brain size and human intellect, craniometrists both weighed actual human brains and compared the volumetric capacity of empty skulls. Using an array of dubious methods that guaranteed the desired results, they found the brain size as well as skull capacity of blacks smaller than those of whites. In the words of Gould once again, their findings "matched every good Yankee's prejudice—whites on top, Indians in the middle, and blacks at the bottom" (53–4).

With slavery now abolished and blacks at least nominal members of white American society, feminism began to supplant abolitionism as a topic of national concern. In the words of Carroll Smith-Rosenberg, the New Woman represented "the quintessential symbol of social danger and disorder" (*Disorderly* 181). Indeed, bell hooks has argued that the backlash launched against feminist figures in the 1870s and 1880s constituted "a sexism that was at a brief moment in American history greater than [its] racism" (3). Perhaps because the color line had already been breached, maintaining the gender line assumed even greater significance.

The social and scientific controversy surrounding the white New Woman may have begun to overshadow the newly emancipated black race, but these two phenomena were related. In an often overlooked detail, arguments used to pathologize postbellum white gender difference were patterned after ones that had been used to denigrate antebellum black racial difference. In the words of Gould once again, "'Inferior' groups are interchangeable in the general theory of biological determinism. They are continually juxtaposed, and one is made to serve as a surrogate for all" (135). Illustrating this phenomenon, craniometrists, comparative anatomists and human biologists during the 1880s and 1890s made pronouncements about white women that were uncannily similar to those previously made about nonwhite men in the 1840s and 1850s. For example, Jean Matthews notes, "European and American scientists measured thousands of skulls and weighed numerous brains and found female brains were consistently smaller than those of men'" (72). Many argued that this detail made white women physiologically closer to apes than to men, echoing the scientific conclusions drawn from analogous information regarding blacks a few decades before. In 1879, for instance, French social psychologist and sociologist Gustave LeBon expressed this position in language that closely resembled that of Nott and Gliddon's 1854 pronouncement regarding blacks:

> In the most intelligent races, as among the Parisians, there are a large number of women whose brains are closer in size to those of gorillas than to the most developed male brains. This inferiority is so obvious that no one can contest it for a moment; only its degree is worth discussion. (quoted in Gould 136)

Coupled with a smaller cranial capacity, white women were also associated with another popular mid-century argument regarding the inherent inferiority of blacks: a stagnated state of evolutionary development. In the minds of many *fin-de-siecle* biologists, anthropologists and comparative anatomists, "Woman . . . in her emotionality as well as in her morphology, remained nearer to the child and to 'savage races'" (Matthews 72–73).

Such areas of biological continuity between white women and the black race gave rise to behavioral ones. Whereas African Americans had been associated with immaturity and irrationality during the 1840s and 1850s, women were now said to possess these exact same characteristics. As one scientist asserted of the "fair sex": "'They excel in fickleness, inconsistency, absence of thought and logic, and incapacity to reason'" (quoted in Gould 137). As a result of such sentiments, postbellum physicians, sociologists and anthropologists now asserted that white women inhabited the lowest rung on the ladder of evolutionary development. According to LeBon once again: "All psychologists who have studied the intelligence of woman . . . recognize today that they represent the most inferior forms of human evolution and that they are closer to children and savages than to an adult civilized man'" (quoted in Gould 136–137).

In a paradoxical detail, white feminists rejected these literal assertions about women's physical and mental inferiority, but they cultivated numerous metaphoric comparisons between themselves and people of color. Arguing for decades that middle- and upper-class white women were "fettered" by harmful fashion trends, "enslaved" by sexist patriarchal practices, and considered mere "chattel" in the eyes of the law, they established a rhetorical kinship between themselves and black slaves that continued even after abolition. As William Chafe has written, in the years directly following the Civil War, some leaders in the movement argued that white women were no longer the social and political equivalents of blacks; they were now even more disempowered than them (Chafe 17–18). As they frequently pointed out, newly emancipated African American males could vote and own property while white women were still denied these rights. In a conscious or unconscious effort to call attention to the continued disenfranchisement of white women, an array of feminist journals adopted names that mirrored those used by abolitionist publications. Whereas antebellum periodicals such as *The Pennsylvania Freeman* had addressed the emancipation of blacks from slavery, postbellum ones like *The Freewoman* and *The New Freewoman* were dedicated to the emancipation of white women from patriarchal oppression.[10]

10. *The Pennsylvania Freeman* was published in Philadelphia by the Eastern District Executive Committee of the Anti-Slavery Society of Pennsylvania, and appeared weekly from March 15, 1838 to June 29, 1854. Meanwhile, *The Freewoman: A Weekly Feminist Review*, was printed in London by the New International Publishing Company and was released weekly in the United States from November 23, 1911 to October 10, 1912. Finally, *The New Freewoman: An Individualist Review*, which was also printed by the

In the pages that follow I argue that, far from distancing itself from the social and scientific links between postbellum white femaleness and antebellum racial blackness, *A Country Doctor* embraces them. Drawing on arguments by both the era's sexologists and its white feminists, Jewett crafts a compelling defense of her tomboyish female physician that is grounded in the period's belief about the biological similarities between gender and race. Although the novel's main character is ostensibly named after her white paternal aunt, Anna—or, as she is called more than twenty times in the text, "Nancy"—Prince, she shares this appellation with a prominent black travel writer from the 1850s. Discussions of the life and career of Nancy Prince appear in such well-known studies as Hazel Carby's *Reconstructing Womanhood*, Carla Peterson's *"Doers of the Word,"* and Francis Smith Foster's *Written by Herself.* As these texts discuss, the New England-born Prince published her reflections on visiting Russia and Jamaica during one of the most turbulent times in these nation's histories. While she was in St. Petersburg with her husband in 1825, she became an eyewitness to the bloody Decembrist Revolt. Then, in an effort to help the newly emancipated people of Jamaica in 1830, she sailed to the West Indies and saw firsthand the devastating social, political and economic effects of slavery. Finally, when illness and widowhood thrust her into financial hardship, she published an account of her experiences. Originally appearing in 1850, *A Narrative of the Life and Travels of Mrs. Nancy Prince* was reprinted twice: in 1853 and again in 1856. While Prince's narrative was never a bestseller that enjoyed a wide national readership, it was—as the multiple printings indicate—well known among New England literary circles. In fact, an article in an 1894 issue of *The Women's Era* attests that the text could be "found in the houses of many of the old residents of Boston, as well as other places all over Massachusetts" (Hilton 4).

Both Jewett's residence in South Berwick and the Fields' abode in Boston, where the author lived for many years, were among the most established as well as bookish. If it is likely that at least one of these households owned a copy of Prince's *Life and Travels*, then it is even more likely that Jewett examined it, given her voracious reading habits. Together with this point of possible contact, Jewett also had an acute interest in travel literature, the genre in which Prince's narrative is commonly classified. In addition, the New England author made two separate trips to one of the nations discussed in *Life and Travels*, Jamaica. Significantly, the first of these excursions occurred in 1882, only two years before the publication of *A Country Doctor*. Finally, as Elizabeth Silverthorne has noted, in the years following the War of 1812, Jewett's paternal grandfather "grew rich from

---

New International Publishing Co., was published semimonthly from January 15, 1913 to December 15, 1913.

the West Indies trade" (20), another topic addressed in Prince's writings. In fact, the sizable fortune Jewett's family amassed from these ventures made her writing career possible: it gave her both the leisure time to write and the freedom to write what she wished. Thus, Jewett's interest in the region and publications about it may have arisen from personal reasons as much as literary ones.

Although nearly forty years separate the publication of *A Narrative of the Life and Travels* and *A Country Doctor*, striking similarities exist between factual black travel writer Nancy Prince and the fictional character Nan Prince beyond the mere sharing of a name. These elements include the women's ostracization from white female gender roles, their experience of familial, spiritual and even geographic alienation and, finally, their incorporation of religious rhetoric to justify their unconventional choices. As a result of such areas of overlap, these seemingly historically, racially and economically disparate figures are similar in many ways. Together with continuing the historical association of white tomboys with various forms of nonwhiteness, what may be called this "case of the two Nancy Princes" in *A Country Doctor* complicates Jewett's construction of white womanhood, her exploration of the historical past, and her deployment of the journey motif. Recalling a recurring trope in *A Narrative of the Life and Travels*, the 1884 narrative interrogates the way in which one's gender and racial identity can dictate the adoption of unconventional social roles as well as necessitate forms of travel that are both forced and chosen.

From the first time that readers are introduced to Nan Prince, she is associated with an array of what Toni Morrison would characterize as American Africanist features. As the country physician notes, the young girl has a brown face (175). In addition, echoing Capitola Black, Nan is often described with such racially charged terms as "wild" and "monkey" because of her gender-bending antics. Mrs. Thatcher, for instance, characterizes her rambunctious granddaughter as a "wild creature," "wild as a hawk" and "wild as ever" (186, 192, 186). Similarly, recalling the association of blacks with simian qualities, a housekeeper deems the tomboyish girl's disheveled room a "monkey's wedding" and the kitchen after she finishes eating a "monkey's wedding breakfast" (324).

Together with possessing physical links to racial blackness or at least nonwhiteness, Nan possesses behavioral ones as well. Among the most notable is her shared ostracization from white women's gender roles. As discussed in the opening chapter on E. D. E. N. Southworth, with many black women compelled to work in either the fields or, ironically, in the homes of genteel white women who were considered too delicate to perform such labor, they were unable to conform to prevailing notions of ladylike conduct and were often seen as mannish. In keeping with such stereotypes about the masculine nature of black women, Nancy Prince is repeatedly excluded from traditional notions of womanhood. While working as a domestic in the home of a well-to-do family, for instance, she is assigned grueling physical work. "Hard labor and unkindness was too much for me; in three months, my health and strength were gone. . . . I did not wonder that the girl who had lived there previous to myself, went home to die" (Prince 7). Likewise, during a stormy return voyage from Jamaica in 1842, she is ostracized from notions about feminine comfort and courtesy because of her race. As Prince notes, once their badly damaged ship made an emergency docking in New Orleans, "the whites went on shore and made themselves comfortable while we poor blacks were obliged to remain on that broken, wet vessel" (78).

In light of Prince's exclusion from prevailing conceptions of woman-hood, she goes to great lengths to demonstrate her adherence to them. While working as a domestic, for example, she is careful to labor for "a respectable colored family" and refuse a position in the home of people "I knew were not very good" (Prince 6). Likewise, while in living in St. Petersburg, Prince notes that most of her time "was taken up in domestic affairs" and attending church "twice every Sabbath, and evening prayer meeting, also a female society, so that I was occupied at all times" (32). As Francis Smith Foster has noted, the free black woman does not engage in any "activities which would have been unacceptable in New England polite society" (*Written* 85).

Nan Prince faces a similar struggle in *A Country Doctor*. Although not excluded from conventional notions of womanhood on the basis of her race, she is exiled from them on the basis of her tomboyish desire to be a physician. As Mrs. Farley asserts, "'In my time . . . it was thought proper for young women to show an interest in household affairs. When I was married it was not asked whether I was acquainted with dissecting-rooms'" (325). After declaring "a woman's place was at home, and that a strong minded woman was out of place, and unwelcome everywhere," she tells Nan: "'I shall look forward in spite of it all to seeing you happily married'" (326, 327).

Akin to antebellum black free woman Nancy Prince, Jewett's postbellum white New Woman Nan Prince refutes assertions that she is unladylike. In contrast to the pronouncements that participation in male professional activities would unsex young women and make them masculine, the novel calls repeated attention to Nan's femininity. Unlike predecessor Jo March, the young woman does not refer to herself by masculine pronouns, wear male attire or bemoan being born female.[11] As her classmates assert, Nan

---

11. The only possible exception to this occurs when the young girl confesses to Dr. Leslie "'I used to wish over and over again that I was a boy, when I was a little thing down at the farm,'" (262). But, as she makes clear: "'the only reason I had in the world [for doing so] was so that I could be a doctor'" (262). Upon realizing that she can be both female and a doctor, she abandons this attitude.

"showed no sign of being that sort of girl who tried to be mannish and to forsake her natural vocation for a profession" (249). On the contrary, Jewett suggests that the young girl's interest of medicine can actually be seen as feminine in many ways: Nan's profession will allow her to provide womanly nurturance to the ill in the community. As the young girl tells Mrs. Fraley, "'I do think that if I can *help* my neighbors in this way it will be a *great kindness*'" [italics mine] (328).

Closely related to the exclusion of Nan and Nancy Prince from conventional notions of womanhood is their exclusion from conventional notions of women's sexuality. As both Hazel Carby and Frances Smith Foster have written, racist stereotypes about the erotic nature of non-white peoples along with the lack of autonomy that black slaves had over their bodies gave rise to powerful stereotypes about the libidinous black Jezebel. In the words of Frances Smith Foster, "the black woman became closely identified with illicit sex. If the 'negress' were not a hot-blooded, exotic whore, she was a cringing terrified victim. Either way she was not pure and thus not a model of womanhood" (*Witnessing* 31). In light of such attitudes, Hazel Carby has asserted, "Black womanhood was polarized against white womanhood in the structure of the metaphoric system of female sexuality, particularly through the association of black women with overt sexuality and taboo sexual practices" (32).

At numerous points in *Life and Travels*, Nancy Prince encounters these attitudes. While on a ship docked in New Orleans, for instance, she recalls, "The people were very busy about me; one man asked me who I belonged to, and many other rude questions . . ." (Prince 78). In a possible reference to rape, many of these men were so persistent, she explains, "I found it necessary to be very stern with them; they were very rude; if I had not been so, I know not what would have been the consequences" (Prince 80).

Keenly aware of negative stereotypes about black women's sexuality, Nancy Prince goes to great lengths to demonstrate her modesty. The writer avoids any discussions about her physical body or disclosures about her personal life. As Carla Peterson has noted, such omissions allow her to combat the dual vulnerability that is associated with being both black and female: "Decorporealizing her body makes sense as a strategy for negotiating her public exposure as a writer, and it allows her to shift the focus of her mission to racial uplift, away from the stereotyped sexualization of the black female body" (192). Indeed, Ronald Walters has written, "The most striking example of her reticence is her failure to give her husband's first name, and the flat, sparse tone in which she writes about the marriage" (xx). Living abroad with her spouse for nine years, Prince returns to the United States only when ill health forces her to do so. In keeping with the stance of a dutiful wife, she explains, "However painful it was to me to return without my husband . . . [i]t was the advice of the best physicians that I had better not remain in Russia during another cold season" (Prince 45).

Although postbellum white New Women were not associated with the promiscuous heterosexuality of antebellum black women, they were linked with another equally stigmatized erotic activity: sexual inversion. Throughout *A Country Doctor*, repeated reference is made to Nan's inherent unsuitability for marriage. In keeping with stereotypes about the female invert, the young ward does not take a romantic interest in the opposite sex. As Dr. Leslie observes, "'Nan's feeling toward her boy-playmates is exactly the same as toward the girls she knows'" (234).

In spite of this characterization, Jewett's novel emphasizes that the tomboyish girl must choose between marriage and a career, not between heterosexuality and homosexuality. When Nan first meets potential suitor George Gerry, her sisterly fondness for him quickly turns into romantic affection. "So this was love, at last, this fear, this change, this strange relation to another soul" (342). When Nan eventually decides to pursue her studies instead of marrying, the narrator stresses that this choice arises from her inclination for medicine rather than her disinclination for heterosexuality. As Nan reflects: " . . . as the night waned, the certainty of her duty grew clearer and clearer. She had long ago made up her mind that she must not marry. She might be happy, it was true, and make other people so, but her duty was not this" (344).

In large part because both Nan and Nancy Prince are excluded from prevailing notions about female gender roles and sexual identities, they experience similar senses of familial, geographic and even spiritual dislocation. As Hazel Carby argues in *Reconstructing Womanhood*, "Prince made clear her double position inside U. S. society as a citizen and outside it as an outcast because of her color" (42). Given Prince's status as a free black woman in a patriarchal slave society, the very notion of traveling was fraught with complications. Indeed, bell hooks has written that for blacks whose ancestors were forcibly brought to this country, "travel is not a word that can be easily evoked to talk about" (173). In light of this historical reality, Carla Peterson notes that the existence of "colored tourists" such as Nancy Prince:

> raises a host of theoretical questions surrounding the African-American traveler and his or her strategies of displacement. . . . If African Americans were indeed on tour, where then was home? Can home ever be specified for the African transplanted to American soil? Can he or she ever tour at leisure, or is the tour always in some sense an enforced one?" (88–89)

Together with detailing her experiences as a "foreigner" in Russia and Jamaica, Nancy Prince conveys her feelings about being a "foreigner" in the United States. The first segment of *Life and Travels*, in fact, is devoted to the forced travels of her ancestors: how her grandfather Tobias Wornton was "stolen from Africa" and how her American Indian grandmother "became a captive to the English" (1). In this way, coupled with describing the countries that she visits, *Life and Travels* describes her negotiation of dual alienation. An outsider while in Russia and Jamaica, Nancy Prince has an equally strong sense of estrangement from the country of her birth.

Although Jewett's postbellum white New Woman lives in a different historical era and faces a different set of obstacles, her experiences in many ways echo those of the antebellum black free woman. Akin to the travel author, Nan is doubly alienated throughout the novel: death and resentment have ostracized her from her biological family, while her tomboyish ambition to be a doctor impedes a kinship with others. Consequently, the young woman embarks on a series of journeys that are forced and chosen, physical as well as spiritual, in her effort to find a sense of purpose and belonging. Like Nancy Prince, the first portion of Nan's journey is physical: the young girl travels to Dunport to reconnect with her paternal aunt and namesake Anna "Nancy" Prince. This physical journey likewise leads to a spiritual one. Looking through her Aunt's bible one day, she comes across "her grandfather's name in the prayer-book" which "gave her a feeling of security as being a link with her past experiences" (294).

In light of the strong spiritual component to their quests, both the fictional and factual Nancy Prince use the divine to justify their iconoclastic actions. As Cheryl Fish has written, throughout *Life and Travels*, Nancy Prince "claims authority from God" (*Black* 37). Drawing on the style of African American preachers and frequently incorporating biblical passages into her narrative, she asserts that her behavior is being facilitated by the divine. Discussing her survival during the St. Petersburg flood, for instance, she remarks, "Thus through the providence of God, I escaped from the flood and the pit" (22). Coupled with giving blessing to moments of survival, Prince uses this strategy to justify instances of rebellion. While questioning a group of Christian men about their decidedly un-Christian practice of slave trading, for instance, "I asked them if they believed there was a God. 'Of course we do,' they replied. 'Then why not obey him?' 'We do.' 'You do not'" (Prince 80).

Nan engages in a similar tactic. Because her skill for medicine emanates from inheritance, it can be seen as a gift bestowed from not simply her biological father but the Heavenly one. As the young woman points out: "'God would not give us the same talents if what were right for men were wrong for women'" (327). Thus, Nan defends her decision by asking the rhetorical question: "'would you have me bury the talent God has given me?'" (328). As Nan's remarks indicate, if God did not intend for her to be a doctor, He would not have bestowed on her such talents. Interfering with her career path, then, is interfering with the divine.

The Tomboyish New Woman Defends
the Old Racial Order

Nan Prince may embody many suggestive echoes of Nancy Prince and her *Life and Travels*, but—akin to all previous discussions—these elements do not blur the distinctions between tomboyish whiteness and racial blackness. In contrast to social and scientific fears about the New Woman precipitating the "race suicide" of Anglo-Americans, Jewett demonstrates that this figure can still be a productive asset to white American society and—perhaps more importantly—the maintenance of a white racial status quo even if she does not become a reproductive wife and mother.

Although seldom discussed by critics or biographers, Jewett held a firm belief in the superiority of white peoples in general and her own Norman ancestry in particular. In both her personal and professional writings, she repeatedly asserted that the best of America was Anglo-Norman. In an effort to showcase the numerous accomplishments of this racial group, in fact, Jewett began research for a nonfiction book about the history of the Norman people in 1883, one year before releasing *A Country Doctor*. Completed in 1887, *The Story of the Normans* asserted that the imperial prowess of England can be credited to their infusion of Norman blood. As she wrote, "The Norman spirit leads England to be self-confident or headstrong and willful" (Jewett *Normans* 365). Hence, she privileged the "Normans' brighter, more enthusiastic, and visionary nature [over] the stolid, dogged, prudent, and resolute Anglo-Saxons" (Jewett *Normans* 364).[12]

Given Jewett's belief in a racial hierarchy in general and Anglo-Norman superiority in particular, she envisioned the tomboyish New Woman as not simply an important gender development but an essential racial strategy. Her portrayal of Nan Prince demonstrates that this seemingly progressive figure could play a vital role in reactionary efforts to maintain the current racial order. Instead of refuting assertions that tomboyish New Women were biological anomalies who possessed genetic defects, Jewett embraced these views and used them as a means to defend these figures. In the same way that abolitionists often argued that blacks ought not to be enslaved because they were born with a certain racial identity, *A Country Doctor* asserts that the New Woman ought not to be disenfranchised because she

12. For more information on Jewett's views about her Norman ancestry and her book *The Story of the Normans* in particular, see Ferman Bishop's "Sarah Orne Jewett's Ideas of Race," in *The New England Quarterly*, 30.2 (June 1957): 243–249, along with Josephine Donovan's "Jewett on Race, Class, Ethnicity, and Imperialism: A Reply to Her Critics," *Colby Quarterly*, 38.4 (December 2002): 403–416, and Marjorie Pryse's "Sex, Class, and 'Category Crisis': Jewett's Transitivity," in *Jewett and Her Contemporaries: Reshaping the Canon* (Eds. Karen Kilcup and Thomas Edwards, Gainesville: University of Florida, 1999): 31–62.

was born with a tomboyish gender identity. Far from threatening the status quo, this figure can serve a vitally important role in supporting it.

Assertions that Jewett's tomboyish main character possesses an innate inclination for medicine are not exclusively rooted in the positive inheritances from her father; they also emerge from the negative inheritances from her mother. Unable to support herself after the death of her husband and unwilling to live with her in-laws, Adeline Prince returned home "'worse than defeated'" (168). At one point, the young woman became so desperate that she considered drowning herself and her small child. Rather than being simply the actions of a distraught woman, Adeline's behavior may have had a more clinical origin. Discussing the young woman's brief life and tragic death later in the narrative, Dr. Leslie asserts that Nan's mother seemed to possess "'a touch of insanity'" and may have even been alcoholic (210). As the physician reveals, "'I know she had been drinking'" (210).

Although Nan is often seen as patterned more closely after her father, she possesses some of her mother's more disturbing qualities. Whenever Nan lacks structured activity, Adeline's traits of irrationality and restlessness emerge. During one period of idleness, for instance, she becomes infuriated by a minor incident at home and runs away. After the young woman spends the entire night wandering the woods alone, the country doctor muses about the episode: it was "'the first time he had noticed distinctly the mother's nature in her daughter'" (256).

Jewett does not include these elements to aver assertions that the New Woman is biologically defective; she incorporates them to mount a powerful defense of her tomboyish main character. Inverting the opinions of the male medical establishment (or, perhaps more accurately, using their own arguments against them), A Country Doctor argues that the possible presence of these genetic defects may render the tomboyish young girl unfit for marriage and better suited for a career. As the country physician observes of his young ward: "'I see plainly that Nan is not the sort of girl who will be likely to marry'" (234). Although marriage and motherhood bring happiness for many women, they have the potential to bring ruin for Nan. The lack of intellectual stimulation and structured activity could spark the emergence of her mother's qualities and spell disaster for her and her spouse. In the words of Dr. Leslie, "'Only one thing will help her through safely, and that is her usefulness'" (244).

Keenly aware of this aspect of her nature, Nan makes a series of compelling, albeit coded, references to it when she is pressured to abandon her studies and settle down with a husband. When Aunt Anna urges Nan to accept the advances of George Gerry, for instance, she soberly remarks, "'I should only wreck my life, and other people's [if I were to wed]'" (351). Several pages later, when George proposes, she expands upon these sentiments. Although acknowledging that "'[m]ost girls have an instinct toward marrying,'" she tells him "'mine is all against it'" (355). As she goes on to explain, "'There are many reasons that have forbidden me to marry, and I have a certainty as sure as the stars that the only right condition of life for me is to follow the way that everything until now has pointed out'" (355). George is heartbroken that Nan has refused him, but she assures him, "'I would rather spoil your life in this way than in a far worse fashion. . . . I will always be your friend, but if I married you I might seem by and by to be your enemy'" (354).

Together with ensuring her own happiness, Nan's decision to refrain from marriage and motherhood has the broader implication of ensuring the felicity of the race. If the young woman has inherited the traits of recklessness, insanity and alcoholism from her mother, she has the potential to pass along these qualities to her offspring. Instead of shirking her racial duty to produce the next generation of white male leaders, Nan is actually able to better satisfy this role by refraining from doing so. In a complete reversal of common accusations against the New Woman, Jewett suggests that her main character would be contributing to the "race suicide" of Anglo-Americans by marrying.

Dr. Leslie's commitment to training Nan in the old medical ways further underscores the hegemonic potential of her desires. Although Nan's decision to study medicine and become a female physician is a seemingly progressive act, it serves a reactionary or at least conservative purpose in *A Country Doctor*. In light of Dr. Leslie's belief about the wisdom of the old medical ways and the folly of modern scientific methods, he instructs Nan in all of the traditional techniques. Finding this information to be the most valuable of her training, the young woman turns down a position at a prestigious institution in Zurich and decides to "spend a year in Oldfields with the doctor, studying again with him, *since she knew better than ever before that she could find no wiser teacher*" [my italics] (364). As a result, Jewett's ostensibly forward-looking female physician is actually a backward-looking figure. Nan's choice of profession may make her a *New* Woman, but she is schooled in the *old* ways.

Nan Prince does more than simply learn the traditional ways as part of her early training; she makes them the basis for her later career. As the narrator notes, "More than one appointment had been offered the heroine of this story in the city hospitals" (364), but she elects to remain in the small rural community. Taking over Dr. Leslie's country practice, Nan works to improve the literal as well as figurative health of her hometown which bears the appropriate name of *Old*fields. During the time that Nan attends medical school, the region experiences some of the massive transformations that are taking place in late-nineteenth-century America. As the narrator notes, "There was a great change in the village; there were more small factories now which employed large numbers" (364).

Given the demographic composition of Oldfields, Nan's decision to remain the small rural community goes beyond mere love for her guardian or loyalty to her hometown; it is also a strategy to help fortify this endangered white community. Rather than embarking on a career in a diverse modern city, Nan will remain in the racially homogenous country settlement. By doing so, she will help to stave off the encroachment of the technological on the traditional, the urban on the rural, and—perhaps most importantly—the multicultural upon the monolithic. In this way, this ostensible New Woman will help to preserve and protect the old racial order. Instead of being a threat to the maintenance of white racial supremacy, tomboyish figures like Jewett's Nan are an asset to it.

The Tomboy Goes from Giving Physicals to Getting Physical: The Dawn of the Progressive Era and the Rise of the Physical Culture Movement

Although this chapter has focused on the intellectual advances of the New Woman, she was not merely a creature of the mind. In addition to exercising her brain through the pursuit of higher education and the entrance into formerly all-male professions, this figure was interested in exercising her body through the tomboyish participation in athletics and entrance into sporting activities. As Martha Banta and Carroll Smith-Rosenberg have each written, the academically talented and professionally ambitious New Woman was also physically fit and unmistakably athletic. Playing tennis, going swimming, enjoying golf, engaging in gymnastics, forming basketball teams and—in a trait that came to be considered one of her hallmarks—riding bicycles, the New Women enjoyed encroaching on male sporting activities almost as much as socio-economic ones.

Not surprisingly, some of the most ardent advocates for female athleticism could be found among the new crop of women doctors. Arguing that they were better judges of women's physical abilities, they challenged previous arguments that the "fair sex" was physiologically unfit for sports. Rather than endorsing the belief that women would harm their reproductive capabilities if they engaged in athletics, women doctors asserted that the opposite was true: adolescent girls and young women would imperil their health if they remained sedentary. Exercise had long been considered an essential part of men's well-being, and female doctors lobbied that the same was true for women.

Of all the female physicians who worked to dismantle *fin-de-siecle* taboos about women and exercise, Mary Putnam Jacobi was one of the most vocal. In an 1874 paper titled "Mental Action and Physical Health," Jacobi "provided convincing scientific evidence to refute that too much mental and physical exertion was debilitating the reproductive vigor of American middle-class women" (quoted in Vertinsky 141). In many cases, in fact, participation in athletics helped improve women's physical well-being as well as mental stamina. Awarded Harvard's Boylston Medical Prize for her work, Jacobi convinced both medical specialists and average citizens that women could not only give physicals as licensed medical doctors but—in the words of a popular song from the 1980s—"get physical" as athletes. Propelled by this shift in attitude, what would come to be known as the physical culture movement was born in the United States. As the title of this phenomenon suggests, it had the tomboyish aim of privileging female athleticism over aestheticism, strength over weakness, and fortitude over frailty.

The next chapter explores the dawn of the Progressive Era and the rise of the tomboyish physical culture movement through a figure who was a lifelong exercise enthusiast and a patient of Mary Putnam Jacobi: Charlotte Perkins Gilman. In an oft-quoted biographical detail that also forms the basis for one of her most well known short stories, "The Yellow Wallpaper" (1892), Gilman underwent Silas Weir Mitchell's infamous rest cure after suffering from postpartum depression in 1887. Forbidden to rise from bed, engage in any activity, or even feed herself, the experience made the writer vividly aware of not only the need for female physicians who better understood women's ailments, but also the importance of daily mental stimulation and physical exercise. As Gilman noted in her autobiography, after following Mitchell's prescription to avoid exercise and "never touch pen, brush, or pencil as long as you live . . . I came perilously near to losing my mind" (*Living* 96). Realizing that medicine could be a form of social control and, in the hands of male scientific community, even patriarchal oppression, Gilman placed herself in the care of female physicians such as Jacobi and also filled her life with intellectual and physical activities.

Focusing on the life and work of this tireless writer, reformer, and intellectual, the next chapter explores the influence of tomboyism on the social, sexual and intellectual climate of the Progressive Era. After decades of intense criticism, this gender-bending code of conduct experienced a type of rebirth during the early twentieth century. As both an avid practitioner of and an eloquent proselytizer about women's athletics, Gilman was at the center of this phenomenon. As my discussion will illustrate, she was so convinced of the centrality of exercise for the health of the white female body and, by extension, that of the national body politic that she did more than simply craft one tomboyish character who participated in the physical culture movement. Instead, in her 1915 utopian novel *Herland*, Gilman presented her fantasy of an entire nation of them.

4

The Tomboy is Reinvented as the Exercise Enthusiast

Charlotte Perkins Gilman's Herland

The assault launched against the adult New Woman and her adolescent precursor, the tomboy, did not end with the *fin-de-siecle*. As the nineteenth century turned into the twentieth, social and scientific condemnation of these figures not only continued, they broadened in scope. As Laura Doan notes, "The potentially explosive topic of women who desire women or women with no interest in men, was a tinderbox waiting to happen" (63). In the United States, this volatile issue found its spark in 1892 with the murder of Freda Ward and the subsequent trial of her killer—and lover—Alice Mitchell. The event received unprecedented media coverage and caused a national sensation. As Carroll Smith-Rosenberg noted, it "catapulted the discussion of lesbianism" from "a minor theme in medical and asylum journals, into polite and influential circles" (*Disorderly* 273).[1] For a nation that was already uneasy about iconoclastic behavior among women, the crime strengthened the connection between childhood gender nonconformity and adult sexual perversion. Exemplifying this position, Dr. F. L. Sim, who testified on Mitchell's behalf during preliminary hearings and was instrumental in declaring her mentally unfit to stand trial,

---

1. For more information about Alice Mitchell, see Carroll Smith-Rosenberg's *Disorderly Conduct: Visions of Gender in Victorians America* (New York: Oxford UP, 1985) and Jonathan Ned Katz's *Gay American History: Lesbians and Gay Men in the U.S.A.* (New York: Meridian, 1976).

noted later that although the young woman was suffering from acute mental illness, "To the family, she seemed a regular tomboy" (53).

At the same time that events like the Alice Mitchell murder trial were illustrating the need to eradicate tomboyish behavior among women, another phenomenon—immigration—was emphasizing the need for its rejuvenation. During the early twentieth century, both the quantity and perceived quality of immigrants entering the United States changed dramatically. Not only were foreign-born men and women coming in increasing numbers to America—18.2 million between 1890 and 1920, an increase of roughly ten million over the previous thirty-year period (Archdeacon 113)—but they were also arriving from new points of origin: Southern and Eastern Europe along with Asia. These new types of immigrants were radically different from their nineteenth-century predecessors: they spoke languages that were not Romance, practiced religions that were not Judeo-Christian, and hailed from countries that were considered non-Western and whose populations were also classified as nonwhite.

This potent combination of new ethnographic types and their increasing visibility threatened many native-born U.S. citizens. Fearful about the high rates of reproduction among these groups and questioning their ability to melt into white American society, these men and women began to speculate that the unrestricted influx of these "mongrel" peoples would precipitate the extinction of the white race. As a result, nativism and xenophobia were not merely the standpoints of radical fringe groups, they became part of mainstream U.S. sentiment. From the influential opinions of popular author and Ku Klux Klan supporter Thomas Dixon to the reactionary attitudes of President Theodore Roosevelt, a "pervasive ideology of Anglo-Saxon hegemony maintained that there were inferior and superior races, that superior races produced higher cultures, and that the amalgamation of superior and inferior races would bring about the deterioration of the superior race and its loftier culture" (P. W. Allen 18).

Such heightened emphasis on maintaining white racial supremacy placed a heightened emphasis on the health, vigor and reproductive capabilities of middle- and upper-class white women. As everyone from family physicians to political leaders asserted, the fate of the race and, by extension, the nation lay in their hands. To the dismay of the era's nativists, however, adolescent girls and young women were not strong, fit nor, especially, fertile. Since the demonization of tomboyism during the late-nineteenth century, they had resumed many injurious behaviors: from wearing tight corsets and eating too many sweets to refraining from exercise and equating femininity with fragility. As a consequence, increasing numbers of the nation's female population were invalids. As Charlotte Perkins Gilman argued in *Women and Economics* (1898), one of the gravest problems of her generation was "the degree of feebleness and clumsiness common to women, the comparative inability to stand, walk, run, jump, climb" (24).

This combination of the declining state of white women's health and the increasing population of nonwhite immigrants made a persuasive case for the rejuvenation of tomboyism. After all, if this code of conduct could strengthen the health of middle- and upper-class white women during the mid-nineteenth century, it surely could do the same for those in the early twentieth century. However, the lesbianism and transvestism that had come to be associated with tomboyism posed a problem for this plan. While white Americans wanted to bolster the health of their women, they also wanted to bolster their connection to femininity and especially heterosexuality. If adolescent tomboyism produced mannish and inverted adult women like the murderous Alice Mitchell, it would defeat the purpose. Therefore, rather than simply reinstate this code of conduct, parents and physicians sought to reinstate a specific type of it: one that retained the desirable antebellum elements of women's health and hygiene, but sloughed off the undesirable postbellum ones of female masculinity and sexual inversion.

As a result, what came to be known as the physical culture movement was born. Retaining the spirit if not the actuality of tomboyism, it allowed women in the early twentieth century to become physically strong but remain within the bounds of societal approval. While adherents engaged in such tomboyish activities as running sprints and lifting weights, they were not attempting to co-opt masculine behavior or challenge patriarchal authority. Recalling the antebellum origins of white tomboyism, women used these activities to better prepare themselves for their roles as wives, mothers and—with the era's rapid influx of nonwhite immigrants—preservers of the race. As Dr. Andrew Wilson, a popular commentator on medical issues, remarked in a 1906 symposium on health: "I regard the great attention paid today to women's exercise and calisthenics, as an admirable aid to their better physical development" ("Symposium" 308). Likewise, an observation by Dr. Yorke-Davies called attention to the ethos of feminine moderation at the heart of the physical culture movement: "Outdoor exercise is undoubtedly essential to robust health and in all cases, when taken regularly and with discretion, tends to increase strength and improve condition" ("Symposium" 308).

Echoing the antebellum origins of tomboyism, literature in general and girls' fiction in particular became a popular means to disseminate information about physical culture and convert young women to the movement. Some juvenile series books, in fact, seem written solely for this purpose. Laura Lee Hope's aptly titled The Outdoor Girls books (1913–1933) showcased a group of young women who motor around the countryside, participate in various open-air activities and have adventures; in short, do anything but be sedentary. Likewise, in Janet Aldridge's The Meadow-Brook Girls series (1913–1914), the four main characters have markedly different personalities, but they are united by a common interest in physical culture. Taking vigorous hikes, going on boating expeditions and partaking in tennis tournaments, they remark about how such activities have improved their health, their spirits and—of course—their appearance. Finally, as Sherrie A. Inness has written, discussion of physical culture and female athletics was especially pervasive in series books featuring life at women's college ("Pluck"). In Margaret Warde's novel *Betty Wales, Sophomore* (1909), for example, the central female character asserts of her newfound devotion to gymnasium exercises: "I'm hoping that it will cure my slouchy walk, and turn me out 'a marvel of grace and beauty' as the physical culture advertisements always say" (45). Inness goes on to note that not only did women's colleges make physical education compulsory during the Progressive Era, but many began taking meticulous body measurements of their students and charting improvements to their stamina over time ("Pluck" 219).

This chapter explores the resurrection of tomboyism through the guise of the physical culture movement during the early twentieth century by focusing on a figure who was a catalyst for the movement in many ways: feminist author and activist Charlotte Perkins Gilman. Although commonly remembered for her ideas about social reform, she was also a lifelong devotee of, and outspoken advocate for, female athletics. Raised by a mother whose poor health had a profoundly negative impact on the family—Gilman's father abandoned the household soon after learning that his invalid wife was unable to have more children—the future writer and intellectual understood the importance of proper nutrition, regular exercise and sensible clothing for women from an early age. In her autobiography, Gilman discusses how as an adolescent she took brisk outdoor walks and volunteered for such chores as scrubbing floors and bringing in wood because of the physical exertion that these tasks provided (*Living* 64). Then, at the age of seventeen, she received a copy of a book that would change her life and make her a bona fide member of physical culture movement: William Blaikie's *How to Get Strong and How to Stay So* (1877). Viewing Blaikie's manual as her "bible" (Vertinsky 207), Gilman began a daily routine of running, calisthenics and weightlifting: "each day I ran a mile, not for speed but for wind. . . . I could vault and jump, go up a knotted rope, walk on my hands under a ladder, kick as high as my head, and revel in the flying ring" (Gilman *Living* 67). Matching these routines with a careful diet, good hygiene, and sensible clothing, Gilman took great pride in her health. As she would confess later in life, "I was never vain of my looks, nor of any of my professional achievements, but am absurdly vain of my physical strength and agility" (quoted in P. W. Allen 33). Indeed, Gilman remained firmly committed to physical culture, bragging while in her late sixties, "I . . . can still run better than many younger women" (*Living* 67).[2]

---

2. Many of Gilman's letters and journal entries, in fact, give nearly as much attention to her exercise and weightlifting regimens as they do to her ideas and treatises. In a diary passage from March 1883, for instance, the author not only proudly records the

Gilman's interest in the physical culture movement went beyond merely improving her own physical body; it also had the larger aim of helping to improve the national body politic. Akin to contemporaries like Theodore Roosevelt, she was deeply concerned about the rising number of nonwhite immigrants in the United States. An avid reader of anthropology and sociology, Gilman believed in a hierarchy of racial and ethnic groups. Placing Anglo-Saxon Americans in general and individuals of Aryan descent (such as herself) in particular on the highest tier of development, she was alarmed by the number of "low" and even "degenerate" races that were flooding the nation's shores. In a 1923 essay entitled "Is America Too Hospitable?," she expressed her amazement at "the cheerful willingness with which the American people are giving up their country to other people, so rapidly that they are already reduced to a scant half of the population" (289). Gilman felt that these men and women were unlikely to "melt" or "mix" into "good Americans," and, even if they did, they would "pollute" the nation's racial stock. As she asserted, "If you put into a melting pot promiscuous shovelfuls of anything that comes handy you do not get out of it anything of value" ("Hospitable" 290). As a result, Gilman called for an end to unrestricted immigration. In words that encapsulated her view on the subject, she declared: "Since *genus homo* is one species, it is physically possible for all races to interbreed, but not desirable" (Gilman "Hospitable" 291).[3]

Gilman's firm convictions about gender, health and race were coupled with an equally vivid awareness about the sexual "perversion" commonly ascribed to women who engaged in iconoclastic behavior. During her life, the writer and intellectual was involved in at least three same-sex affairs. The first—and by far most tender—was with childhood friend Martha Luther. Commencing in 1877 and lasting until 1881, their relationship was filled with passionate declarations of love and vows of lifelong devotion. In one letter, for instance, Gilman told Martha, "I could spend hours in cuddling if I had you here. . . . [Y]ou will make up to me for husband and children and all that I shall miss" (quoted in Hill *Making* 77). Given these feelings, Gilman became extremely jealous of the male suitor who courted and eventually married Martha. In letters and journal entries, in fact, she referred to him as "the interloper" (Lane *Herland* 77–8). Moreover, when he proposed to Martha, Gilman instructed her beloved, "tell him you are

---

measurements of her lower leg and upper arm muscles, but boasts that she had become so strong that she had "carried a girl on *one arm* and hip easily!" [her emphasis] (C. P. Gilman *Abridged* 91).

3. For more on Gilman's views of race and immigration, see her essays "Race Pride" in *The Forerunner*, (April 1913): 89–90, along with "A Suggestion on the Negro Problem" in *American Journal of Sociology*, 14.1 (July 1908): 78–85. For secondary analysis, see Lisa Ganobcsik-Williams's "The Intellectualism of Charlotte Perkins Gilman: Evolutionary Perspectives on Race, Ethnicity and Class" in *Charlotte Perkins Gilman: Optimist Reformer*, Ed. Jill Rudd and Val Gough (Iowa City, IA: U of Iowa P, 1999): 16–41.

spoken for by a female in Providence, and can't marry just yet" (quoted in Hill *Making* 88). After their nuptials, Gilman remarked in the language of a jilted lover, "the little girl is very happy. And all the family . . . are well-pleased. Wherein—I am, Finis" (quoted in Lane *Herland* 78).

As Barbara A. White has written, biographers might be willing to view Gilman's relationship with Martha "as an 'episode' in an otherwise unblemished heterosexual life if it were not for [her] subsequent relationships with women" (197–8). In 1890, after the dissolution of her marriage to Walter Stetson, she became involved with Grace Channing, a longtime friend who—in a bizarre detail—was engaged to her ex-husband. Before the couple's wedding, in fact, the aspiring author wrote Grace a passionate letter: "When Martha married it cracked my heart a good deal—your loss will finish it. I think of you with a great howling selfish heartache. *I want you—I love you—I need you myself!*" [italics in original]. (Gilman *Journey* 404).

Within a year after Grace married, Gilman entered into her third and final same-sex affair, with journalist Adeline E. Knapp. Unlike her relationship with Martha, which Gilman asserted contained love but not sex,[4] her involvement with Adeline was physical. In addition to sharing a home together in California, the two shared a bed. Years after their stormy four-year relationship ended, Gilman confessed to her soon-to-be-second husband, Houghton Gilman, "I loved her, trusted her, wrote her as freely as I wrote to you. I told you that I loved her that way" (quoted in Lane *Herland* 66).

Although Gilman remained happily married to Houghton until his death in 1934, she continued to speak tenderly about her relationships with women. In her autobiography, which she asked to be published after her death, she wrote that her relationship with Martha Luther was the most loving of her life: "With Martha I knew perfect happiness. . . . Four years of satisfying happiness" (Gilman *Living* 78). For these reasons, Barbara White has argued that although Gilman is most often presented as a heterosexual figure, she is more accurately described as a bisexual one (197).

In the discussion that follows, I examine the way in which Gilman's nativist sentiments along with her awareness of the anxiety surrounding female homosexuality influenced her attraction to, as well as advocacy of, the tomboyish physical culture movement. Fueled by her xenophobic interest in bolstering the white race, but also by her recognition of the fears regarding female gender and sexual "perversion," her representative vision of women's athleticism advocated health and hygiene as well as femininity and reproductive heterosexuality. Of the numerous prose and poetic works

---

4. In her autobiography, for instance, Gilman insisted about her relationship with Luther: "In our perfect concord there was no Freudian taint" (*Living* 80).

that Gilman penned addressing physical culture,[5] I focus on one of her most famous: the 1915 novel *Herland*. A utopian narrative about three male adventurers—sociologist Vandyke Jennings, biologist Jeff Margrave and wealthy entrepreneur Terry O. Nicholson—who brave an uncharted jungle to find a "lost" female settlement, the book charts the new but simultaneously old characteristics associated with physical culture during the early twentieth century. From its belief in the malleability of human behavior and emphasis on dress reform to its realignment with femininity and veneration for marriage and motherhood, the early-twentieth-century exercise movement was largely a repackaged form of mid-nineteenth-century tomboyism. Given the racial ramifications associated with the resurrection of gender-bending behavior for women, it is no coincidence that Gilman's utopian land of tomboys is also one of Aryan mothers.

"Everything Old Is New Again": Progressive Era Physical Culture as a Regression to Antebellum Tomboyism

Perhaps the most important element that the tomboyish physical culture movement resurrected from the antebellum origins of this code of conduct was also the most subtle: the belief that gender-bending behavior was a voluntary choice rather than a biological compulsion. Although the early twentieth century remained heavily influenced by Darwinian thinking, it no longer asserted that biology was destiny. Inheritance may determine the basic traits that an individual possessed, but these elements could be modified by environmental forces. Indeed, as Thomas Peyser has written about the era, the belief that society and the individuals who comprised it "was in some fundamental way a construction (like a building) rather than a natural formation (like a leaf) lay behind the progressive impulse" (3).

Charlotte Perkins Gilman was an adamant believer in the human capacity for change. On the opening page of *Women and Economics*, she asserted, "The power of the individual will to resist natural law is well proven. . . . [T]he social environment . . . is of enormous force as a modifier of human life" (1). Although her utopian novel *Herland* is commonly seen as being inspired by new directions in American feminism, it was also fueled by new beliefs regarding the basis for human behavior. Echoing Gilman's assertion in *Women and Economics* that "physical organs are developed by use, that what we use most is developed most" (3), the utopian women successfully shape their physical, mental and even emotional characteristics. As one of the three male adventurers observes, "they recognized that however the children differed at birth, the real growth lay later—through education"

5. See the Tomboy Bibliography at the end of this study for a list of her many writings on the subject.

(61). This process is perhaps most powerfully illustrated in their ability to shape bodies: the Herland women are all in astounding physical condition. Both young and old attend regular gymnasium sessions and make a national pastime out of running and jumping. Indeed, the narrator notes, "Each was in the full bloom of health, erect, serene, standing sure-footed and light as any pugilist" (22). Even the seemingly most physiological of processes—their parthenogenetic form of reproduction—can be voluntarily controlled by the Herlanders. Women who have been asked to refrain from childbearing for either eugenic reasons or in the interest of population control are able to thwart the powerful instinctual urge to conceive a baby. As one of the women of Herland explains, "'When that deep inner demand for a child began to be felt she would deliberately engage in the most active work, physical and mental; and even more important, would solace her longing by the direct care and service of the babies we already had'" (71). Over time, such tactics allow the young woman to "voluntarily defer" motherhood (Gilman *Herland* 71).

Because the tomboyish physical culture movement was a eugenic strategy for improving the health of white women and, by extension, the white race, it became associated with more than simply physical exercise. The hygienic, nutritional and clothing components which had long been seen as ancillary to this code of conduct became integral once again.[6] Accordingly, one of the first traits that the three male adventurers note about the Herland women is their attire: they forgo heavy dresses and constricting corsets, and instead wear tunic-like clothing. Allowing for a full range of motion and possessing many useful pockets, the men concede "The garments were simple in the extreme, and absolutely comfortable" (28). The same ethos applies to their hairstyles. As Van notes, "all wore short hair, some few inches at most; some curly, some not; all light and clean and fresh-looking" (32).

Of course, the racial benefit of improving the health of middle- and upper-class white women would be lost if these figures did not have children. In addition to being reconnected with the eugenic aim of antebellum tomboyism, therefore, the physical culture movement was firmly associated with its mid-nineteenth-century origins as a preparatory stage for marriage and motherhood. In *Herland*, the three adventurers quickly realize that

---

6. In sentiments that recall antebellum dress reformers in general and novelist E. D. E. N. Southworth in particular, for instance, Gilman routinely raged against the harmful nature of women's fashions. In an essay titled "Why Women Do Not Reform Their Dress" (1886), for instance, she asserted: "The present style of dress means, with varying limits, backache, side ache, headache, and many other ache; corns, lame, tender, or swollen feet, weak clumsy, and useless compared to what they should be; a crowd of diseases, heavy and light; a general condition of feebleness and awkwardness and total inferiority as an animal organism; with a thousand attendant inconveniences and unnatural distortions amounting to hideousness" (24).

motherhood is at the center of their society. After acquiring the ability to reproduce parthenogenetically, children became "the *raison d'être* in this country" (Gilman *Herland* 53). Their tutor Moadine remarks, "'The children . . . are the one center and focus of all our thoughts'" (67). Motherhood even forms the basis for the settlement's religious beliefs. The women practice what Van characterizes as a type of "Maternal Pantheism": "Here was Mother Earth, bearing fruit. All that they ate was fruit of motherhood, from seed or egg or their product. By motherhood they were born and by motherhood they lived—life was, to them, just the long cycle of motherhood" (61).

While the utopian inhabitants of Herland have developed an effective form of parthenogenetic reproduction, they are eager to replace it with what they term "bisexual reproduction" after Terry, Van and Jeff arrive. In a detail that recalls the antebellum origins of white tomboyism once again, the women are only willing to resume traditional motherhood within the confines of traditional marriage. While Alima, Ellador and Celis refuse to live in the same abode or take the same last name as their husbands, they do not dispute the importance of being married before engaging in procreation. Consequently, the three women wed their respective spouses during a momentous triple ceremony. As Van notes, "before that vast multitude of calm-faced mothers and holy-eyed maidens, came forward our own three chosen ones" (120).

The strong connection between the tomboyish physical culture movement and marriage and motherhood was matched by its equally strong disconnection from sexual inversion. In light of *fin-de-siecle* fears about lesbianism, Gilman stresses that although her utopian inhabitants live in a homosocial society, it is not a homoerotic one. At numerous points, the three male adventurers call attention to the Herlanders' complete lack of sex drive: "[T]hey hadn't the faintest idea of love—sex-love, that is" (89). Lest this comment go unnoticed, it is reiterated. When narrator Vandyke Jennings discusses his frustration with the courtship process, for instance, he explains: "You see, they lacked the sex motive" (100). Living in what Barbara A. White has characterized as "a state of compulsory celibacy" (199), the Herlanders do not simply passively lack a sex drive, they actively breed it out: "There was no sex-feeling to appeal to, or practically none. Two thousand years' disuse had left very little of the instinct; also we must remember that those who had times manifested it as atavistic exceptions were often, by that very fact, denied motherhood" (93).[7]

---

7. In spite of the asexual nature of the Herland women, Barbara A. White aptly notes that the sensation they experience when expecting a child is reminiscent of an orgasm. As Somel explains to Van, "'You see, before a child comes to one of us, there is a period of utter exhalation—the whole being is uplifted and filled with a concentrated desire for that child'" (71).

The physical culture movement was equally concerned with eradicating its potential link to mannish gender abnormality. As Patricia Vertinksy has discussed, from the personality traits that practitioners of this code of conduct cultivated to the sporting activities in which they engaged, they affirmed their connection to femininity or at least biological femaleness. In *Herland*, the utopian inhabitants are in dialogue with an array of Western stereotypes about femininity. Even though Van does not have a clear view of the inhabitants when he first enters Herland, he nonetheless asserts: "They were girls, of course, no boys could ever have shown that sparkling beauty" (17). This declaration about their girlish rather than boyish nature is confirmed several chapters later. In an observation that forms a direct refutation of *fin-de-siecle* accusations that New Women were becoming so mannish that they would begin growing beards, "Jeff pointed out that he never before had seen such a complete lack of facial hair on women. . . . 'Looks to me as if the absence of men made them more feminine in that regard, anyhow'" (74).

The feminine external appearance of Gilman's Herlanders is matched by their internal personality traits. Not only do the utopian inhabitants venerate motherhood, but in keeping with Victorian stereotypes about women, they dislike competition and display deference to men. As Moadine tells Van, they do not wish to see their children "suffer, sin, and die, fighting horrible with one another" (69). Although Herland society is clearly superior to the patriarchal one from which Van, Jeff and Terry hail, the women repeatedly defer to it. When the adventurers' biplane was first spotted overhead, in fact, "they had instantly accepted it as proof of the high development of Some Where Else" (65). Likewise, echoing Western stereotypes about women's intellectual inferiority, Somel tells Jeff, "'You know so much, you see, and we know only about our own land'" (48). Even seemingly gender-neutral aspects of Herland like their linguistic development, land usage and architectural style echo Western stereotypes about femininity. Van describes the country's dialect via essentialist views of women's mellifluous language: a "torrent of soft talk . . . clear musical fluent speech" (17). Moreover, the women have chosen to cultivate their country with fruit-bearing trees, shaded paths and "flowers everywhere" (20). Finally, the houses in which the Herland women live are constructed of appropriately rose-colored stone (19).

This heightened emphasis on feminization likewise shapes the type of athletic activity in which the Herlanders engage. While tomboyish girls in previous generations had participated in all kinds of rough-and-tumble play, devotees of physical culture during the Progressive Era were restricted to selected ones. As Patricia Vertinsky has written, the movement placed almost as much emphasis on engaging in the proper type of activity as it did on engaging in athletic activity at all (22). From its inception, advocates created a list of sports that were considered appropriately feminine. Gone were the more masculine activities of hunting, fishing and climbing, and in their place were the more ladylike ones of running, calisthenics and especially gymnastics.[8]

Although Gilman is commonly remembered for her efforts to eradicate gender barriers, her views on athletics routinely reinforced them. The author believed that women should engage in sporting activities, but she also believed that these activities should remain within certain gendered limitations. In *The Man-Made World* (1911), for instance, she argued that since women do not "find ceaseless pleasure in throwing, batting or kicking things," they would never take an interest in baseball or soccer (153). Likewise, because women "are not built for physical combat" (*Man-Made* 153), she believed contact sports would never appeal to them. Echoing these observations, the inhabitants of Herland do not receive their physical activity from aggressive sporting matches or endurance competitions. On the contrary, they exercise in a venue that was the hallmark of the physical culture movement in many ways: a gymnasium. As Van observes, "There were no spectacular acrobatics, such as only the young can perform, but for all-around development they had a most excellent system. A good deal of music went with it, with posture dancing and, sometimes, gravely beautiful processional performances" (34).[9]

Because the tomboyish physical culture movement associated itself with femininity and heterosexuality, and dissociated itself from female masculinity and sexual inversion, it was seen as desirable and even beautiful once again. Akin to the way in which Capitola Black's tomboyish antics made her acutely appealing, the three male adventurers find themselves envious of, and even aroused by, the Herlander's abilities. Upon first seeing the physically fit inhabitants, Terry exclaims: "Mother of Mike, boys. . . . To climb like that! to run like that! and afraid of nothing. This country suits me all right" (19).

8. For more information on the gendered ideology of the physical culture movement, see Patricia A. Vertinsky's *The Eternally Wounded Woman: Women, Doctors and Exercise in the Late Nineteenth Century* (Urbana: University of Illinois, 1989).

9. The segregation of sporting activities into masculine and feminine was accompanied by the segregation of the sexes while they engaged in them. Physical exercise became a single-sex rather than a co-ed activity as women's gymnasiums, bicycling expeditions and athletic teams emerged. In a seemingly paradoxical stance, Gilman supported this division. During the 1880s, for example, she lobbied for the creation of a women's gymnasium in Rhode Island, rather than their right to use the one designated for men. In an article for the *Provincial Daily Journal* to demonstrate the benefits of all-women's facilities, she argued that they enhanced their appearance: "'the increase in health and beauty has been most encouraging, to see the back straighten, shoulders fall into place, narrow chests expand and weak muscles grow firm and round'" (quoted in Vertinsky 208).

Becoming the Aryan Savage: Getting Physical as Going Primitive in *Herland*

Although the physical culture movement drew heavily on the antebellum origins of white tomboyism, this was not its sole source of inspiration. The phenomenon also culled elements from a far earlier and more primordial period that was likewise seen as having a restorative effect on a beleaguered white race: primitivism.

While Westerners routinely disparaged tribal peoples for their "uncivilized" ways and "backwards" customs, they also often romanticized this way of life. During the early twentieth century, many began to find Western society stale and stifling. As T. J. Jackson Lears has written, for them, "authentic experience of any sort seemed ever more elusive" (5). Especially for the wealthy elite, "life seem[ed] increasingly confined to the air parlor of material comfort and moral complacency" (Lears 5). Living in sterile abodes that disconnected them from nature, adorning themselves in elaborate and often ridiculous garments, and behaving according to artificial codes of decorum, they had lost touch with their natural instincts.

Primitives lived in contrast to this condition. Uninhibited by the trappings of an overly civilized society, tribal peoples had a more natural and unfettered way of life. Instead of positioning themselves in opposition to nature, they lived in harmony with their surroundings. Similarly, rather than confining themselves to either restrictive attire or societal mores, they were physically and emotionally unrestrained. For these reasons, primitive cultures came to be viewed as sites of rejuvenation and even reinvigoration for an overly civilized Western society. As Marianna Torgovnick has written, they represented a "utopian desire to go back and recover irreducible features of the psyche, body, land, and community—to reinhabit core experiences" (*Passions* 5). From the African masks in Picasso's cubist painting *Les Demoiselles d'Avignon* (1907) to the tribal movements in Nijinsky's choreography for the ballet *The Rite of Spring* (*Le Sacre du Printemps*, 1913), primitivism "became a medium for soul-searching and self-transformation" (Torgovnick *Passions* 8).

In an often-overlooked detail, the physical culture movement also drew on the liberating power of primitivism in its quest to rejuvenate an "overcivilized" white race. Advocates believed that the adoption of tribal traits would allow individuals "to smash the glass and breathe freely—to experience 'real life' in all its intensity" (Lears 5). Theodore Roosevelt, for instance, in his advocacy for the male counterpart to the physical culture movement—a phenomenon he deemed "the cult of the strenuous life"—encouraged boys to embrace their primal instincts towards physicality. Believing that modern young men had become so overly civilized that they were weak and effeminate, he sought to make them more "savage." Through rough-and-tumble athletics like football, wrestling and boxing,

Roosevelt believed "a delicate, indoor race" would receive "a saving touch of honest, old-fashioned barbarism" (quoted in Lears 108).

Primtivism had an equally rejuvenative power for white, middle-class women, as the utopian inhabitants of *Herland* demonstrate. Since the publication of Gilman's novel, in fact, readers and critics have typically viewed it as a feminist response to H. Rider Haggard's 1887 novel *She*.[10] An adventure book about two men who travel deep into the jungles of Africa to explore a lost white civilization that is ruled by an all-powerful female nearly 2,000 years old, Haggard's narrative was among the most popular and influential of its day, and *Herland* is seen as a product of mimesis. Presenting a group of male travelers who likewise traverse an uncharted jungle to explore an all-female civilization that is also reportedly 2,000 years old, Gilman's narrative offers a retort to the misogynist portrait of women in Haggard's text. As Sandra Gilbert and Susan Gubar have argued, "*She*'s power and popularity transformed the colonized contents into the heart of female darkness that Charlotte Perkins Gilman would rename and reclaim in a utopian feminist revision of Haggard's romance" (*No Man's Land* 192).

Although the basic narrative structure for *Herland* may have been modeled after Haggard's *She*, I argue in this section that its use of primitivism is more closely patterned after another well-known and slightly more contemporaneous adventure book: Edgar Rice Burroughs's *Tarzan of the Apes*. Chronicling the experiences of an orphaned white English aristocrat who is raised by a band of black apes in the African jungle, Burroughs's story was serialized in 1912 before being published in book form in 1914. A commercial success from the moment *Tarzan* appeared on bookstore shelves, it became a powerful cultural myth and sparked a profitable series. During the next twenty years, Burroughs published more than two dozen novels about the fictional Lord Greystoke. An astounding four of these narratives—*The Return of Tarzan* in 1913, *The Son of Tarzan* and *The Jungle Tales of Tarzan* in 1915 and *Tarzan and the Jewels of Opar* in 1916—appeared in the four years following the novel's initial serialization alone.

Although the utopian inhabitants of Herland develop a highly advanced civilization, they also possess many suggestive echoes of Tarzan's unique form of white primitivism. Akin to Burroughs's "White Ape," Gilman's tomboyish inhabitants embody the "Aryan savage" in many ways. From their close connection with nature and participation in active physicality to their history of bellicosity and almost childlike innocence, they traffic

---

10. In addition to Sandra Gilbert and Susan Gubar's well-known discussion about the connections between these two books, see also Aleta Cane's "Charlotte Perkins Gilman's *Herland* as a Feminist Response to Male Quest Romance," *Jack London Journal*, 2 (1995): 25–38.

in a parallel version of modernist white fantasies about tribal peoples and cultures. Indeed, Marianna Torgovnick has written about the gendered readership of the *Tarzan* novels: "Women usually had not read the Tarzan books, in fact usually did not know anything more than the bare facts of Tarzan's story. The rare exceptions among the women who had read the Tarzan books usually attributed their reading to older brothers or to *a rebellious, tomboy past*" [my emphasis] (*Gone* 70).

Building on this observation about the gender-bending appeal of Burroughs's text, this section reveals the previously overlooked connections between *Herland* and *Tarzan*. The links between these two narratives add a new dimension to Gilman's oft-discussed engagement with popular literary forms, while they also shed new light on the racialized implications of the tomboyish physical culture movement. Unlike H. Rider Haggard's simian and degenerative She-Who-Must-Be-Obeyed,[11] Tarzan's primitive upbringing in the jungles of Africa did not make him an atavistic figure. As Gail Bederman has written, his life among a band of wild apes rendered him "a powerfully appealing fantasy of perfect, invincible manhood" (219). Tarzan's seemingly savage traits embody an effective way to rejuvenate an enfeebled white Western manhood. Akin to Theodore Roosevelt's famous hunting safaris, "Burroughs . . . constructed Africa as a place where 'the white man' could prove his superior manhood by reliving the primitive, masculine life of his most distant evolutionary forefathers" (Bederman 220).

It is this view of "uncivilized" behaviors as having positive, desirous and even rejuvenative effects—rather than atavistic or degenerative ones as in Haggard's *She*—that underwrites the construction of tomboyish white characters in *Herland*. By embracing various elements of tribalism and even "savagery," Burroughs's White Ape is able to become "King of the Jungle" and Gilman's Aryan settlers are able to create a superior society. In this way, although *Herland* is commonly seen as repudiating early-twentieth-century beliefs that women were "primitive" beings who lacked the intellectual capacity to create a sophisticated society, it is actually participating in a more complex project. Given prevailing beliefs in the rejuvenative power of primitivism along with the cultural popularity of *Tarzan*, the 1915 novel argues that the key to creating an advanced society is not the wholesale rejection of primitivism, but the embrace of strategic facets of it.

---

11. In a powerful indication of the way in which Ayesha's adoption of primitive qualities has caused evolutionary backsliding, her destruction occurs in a manner as savage as this figure herself. Consumed by a "revolving pillar of flame," her body shrinks to a size "no bigger . . . than that of a two-month's child" and her skin resembles "crinkled yellow parchment" (Haggard 294–295). In case these atavistic implications went unnoticed, the formerly beautiful white queen is compared to a "monkey" and a "baboon" (Haggard 293–295).

In their desire to bolster the health of the Aryan race, Gilman's inhabitants are doing more than simply "getting physical." Akin to one of the underlying tenets of the physical culture movement in general, and Tarzan in particular, they are also selectively "going primitive."

The suggestive echoes between *Herland* and the modern white fantasies about primitivism that permeate *Tarzan* emerge from the opening pages of Gilman's text. As local guides tell the three male adventurers before leading them to the isolated female settlement, "this strange country where no men lived—only women and girl children" is rumored to be extraordinarily savage: "It was dangerous, deadly, they said, for any man to go there" (4). Going beyond mere local legend, such remarks reflect what Rita Felski has termed "the gender of modernity." Because women were confined to the domestic sphere, many argued that they existed in a pre-industrial and even prelapsarian state. Seen as disconnected from the "masculine" technological changes of modern society, they were regarded, in the words of Rita Felski, as "a mythic referent untouched by the strictures of social and symbolic mediation" (38). Primitives shared this condition. Removed from the flux and turmoil of the modern world, they seemed frozen in time. As a result, middle- and upper-class white women and modernity's understanding of the primitive became linked. As Torgovnick notes, the concept was "coded metaphorically as feminine. . . . [F]amiliar tropes for primitives became the tropes conventionally used for women" (*Passions* 8).

The three male adventurers in Gilman's *Herland* subscribe to these attitudes. From the opening pages of the novel, Jeff, Terry and Van associate primitivism with femininity and civilization with masculinity. Speculating on the conditions in the all-female settlement before their arrival, for instance, Terry asserts, "'[W]e mustn't look for inventions or progress; it'll be awfully primitive'" (10). Then, when the trio sees evidence of technological advancements, they insist that males are hidden somewhere: "'[W]hy, this is a *civilized* country. . . . There must be men'" [italics in original] (12).

Even though Gilman sharply criticizes these attitudes, she does not have her utopian inhabitants repudiate all vestiges of primitivism. In fact, upon first entering the all-female utopia, the men find an array of elements that seem to confirm their initial assumption. The first of these details recalls not only the era's belief in the simian character of "low" races but also one of Tarzan's hallmarks: an arboreal nature. Raised in the jungle by apes, Burroughs's title character feels at home in the tree-tops. Providing protection from the hazards of the jungle floor, and allowing him to commune with the other apes in his band, it constitutes one of his most important survival skills and memorable qualities. As the narrator notes, "He could swing twenty feet across space at the dizzy heights of the forest top, and grasp with unerring precision, and without apparent jar, a limb waving wildly in the path of an approaching tornado" (38). The utopian inhabitants in *Herland* share this trait. In the opening pages of the novel, Alima, Celis and Ellador perch in a treetop. While the three male adventurers must concentrate to keep their balance, the women—like Tarzan—seem at home in this terrain. As Van observes, they "swung before us, wholly at ease" (17). Consequently, the men conclude, "'Inhabitants evidently arboreal'" (19).

Although this assertion ultimately proves inaccurate, the inhabitants' connection to another common tenet of primitivism—active physicality—is not. Whereas Westerners were associated with the cerebral, primitives were associated with the corporeal. Tribal peoples did not sit behind desks or lounge in parlors; they roamed through nature. Unlike the sedentary habits of modern men and women, running, jumping and climbing were a part of their daily activities. For these reasons, Marianna Torgovnick has pointed out that "Within the context of such thinking, 'going primitive' and 'getting physical' slide together" (*Gone* 228).

Exceedingly muscular and exceptionally athletic, Tarzan illustrates this conflation. As the narrator says of the untamed title character, he was the "personification . . . of the primitive man, the hunter, the warrior" (108). Although not as brawny as the apes, his active, outdoor existence has rendered him stronger and more robust than the typical white man. When Tarzan was only ten years old, the narrator notes, "he was fully as strong as the average man of thirty, and far more agile than the most practiced athlete ever becomes. And day by day his strength was increasing" (39). For these reasons, both Richard Dyer and, more recently, John F. Kasson have argued that Burroughs's King of the Apes constitutes a defining cultural symbol of white male muscularity.

Even though Gilman's Herlanders obtain their healthy physiques through carefully planned exercise regimens rather than the physical demands of their daily lives, the end result is the same. The athletic skills of even the older women greatly exceed that of the three male adventurers: "Terry was the strongest of us, though I was wiry and had good staying power, and Jeff was a great sprinter and hurdler, but I can tell you those old ladies gave us cards and spades" (34). Recalling Tarzan's strength and muscularity, the Herland women lift the men at one point "like children, straddling helpless children, and borne onward, wriggling indeed, but most ineffectually" (25).

Although primitives were associated with an advanced state of physical development, the same could not be said for attitudes regarding their mental and emotional condition. Unaware of the corruption, hardship and injustices of the modern world, they were thought to live in a state of childlike ignorance. For these reasons, psychologists and anthropologists frequently made connections between adult tribal peoples and white Western children. As Sander Gilman has observed, many leading scientists during the early twentieth century asserted, "The child is the primitive form of man" and vice versa ("Sexology" 73).

In one of the many paradoxes that permeate his character, Tarzan is simultaneously adult and childlike. Although a savage figure who slaughters wild animals and becomes "King of the Jungle," he seems more like a timid boy than a powerful man. Tarzan has simple thoughts that seldom go beyond the biological necessities of eating and sleeping. On the rare occasion when they do—such as with his desire to learn how to read and write—his mental processes retain a childlike quality. For example, when Tarzan finds a primer in the abandoned cabin that once belonged to his parents, he spells out words like "M-A-N" and "M-O-N-K-E-Y-S" as if he were a young child (56). The method by which he learns to write is similar. Holding the pencil "as one would grasp the hilt of a dagger," Tarzan "would attempt to reproduce some of the little bugs that scrambled over the pages of his book" (55). These details combined with Tarzan's age and exceptional strength prompt the narrator to deem him a "man-child" (41).

Separated from the outside world for more than 2,000 years, Gilman's Herlanders can be viewed in an analogous way. Although they have created a sophisticated society, they paradoxically reflect the ignorant nature of primitives like Tarzan. In spite of their vast knowledge of select subjects, the utopian women are unaware of even the most basic facts about Western life and naïvely shocked by its most mild forms of injustice. When Jeff, Vandyck and Terry explain dairy farming, for instance, the Herlanders become physically ill. Believing that the process "robs the cow of her calf, and the calf of its true food . . . [t]hey heard it out, looking very white, and presently begged to be excused" (50).

In the same way that lack of knowledge about the modern world made primitive peoples more innocent, it also made them more free. Unlike "civilized" men and women, who are hampered by restrictive manners and mores, tribal peoples are unfettered by social codes and thus live more naturally. Indeed, as Torgovnick argues, "[p]rimitives are our untamed selves, our id forces. . . . Primitives are free" (*Gone* 8).

Tarzan, who lives outside of human society, is unencumbered by rules and restrictions. Exemplifying the character's distance from his aristocratic heritage, "he gobbled down a great quantity of raw flesh" at most meals and then "wiped his greasy fingers upon his naked thighs" (77). Tarzan's lack of refinement, however, goes beyond mere table manners. Together with eating like a savage, Tarzan also behaves like one. Unlike modern men and women, who carefully consider each decision, he privileges action over thought. Doing what comes naturally or instinctually, he sleeps when he is tired, eats when hungry and fights when angry. In an act that epitomizes Tarzan's freedom from the conventions of civilized society, he commits the ultimate taboo: killing his ape father. In a savage fight, Tarzan slays Kerchak to become king of the jungle (97).

Although Gilman's Herlanders would be horrified by Tarzan's lack of personal restraint and especially by his participation in patricide, their tomboyish behavior affords them abundant physical freedom and personal autonomy. As Gilman frequently argued, tomboyism was the most natural form of female conduct. In the opening segment of *Women and Economics*, for instance, she asserted: "The most normal girl is the tom-boy—whose numbers increase among us in these wiser days—a healthy young creature, who is human through and through; not feminine until it is time to be" (29). *Herland* calls similar attention to the naturalness of tomboyish behavior. Even for the older women, strength and agility were commonplace rather than atypical. As Vandyck asserts, "They ran like deer, by which I mean that they ran not as if it was a performance, but as if it was their natural gait" (34).

Closely related to the Herlander's engagement in more natural and therefore tomboyish activities is their embrace of a more natural and thus androgynous appearance. Together with thinking that women's behaviors had become overly civilized, Charlotte Perkins Gilman believed that their physical appearance had done so as well. As she commented in *Women and Economics*: "Our distinctions of sex are carried to such a degree as to be disadvantageous to our progress" (17). With one sex limited to a certain set of behaviors and the other sex restricted to the opposite, both suffered. Gilman asserted that when men and women adhered to these rigid divisions, they were only "half a complete person" (*Women* 26).

Primitives lived in contrast to this condition. They lacked the excessive distinctions of sex that were present in so-called modern society and were thus often seen as androgynous. As Gail Bederman has written about early-twentieth-century attitudes regarding the gender-bending nature of primitive peoples, "'Savage' (that is, nonwhite) race . . . had not yet evolved pronounced sexual differences—and, to some extent, this was precisely what made them savage" (28). Far from seeing this lack of a specialized sex distinction as a negative attribute, Gilman considered it a positive asset. Advocating for a new gender system that allowed for a fuller and more natural range of behavior, she believed that individuals should be seen as human first and men or women only secondarily. To further emphasize this point, Gilman identified herself as a "humanist" rather than a "feminist" throughout her career. As she asserted, her aim was to free both sexes and not merely women from the oppressions of gender.[12]

Herland incorporates these attitudes. While the tomboyish characters possess more feminine traits than their *fin-de-siecle* counterparts, they also

---

12. For more information about Gilman's critique of both male and female gender roles, see Mary A. Hill, *Charlotte Perkins Gilman: The Making of a Radical Feminist* (Philadelphia: Temple UP, 1980) and Ann J. Lane, *To Herland and Beyond: The Life and Work of Charlotte Perkins Gilman* (New York: Pantheon, 1990).

display a large number of androgynous elements. Straddling traditional Western gender roles with their short hairstyles and tunic-like attire, the women frustrate and often even unsettle the three male adventurers. Aggravated by their combination of male and female signifiers, Terry refers to them as "Sexless, epicene, undeveloped neuters" (140). A less judgmental Van comments on the androgynous nature of their culture: "There was no accepted standard of what was 'manly' and what was 'womanly'" (93).

Not surprisingly, given that primitives lived in tune with human nature, they also lived in harmony with the natural world. Unlike "civilized" men and women, who constructed elaborate structures to shield them from the elements, tribal peoples had direct contact with flora and fauna. Often living outdoors or in homes made directly from earthen materials like mud or leaves, they were frequently regarded as "mystics, in tune with nature, part of its harmonies" (Torgovnick Gone 8).

Tarzan, who wears little more than a loincloth made of animal pelt for much of the novel, is one with his environment. He lives in the trees, feeds on the local plants and animals, and makes his home in the jungle. In a passage that indicates the close connection that Tarzan and his ape pack have with nature, the narrator describes one of their typical evenings: "At night they slept where darkness overtook them, lying upon the ground, and sometimes covering their heads, and more seldom their bodies, with the great leaves of the elephant's ear" (43).

Although Gilman's Herlanders do not sleep on the ground, Amanda Graham as well as Susan Stratton have noted that they are astute environmentalists.[13] One of the first characteristics Jeff, Terry and Van notice about Herland society, in fact, is its symbiotic relationship with nature. Unlike the filth, noise and pollution of most Western cities, their settlement was "in a state of perfect cultivation, where even the forests looked as if they were cared for; a land that looked like an enormous park, only it was even more evidently an enormous garden" (13). Even on close inspection, Van notes, "Everything was beauty, order, perfect cleanness, and the pleasant sense of home over it all" (21).

The absence of a formal social structure may have allowed tribal peoples to be more natural and free, but it also made them more unpredictable. Without a codified system of manners and mores, primitives often acted rashly and behaved violently. In contrast to the primacy that Western society placed on physical and emotional restraint, they lacked self-control. If angered by another person, they did not hesitate to fight and even kill them. However, even this seemingly undesirable trait came to be seen as

13. For more on Herland's environmentalism in general and ecofeminism in particular, see Amanda Graham's "Herland: Definitive Ecofemininst Fiction?" in A Very Different Story, Eds. Val Gough and Jill Rudd (Liverpool UP, 1988) and Susan Stratton's "Intersubjectivity and Difference in Feminist Ecotopias" in FEMSPEC, 3.1 (2001): 33–43.

having positive rejuvenative qualities during the early twentieth century. As T. J. Jackson Lears notes, "War promised both social and personal regeneration" for a stale and stagnated white Western society (100). As a result, many "began to hope that the warrior might return to redeem them from enervation and impotence" (Lears 100). In fact, when the First World War initially erupted in 1914—and, of course, the conflict was still raging when *Herland* was published the following year—many heralded it as a positive event that would bring rejuvenation.

Once again, Tarzan embodies this trait; rather than being intimidated by bellicosity, he is invigorated by it. Every day, Tarzan must fight with either the other apes or with the other wild beasts for survival. Uninhibited by the conventions of "civilized" warfare, he uses any means necessary to defeat his opponents. Crushing skulls and slicing off limbs along with routinely strangling, clawing and biting, Tarzan is truly a warrior savage. In one of the many graphic descriptions of his battles, for instance, the narrator notes, "as the tearing, striking beast dragged [Tarzan] to the earth he plunged the blade repeatedly and to the hilt into its breast" (49).

In a detail that is less often discussed about Gilman's Herlanders, they share this trait. While the settlement is currently a peaceful utopia that is appalled by the bellicosity of the Western world, Herland was born in the bloody crucible of war. When their men left for war, the slaves initiated a revolt and the women of Herland did not hesitate to fight back. Indeed, they "rose . . . and slew their brutal conquerors" (56). More than simply executing the participants in the revolt, the women decimated the entire population. Vandyke justifies their act of brutal bellicosity, explaining that the "succession of misfortunes was too much for those infuriated virgins" (56). Akin to Tarzan's belligerent behavior, these events brought out the "savage" in the Herlanders.[14]

Cultural Progression from Behavioral Regression: Using Dark Primitivism as a White Racial Strategy

In spite of the numerous elements that both Tarzan and the Herlanders incorporate from modernist stereotypes about the primitive, one important difference remains: their racial identities. Whatever characteristics primitives were thought to possess, and from whatever geographic region they were believed to hail, they were always nonwhite. As Patrick Brantlinger

14. The asexual form of reproduction that the Herlander's develop can also be linked with primitivism. Although parthenogenesis was an evolutionary development in the settlement, the adventurers see it as an atavistic throwback. When one of the women asks the biologist Jeff tutors if any other animal species use this method to breed, he responds: "'Why, yes—some low forms, of course'" (47).

has discussed in an oft-referenced article, tribal men and women inhabited not simply a figurative but a literal "Dark Continent."[15]

Although Tarzan contains many characteristics of primitivism, the narrator makes it clear that his "savage" behavior has not led to racial atavism. The "King of the Apes" may swing through the trees and wear an animal skin loincloth, but he is not a racial Other. In the opening pages of the narrative, in fact, much attention is given to the white racial heritage and genetic pedigree of Tarzan's parents in general and his father—Lord Greystoke—in particular:

> Clayton was the type of Englishman that one likes best to associate with the noblest monuments of historic achievement upon a thousand victorious battle fields—a strong, virile man—mentally, morally, physically. In stature he was above average height: his eyes were gray, his features regular and strong: his carriage that of perfect, robust health influenced by his many years of [military] training. (2)

As the orphaned son of a British aristocrat, repeated emphasis is placed on Tarzan's whiteness. Although "burned brown by exposure" to the sun (39), the future "King of the Apes" knows that he is not one of the dark creatures with whom he has been living. Possessing an astounding sense of racial awareness and even race pride, he sees a picture of humans in a book and instantly identifies with them: "No longer did he feel shame for his hairless body or his human features, for now his reason told him that he was of a different race from his wild and hairy companions. He was a M-A-N, they were A-P-E-S" (56). Over time, Tarzan's sense of racial identity increases. Upon encountering the leader of a displaced African tribe, he recognizes the black man as a member of his species but not his race: "Tarzan looked with wonder upon the strange creature beneath him—so like him in form and yet so different in face and color. His books had portrayed the Negro, but how different had been the dull, dead print to this sleek thing of ebony" (68). Similarly, when Tarzan posts a note marking his domain and threatening any potential trespassers, he demonstrates his race consciousness:

> "THIS IS THE HOUSE OF TARZAN, THE KILLER OF BEASTS AND MANY BLACK MEN" [my italics] (115).

Several chapters later, an expedition of white scientists comes to the region and Tarzan instantly recognizes them as members of his race: "Here at last

15. See Patrick Brantlinger, "Victorians and Africans: The Genealogy of the Myth of the Dark Continent," "Race," Writing and Difference, Ed. Henry Louis Gates, Jr. (Chicago: U of Chicago Press, 1986): 185–222.

was his own kind; of that he was positive" (122). In an act of astounding race loyalty, he endangers his own life to save theirs: "He wondered why he felt so great an interest in these people—why he had gone to such pains to save the three men" (150). Even the name "Tarzan," which was given to him by his ape mother, calls attention to his racial identity. Meaning "White Skin," the appellation is itself a marker of difference (38). Indeed, as the title of one of Burroughs's chapters announces—and as the other animals repeatedly call him—Tarzan is the "White Ape."

Gilman's Herlanders possess an analogous sense of racial identity and even race pride. Akin to Tarzan, the women have been burned brown from the sun. As Vandyck Jennings notes, they were "somewhat darker than our northern races because of their constant exposure to the sun and air" (55). At various points throughout the novel, in fact, the men call attention to the women's tanned and colorized bodies. Terry's bride Alima, for instance, possesses "brown hands" (92). Similarly, Van's wife Ellador has hair so dark that it resembles "a seal coat," but she also has "clear brown skin" (92). Finally, Terry frequently calls Jeff's tutor Zava by such racially suggestive nicknames as "Java," "Mocha," "Coffee," or—when he is feeling "especially mischievous"—"Chicory" and even "Postum" (75–76). Although these details seemingly indicate their status as racial Others, the opposite is ultimately true. As Thomas Peyser has aptly noted, the whiteness of the Herland women "persists even when it disappears" (82). In spite of the utopian inhabitants' brown skin and racialized features, Van asserts, "there was no doubt in my mind that these people were of Aryan stock, and were once in contact with the best civilization of the old world. They were 'white'" (55). Like Tarzan once again, the inhabitants possess an amazing awareness of, and even pride in, their racial pedigree. Bolstering their offspring through education and breeding out "all morbid and excessive types" (78), they have created what the three male adventurers frequently identify as a superior race.

Closely related to the maintenance of white racial supremacy in *Herland* and *Tarzan* is the fear of miscegenation. Although Tarzan's strength and prowess make him an attractive mate, he refuses to form a sexual union with any of the female apes. Nowhere, perhaps, is this phenomenon more clearly articulated than in a scene from the sixth narrative of the series, *Jungle Tales of Tarzan* (1916), which is actually a prequel to Burroughs's first novel. In a sequence entitled "Tarzan's First Love," the future King of the Jungle becomes enamored with a fellow ape named Teeka, but their tender interactions only reinforce the differences between them:

[Teeka] came quite close and snuggled against him, and Tarzan, Lord Greystoke, put his arm around her. As he did so he noticed, with a start, the strange incongruity of that smooth, brown arm against the black and hairy coat of his lady-love. He recalled the paw of Sheeta's mate across the face—no incongruity there. . . . The males and females differed, it was true; but not with such differences as existed between Tarzan and Teeka. (Burroughs *Jungle Tales* 21) .

As Marianna Torgovnick has written, the references to species difference in this passage serve as stand-in for racial difference (*Gone* 55). As a result, Tarzan allows his male rival, the ape Taug, to win her affections. Meanwhile, the son of a British aristocrat waits until the arrival of one of his "own kind" for a mate: the white woman Jane Porter.

A parallel situation occurs in Gilman's novel. Although the Herlanders tell Van, Terry and Jeff that they learned to reproduce parthenogenetically after all of the men in their settlement were killed off through a combination of war and natural disaster, this explanation is not entirely accurate. The men of Herland may have disappeared, but their access to males has not: the tribe that lives in the region below the mountaintop community has male members. Not only are these primitive peoples aware of the all-female settlement—a small group of them, in fact, guides Terry, Vandyck and Jeff to the region—but the Herland women are similarly cognizant of their existence. In a throwback to the hegemonic purpose of white tomboyism, the Herlanders do not wish to procreate with these nonwhite peoples. In the words of Peyser, they establish an "imperial white ghetto" (43). With their interest in strengthening the Aryan race, the Herlanders develop a parthenogenetic form of reproduction and wait more than 2,000 years for the arrival of white men. For these reasons, Gilman's novel becomes a narrative about "whites becoming reacquainted with their own essential whiteness, a rediscovery of an unsullied culture from the past that has miraculously survived the convulsions of history intact" (Peyser 82–83). Parthenogenesis allows the inhabitants not only to reproduce without men, but also without going outside of their race. As a result, Herland may be an ostensible utopia of women, but it is also one for whites. In contrast to the "flood of low-grade humanity" that Gilman believed was polluting the United States ("Hospitable" 290), perversions of any kind, either racial or sexual, are unknown in Herland. Indeed, in a remark that embodies a nativist's dream, Vandyke notes, "they were a 'pure stock' of two thousand uninterrupted years" (121).

By retaining this firm link to whiteness and the privileges that it affords, the title characters in both *Herland* and *Tarzan* are able to turn dark primitivism into a white racial strategy. In short, they are able to become "Aryan savages." Tarzan's experiences in the jungle augment rather than detract from his impressive racial heritage, cultural background and class pedigree. His warrior nature and especially active physicality make him even more potent, powerful and imposing than his father. As Torgovnick notes, "Tarzan always rises to the top of the hierarchies. In the first two volumes of the series, Tarzan becomes a king not once, but twice" (*Gone* 55–56).

Likewise, the titles of subsequent novels like *Tarzan Triumphant* (1931), *Tarzan the Invincible* (1930) and *Tarzan, Lord of the Jungle* (1927) showcase his superiority. In keeping with this stature, the apes begin calling Tarzan by the colonialist title "Big Bwana" in later novels; meanwhile, he refers to them as "my children" (Torgovnick *Gone* 57).

Although the utopian inhabitants of Herland repudiate beliefs that women are too "primitive" to create a sophisticated society, they simultaneously demonstrate that adopting strategic facets of primitivism is beneficial. Through such seemingly "uncivilized" traits as living in close harmony with nature, adopting a more androgynous gender identity and engaging in active physicality, the Herlanders paradoxically become, in the words of the narrator, a group of "highly civilized women" (27). Even their use of primitive bellicosity furthers this goal. In the same way that Tarzan uses violence to kill rival apes and establish himself as King of the Jungle, the Herlanders do the same when they quell the slave revolt. Eliminating their black population and giving their now all-white settlement a reputation for "savagery," their bellicose past keeps the Herland community culturally closed and racially protected.

In a final and more broad cultural implication, the primitivism present in *Herland* and the physical culture movement of which it was a product transformed the connection of tomboyish characters to history. On the whole, the spunky female figures in works by Southworth, Alcott and Jewett are forward-looking. As a group of strong, independent individuals who are unfettered by the confines of their mother's femininity, they represented the next generation of American women. The tomboyish physical culture movement during the early twentieth century, however, changed this trait. Instead of offering a glimpse into possible gender roles of the future, tomboyish figures like Gilman's Herlanders became products of nostalgia for the past, be it the antebellum period or a primordial one. Untainted by the fakery, artifice and superficiality that many associated with the modern period, they harkened back to an earlier era when human behavior was more "authentic." Frozen in time for the past 2,000 years, the seemingly primitive regression of the Herland women paradoxically embodies a strategy for cultural progression.

The Tomboy Goes from Native-Born to Foreign Immigrant: An American Code of Conduct Becomes Americanizing

The following chapter on Willa Cather's *O Pioneers!* (1913) and *My Antonia* (1918) addresses the same chronological era, but it focuses on many of the opposite concerns. Whereas the tomboyish characters in *Herland* emerged in response to nativist fears, these prairie novels were written in response to the struggle of newly arrived nonwhite immigrants who were the targets of xenophobia. Spotlighting some of the "seething foreign masses" that disturbed nativists like Gilman, *O Pioneers!* and *My Antonia* invert the message of *Herland* in many ways.

Continuing with themes of class, acculturation and citizenship raised in this chapter, the next one explores what happens when tomboyism serves not as a eugenic strategy for middle- and upper-class white Americans but an economic necessity for poor, nonwhite immigrants. Unlike the untaintedly Aryan Herlanders, who engage in a voluntary form of physical culture to maintain their racial prowess, European immigrants Alexandra Bergson and Antonia Shimerda are thrust into an involuntary type of female masculinity to ensure their basic survival. After the deaths of their fathers and the overwhelming difficulty of cultivating the prairie soil, these young women are compelled to engage in such traditionally male tasks as plowing the fields, planting the crops and performing heavy farm labor. Given the longstanding association of this code of conduct with the Anglo-American ruling class, it becomes a powerful agent for assimilation, acculturation and even citizenship for the immigrant underclass. The next chapter will demonstrate that tomboyism in Willa Cather's prairie novels serves not as a means to preserve the whiteness and Americanness of native-born citizens, but as a way for foreign-born immigrant characters to obtain them.

5

The Tomboy Becomes the All-Americanizing Girl

Willa Cather's O Pioneers! *and* My Antonia

Perhaps more than any other region in the United States, the "wild West" is associated with female gender iconoclasm. As Mary Paniccia Carden has written, "the frontier appears not as the site where forms and practices of male hegemony are enacted, but rather as a liminal space where binary delineations of gender loosen their hold" (283). On the unsettled prairie, adolescent girls and young women were called upon to perform an array of tasks that fell outside of their traditional gender roles. From chopping wood and clearing fields to butchering meat and protecting their families from wild animals and neighboring American Indian tribes, female figures from all races, classes and geographic backgrounds engaged in some form of gender bending.

Given the strong connection between tomboyism and rugged frontier life, some of the most well-known literary tomboys are also frontier figures, including Calamity Jane in Edward Wheeler's *Deadwood Dick* series (1877–1885) and the main characters in Laura Ingalls Wilder's *Little House* series (1932–1943) and Carol Ryrie Brink's *Caddie Woodlawn* (1935). By the mid-twentieth century, in fact, this locale had become so strongly associated with this code of female conduct that an entire sub-genre of frontier tomboy texts began to emerge. In *Texas Tomboy* (1950), *Lone Star Tomboy* (1951), *Yosemite Tomboy* (1967), *Kansas Tomboy* (1968) and *Tomboy Ranch* (1981), the "wild West" and this code of conduct were practically synonymous.

Of the male and female writers who presented female gender iconoclasm on the frontier, this chapter focuses on a particularly prominent one:
Willa Cather. As Marilee Lindemann asserts in a recent book, this popular
Midwestern author was "the Tomboy of the Prairie" (79). Spending the
bulk of her childhood on the plains of Nebraska, Cather reveled in the
"wild" behavior that was made possible by her residence in this similarly
"wild" land. Cropping her hair, calling herself "William" and engaging in
boys' activities, her gender iconoclasm was infamous. Deborah Lambert has
written that when the future author was an adolescent girl, she composed
what could have served as a guidebook to frontier tomboyism: "In a list
that might have been completed by Tom Sawyer, she cites 'slicing toads' as
a favorite summer occupation; doing fancy work as 'real misery'; ampu-
tating limbs as 'perfect happiness'; and dressing in skirts as 'the greatest
folly of the Nineteenth Century'" (677). The Western component to Cather's gender identity persisted even if her penchant for slicing toads did not.
When Grant Reynard met the famous author in 1928, he remarked that
her military-style coat and festooned cuffs reminded him of "Annie Oakley
from Buffalo Bill's Wild West Show" (Wagenknecht 137).

Coupled with being a tomboyish figure in her personal life, Cather
showcased gender-bending young women in her professional writings.
Some of her early literary efforts, in fact, presented tomboyish Western
figures. In her short stories "Tommy, the Unsentimental" (1897) and "The
Way of the World" (1898), the author featured adolescent girls whose
gender iconoclasm is heavily informed by their residence on the frontier.
The central character Theodosia "Tommy" Shirley from her 1897 narrative
drinks whiskey, plays poker, and halts a run on a bank. Likewise, in "The
Way of the World," the narrator remarks of tomboyish central character
Mary Eliza Jenkins, "there are some girls who would make the best boys in
the world—if they were not girls" (401).

Tomboyism continued as a theme in Cather's later and more well-known
novels. Two of the narratives with which she established her reputation
and for which she is commonly remembered today—the prairie novels O
Pioneers! (1913) and My Antonia (1918)—showcase tomboyish main characters. The first time readers meet Alexandra Bergson in O Pioneers!, for
instance, she is wearing "a man's long ulster . . . not as if it were an afflic-
tion, but as if it were very comfortable and belonged to her" (5). Similarly,
at various points throughout My Antonia, Antonia "Tony" Shimerda flexes
her muscles and prides herself on being able to "work like a mans" (80).

Cather's residence on the Nebraska frontier did more than simply shape
her childhood gender identity and professional literary subject matter; it
influenced her views about the era's rapid influx of immigrants. Living on
the prairie from the age of nine, she was immersed in a multicultural and
even multilingual society that was comprised largely of immigrants. As
biographer James Woodress notes, when the future writer and her family

arrived on the Divide in the 1880s, the foreign-born population outnumbered the native-born one by nearly three to one (38). In this environment, Cather recalled "walking about the streets of Wilbur, only about thirty miles from Lincoln, for a whole day without hearing a word of English spoken" (Woodress 38). Rather than feeling threatened by immigrants and their "foreign" ways, she was fascinated by them. As a young girl, she befriended many of their European neighbors; she loved listening to them converse in their native tongue, tell stories about life in the old country and discuss European culture and customs. In fact, the author would recall that there were many afternoons when she arrived home "in the most unreasonable state of excitement" after visiting with the immigrant neighbors (Cather *Person* 9).

Years later, Cather drew on these memories as the basis of her fiction. In works ranging from the one that is commonly considered her masterpiece, *My Antonia* (1918), to the one for which she was awarded the Pulitzer Prize, *One of Ours* (1922), they became the defining trope of her fiction and a rare point of engagement with contemporaneous issues. Indeed, although Cather is often accused of avoiding the concerns of her day by retreating to the past,[1] she was not reticent about matters of immigration, acculturation and assimilation. Disgusted by the intolerance of many native-born Americans towards new arrivals, Cather was an outspoken critic of what came to be known as the Americanization Movement. Founded at the turn of the century and enjoying its heyday amidst the xenophobia that followed the outbreak of World War I, the organization did just as its name suggested: it sought to "Americanize" the nation's foreign-born immigrants by stripping them of their European ways. As Frank Van Nuys has written, members of the movement were united by a common purpose: "the welding of the many races and classes in this country into one" (45).[2]

Whereas the Americanization Movement saw immigrant cultures as a liability, Cather viewed them as an asset. Finding U.S. society stale and conformist, she welcomed the diversity brought by immigrant men and women. As a result, during an era in which many of her compatriots strove to eradicate foreign customs, Cather championed them. In a 1924 interview in *The New York Times* Book Review, for instance, she chastised the "social workers" and "missionaries" who dedicated their lives to transforming newly arrived immigrants into "stupid replicas of smug American citizens" (Cather *Person* 148). For the author, "this passion

---

1. See especially Granville Hicks's essay "The Case Against Willa Cather," which appeared in *English Journal*, XXII, no 9 (November 1933): 703–710, and is one of the first and most famous articulations of this viewpoint.

2. For more on the Americanization Movement, along with its many offshoots, see Frank Van Nuys's *Americanizing the West: Race, Immigrants and Citizenship, 1890–1930* (Kansas City: U of Kansas, 2002).

for Americanizing everything and everybody is a deadly disease with us" (Cather *Person* 148).

In the pages that follow, I explore the way in which Willa Cather's unique view of immigrant culture combined with her unique gender identity to reveal a new function for tomboyism. A code of conduct that was commonly associated with what Frances Cogan has deemed the "All-American Girl," I demonstrate how it served as an agent for those desiring to be the all-Americanized one during the 1910s. In a radical break from the white, middle class, Protestant and native-born tomboys populating previous narratives, the gender-bending figures in *O Pioneers!* and *My Antonia* are foreign born, working class, and—in the case of Antonia Shimerda—even Catholic. This shift in the demographic coordinates of this code of conduct precipitated a shift in its societal purpose. Changing patterns of immigration, along with changing attitudes about race, caused tomboyish behavior to acquire a drastically different meaning for Cather's immigrant main characters. This chapter explores the way in which immigrant groups from Europe became both white and American in the context of the West, and the role that tomboyism played in this process. Being a tomboy in Willa Cather's prairie novels goes far beyond simply being a cowgirl. For Alexandra Bergson and Antonia Shimerda, it also helps signify being an American.

Tomboyism and the Making of an American: Defying Gender to Embrace Citizenship in *O Pioneers!*

As Susan Rosowski has noted, "From the beginning of discussions about American literature, writers have identified its 'Americanness' with the West" (1). In what has become an oft-quoted remark from Frederick Jackson Turner's *The Significance of the Frontier in American History* (1893), "The frontier is the line of most rapid and effective Americanization" (5). European settlers did more than simply change the land upon their arrival; they were changed by it. Sloughing off their Old World ways, they became a new type of individual, "the American" (Turner 5).

Although the West has commonly been regarded as an agent of Americanization, tomboyism also performed this function. As a code of conduct that has long been associated with white middle-class American women, it helped participants like Capitola Black and Nan Prince assert this status and the privileges that it affords. *O Pioneers!* expanded on the scope of this phenomenon, transforming tomboyism from a means to affirm a certain race and class position to a way to attain them. The central character Antonia Bergson is working class, foreign born and culturally "other" at the start of the narrative, but by its conclusion she embodies the American Dream and is an exemplar of the national spirit. Alexandra's participation in tomboyism forms an integral part of this process. This code of conduct helps her to cultivate such quintessential American qualities as a patriotic love of the land, a firm commitment to the Puritan work ethic, a Franklin-like aptitude for ingenuity and—echoing Walt Whitman's poem "Pioneers! O Pioneers!" from which Cather took the title for her book—a Whitman-esque commitment to individualism. Perhaps more importantly though, Alexandra's connection to tomboyism also solidifies her connection with whiteness and, by extension, Americanness. In *O Pioneers!*, the main character is transformed from an impoverished European immigrant into the archetypal American citizen—the Jeffersonian farmer—largely because of her participation in tomboyism.

• • •

The opening pages of *O Pioneers!* read like the beginning of many other tomboy narratives, as Cather's main character possesses an array of traits commonly associated with this code of conduct. Recalling the gender-bending physical appearance of Capitola Black and Jo March, for example, the young woman is "a tall, strong girl" who is cross-dressed when first introduced to readers (5). Similarly, echoing the long-standing rebellion of tomboys from the historically subordinated status of women, Alexandra repudiates the male gaze. When a traveling salesman flirtatiously compliments her beautiful hair, "She stabbed him with a glance of Amazonian fierceness" (6).

Although Alexandra Bergson may possess many of the same physical traits as tomboyish figures discussed in previous chapters, she has little else in common with them. Unlike the central characters in *The Hidden Hand* and *Little Women*, she belongs to a different socio-economic class and, more importantly, ethnic culture. In the opening pages of *O Pioneers!*, in fact, the narrator calls attention to the foreign nature of both the nineteen-year-old girl and her Swedish family. Alexandra's five-year-old brother, Emil, is the only American-born Bergson, but he is nonetheless presented as "a little Swede boy" who speaks in broken English (4). If the American-born Emil employs such broken phraseology as "My kitten, oh, my kitten! Her will fweeze!'" (4), readers can only surmise the low level of fluency among the family's foreign-born members.

This difference in nationality is mirrored by a difference in socio-economic status. Although many gender-bending figures have been in strained economic circumstances, the Bergsons are experiencing a full-fledged crisis. Spending their "first five years on the Divide getting into debt, and the last six getting out" (14), Mr. Bergson and his family have barely attained a subsistence level of living. Exacerbating the family's already difficult financial situation, Alexandra's father is now terminally ill. Struggling economically while Mr. Bergson was alive, Alexandra fears that the family may be unable to survive once he dies: "'[T]he boys are strong and work hard, but we've always depended so on father that I don't see how we can go ahead'" (11).

These bleak economic conditions precipitate Alexandra's participation in tomboyism. Rather than voluntarily choosing this code of conduct to protect her family's privileged socio-economic position, she adopts it out of circumstantial necessity to ensure their basic survival. The struggle to keep the Bergson farm afloat is a gender-blind one that requires the help of every member. As a result, in keeping with observations by Ann Gordon and Mari Jo Buhle that lower-class women were often compelled to engage in labor that was considered "masculine" (290–291), the narrator notes, "Before Alexandra was twelve years old she had begun to be a help to [her father], and as she grew older he had come to depend more and more upon her resourcefulness and good judgment" (15). Although the young woman's brothers, Lou and Oscar, work physically hard in the fields, she works intellectually hard on the financial aspects of the family business. "It was Alexandra who read the papers and followed the markets, and who learned by the mistakes of their neighbors" (15). Memorizing yearly seed prices, average annual crop yields and daily operating expenses, "It was Alexandra who could always tell about what it had cost to fatten each steer, and who could guess the weight of a hog before it went on the scales closer than John Bergson himself" (15).

Recalling *fin-de-siecle* beliefs in the biological basis for human behavior, Alexandra's father attributes her talent for farming and finances to family genetics: "In his daughter, John Bergson recognized the strength of will, and the simply direct way of thinking things out, that had characterized his father in his better days" (16). The young woman, however, realizes that these qualities can be more realistically attributed to necessity than inheritance. When Lou accuses his sister of being "unwomanly" later in the novel, for instance, Alexandra asserts that the conditions on the Divide dictated such behavior: "'I never meant to be hard. Conditions were hard. Maybe I would never have been very soft, anyhow; but certainly I didn't choose to be the kind of girl I was'" (114).

Difficult economic conditions may have made Alexandra tomboy-ishly "hard," but they have also made her an exceptional farmer. When Mr. Bergson dies, he leaves the farm to his daughter instead of his sons. While this decision emphasizes his confidence in Alexandra's abilities, it also heightens the circumstantial necessity of her behavior. Whereas many female figures are compelled to abandon their iconoclastic ways as they grow older, Alexandra's situation dictates that she hone them.

In the coming years, Alexandra does more than simply keep the promise to her father about not getting discouraged and selling the land; she actualizes his dream of creating a prosperous farm. As the narrator notes at the start of the novel's second section, "Any one thereabouts would have told you that this was one of the richest farms on the Divide, and that the farmer was a woman, Alexandra Bergson" (56). Alexandra's tomboyism, however, yields something much more valuable than simply successful crops and plump livestock; it also helps her with the process of assimilation and acculturation. By affiliating herself with a code of conduct that has a longstanding association with white, middle-class American women, the Swedish-born girl is able to attain these attributes for herself. Foreign-born, working-class and culturally Other at the start of the narrative, she becomes not simply an exemplary prairie farmer, but an exemplary American citizen. For these reasons, while O Pioneers! is commonly read as a narrative about the cultivation of the frontier soil, it can also be seen as one about the Americanization of an immigrant through tomboyism.

Alexandra obtains an array of distinctly American qualities through her connection with tomboyism. Arguably, the first among these is a strong Protestant work ethic and Ben Franklin-like sense of ingenuity. Akin to both her biological father and the U.S. Founding Fathers, the young woman believes that hard work is the key to success. Hence, she often works in the fields until "her body [is] actually aching with fatigue" (137). The smart and savvy Alexandra knows, however, that diligent labor alone is not sufficient; in addition to working hard, she must also work smart. Unlike her brothers, who crave conformity, she recognizes that new approaches will be required to farm this new land. Therefore, Alexandra implements fresh ideas and innovative agricultural practices. Early in the novel, for instance, she heeds the advice of an eccentric neighbor about a better way to care for hogs after a cholera epidemic has decimated the stock of nearby neighbors (29–30). Although her brothers laugh at the unconventional approach, she is aware that it will save the animals in their pen. Later, Alexandra meets a university-educated farmer and learns about alfalfa, a new type of clover hay. Lou cries when he first plants the crop because he is convinced that their neighbors are laughing at them, but she realizes that it will transform the prairie. Within a few years, the land that was once "a horse that no one knows how to break to harness" becomes the richest and most prosperous in the country because of alfalfa (43).[3]

Another of Alexandra's qualities that illustrate her Americanness and can be linked to her tomboyishness is her patriotism. While numerous critics discuss Alexandra's strong connection to the soil, they often neglect to mention that her beloved prairie is also, of course, America. As she notes, the land "seemed beautiful to her, rich and strong and glorious" (44). At one point, Alexandra is so overcome by the landscape that she begins to cry: "Her eyes drank in the breadth of it, until the tears blinded her" (44).

---

3. Rather than abandoning her unconventional ways when she becomes a successful farmer, Alexandra continues to operate by the methods that brought her prosperity. When Carl Linstrum returns to the prairie, for instance, his childhood friend has just begun building the first silo on the Divide (60).

Over time, her patriotic love of the land expands to include a patriotic love of the national culture. Whereas, before, even the American-born member of the Bergson family spoke in broken English, all are fluent by the conclusion of the book. Echoing the wishes of the Americanization Movement, even in the privacy of Alexandra's home, "The conversation at the table was all in English" (67).

For these reasons, passages in the novel lament the circumstantial reason for Alexandra's lack of romantic involvements—"She had never been in love, she had never indulged in sentimental reveries. Even as a girl she had looked upon men as work-fellows. . . . She had grown up in serious times" (136)—but her failure to have children is not cast as a cause for sadness. Even though the gender-bending woman never gives birth to actual offspring, she remains a fertile figure. In the words of Mary Paniccia Carden, "The narrator does not mourn her childlessness or suggest that her biological destiny remains unfulfilled—her farms stand in as evidence of her fertility" (283). In this way, Alexandra's tomboyism remains linked to the original societal purpose of this code of conduct. Whereas the native-born tomboys in previous chapters had a fertile union with a male spouse, this foreign-born immigrant character has one with the prairie soil. Alexandra may not give birth to the future leaders of the United States, but her tomboyish cultivation of the frontier allows her to help give birth to the nation itself.

Alexandra's tomboyism also aids in the cultivation of a final American trait that is arguably even more valuable: a white racial identity. From the foundation of the United States, citizenship was predicated on whiteness. In 1790, only months after the ratification of the Constitution, Congress restricted naturalization to "free white persons who, have [sic], shall migrate into the United States, and shall give satisfactory proof, before a magistrate, by oath, that they intend to reside therein, and shall take an oath of allegiance, and shall have resided in the United States for one whole year" (*Annals of Congress* 184). Commenting on the impact of this provision, Ian F. Haney López has written, "Though the requirements for naturalization changed frequently thereafter, this racial prerequisite endured for over a century" (1).[4]

The legal provision about "free white persons" shaped not only the nature of American citizenship, but patterns of immigration. Although religious persecution, economic strife, and political upheaval are commonly identified as precipitating the massive influx of immigrants to the United

---

4. Not until 1952 with the passage of the Immigration and Nationality Act, in fact, was whiteness eliminated as a legal prerequisite for naturalization. Thus, for more than 150 years, federal law assured that whatever qualities naturalized Americans possessed—whether they were rich or poor, male or female—they would all share one trait: whiteness.

States that occurred during the late eighteenth and early nineteenth centuries, the 1790 racial stipulation was an important factor. As Matthew Jacobson has written, "It was the racial appellation 'white persons' in the nation's naturalization law that allowed migrations from Europe in the first place" (8). Because these peoples were considered white and therefore eligible for citizenship, they were able to enter the United States.

Given the connection between Americanness and whiteness, the process of becoming an American was synonymous with the process of becoming white for many immigrant groups. As George Lipsitz has demonstrated, one of the motivating factors for many Europeans to immigrate to the United States was to gain access to this racial classification and the social, cultural and economic privileges that it afforded. Often denigrated as religious, socio-economic or cultural "Others" in their homelands, immigrants "became something called 'whites' when they got to America" and "that designation made all the difference in the world" (Lipsitz 370). Individuals who had been members of a disparaged underclass in the Old World became part of the dominant ruling class upon arriving in the United States. For these reasons, Matthew Jacobson has observed, "The European immigrants experience was decisively shaped by their entering an arena where Europeanness—that is to say, whiteness—was among the most important possessions one could lay claim to. It was their *whiteness*, not any kind of New World Magnamity, that opened the Golden Door" [italics in original] (8).

O Pioneers! encodes the racial prerequisite for citizenship. These details, in fact, play a major role in both the presentation of the text's gender-bending main character and, perhaps more importantly, in her fate. Not coincidentally, the novel's tomboyish European immigrant who goes on to become a model American citizen is presented as an unequivocally white person. In contrast to the gender-bending figures highlighted in previous chapters, Alexandra lacks any hint of nonwhiteness or even "dark whiteness." Hailing from the Northern European country of Sweden—a region that was considered during this era to have a close racial kinship with the Aryan or Teutonic races[5]—she is described as an unambiguously white character. Numerous passages call attention to her "clear deep blue eyes," "reddish yellow curls," and "gleaming white body" (5, 6, 137). When Carl Linstrum is reunited with his childhood friend, in fact, he remarks on her ivory coloration. Although her hands and neck are sunburned from working outdoors, the skin on the rest of her body has "the freshness of snow itself" (60). Making a connection between Alexandra's exemplary

5. For more information on the racial hierarchy established during the early twentieth century and the relationship between various groups, see Matthew Jacobson's *Whiteness of a Different Color: European Immigrants and the Alchemy of Race* (Cambridge: Harvard UP, 1998).

whiteness and her European heritage, Carl asserts that his childhood friend has "skin of such smoothness and whiteness as none but Swedish women ever possess" (60).

Alexandra's participation in tomboyism accentuates this quality. As a mode of behavior that was conceived by white women for white women to protect and preserve white racial supremacy, it verifies her claim to whiteness and, thus, her ability to become a "true" (i.e., white) American. Possessing the same racial prerequisite, the two entities are interrelated; participation in one facilitates inclusion in the other.

In keeping with Willa Cather's interest in cultural pluralism, Alexandra's assimilation into white, middle-class American society does not mandate the eradication of her Old World ways. While her brothers are ashamed of their European heritage—one forbids Swedish from being spoken in his house while the other has trained himself to sound "like anybody from Iowa" (67)—Alexandra preserves it. She instructs her neighbor, Crazy Ivar, to read the Bible to her in his native Norwegian (61). Likewise, when her brother's mother-in-law comes to visit, she allows the elderly woman to adhere to traditional European ways rather than modern American customs. "'Now we be yust-a like old times!,'" Mrs. Lee gleefully exclaims upon entering Alexandra's house (126). In this way, Alexandra embodies a more pluralistic vision of the "American Girl" than both Frances Cogan and Martha Banta have discussed. Rather than rigidly conforming to the traits commonly associated with this figure, Alexandra raises the possibility of diversity. Valuing her European heritage, the tomboyish character highlights an approach to American culture that includes multiculturalism. As a result, O Pioneers! highlights a new social function for tomboyism. This code of conduct had long been an asset to native-born citizens, and the 1913 novel demonstrates that it could be a beneficial trait for newly naturalized ethnic Americans as well.

This change in the demographic coordinates of tomboyism points to an important change in early twentieth-century attitudes about race. Whereas whiteness was an unmarked category in previous historical eras, it now came to be seen as a distinct racial construct. In the same way that tomboyish figures in previous narratives were racialized as American Africanist, Cather's immigrant character becomes racialized via American whiteness.

The White Tomboy Becomes Caucasian: European Ethnic Whiteness via Southern American Blackness in My Antonia

Four years after the appearance of O Pioneers!, Willa Cather published a second novel about a tomboyish immigrant on the prairie: My Antonia. The 1918 narrative, however, did not simply repeat the trope of a foreign-born young woman being transformed into an American via this gender-bending code of conduct. Instead, it offered a variation on this theme that explored the era's changing patterns of immigration and changing conceptions of race. As Ian F. Haney López has written, although the Founding Fathers had lengthy and often heated debates about every word used in the Constitution, they did not discuss the meaning of the phrase "free white persons." To them, the class of persons who were "free" and especially who were "white" was clear and understood (22).

While whiteness may have been a self-evident and even monolithic category at the end of the eighteenth century, it would not always remain this way. During the late nineteenth and early twentieth centuries, shifting patterns of immigration would call into question the meaning of this classification. Immigrant groups began appearing on the nation's shores that the Forefathers never anticipated, from Chinese and Japanese immigrants to individuals from Southern and Eastern Europe.

In addition to sparking a xenophobic backlash from many native-born Americans, these arrivals also sparked a crisis in racial categorization and the concept of whiteness. In a country that had been largely bifurcated into the binary of whiteness and blackness by the importation of African slaves, many began to wonder how these new and decidedly more "alien" immigrant groups were to be classified. While Turkish, Armenian, and Slavic peoples were not Africanist and therefore "black," they also did not seem like Anglo-Saxons and therefore "white" either. Could these men and women be placed under the category of "free white persons" and be eligible for citizenship? If not, to what race did they belong? Possessing different physical, cultural and religious traits from their Northern and Eastern European counterparts, they had a quality of Otherness.

The uncertainty that these new and indeterminate groups raised about racial classification eroded the monolithic nature of whiteness. Whereas this category was once static and self-evident, it now became splintered and indeterminate. Ian F. Haney López has discussed that for the first time in the nation's history, cases began to be brought before state and federal courts by individuals who wanted to be legally designated as white and thus as potential citizens.[6] Beginning in 1878 with the landmark case *In re Ah Yup*, the trend continued with cases brought by men and women of Arab, Slavic and Asian Indian descent. Although whiteness had formerly been a clear and constant category, it was now contested and uncertain. Indeed, the basic meaning of the concept was up for debate.

6. For a discussion of these various cases and their impact on changing legal definitions of race and especially whiteness, see Ian F. Haney López's *White by Law: The Legal Construction of Race* (New York: NYU, 1996). In an especially valuable feature of his book, the appendix reprints the original case briefs, court proceedings and judge's decisions.

In this section, I explore the transformations to whiteness that occurred as a result of changing patterns of immigration, and the impact that this phenomenon had on the racially marked phenomenon of tomboyism. Whereas Willa Cather's tomboyish main character in O Pioneers! was unequivocally white, the central one in My Antonia is only marginally so. Hailing from the Southern European nation of Bohemia, her connection to this classification is tenuous. Although white enough to come ashore as a "free white person," Antonia's racial credentials are, as Matthew Jacobson has observed about immigrants from Southern Europe, "not equivalent to those of the Anglo-Saxon 'old stock'" (4). Thought to possess a distant connection to the Teutonic or Nordic race, these individuals were thought to possess a distant connection to whiteness. As a result, groups that we would now consider different white ethnicities—such as Poles, Syrians, Greeks, Armenians and Sicilians—were seen as different races during this era. Echoing this attitude, the native-born narrator in My Antonia identifies his Bohemian neighbor as a marginally white person at best. Associating Antonia with various forms of nonwhiteness or, at least, "dark whiteness," Jim describes her and the immigrant girls like her as "almost a race apart" (Cather Antonia 127). Echoing Matthew Jacobson's observation about a paradoxical but very real racial designation that emerged during this era, she is "both white *and* racially distinct from other whites" [italics in original] (6).

The pages that follow explore the impact that Antonia's status as a dark white person has on her participation in tomboyism and, in turn, the impact that her tomboyism has on her racial classification. Significantly, the relationship between these two elements is not mediated by the split between native-born Americans and foreign-born immigrants in the West. Given Cather's Virginia heritage, the often-overlooked Southern origins of her adolescent tomboyism, and My Antonia's possession of a Southern narrator, it is predicated on the black-white dyad in the American South. While the ostensible setting of Cather's 1918 narrative may be the plains of Nebraska, the racial characterization of its tomboyish main character more accurately suggests the hills of Virginia. Against this backdrop, Antonia Shimerda may not be unequivocally white like her Northern European predecessor in O Pioneers!, but she gains access to a new racial classification that was forming during this era. In My Antonia, the formerly white tomboy becomes Caucasian.

• • •

Although Willa Cather is often remembered as a Midwestern writer who immortalized the prairie, she spent the first nine years of her life in the South. Born in Winchester, Virginia during the height of Reconstruction, the author was raised on land in the Shenandoah Valley that had been in her family for more than six generations. The oft-discussed difficulty that the future author experienced when her parents relocated to Nebraska arose in part from her attachment to the lush landscape of Virginia. In a 1913 interview, she remarked, "I would not know how much a child's life is bound up in the woods and hills and meadows around it, if I had not been jerked away from all these and thrown into a country as bare as a piece of sheet iron" (Cather *Person* 10).

Together with being emotionally attached to the landscape of Virginia, Cather was also intellectually influenced by its racial economy. As Anne Goodwyn Jones notes, even as a young girl, "she learned her situation in a deeply hierarchical social world" ("Dixie" 86). In what has become an oft-quoted passage from Edith Lewis's *Willa Cather Living*, a young Cather rebuffed the patronizing behavior of an elderly judge by exclaiming, "'I'se a dang'ous nigger I is!'" (E. Lewis 13). In the words of Tomoyuki Zettsu, the future author "was distinctively aware of the extent to which the idea of a 'nigger'—when adopted by a well-bred white young lady—could be 'dang-ous' to the ordered and genteel Southern community in which she lived" (87).

This childhood outburst was not the only time when Cather employed Southern racial tensions as a conduit for female gender rebellion. As biographers Sharon O'Brien (*Emerging*) and Phyllis C. Robinson have noted, the future author's family was deeply divided over slavery. While her father's relatives were staunchly against the institution, her mother's family endorsed it; a number of them owned slaves and sided with the Confederacy. Interestingly, given both the anti-slavery views of Cather's parents and her family's relocation to Nebraska, she held an affiliation with her Confederate kin. Many of the journalistic pieces that she wrote while a student at the University of Nebraska romanticized and even defended the South. In an 1894 review of a theatrical version of *Uncle Tom's Cabin*, for instance, Cather called Stowe "a Puritan bluestocking" who "sat up under cold skies of the north and tried to write of one of the warmest, richest and most highly colored civilizations the world has ever known" (quoted in Slote 270).

Cather's Southern heritage, however, did more than simply influence her literary tastes; it also shaped her gender identity. While this Midwestern writer is often hailed as the "Tomboy of the Prairie," her gender iconoclasm was rooted in white Confederate masculinity. Paralleling the centrality of Jo March's Union army boots in the construction of her tomboyish identity, a teenaged Cather wore a Confederate cap that belonged to maternal uncle, William Seibert Boak, who had been killed fighting for the South in the Civil War. In fact, the hat embodied such an important part of the future author's self-image that she not only embroidered her initials "W.C." on it, but even had her portrait taken by a professional photographer while wearing it. As O'Brien has noted, this act marked an important shift from her cultivation of a private alter ego to her debut of a new public persona (*Emerging* 101).

Together with wearing her uncle's Confederate cap, Cather adopted facets of his identity. Throughout adolescence, she signed her name "William Cather, Jr." and liked to tell people that she had been named after this relative who had died at Manassas. One of Cather's early literary efforts, in fact—a poem that she wrote in 1902 and included in *April Twilights* (1903)—eulogized her fallen uncle and further underscored this connection. Appropriately titled "The Namesake," the poem refers to his grave as a "bed of glory" (25). Likewise, in the final stanza, it reaffirms Cather's solidarity with the man who wore the "jacket grey" along with the cause for which he died: "Proud as I am to know / In my veins there still must flow, / There to burn and bite away; / And I'll be the winner at the game / Enough for two who bore the name" ("Namesake" 26). In light of these passages, O'Brien has observed that at the core of the future author's Midwestern gender rebellion was the image of a Confederate rebel (*Emerging* 96–113).

The strong connection that Cather felt with her Southern ancestry continued into her early adulthood. As a young author, she adopted the last name of her mother's slave-owning relations—the Seiberts—as her own middle name. Although spelling it "Sibert," she included the appellation in the majority of her journalistic writings and early fictional narratives. The original title pages for both *O Pioneers!* and *My Antonia*, in fact, contain the moniker.

In light of these details, it comes as no surprise that traces of Cather's Southern heritage surface in *My Antonia* in general and the racial dynamics at play within its gender-bending immigrant character in particular. Hailing from the Southern European nation of Bohemia, Antonia is already a racial Other. A foreign-born immigrant and a Roman Catholic in a predominantly Protestant country, the tomboyish young woman and her family exist outside of conventional conceptions of both whiteness and Americanness. Although the young woman is eager to learn both American customs and the English language, she does not experience the cultural "whitewashing" that permeated *O Pioneers!* On the contrary, Antonia remains socially, racially and culturally alien.

Antonia's status as an outsider, however, does not have its root exclusively in her European nationality. Recalling Cather's Southern heritage and the Confederate source of her gender iconoclasm, the Bohemian young woman's difference is also closely linked to African American-inflected sources and the black-white dyad of the South. Unlike the third-person narration in *O Pioneers!*, Antonia's story is told from the perspective of a specific character with a specific regional background: Jim Burden, who like Cather is a displaced Virginian. Together with bringing his father's field hand with him, Jim has also brought his Southern values. As Anne Goodwyn Jones has written, while the young man makes scant literal reference to Virginia, he repeatedly uses the region's culture, customs and even racial economy as the figurative lens through which to view Nebraska in general and his Bohemian neighbors in particular. Indeed, Jim's affection for Mr. Shimerda is heavily informed by his Virginia ancestry:

> When Jim sees Mr. Shimerda's hair . . . he is reminded of portraits on the walls in Virginia. He observes carefully Mr. Shimerda's pride in the details of his appearance; his scarf and pin in place even after death. Mr. Shimerda's violin, and the sense of culture it represents, are foreign to the practical prairie but familiar to Virginia. (Jones "Displacing" 99)

The pages that follow push such arguments about the Southern basis of Cather's ostensibly Western novel even further. They demonstrate that Jim's Virginia heritage also influences his attitude about the tomboyish Antonia Shimerda. To a young man who has been raised in the binary of black and white, Antonia's unfamiliar ethnic heritage becomes mapped onto a more familiar racial one. With her brown skin tone, participation in heavy field labor, and erotic sexual allure, the tomboyish girl shares many traits with Jim's Southern stereotypes about African Americans. As a result, Antonia's white European ethnicity often becomes blurred with Southern racial blackness.

In the same way that Cather's *O Pioneers!* begins in a manner that is similar to many other tomboy narratives, *My Antonia* commences in a way that is analogous to it. Recalling its literary predecessor, the 1918 narrative recounts the story of a young European immigrant whose economic circumstances compel her to adopt tomboyish behaviors. Whereas Alexandra and her family experience material want, Antonia Shimerda and her kin live in a state of abject poverty. Swindled out of much of their money by a dishonest countryman and grossly ill-prepared for farm life, their first winter on the prairie is horrific. When the Burdens come to visit their new neighbors on a frigid afternoon, in fact, Antonia is wearing only a thin cotton dress, her mother's feet are tied up in rags, and her father and brothers share a single winter jacket. Moreover, the Shimerdas are living in a sod dugout that Grandmother Burden describes as "'no better than a badger hole'" (16). Their main source of food is the rotten potatoes that the postmaster has discarded. For meat, the family has been shooting prairie dogs which, as one of the Burden's field hands grimly notes, "belonged to the rat family" (47).

As in *O Pioneers!*, this dire economic situation is exacerbated by the death of the family patriarch. Whereas John Bergson died of exhaustion after a decade of hard physical labor, Mr. Shimerda dies of suicide prompted by homesickness. The old man was so unhappy, Jim explains, "that he could not live anymore" (67). Nonetheless, his death has the same impact on his daughter. When Mr. Shimerda was alive, fourteen-year-old Antonia was his precious little girl. Jim notices how the old man would lovingly coo "My Án-tonia" whenever he talked about her (81). As a result of this strong affection, Mr. Shimerda selects Antonia for the important task of learning English. As Jim recalls, "Almost every day, she came running across the prairie to have her reading lesson with me" (22). Before long, the young girl who previously did not even know the word for *sky* "could talk to me about almost anything" (27).

Together with learning American English, Antonia learns American domestic skills. While at the Burden's house studying, "Antonia loved to help grandmother in the kitchen and to learn about cooking and house-keeping. She would stand beside her, watching her every movement" (22). When not engaged in such industrious tasks, Antonia behaves like any other typical young girl: she plays. Numerous passages recount Jim and his immigrant friend romping in sun-drenched fields, listening to crickets, and marveling at the prairie dogs that dot the landscape.

The death of Antonia's father, however, radically changes the young girl's life. Now that this family, who nearly starved during the winter, has lost its primary breadwinner, they cannot afford to have their eldest daughter spending time learning English or playing with the neighboring boy. Like Alexandra Bergson, she must now help work the family farm. Donning her father's boots and fur hat, Antonia literally takes her father's place in the fields. Indicating both the personal pride and economic urgency involved in her labor, she inquires competitively, "'Jim, you ask Jake how much he ploughed to-day. I don't want Jake to get more done in one day than me. I want we have very much corn this fall'" (79).

During the ensuing months, Antonia continues to help with the farm work and, as a result, continues to grow progressively more tomboyish: "She was out in the fields from sunup to sundown. If I rode over to see her where she was ploughing, she stopped at the end of the row to chat for a moment, then gripped her plough-handles, clucked to her team, and waded on down the furrow, making me feel that she was now grown up and had no time for me" (81). Indeed, Jim complains how Antonia "could talk of nothing but the prices of things, or how much she could lift or endure. She was too proud of her strength" (81). As a result, the gender-bending character acquires something that her predecessor Alexandra did not: a boyish nickname. Although Antonia is dubbed "Tony" before her involvement in field labor, she is known almost exclusively by it after she begins working in the fields.

Like Alexandra, Antonia is acutely aware of the situational need for her gender-bending behavior. When Jim inquires if she will be attending school come September, she scoffs at the idea. Calling attention to the way in which education is a luxury that she can no longer afford, she asserts: "'I ain't got time to learn. I can work like a mans now. . . . School is all right for little boys. I help make this land one good farm'" (80). Later, when Jim asks his former playmate why she must "'all the time try to be like [her cruel bother] Ambrosch'" (90), Antonia responds by calling attention to their differing economic status. Gesturing towards the Burden's beautiful house and successful farm, she says, "'If I live here, like you, that is different. Things will be easy for you. But they will be hard for us'" (90). Grandmother Burden agrees, lamenting later, "'Things would have been very different with poor Antonia if her father had lived'" (99–100).

Although Antonia may be a European immigrant whose economic circumstances compel her to engage in various forms of tomboyish behavior, this is where her similarity to Alexandra Bergson ends. Hailing from the Southern European nation of Bohemia, Antonia has a different cultural heritage and racial identity. Even though the young woman is considered white enough to enter the United States under the naturalization laws, she does not have the same racial pedigree as her Northern European counterpart. Possessing a distant connection to the Nordic or Teutonic race, the Bohemian woman is associated with various forms of dark whiteness, or what Matthew Jacobson would characterize as "probationary whiteness." In contrast to assertions about Alexandra's ivory hue, repeated reference is made to Antonia's "brown skin," the "rich, dark color" in her cheeks and her "wild-looking" hair (17, 79, 89). Rather than arising from Antonia's exposure to the sun, her dark hue is independent of it. When the young woman serves as a domestic in Black Hawk, she retains this coloration. Although Antonia is now indoors, she still has "brown legs and arms, and splendid colour [sic] in her cheeks" (99).

To Jim Burden, who has been born in Virginia and raised amidst the Southern racial economy, Antonia's dark whiteness acquires a racially charged significance. In the South, where he was raised, foreigners with brown skin and dark features are not newly arrived European immigrants. As Anne Goodwyn Jones has noted, "they are African Americans—within memory, slaves" (98). Consequently, Jim frequently maps Antonia's European ethnic whiteness onto Southern racial blackness. Coupled with possessing various physical links with Southern stereotypes about blacks, the young woman possess behavioral ones as well. Perhaps the strongest amongst these is Antonia's participation in heavy field labor. In contrast to a proper white Southern belle, his Bohemian friend is "sunburned, sweaty, her dress open at the neck, and her throat and chest dust-plastered" (81). As a consequence, whereas Alexandra's gender-bending behavior in O Pioneers! was lauded, Antonia's is criticized. Jim grumbles: "Everything [about her] was disagreeable to me. Antonia ate so noisily now, like a man, and she yawned often at the table and kept stretching her arms over her head, as if they ached" (81). Even when Antonia abandons field labor and begins working in Black Hawk, she is still seen in racially suggestive ways. As Jean Schwind has written, in the spirit of "the old plantation South,"

Jim refers to the hired girls such as his Bohemian friend "as if they were the property of their employers," making repeated reference to the "Harlings' Tony" and the "Marshalls' Mary" (58).

Another central difference between Antonia and Alexandra is their status as sexual beings. Whereas the tomboyish central character in O Pioneers! was a largely asexual figure, her counterpart in My Antonia recalls stereotypes about the exoticism associated with the black racial Other. From the moment Jim meets his new immigrant neighbor, he is struck by her beauty. Commenting that her eyes "were big and warm and full of light" (17), he is instantly attracted to her, an attraction that even their twenty-year separation cannot diminish. As Jim tells Antonia's sons in the closing section of the novel, "'Your mother, you know, was very much loved by all of us. She was a beautiful girl'" (222).

Paradoxically, Jim deems Antonia's tomboyish actions detrimental to her gender identity, but he considers them highly beneficial to her sexual one. As he comments, in these days before compulsory physical education, "Girls who had to walk more than a half mile to school were pitied. There was not a tennis court in town; physical exercise was thought rather inelegant for the daughters of well-to-do families" (127). As a result, the white native-born American girls from town were pale, thin and frail. According to Jim, "[w]hen one danced with them . . . their muscles seemed to ask but one thing—not to be disturbed" (128). In contrast, the daughters of immigrant farmers were strong and robust. Their "out-of-doors work had given them a vigor which, when they got over their first shyness on coming to town, developed into a positive carriage and freedom of movement" (127). In light of this difference in health and appearance, "The country girls were considered a menace to the social order. Their beauty shone out too boldly against a conventional background" (127).

As both Patricia Hill Collins and Hazel Carby have written—and Cather herself would explore in Sapphira and the Slave Girl—many Southern white women felt threatened by the exotic allure of black female slaves. Reflecting the way in which slavery permitted white men to take sexual liberties with black women, many native-born American men in Cather's novel take sexual liberties with immigrant girls like Antonia. For instance, one night after the tent dance, "Young Harry Paine, who was to marry his employer's daughter on Monday tried to kiss [Antonia], and when she protested . . . caught and kissed her until she got one hand free and slapped him" (132). Likewise, in what has become an oft-discussed scene later in the novel, Wick Cutter tries to force himself on the Bohemian girl. Even Antonia's fiancé, native-born train conductor Larry Donovan, seduces and abandons her. Characterized as "a kind of professional ladies' man" by Jim (143), he spends the young woman's money, impregnates her and then flees to Mexico.

Antonia's racialized status renders her a sexualized object while it simultaneously changes the meaning of her participation in tomboyism.

Unlike Alexandra Bergson, whose gender-bending behavior makes her a successful farmer and quintessential American, Antonia is poor at the end of the novel. As Jim notes, "When I met Tiny Soderball in Salt Lake, she told me that Antonia had not 'done very well'; that her husband was not a man of much force, and she had had a hard life" (211).

In the same way that Antonia does not attain the American Dream, she also does not attain the status of an exemplary citizen. Whereas her tomboyish predecessor preserved elements of her European heritage while largely adopting American culture, the opposite is true for Antonia. Her home in the final pages of the narrative is a model of European rather than American life. As Jim learns, Anotnia's family "always spoke Bohemian at home. The little ones could not speak English at all—didn't learn until they went to school" (216). Marrying a Bohemian man, reading Bohemian newspapers and socializing within the Bohemian community, Antonia has undergone a type of reverse assimilation. Whereas Alexandra Bergson fell in love with her new country and adopted it as her own, Antonia's affectionate ties remain with Europe. Although the immigrant woman has lived in Nebraska for more than twenty years, she says of Bohemia, "'I ain't never forgot *my own country*'" [my emphasis] (150).[7]

Antonia may only have a proprietary claim to whiteness and the privileges that it affords, but she is folded into a new racial categorization that was forming during this era: Caucasian. With the steady fracturing of whiteness amidst the influx of "dark white" and "probationary white" peoples, its meaning and—more importantly—authority was crumbling. In an effort to preserve the societal power of whiteness, the category underwent a radical reconfiguration, and the concept of Caucasian was born. A term that literally refers to the mountain region of Caucasus between the Caspian and the Black Seas, it came to signify anyone who had a connection, however distant, with whiteness. In the words of the *Oxford English Dictionary*, "A member of the 'Caucasian' family, an Indo-European; spec. a member of the 'white race,' opp. one of other ethnic descent" ("Caucasian" 995). As a more expansive category, Caucasian included not only

---

7. Antonia's status as a cultural outsider and even racial Other is underscored by the presence of another gender-bending character in the novel who is also a circumstantial tomboy, and who is repeatedly cast as a counterpoint to Antonia: Lena Lingard. Unlike the Bohemian new immigrant Tony, Lena is Norwegian and, as a member of "old" type of immigrants, has an undisputed connection with whiteness. While Lena is outside in the sun all day, for instance, her skin remains ivory. As Jim notes, the young woman's "legs and arms, curiously enough, in spite of their constant exposure to the sun, kept a miraculous whiteness" (106). Because Lena has access to whiteness, she has access to Americanness. Drawing on her tomboyish individualism, self-reliance and ingenuity, she matures into a figure who becomes another type of quintessential American: the New Woman. Refraining from marriage and motherhood, Lena operates a successful dress shop in San Francisco and, as a result, attains not simply the American Dream but a particularly modern and feminist form of it.

native Anglo-Americans and Northern and Western European immigrants who had an unquestioned link with whiteness, but individuals from new immigrant groups who were thought to have a distant connection with it. Shades of whiteness, such as those possessed by the Celts, Turks and Slavs that were previously seen as separate, were now unified under the term Caucasian. In this way, "The eighteenth century's 'free white persons' became the nineteenth century's Celts, Slavs, Hebrews, and Anglo-Saxons, who, in turn, became the twentieth century's Caucasians" (Jacobson 22).

Although the struggles of ethnic whites for inclusion in the United States is often seen as separate from the plight of other racial minorities, they were interrelated. Historians Lisa Lowe, Frank Van Nuys and David Roediger have each written that a crucial backdrop for the reconsolidation of whiteness as Caucasian was the presence of other, more "undeniably nonwhite," groups. The Irish, Italians and Germans possessed a more distant connection to whiteness than native-born Anglo-Americans, but they had a much stronger connection to it than their Asian, African or American Indian counterparts. For this reason, a crucial facet to becoming white for many newly arrived immigrants was demonstrating their difference from these groups. As Frank Van Nuys has written, by illustrating that they were not "yellow," not "red" and especially not "black," they could aver that they were white or, at least, Caucasian, and thus enjoy the social, political, and economic privileges that this status afforded (35). In a representative example of this phenomenon, "an Irish immigrant in 1877 could be a displaced Celt in Boston—a threat to the republic—and yet a solid member of The Order of Caucasians for the Extermination of the Chinaman in San Francisco, gallantly defending U.S. shores from an invasion of 'Mongolians'" (Jacobson 5).

Largely predicated on Asian immigrants in California, the process was based on American Indians on the prairie and African Americans in the Southern states and East Coast. As Frank Van Nuys has written, many immigrants on the frontier asserted their status as white Americans by joining the federal Indian wars and killing the nation's indigenous peoples (Van Nuys 9–12). Likewise, on the Eastern seaboard and especially in the South, this phenomenon took place against the backdrop of African Americans. In the words of Jacobson again, because of "the power of Jim Crow to create or enforce racial distinctions along strict, binary lines, a number of hitherto probationary races became more decisively white" (110). Within this environment, "Immigrants to this country quickly learn[ed] the value of being White rather than Black, and thereby learn[ed] to cast themselves as Whites" (López 52). Indeed, as Walter Benn Michaels has written, "because (under Jim Crow) no black person could become a citizen, any white person could" (33).

First published in 1918, *My Antonia* was both written and set during the period when the racial cauldron of whiteness was being stirred and the concept of Caucasian was beginning to form: the narrative commences in 1885 and ends in 1916. During this time, the book's Bohemian central character sheds her probationary whiteness and gains entrance into this new categorization. Significantly, even though Cather's novel takes place in the Midwest, this process does not occur against the backdrop of American Indians. As Mike Fischer has discussed in an oft-referenced essay, *My Antonia* is devoid of references to tribal peoples "whose removal was seen as a *sine qua non* for successful white settlement" on the prairie (31). Instead, given the author's Virginia ancestry and her use of a Southern-born narrator, this process occurs against the backdrop of a black character: the mulatto musician Blind d'Arnault, who Elizabeth Ammons aptly notes seem to "erupt out of nowhere in Cather's novel set in the heartland" ("*Antonia*" 59). Whereas Antonia's brown skin and gender-bending behaviors figuratively recall Jim's Virginia heritage, d'Arnault does so literally. When the black musician welcomes everyone to Mrs. Gardiner's hotel and promises an evening of enjoyable music, Jim is transported back to his pre-prairie youth: "It was the soft Negro voice, like those I remembered from childhood" (119). In keeping with this assertion, the young man's discussion of d'Arnault reveals his inculcation of Southern racial attitudes. In keeping with prevailing stereotypes about the "primitive" nature of blacks, Jim notes that the mulatto musician "played barbarously" (121). The Virginia-born narrator describes d'Arnault's appearance via equally racist language: "He had the Negro head, too; almost no head at all; nothing behind the ears but folds of neck under close-clipped wool. He would have been repulsive if his face had not been so kindly and happy. It was the happiest face I had seen since I left Virginia" (118). Although Blind d'Arnault is of mixed blood, Jim makes it clear that the Southern one-drop rule applies: "He looked like some glistening African god of pleasure, full of strong savage blood" (123).

D'Arnault has a more subtle but arguably more important effect on the immigrant girls who populate this scene. Tiny Soderball, Mary Dusak and Antonia Shimerda are dancing to the music in an adjacent room, but they are quickly discovered by the blind pianist's keen ear. "Kirkpatrick caught Tiny by the elbows, 'What's the matter with you girls? Dancing out here by yourselves, when there's a roomful of lonesome men on the other side of the partition!'" (122). Whereas the native-born men had previously resisted carousing with "foreigners," their attitude now changes. Against the backdrop of the black musician and his "good old plantation songs" (184), Antonia, along with the other hired girls who Jim had previously categorized as "almost a race apart," become acceptably white or at least Caucasian. As Blythe Tellefsen has pointed out, for the first time in the novel, they are able to interact with the native-born men like equals (237).

Antonia's inclusion in the newly created concept of Caucasian may come too late to allow her to become a quintessential American or recipient of the American Dream, but it does allows her to become a symbol for something more significant: America.

As Jim asserts in the Introduction to the novel and at repeated points throughout the narrative, his Bohemian friend represents the nation's frontier: "More than any other person we remembered, this girl seemed to mean to us the country, the conditions, the whole adventure of our childhood" (2). With her large family and strong affiliation with European culture, she is like the crucible out of which the nation has formed. In fact, Jim muses in the final pages of the narrative: "It was no wonder that her sons stood straight and tall. She was like a rich mine of life, like the founders of early races" (227).

The Tomboy Migrates Even Further West and Arrives in Hollywood: Mary Pickford and Tomboyism in Early American Silent Film

During the same time that Willa Cather was crafting the tomboyish characters of *My Antonia* and *O Pioneers!*, gender-bending female figures were making their way into an entirely new medium: film. From the earliest days of commercial motion pictures in the United States, the tomboy appeared as a distinct screen persona. Films like Wilfrid North's *Miss Tomboy and Freckles* (1914), Carl Harbaugh's *The Tomboy* (1921) and Edward Ludwig's *Some Tomboy* (1924) featured female figures who engaged in such tomboyish actions as playing sports and climbing trees.

Of the many silent era actresses who played tomboys, Mary Pickford was perhaps the most famous. From her starring role in Marshall Neilan's 1917 film adaptation of *Rebecca of Sunnybrook Farm*, she went on to portray an array of scruffy gender-bending imps. In *Tess of Storm Country* (1922), for instance, Pickford played seventeen-year-old Tessibel "Tess" Skinner, who runs barefoot, refuses to take a bath and even gets into fights. Two years later, in *Little Annie Rooney* (1925), Pickford appeared as Annabelle Rooney, a tough young girl who lives in a New York slum. For nearly the first twenty minutes of the film, "Little Annie" engages in a street brawl with a warring gang of neighborhood boys. She throws bricks, leaps over fences and engages in fistfights.

Mary Pickford's cinematic portrayals of tomboyish characters recalled the antebellum origins of tomboyism as both a feminine and heteronormative institution. Although her on-screen personas may run wild and be mischievous, they also wear dresses and have long hair. Moreover, at the end of the films, they are all "tamed" by heterosexual romance and traditional marriage. In *Little Annie Rooney*, for example, the title character cooks, cleans and even knits a necktie for her father's birthday. Moreover, she falls in love with the leader of a neighborhood Irish gang who is the bane of her policeman father's existence. The final scene of the film shows Annie and Joe happily married and also tamed: she has stopped street fighting while he has abandoned his life as a gangster and now has a respectable job driving a delivery truck.

In the chapter that follows, I demonstrate that what began as an ostensible passing fad with Mary Pickford's presentation of tomboyish characters emerged as an enduring cinematic phenomenon by the following decade. Of all the periods in American history, in fact, perhaps none has been more heavily romanticized or often mythologized than the 1920s. Seen as a time of lavish parties, boisterous fun and unbridled hedonism, it is the era to which many contemporary men and women wish they could be transported back in time to experience.

Inextricable from the widespread appeal of the Twenties was a new female personality type that emerged during it: the flapper. Without any explanation, her name evokes the excitement that gave the Roaring Twenties its name. Rather than trying to resist the allure of the flapper, the next chapter surrenders to it. Drawing on elements such as the carefree exuberance that infected the younger generation in the years following the First World War, the flush economic times that fueled such behavior, and the passage of the Nineteenth Amendment that forever changed the status of women in the United States, I explore the important but previously overlooked role that tomboyism played in the creation of the Twenties flapper. With her shortly cropped hair, androgynous Coco Chanel attire and participation in such formerly masculine activities as smoking and drinking, many of the primary signifiers of this Twenties icon were variations on this gender-bending code of female conduct. Indeed, although this figure is frequently referred to as the "boyish flapper," the chapter that follows demonstrates that she may be more accurately characterized as the tomboyish one.

6

The Tomboy Shifts
From Feminist to Flapper

Clara Bow in Victor Fleming's Hula

T he deaths of nearly nine million soldiers and the decimation of hundreds of square miles of French countryside were not the only casualties of the First World War; so too was the Victorian way of life in the United States. As Amos St. Germain has written, "The universal presumptions of Western Civilizations—beliefs in progress, order, and culture—had been blown to pieces by the World War" (15). The sheer length of the conflict, its use of more lethal forms of warfare and its quick stalemate in the trenches of France left many Americans "restless and discontented, in a mood to question everything that had once seemed to them true and worthy and of good report" (F. L. Allen 79). As a result, Frederick Lewis Allen notes, "A first-class revolt against the accepted American order was certainly taking place during those early years of the Post-war Decade" (73).

While hardly any aspect of American life was immune from this phenomenon, perhaps nowhere was it more pervasive than in the realm of female gender roles. In the words of Allen once again, whereas middle- and upper-class white young women had generally adhered to some version of Victorian mores prior to the First World War, they were "making mincemeat of this code" in the period that followed it (74). From reconfiguring new protocols for courtship and re-envisioning popular fashion codes to questioning established beliefs about the "woman's sphere" and experimenting with new behaviors like smoking and drinking, these young women were radically reinventing their place during the 1920s. Before long, the colloquial term "flapper," previously used to refer to "a young girl in her late teens" who possessed a "flightiness or lack of decorum" ("flapper" 1008), came to connote this new type of rebellious female figure. While literary works like F. Scott Fitzgerald's *This Side of Paradise* (1920), Anita Loos's *Gentlemen Prefer Blondes* (1925) and Percy Marks's *The Plastic Age* (1924) showcased her, the nation's burgeoning film industry also became an important locus of representation. As Patricia Erens has argued, the construction, dissemination and especially popularization of the flapper "was definitely related to the movies" (133). Indeed, more than a dozen films released during the decade contained this word in the title alone.[1] In light of the frequency of flappers on the silver screen, a 1924 article aptly quipped, "You cannot find the word 'flapper' in the dictionary, but you can find it in nine out of ten comedies. Next to talk of breaking the Volstead Act I am convinced that the flapper is the most popular movie subject today" (quoted in S. Ross 1).

While flappers were infamous for their possession of hyper-feminine qualities like wearing short dresses and being flirtatious, they were simultaneously known for being boyish and, frankly, even tomboyish. In an often-overlooked facet of this figure, many of the traits associated with flappers were variations on this gender-bending code of female conduct. In words that are reminiscent of tomboyism, Ann Douglas has said of the shifting fashion sensibility among middle- and upper-class white women during the 1920s: "Waists and breasts disappeared: long hair was banished along with the old-fashioned corset. Frills were out, sport clothes, [and] crisp suits . . . were in" (*Terrible* 248). With their short bobs, androgynous Coco Chanel clothes and engagement in formerly male prerogatives like driving automobiles, smoking cigarettes and drinking now-illegal alcohol, flappers blurred the line between masculinity and femininity.

Focusing on the female gender rebellion that permeated the 1920s, this chapter recoups the lost tomboyish root of the Twenties flapper. Although this figure is commonly characterized as an off-shoot of the cinematic "vamp," she was actually an enticing if somewhat paradoxical combination of adolescent tomboyish androgyny and adult feminine sexuality. Indeed, while cultural critics today do not commonly see the tomboy and flapper as linked figures, individuals in the United States and Great Britain during the 1920s were acutely aware of their overlap. An article in the British newspaper *Daily Mail*, for instance, described the postwar changes in women's fashion as "ultra-tomboyish" ("Boyette" 7). Similarly, in her

---

1. See, for example, *The Flapper* (1920), *The Flip Flapper* (1920), *The Married Flapper* (1922), *Fans and Flappers* (1922), *The Country Flapper* (1922), *The Cowboy and the Flapper* (1924), *Flapper Fever* (1924), *The Perfect Flapper* (1924), *Flapper Wives* (1924), *The Painted Flapper* (1924), *Flaming Flappers* (1925), *An Alpine Flapper* (1926), and *The Exalted Flapper* (1929).

well-known autobiography *Confessions and Impressions* (1930), popular British novelist and travel writer Ethel Mannin used an archaic synonym for tomboyism to describe the gender-bending appearance of young women in years following the First World War: "clumsy, thick-ankled, untidily tweed-clothed hoyden" (227). Finally, in a development that belied both the flapper's connection to tomboyism and the role that the era's new automobiles played in the construction of this figure, the Jordan Motor Company began producing "The Little Tomboy" model in 1927. Echoing its namesake, the vehicle was small, sleek and sporty. Moreover, it was one of the first automobiles that was specifically marketed not only to the growing legion of female drivers, but to the younger generation of flapperesque ones.

Of all the individuals who both embodied the flapper and exemplified her connection to tomboyism, I spotlight the one who is perhaps the most well known: actress Clara Bow. As F. Scott Fitzgerald said of her, "Clara Bow is the quintessence of what the term 'flapper' signifies as a definite description: pretty, imprudent, superbly assured, as worldly-wise, briefly-clad, and 'hard berled' as possible" (quoted in Higashi 125–126). Given Bow's on-screen roles in quintessential flapper films like *The Plastic Age* and her notorious off-screen penchant for partying, Sara Ross has observed, "When the word 'flapper' is mentioned today, if the image of any star is called to mind it is likely to be that of Clara Bow" (241).

Echoing the strong links between flapperism and tomboyism, Bow was a rough-and-tumble girl when she was young and began her cinematic career by playing tomboyish roles. The only child from a working-class Brooklyn family plagued by alcoholism, domestic violence and mental illness, Bow had a home life that was as tough as the neighborhood in which she lived. As biographer David Stenn has written about the future starlet, "Scorned 'cause [she] was the worst-lookin' kid on the street,' Clara became a tomboy, roving streets where packs of teenage ruffians fought neighboring gangs with knives, bricks, or stones hauled in onion sacks" (12). Often forced to defend herself, "Clara's favorite weapon was her fists. 'I could lick any boy my size,' she recalled with pride. 'My right was famous'" (Stenn 12). Together with partaking in tomboyish pursuits like fighting, Bow was involved in equally gender-bending sporting activities. In the words of Stenn once again, "When boys organized stickball games in the streets, she was chosen first" (12).

Although Bow could not have known it at the time, her tomboyish childhood identity was an excellent training ground for her future career as an actress. One of her first film roles was playing a tomboy in Elmer Clifton's *Down to the Sea in Ships* (1922). Her character, the unruly "Dot" Morgan, gets into fistfights, pesters her close friend Jimmy about her ability to do "man's work" and even cross-dresses as a boy to stow away on a whaling ship. Given these activities, she is described in one of the film's intertitles as a "restless, mischievous child of the sea."

In the same way that Bow began her career playing tomboyish parts, she ended it with such roles as well. When the flapper as both a cultural type and cinematic stereotype was beginning to wane in the early 1930s, Bow attempted to reinvent herself by returning to more tomboyish figures. In John Francis Dillon's *Call Her Savage* (1932), she embodied one of the most popular and pervasive tomboyish types: the frontierswoman. Bow's character, Nasa "Dynamite" Springer, leaves all remnants of the flapper formula behind. Recalling such tomboyish icons as Calamity Jane, she boozes and brawls her way through the West.

Highlighting this well-known actress, who was arguably the most famous embodiment of the Twenties flapper both on and off the screen, I examine the connections between this early-twentieth-century symbol of modern womanhood and the now almost century-old phenomenon of tomboyhood. Although nearly all of the iconoclastic female figures that Bow played possess some links to this code of conduct, I focus on the one who had an especially strong connection to it: Hula Calhoun from Victor Fleming's *Hula* (1927). A silent film about the rough-and-tumble daughter of a wealthy Honolulu pineapple plantation owner who falls in love with an unhappily married man, *Hula* is as a much a tomboy film as a flapper one. The 1927 production is not one of the films for which the "It Girl" (or, for that matter, director Victor Fleming) is commonly remembered today,[2] but the production is significant because it combines Bow's early roles where she epitomized the flapper formula with her later ones where she embodied rough-and-tumble women. Indeed, with her title character in *Hula* wearing men's pants instead of fashionable dresses, preferring to swim in a secluded lagoon over attending fancy parties, and riding her horse into a formal dining room rather than making a "ladylike" entrance, Bow demonstrates that although the flapper is commonly seen as a unique product of the 1920s, it actually had its root in the longstanding phenomenon of tomboyism.

"I've Met the Most Gorgeous Man!": The Tomboyish Flapper and the Return of Hyper-Heterosexuality

Although the title character in *Hula* was heralded as "the flapper of Hawai'i" in commercial advertisements about the movie (S. Ross 286), she engages in an array of well-known elements of tomboyism. An early

---

2. To be sure, *Hula* received several less-than-enthusiastic reviews upon its theatrical release. Mordaunt Hall, writing for *The New York Times*, for example, called the production "a silly affair" in which none of the characters are ever "permitted to betray the slightest sign of intelligence" (383). As a result, he lamented the production's waste of screen talents like Bow—who he praised as "vivacious and charming" (384)—and her co-star, Clive Brook.

intertitle of the film announces, "The Calhoun cowboys had ridden in, blossom-laden, for Hula's birthday feast," and then cuts to a shot of a figure arriving on a horse. Carrying a basket of gifts and wearing pants and a straw hat, the individual appears to be one of the men announced in the intertitle. It is not until a close-up a few seconds later that viewers realize this figure is the Calhoun cow*girl* Hula.

As the scene progresses, Hula continues to behave in ways that are more stereotypically boyish than girlish. When presented with a basket of gifts, for instance, she roughly digs through the items, tossing select ones to seemingly random individuals around the table. Similarly, when the feast commemorating her birthday commences, she does not say a dignified grace to start the meal. On the contrary, the moment that the food is served, she shouts "Race you!" to her guests and then commences eating with her hands. When a potential suitor chastises her tomboyish behavior by pointing out "You are a woman now, ready to love," Hula is not dissuaded. The comment only prompts her to eat faster and more aggressively: she plunges her fingers into the bowl and scoops the food even more rapidly into her mouth.

These events serve as an apt indicator of Hula's behavior throughout Victor Fleming's film, for the young woman repeatedly rebels against prevailing gender mores by engaging in a rough-and-tumble form of tomboyism. For example, although Hula's best friend is not a sissy boy, it is an equally tomboyish companion: a dog that accompanies her everywhere. When the young woman first meets British architect—and future fiancé— Anthony Haldane, in fact, she is running after the animal. Barging into the gentleman's room and throwing herself under his bed to retrieve the terrier, she makes a decidedly unladylike first impression.

In many subsequent scenes, Hula's dog is the conduit for her tomboyish actions. She brings the animal to the dinner table one evening, and he promptly begins lapping soup from the bowl of another guest. A few moments later, the terrier falls into a swift-moving stream while chasing after a cat, and Hula must save not only her cherished pet but also its ostensible rescuer, Haldane, who dove in after the canine and was swept away by the current. Indeed, when Hula realizes that both her love interest and beloved dog are in danger of being washed over a steep waterfall, she behaves more like a stereotypical hero than heroine. In a gender reversal, Hula wades into the treacherous waters and pulls both her dog and Anthony to safety. Her dress is torn and dirtied, but, in keeping with her tomboyish nature, she is more concerned with Haldane's well-being than her own. With a look of intense worry, Hula examines his body for injuries.

When Hula is not engaging in such heroics, she embodies many additional facets of tomboyism. Early in the film, she prefers swimming in a secluded lagoon with her dog to attending fancy parties with her father's refined guests. Then, in one of the most oft-mentioned scenes, Hula rides her horse up the steps and into her father's house on a dare, eliciting a combination of shock and consternation from his guests. Finally, throughout the film, Hula gallops all over the Honolulu plantation on horseback: leaping gorges, running down steep ravines and helping her father oversee the family's large pineapple plantation. Especially in long shots, with her trousers, hat and spurs, she looks more like a young man than a young woman.[3]

Rejecting the former association of tomboyish behaviors with gender and sexual inversion, the Twenties flapper in general and Clara Bow's Hula in particular made participation in this code of conduct not simply socially acceptable but heterosexually appealing once again. Recalling the magnetic appeal of Capitola Black, the beautiful and robust Hula is highly attractive to Haldane. As Hula crawls under the bed of the British architect in search of her truant dog, he admires her long, lean legs. When she emerges, the two begin talking and Hula pulls up her skirt to show him a bee sting on her well-toned thigh. As Sara Ross has noted, this scene—along with the later one in which Hula wades into the stream to save Haldane and her terrier—demonstrates a common feature of the flapper film: the titillating "skin show." Numerous cinematic portrayals of this figure employed flimsy plot excuses to depict her as scantily clad and also often even soaking wet, thereby making her already form-fitting attire even more clingy and transparent. Hence, whether the flapper was lauded as a triumphant symbol of women's new freedoms or condemned as proof that the younger generation had lost all sense of decorum, she was, at her core, a sex symbol.

A key component to the erotically appealing nature of Bow's Hula—along with other tomboyish flappers—was her ability to soften and even sexualize her gender-bending nature. Flappers may have cut their hair, worn androgynous clothes and engaged in an array of formerly unladylike activities, but they also retained a firm link to femininity. Flappers eased the gender-bending nature of their appearance with an array of feminizing elements like oversized jewelry, a comely spit curl, finely tweezed eyebrows, and heavy makeup. Throughout Victor Fleming's film, Hula's shirts and pants are exquisitely tailored and thus form-fitting. In addition, her eyebrows are finely sculpted and she is never seen without dark lipstick accentuating her signature pouty lips.

When flappers like Hula did openly defy women's traditional gender roles, they patterned their behavior and appearance after adolescent boys rather than adult men. In the words of Laura Doan, "boyishness denoted a certain fashionable youthfulness that was never threatening" (*Fashioning* 105). Because boys were sexually immature and thus relatively lacking in erotic agency, young women who engaged in boyishness did not embody the same potential threat as those who adopted more masculine behaviors.

---

3. One more element could be added to Hula's tomboyish traits: the young woman is motherless. Mrs. Calhoun died many years ago, and Hula has been raised by her father.

For these reasons, flappers were not associated with the "mannish lesbianism" that was becoming increasingly visible during the 1920s, especially in England and France. On the contrary, figures like Bow's character were firmly located in the realm of heterosexuality and—given their status as sex symbols—even hyper-heterosexuality. Akin to Capitola Black once again, flappers used their boyish traits to enhance rather than hinder their desirability to the opposite sex. As Laura Doan has remarked about the ethos of gender-bending women during this era:

> [T]he Modern Girl's objective is not to pass as a boy but to "look as much like a boy as possible." "The little feminine mannerisms" that demonstrate how the boyette amuses herself "by masquerade" deliberately expose her true gender. If she is mistaken for an actual boy, the "look" has somehow gone wrong. (*Fashioning* 103)

To be sure, Anthony is attracted to Hula in large part because of her rough-and-tumble nature. Together with admiring the finely toned body that her participation in tomboyism has created, he also enjoys sparring with her spirited, outspoken personality. Several scenes show the two flirtatiously chasing each other around the pineapple plantation on horseback, and also engaging in playful discussions and debates.

Anthony's attraction to Hula, however, is far from one-sided. From the moment that the young woman sees the British architect, she is enamored with him. Looking starry-eyed at the gentleman, she admires his profile and declares, "Anthony, you are a beautiful man!" Later, while recounting the incident to her father, she announces "I've met the most gorgeous man!" and adds a few minutes later, "I love him." In many subsequent scenes, Hula uses her tomboyism in general and scrappy dog in particular to further her flirtation with the British architect. When she brings the animal to the dinner table one evening, for instance, he does not simply drink soup from the bowl of a random guest, but from that of a rival for Anthony's affection. Likewise, when the animal falls into the stream, it is part of a carefully orchestrated plot to gain the British gentleman's attention. When Hula sees Anthony flirting with the wealthy coquette Mrs. Bane, she sends the terrier running after a cat and then begs Anthony for assistance.

Twenties flappers like Hula may have used their physical tomboyishness for heterosexual coyishness, but this quality did not prevent them from being associated with another common hallmark: taming. In an attempt to please her suitor near the middle of the film, Hula relinquishes her tomboyish trousers for feminine dresses. An intertitle notes that the steamships arriving from the U.S. mainland brought "gowns for Hula." In keeping with the antebellum origins of tomboyism as a lifelong identity though, this feminization does not last. When Anthony sees the young girl in one of her new dresses and deems her "too splendiferous to kiss," she tears the lace from her garment and musses her hair. In a subsequent scene, she is once again wearing pants, a tie and straw hat. The final sequence of the film presents Hula in gender-bending attire and acting like a tomboy. In an effort to convince Anthony's wife to finally grant him a divorce, she feigns detonating the dam that he has been building on her father's plantation. Once Mrs. Haldane realizes that her husband is going to be bankrupt and has thrown it all away for a "silly little fool," she agrees to sign the papers. Only after Mrs. Haldane has left for the mainland does Hula reveal the ruse: she has not put dynamite to the dam, only some land nearby. As the young woman jokes to Anthony, she "has had to move mountains with dynamite—to get you!"

Even the promiscuous flirtations and occasional marital infidelities with which flapper figures like Hula were associated serve the original heteronormative purpose of tomboyism. Although Bow's character may pursue a man she knows to be married, she is, in keeping with another hallmark of the flapper film formula, presented as a sympathetic figure. Reflecting the era's changing attitudes about both women's gender roles and rules for courtship and marriage, Hula is not seen as a heartless homewrecker. Instead, she is cast as an admirable figure who has the wisdom as well as daring to free two desperately unhappy people from a loveless marriage. When Anthony's wife—who has never really loved her husband, and whose husband has never been particularly enamored with her—finally consents to a divorce, it allows the formerly unhappy couple to form happier marital unions with people whom they actually love. Far from creating a broken home, therefore, Hula's involvement with the married man actually creates two felicitous marriages. In doing so, she joins the ranks of numerous historical tomboy figures who seemingly rejected women's traditional roles only to ultimately embrace them. Indeed, the final scene of the film is a traditional happy ending replete with Anthony's marriage proposal and Hula's gleeful acceptance. In this way, the young woman once more replicates the antebellum origins of tomboyism by demonstrating that her gender-bending ways are actually a method by which to embrace, rather than escape, the roles of wife and mother.

Flappers like Hula may have engaged in many actions that broadened women's gender and sexual roles, but they did not see themselves as continuing the crusade of their historical antecedent, the New Woman. Many flappers distanced themselves from the fight for women's rights, while others took this stance one step further by voicing negative views of the movement. As William Chafe has written,

"Feminism, has become a term of opprobrium for the young" Dorothy Dunbar Bromley noted in 1927. "The word suggests either the old school . . . who wore flat heels and had very little feminine charm, or the current species who antagonize men with their constant clamor about maiden names." (103)

Exemplifying this detail, at no point does Bow's character mention women's rights or even their status in society. She may encroach on many formerly male prerogatives, but these actions are devoid of a politicized consciousness. For the first time in the history of this code of conduct, therefore, with the figure of the tomboyish flapper, female gender iconoclasm distanced itself from feminism.

"A native isn't tied by convention!
Gad, I wish we *were* natives!":
Flapperesque Tomboyism and Hawaiian Tribalism in *Hula*

In the same way that the Twenties flapper incorporated many signature elements of white tomboyism, she also continued this code of conduct's longstanding association with nonwhiteness. As Nathan Huggins and David Levering Lewis have written, the 1920s was a time of unparalleled expansion in nearly all forms of black artistic expression in the United States. From poets Countee Cullen and Langston Hughes, musicians Duke Ellington and Jelly-Roll Morton, and novelists Zora Neale Hurston and James Weldon Johnson, an array of black artists, writers, and performers demonstrated the depth and richness of black culture.

As Ann Douglas has written, although the largely white phenomenon of the Roaring Twenties and the principally black one of the Harlem Renaissance are often cast as two separate cultural phenomena, "they are at bottom . . . inextricable, whites and blacks participated and collaborated in both projects" (*Terrible* 5). African Americans frequented speakeasies and drank bathtub gin, and white Americans listened to Duke Ellington and read James Weldon Johnson. In fact, a key component to the assault on Victorian values during the 1920s arose from this cross-fertilization. Fueled by the disillusionment of the First World War, white Americans longed to be more free, natural and uninhibited, and they saw primitivism once again as the means to do so. Whereas this concept was located within the remote jungles of Africa during the 1910s, it was situated more locally within the nation's African American culture in the 1920s. The flowering of black art, literature and especially music and dance were seen as emerging not simply from a general artistic awakening within the black community, but one that was fueled by a reconnection with its tribal roots. In an article titled "Does Jazz Put the Sin in Syncopation?" in the August 1921 issue of *Ladies' Home Journal*, Anne Shaw Faulkner—the head of the Music Department of the General Federation of Women's Clubs—remarked that jazz was originally played as "the accompaniment of the voodoo dances, stimulating the half-crazed barbarian to the vilest deeds" (16). Similarly, in Percy Marks's novel *The Plastic Age*, the narrator asserts that this new musical form distinguished itself by its "horribly primitive . . . syncopated rhythms" (252–253).

White men and women longed to "go primitive" by listening to these "savage" new musical forms, partaking in these "tribal" dance styles, and visiting African American clubs in neighborhoods like Harlem. In fact, by the mid-1920s,

> Harlem was being advertised as the "Nightclub Capital of the World." About 125 nightclubs, led by the Cotton Club and Connie's Inn, served up African-American music and dancing to white patrons eager to enjoy a little regression back to jungle life and to participate, if only as voyeurs, in what was palpably the most exciting entertainment scene America had ever boasted. (Douglas *Terrible* 74)

The Jazz Age fascination with African American culture permeated all facets of white American society, not merely the hip New Yorkers who frequented Harlem on the weekends. In the words of Douglas once again, "If actual blacking up, Eddie Cantor-style, decreased in the 1920s, blacking up, speaking metaphorically, increased dramatically" (*Terrible* 78). In their personal lives as well as professional careers, many whites "flirted with varying degrees of Negritude" (Douglas *Terrible* 78). Writer Carl Van Vechten, for instance, drew heavily on blackness and black culture in his bestselling novel *Nigger Heaven* (1926). In a popular caricature from the era, Vechten experienced what Susan Gubar calls a "racechange" and appears black. "Ignoring the fair complexion and blond hair of the Midwesterner, Miguel Covarrubias produced several caricatures which capture not so much Van Vechten in blackface as Van Vechten the African American" (*Racechanges* 154). Likewise, black slang and speech patterns became fashionable among middle- and upper-middle-class white youth. "The American National Council of Teachers of English might have established 'Ain't-less Weeks' and 'Final-G Weeks' . . . but using 'ain't' and dropping the final *g* (as in Berlin's 'Ain't you goin'?' or Jolson's 'You ain't heard nothin' yet!')—the most easily recognized characteristics of the Negro dialect—remained immensely popular" [italics in original] (Douglas *Terrible* 376). In light of the numerous ways in which white men and women co-opted various forms of blackness, Cole Porter famously remarked in the lyrics to one of his popular songs during the 1920s, "Black's white today. . . . / Anything goes!" (Douglas *Terrible* 115).

The tomboyish flapper was as much at the epicenter of transformations in white culture during the 1920s as she was at the hub of black ones. This figure, who wore Coco Chanel's androgynous fashions and bobbed her hair, also adored jazz music and reveled in the black-inspired dances like the Charleston. For these reasons, the ostensibly white figure of the flapper was often presented in ways that highlighted her connection to primitive nonwhiteness. In a drawing by Robert Bruce Nugent that was printed in Charles S. Johnson's collection *Ebony and Topaz* (1927), for instance, the white Western flapper and black tribal savage form two halves of the same body. Lest the miscegenated implications of the illustration go unnoticed, the series bears the telling title, "Drawings for Mulattoes."[4] Images of the flapper-as-savage also permeated the nation's mass culture. The cover illustration for the July 15th, 1926, issue of the nationally circulating *Life* magazine presented a young white flapper dancing the Charleston before a background of black tribal "primitives" who are engaged in an identical dance. The shared facial expressions and especially body positions of these figures imply a continuity between them. Moreover, reflecting the link between sexually loose white women and the black Hottentot Venus (discussed in the Introduction to this volume), the cover illustration bears the suggestive caption, "Everything is Hot-tentotsy Now!"

Victor Fleming's 1927 film *Hula* illustrated the tomboyish root of the Twenties flapper while it simultaneously embedded 1920s beliefs about the association between these white figures and nonwhite "savages." As her name suggests, Hula possesses a strong kinship with Hawaiian culture. Yoking the white fascination for tribal "savagery" during the 1920s with the longstanding history of associating white tomboys with various forms of nonwhiteness, Bow's character "goes native" throughout the film.

The connection between the white Western character Hula and the nonwhite peoples of Hawai'i emerges in the opening scene. As soon as the young woman dismounts her horse, guests at her birthday feast begin showering her with a signature item of Hawaiian culture: flower *leis*. Whereas many flappers would prefer Western-styled jewelry, Hula is delighted with this gift. Even when so many *leis* have been placed around the tomboyish girl's neck that her face begins to be obscured, she smiles gleefully.

As an appropriate addition to these items, Hula receives a *ukulele*. Although the instrument is not indigenous to the islands—as Elizabeth Buck notes, it was brought to Hawai'i by Spanish sailors and Portugese cowboys— it is closely associated with them. The *Oxford English Dictionary*, in fact,

---

4. A similar phenomenon permeates a collection of photographs by Man Ray. In the image *Noire et blanc*, the flapperesque model Kiki is posed to closely resemble the African mask that she is holding. As Susan Gubar has written of the photograph, "Because Kiki's hand and cheek now embrace and encircle the mask, the two figures appear in the position of doubles, a twinning that eludes hierarchized racial and sexual categories" (*Racechanges* 48). In the photographic negative of this work, which was also shown, the "switching lights and darks . . . graphically emphasizes the photographer's accord with Booker T. Washington's point that it is sometimes 'difficult . . . to know where the black begins and the white ends'" (*Racechanges* 7).

defines *ukulele* as a "Hawai'ian guitar" ("ukulele" 811). Moreover, the *OED*'s listing for the first English usage of the term spotlights the instrument's connection to the Hawaiian dance from which Bow's character gets her name: "Then comes to twang of the *ukulele*, the soft, melodious cadence of the hula song" [italics in original] (811).

Together with receiving a traditional Hawaiian instrument and wearing traditional Hawaiian *leis*, Hula enjoys a traditional Hawaiian meal at her birthday feast: *poi*, a paste-like food that is made from pounded taro root. The young woman's decision to eat with her hands, therefore, can be seen as not simply tomboyish but tribal, for *poi* is traditionally eaten with the fingers and not with Western utensils. This detail gives the male guest's admonishment that Hula is too old behave in this manner a dual meaning. His remark suggests that the young woman not only refrain from being so tomboyish, and also that she cease behaving like a tribal primitive. Yoking the nearly century-long tradition of tomboy taming with the Western interest in "civilizing" so-called primitive peoples, the gentleman believes that the time has come for the rebellious Hula to begin acting more like a white Western woman and less like a nonwhite native.

Such links between Hula and native Hawaiian culture permeate scenes throughout the remainder of Fleming's film. After the young woman barges into Anthony Haldane's room in pursuit of her dog, for instance, a genteel lady admonishes: "Really—you've lived among natives so much—you've become as primitive as they are." Indeed, the tomboyish young woman not only wears flower *leis* and delights in the gift of a new *ukulele*, she also uses the Hawaiian word *Kahana* to refer to her father. Given the embattled history of the Hawaiian language, Hula's adoption of even this one term represents a daring act of tomboyish rebellion. After the overthrow of the Hawaiian monarchy in 1893, "the Provisional Government of the Republic banned the use of Hawaiian in government offices, courts, and schools" (Buck 133). Hula's employment of the term *Kahana* can thus be viewed as a politicized act, commenting about Hawaiian cultural survival, linguistic integrity and even political sovereignty. Indeed, both Noenoe K. Silva and Huanani-Kay Trask have written that the modern nationalist movement in Hawai'i has centered on the reclamation of the island's native language: local newspapers began printing in Hawaiian, and schools commenced officially or unofficially teaching it to students. As a result of such activist efforts, in 1978, the "*Aloha* state" became the only one in the union to have two official languages: English and Hawaiian.

Together with adopting facets of the Hawaiian language, Hula has inculcated some of its cultural traditions. In an attempt to woo Anthony, she surprises him on the worksite with a homemade lunch. Rather than making an American-style sandwich and putting it in a metal lunch pail, she prepares a more traditional Hawaiian meal: Hula gives him *poi* that she has placed in a hollowed-out pineapple. Later, of course, the young woman accentuates her connection to island customs by performing the *hula*. During a *luau* hosted by her father, she witnesses the erotic effect that the dance has on Western men in general and Haldane in particular. Eager for Anthony to view her as an object of desire, she announces, "If that's what amuses our guests—I'll show them what my name means." Hula jumps up from her seat, grabs the arm of one of the Hawaiian dancers and forcibly pulls her offstage. Behind some bushes, they swap not only material clothing but symbolic cultural identities: Hula literally throws off her Western dress (tossing it over a bush toward the audience) and dons the grass skirt, bandeau top and flower anklets of the native Hawaiian (an act that leaves viewers to speculate what, if anything, the original performer is wearing). Once Hula has successfully completed this transformation, she enters the stage and begins to dance. As she moves and wiggles, the camera pans her body, sexualizing and objectifying her in a manner that recalls the stereotypical treatment of nonwhite women under the white Western male gaze.

In contrast to Clara Bow's character, who embraces Hawaiian culture, Anthony is never depicted eating anything other than Western foods (he refuses Hula's *poi*-in-a-pineapple lunch, claiming that he is too busy to dine) or wearing anything other than Western garb (he dons a tuxedo jacket and tie for much of the first part of the film). Significantly, the only instance in which Anthony expresses any interest in Hawaiian culture is during a conversation with Hula. When she points out, "Even a native knows marriage means nothing without love" in an attempt to persuade him to leave his wife and marry her, he gives a surprising retort. Echoing white Western stereotypes about tribal primitives as carefree and uninhibited, he asserts: "A native isn't tied by conventions. Gad, I wish we *were* natives!" [italics in original intertitle]. Not surprisingly, this scene directly precedes the *luau* in which Hula sloughs off her Western dress, dons the grass skirt and dances the *hula*. The close chronology of these two events suggests their causality. The young woman's decision to "go native" seems inspired or at least precipitated by Anthony's remark about the admirably uninhibited natures of tribal peoples. Through her bold tomboyish actions, she demonstrates that she is also not confined by Western convention.

Cultural Appropriation, Misappropriation and Reappropriation: Flapperesque Tribal Tomboyism in the Service of White American Imperialism

Bow's character may wear grass skirts, eat *poi* and dance the *hula* as a tomboyish means to defy traditional gender roles for white Western women, but she ultimately reasserts her alliance with them. Akin to the white Americans who enjoyed black culture during the 1920s, Hula's tomboyish connection to nonwhite Hawaiian tribalism does not interfere with her genteel race and class status or the privileges that they afford. While Bow's character adopts various facets of the island's indigenous culture, these elements prove to be nothing more than white Western misappropriations of them. For instance, the young woman uses the word *Kahana* to refer her father, but this is not the correct Hawaiian term for this figure. The actual Hawaiian word for "father" is *Makua kane* or simply *makua*. The term *Kahana*, which is based on the root word *kaha*, translates as "cutting." Far from being used to refer to people, it is a common name for geographic places, most notably on Oahu, the island where Victor Fleming's film is ironically set.[5]

A similar observation applies to Hula's signature element of tomboyish cultural transgression: her dance of the *hula*. Although the young woman dons the grass skirt, bandeau top and ankle adornments associated with the *hula*, she does not engage in a culturally accurate performance of it. Like many white Westerners who partake in the dance, she does not understand its symbolic significance. As Elizabeth Buck notes, before Western contact, *hula* was a form of "poetry in motion" (112). Each of the hand gestures, arm movements and body positions conveyed a message. For these reasons, the dance was not an innocuous amusement or pleasing entertainment, but a central facet of the cultural, political and religious life of Hawai'i. Indeed, Noenoe K. Silva has written extensively on the role of *hula* in the formation of the island's collective memory, the transfer of its historical knowledge, and the construction of its cultural identity.[6]

The *hula* that Clara Bow's character performs, however, is devoid of these qualities. Instead of learning the specific movements and symbolic meanings of the island dance, the young woman enacts a white Western misinterpretation of it. Randomly undulating her hands and indiscriminately wiggling her hips, she transforms this highly symbolic ritual into a burlesque parody. Echoing Elizabeth Buck's comments about performances of the *hula* at many white resorts in present-day Hawai'i, the young woman's costume and movements are merely "something to be seen and enjoyed without wondering about the past or its meaning to Hawaiian performers" (4). As a result, what initially seemed like an instance of authentic cultural exchange proves to be merely another moment of white cultural imperialism. Far from respectfully adopting elements of the Hawaiian dance, the flapperesque woman has merely co-opted it for own purposes.

5. I would like to thank Leilani Basham, Coordinator of the Hawaiian Language Program at the University of Hawai'i at Manoa for her kind assistance with the denotative meaning and etymological history of these terms.

6. See, especially, her essay "*He Kanawai E Ho'opau I Na Hula Kuolo Hawai'i*: The Political Economy of Banning the Hula," in *The Hawaiian Journal of History*, vol 34 (2000): 29–48.

Hula's adoption of the island's nonwhite tribal culture to paradoxically reinforce white Western power is perhaps never more vivid than in the conclusion of Fleming's film. The young woman does not use her affection for Hawaiian culture to dismantle her father's imperialist pineapple plantation, release the native workers, and return the colonized land to the indigenous Hawaiians. On the contrary, she wears flower *leis*, makes *poi* and dances the *hula* to woo a genteel English suitor who, as an intertitle asserts, "lived up to Britain's colonial maxim." Rather than seeking to learn from the peoples and places of Hawai'i, Anthony Haldane participates in the imperialist project of subjugating and colonizing them. He is the chief architect of an irrigation project on the plantation, and his job forms an apt metaphor for the historical treatment of Hawaiian peoples by white Westerners in general and by American capitalists in particular. Akin to the U.S. annexation of Hawai'i in 1893 after military troops illegally invaded the islands and overthrew their sovereign queen, the dam that Anthony is building will forcibly change and subdue the land rather than allowing it to maintain its integrity and autonomy.

In this way, while Hula's adoption of Hawaiian customs ostensibly represents cultural hybridity, it ultimately reinforces white American capitalism and Western imperial domination. At the end of the film, the tomboyish young woman who is the sole heir to her father's successful pineapple plantation has become engaged to a man who will ensure its colonialist and capitalist dominance. The union between Hula and Anthony, in fact, is as much a consolidation of imperial power as it is a romantic love story. The pineapple plantation has made the Calhouns one of the wealthiest families in Honolulu, and Anthony has earned a hefty sum to build its new irrigation system. As the young architect reveals in one of the film's intertitles, the dam project has allowed him to make his "fortune." The merging of both Anthony and Hula's estates, coupled with his ability to further expand the plantation's size and scope, leaves little doubt that this commercial empire will remain dominant.

Given the wealth generated and specific crop grown, in fact, the Calhoun plantation reflects a company that played a central role in the imperialist annexation of Hawai'i: Dole Pineapple, originally founded in 1851 as the Hawaiian Pineapple Company. As both Noenoe K. Silva and Huanani-Kay Trask have discussed, protecting the business interests of this company, along with other large American corporations involved in the fruit and sugar industries, was a primary factor in the military overthrow of the Hawaiian monarchy. The founder of Dole Pineapple, James Drummond Dole, was the cousin of Samuel Ballard Dole, the American lawyer and statesman who served as head of the provisional government of Hawai'i after the military removal of Queen Liliuokalani from her throne, and who also infamously ignored demands by the U.S. federal government to return power to the Hawaiians. In spite of President Grover Cleveland's pronouncement that the American-led revolution was an unlawful military overthrow of a sovereign foreign nation, Samuel Dole eventually won annexation, albeit not until five years later when Cleveland's term ended and William McKinley took office. Dole then convened a Congressional commission to draft legislation for Hawai'i, much of which was—not surprisingly—focused on protecting American business interests on the islands, including those of his cousin's successful company.[7]

In keeping with Hula's position as not only a white American woman but also one who is heir to a successful pineapple plantation, characters throughout the film call attention to her privileged race and class status. Although Anthony found the *hula* sensual and exciting when it was performed by nonwhite Hawaiians, he is upset when the wealthy white Hula performs it. When other men begin leering at her, he jumps up from his seat, grabs Hula by the arm and announces, "Get back to Kahana's house—or I'll carry you there!" When she refuses, he forcibly picks her up and carries her, literally kicking and screaming, inside. His actions demonstrate that what may be acceptable behavior for the nonwhite women of Hawai'i is unacceptable for a wealthy white American woman.

Even when Hula is not explicitly participating in Hawaiian customs, she remains more in dialogue with Western stereotypes about nonwhite tribal peoples than culturally accurate understandings of them. When a potential suitor tells her that she is ready for love in the opening scene of the movie, for instance, she responds in a manner that recalls Edgar Rice Burroughs's Tarzan, a figure who in many ways epitomizes the white Western fantasy of "going primitive." Turning to the gentleman, the young woman matter-of-factly tells him, "Hula will know when she is ready for love." Later, she employs this linguistic style again, telling her father about Anthony Haldane: "Some day he will love Hula." By speaking of herself in the third person, Hula reflects Western beliefs about the linguistic infacility of tribal savages while she simultaneously anticipates Johnny Weissmuller's now famous line "Me Tarzan, You Jane" from the 1932 film adaptation of Burroughs's book.

Taken collectively, these details continue the antebellum purpose of tomboyism as a means to buttress white racial supremacy. Hula's efforts affirm the Western colonialist presence in the South Pacific as they simultaneously ease a series of powerful racial fears that emerged in the 1920s. During an era that followed the deaths of millions of primarily white young men in the Great War, maintaining white racial dominance became

7. For more information on James Drummond Dole, Dole Pineapple and the U.S. annexation of Hawai'i, see Paul T. Burlin's *Imperial Maine and Hawai'i: Interpretive Essays in the History of Nineteenth-Century American Expansion* (Lanham, MD: Lexington Books, 2006).

an acute concern and even anxiety. As Walter Benn Michaels has written, many Anglo-Europeans during the 1920s did not see the "lost generation" as the current crop of young men disillusioned by the war, but the millions of children that the fallen soldiers would have sired but would now never be born (29). This decrease in white population—along with its steady amplification with each passing generation—aroused fears once again over the possible loss of white racial supremacy. As a result, nativists like Lothrop Stoddard argued that the conflict ought not to be have been dubbed the "Great War" but the "White Civil War" (Michaels 24, 29).

Although the wartime death toll of American soldiers was precipitously lower given the shorter expanse of time that the nation was involved in the conflict,[8] the United States was not immune from anxiety about maintaining the white racial status quo. As Amos St. Germain has written, the 1920s was a time of heightened racial anxiety in the United States:

> The "we" of the American population of 1920 had come to include a remarkable number of "them," those of immigrant birth. The 1920 census revealed that there were more Americans who were a mixture of native American with immigrant stock than there were citizens who were exclusively of one or the other. (26)

In the wake of these statistics, reversing the "open door" policy of unrestricted foreign immigration that operated in the nation for centuries, Americans "decided in the early 1920s that we really didn't want the 'huddled masses of your teeming shore' that the poetess Emma Lazarus had spoken of. The Emergency Quota Act of May 1921 restricted each country's immigration to 3% of that immigrant population in America according to the census of 1910" (St. Germain 22). As the decade wore on, such sentiments only increased. With the passage of the Immigration Act of 1924, "The number of immigrants was limited to 2% of those populations in America according to the census of 1890. . . . In addition, the law of 1924 virtually excluded all Asians" (St. Germain 22). Echoing the antebellum origins of tomboyism, the flapper was seen as not simply a new female gender identity but racial strategy that would address these dual phenomena. Hula, with her British imperialist husband and powerful pineapple plantation, accomplishes the interrelated goals of maintaining racial and colonial dominance.

---

8. The United States entered the conflict in April 1917, nearly three years after it had commenced. The total number of U.S. soliders killed during World War I was 116,516. By comparison, the death toll for armed service members in Great Britain was 908,371 and in France was 1,357,800. For more information see the comparative chart "World War I Armed Forces and Casualties by Country" in *Facts About the 20ᵗʰ Century* (Eds. George Ocha and Melinda Coreys. New York: H. W. Wilson, 2001): 358.

From the Jazz Age to the Golden Age:
The Stock Market Goes Bust and Tomboyish
Children's Literature Goes Boom

The stock market crash in October 1929 and the economic crisis that ensued brought an abrupt end to the carefree days of the Roaring Twenties and, by extension, to the carefree flapper. In the decade that followed, boyish young women with bobbed hair and a taste for bathtub gin faded as quickly as the fads of flag pole sitting and dance marathons. Akin to nearly all other periods of national crisis, the Great Depression brought a backlash against iconoclastic gender roles and a return to more conservative mores for women. With the nation experiencing unprecedented levels of unemployment and fears over communist revolution, tradition instead of transgression came to characterize American life.

The return to more conventional gender roles did not mean the end of tomboyism, though. Although the stock market bust rang the death knell for the flapper, it precipitated a tomboyish boom in U.S. literature and culture. From hit songs like Red Norvo's "Tomboy" (1934) to theatrical productions such as Boyce Loving's play *Tomboy: A Comedy in Three Acts* (1935), cultural presentations of gender-bending female figures did not simply endure, they broadened in scope. The *dramatis personae* for Loving's drama, in fact, associates its main character, Jacqueline "Jackie" Abbott, with an array of stereotypical tomboyish qualities:

> Jacqueline: The "tomboy," aged sixteen, is a rip-snorting, vigorous, ultra-healthy young girl, with never a romantic notion entering her noodle. . . . Is an expert at fishing, hunting, golf, tennis, swimming, and other sports. Is mannish in her swagger, and speech. Cannot abide love affairs, spooning, and other usual young-girl topics of interest. Pals around with a neighbor boy friend and her father. (Loving 8)

The presence of tomboyism in new cultural venues like the theater and popular music, however, were dwarfed by developments in another genre that had a longstanding connection with this code of conduct: children's literature. During the 1930s, a sizeable number of books for young readers featured gender-bending female figures, from Carol Ryrie Brink's *Caddie Woodlawn* (1935), Kate Seredy's *The Good Master* (1935) and Laura Ingalls Wilder's *Little House* series (1932–1943) to Anne Pence Davis's *Mimi* series (1935–1936), Ruth Sawyer's *Roller Skates* (1936) and Carolyn Keene's Nancy Drew Mysteries (original series 1930–1957). Given the commercial popularity and critical importance of these narratives, the 1930s are often seen as the final phase of the "golden age" of tomboy literature. As Christian McEwan and Elizabeth Segel have written, it was the period when many of the most-well-known narratives in this genre were released.

Rather than a coincidental occurrence, the surge in tomboyish children's literature during the Depression was a direct result of the demands of this turbulent historical era. Amidst this time of national hardship, American men and especially its women needed to be strong, resilient and resourceful. Tomboyism had constituted an effective means to help girls prepare for the physical and psychological demands of life during the 1840s, and it would do the same for those in the 1930s. Exemplifying this phenomenon, in the opening pages of *Caddie Woodlawn*, the father of the title character recounts his decision to change childrearing tactics after the death of a previous daughter who had been weak and sickly:

> "Harriet," he had said, "I want you to let Caddie run wild with the boys. Don't keep her in the house learning to be a lady. I would rather see her learn to plow than make samplers, if she can get her health by doing so." (Brink 15)

Tomboyism enhances Caddie's health and strength while it simultaneously enhances the socio-economic position of her family. The tomboyish title character engages in an array of tasks that are financially lucrative or at least productive: she picks wild hazelnuts while out playing in the fields, gathers cranberries during an excursion with her brothers, plows the fields in the afternoons with the horse team, fixes clocks with her father in the winter, and goes hunting with her uncle during his visits. Through her efforts, the Woodlawn family has additional food to eat, better land to plant and a more pleasant home environment in which to live.

Wilder's *Little House* series took this phenomenon even further. In each novel, the tomboyish Laura receives extended instruction in an array of useful skills. In the first book, *Little House in the Big Woods* (1932), for instance, the narrator provides a lengthy account of the process by which the young girl and her father smoke deer meat:

> Standing on end in the yard was a tall length cut from the trunk of a big hollow tree. Pa had driven nails inside as far as he could reach from end to end. Then he stood it up, put a little roof over the top, and cut a little door on one side near the bottom. On the piece that he cut out he fastened leather hinges; then he fitted it into place, and that was the little door, with the bark still on it.
>
> After the deer meat had been salted several days, Pa cut a hole near the end of each piece and put a string through it. Laura watched him do this, and then she watched him hang the meat on the nails in the hollow log.

He reached up through the little door and hung meat on the nails, as far up as he could reach. Then he put a ladder against the log and climbed to the top, moved the roof to one side, and reached down inside to hang meat on those nails.

Then Pa put the roof back again, climbed down the ladder, and said to Laura:

'Run over to the chopping block and fetch me some of those green hickory chips—new, clean, white ones.'

So Laura ran to the block where Pa chopped wood, and filled her apron with the fresh, sweet-smelling chips.

Just inside the little door in the hollow log Pa built a fire of tiny bits of bark and moss, and he laid some of the chips very carefully.

Instead of burning quickly, the green chips smoldered and filled the hollow log with thick, choking smoke. Pa shut the door, and a little smoke squeezed through the crack around it and a little smoke came out through the roof, but most of it was shut in with the meat. (Wilder 6–9)

This step-by-step analysis reads more like an entry in a factual how-to manual than a passage in a fictional novel. Indeed, after such a long and detailed description, readers almost feel like they could perform the task themselves.

Throughout the remainder of *Little House in the Big Woods* and the rest of the *Little House* series, Wilder routinely interrupts the ostensible plot of her novel to discuss a domestic duty or outdoor task in detail. Lengthy passages in *Big Woods* explain how to churn butter, make cheese, tap syrup from trees, shock wheat, butcher a hog, forge bullets, make candy, smoke venison, weave straw hats and load a rifle. Especially against the backdrop of the hardscrabble conditions of the Great Depression, such information embodied not historical nostalgia but valuable and even necessary life skills for many contemporaneous girls.

Even Carolyn Keene's Nancy Drew can be connected with similar impulses in spite of the fact that the tomboyish title character hails from a family that is well-to-do. In nearly every book of the series, Nancy uses her tomboyish knack for solving mysteries to assist the physically ill, socially disenfranchised or economically impoverished. In *The Secret of the Old Clock* (1930), for instance, she finds a missing will that redirects a sizable inheritance from a group of heartless and already wealthy relatives to a set of kindly and impoverished ones. Likewise, in *The Hidden Staircase* (1930), the female sleuth helps a pair of poor elderly ladies rid their home of a greedy neighbor who was trying to frighten them into selling it. Finally, in *The Secret at Shadow Ranch* (1931), Nancy rescues a young girl who has been kidnapped because she is the heir to a sizable family fortune. As Deborah L. Siegel has written, the wealthy female sleuth's ability to "restore the financially downtrodden to their rightful state of ownership during a historical moment in which the financial order was radically and unexplainably upset" allowed her to become a heroine amidst one of the worst economic depressions in U.S. history (160).

In keeping with the Depression era emphasis on gender normativity, although children's books from the 1930s present tomboyish young girls as capable, productive and industrious, they also present them as both feminine and heterosexually appealing. Recalling antebellum literary and cultural heroine Capitola Black, Nancy Drew is the envy of both men and women. With her trusty roadster, cunning intelligence and sharp sense of intuition, no case is too difficult for her to crack. Even more importantly, Keene's novels emphasize that Nancy's tomboyish ability to solve mysteries does not threaten either patriarchal authority or her status as "a lady." Nancy only takes cases that her father does not have the time to investigate himself. Additionally, repeated passages call attention to her stylish outfits, shapely physique and comely, often bobbed, hair. In this way, while Nancy does not embody the image of a gender-bending female figure that was commonly associated with tomboys by the early twentieth century (this role is reserved for George Fayne), she does possess what Mildred Wirt Benson, the ghostwriter for the first twenty-three books of the original thirty-book series, described as "a tomboy spirit" (quoted in CBS, "Nancy Drew," par. 6). In both Bobbie Ann Mason's influential book about the girl sleuth and Meghan O'Rourke's recent *New Yorker* essay about her, they cite Nancy's adventurous personality, bold temperament and daring nature as largely responsible for the multi-generational appeal of the series.

In books like *Caddie Woodlawn* or the *Little House* series, which focus on younger girls whose gender-bending adolescent behaviors have the potential to encroach on patriarchal authority once they become adults, taming plays an important role. In Carol Ryrie Brink's novel, Caddie's father, who had formerly advocated tomboyism, later urges his daughter to abandon these traits:

> "I don't want you to be the silly, affected person with fine clothes and manners whom folks sometimes call a lady. No, that is not what I want for you, my little girl. I want you to be a woman with a wise and understanding heart, healthy in body and honest in mind. Do you think you would like to be growing up into that woman now? How about it, Caddie, have we run with the colts long enough?" (Brink 245)

Although this conversation initially causes the tomboyish young girl to cry, she quickly embraces her new role: "It was a responsibility, but, as Father spoke of it, it was a beautiful and precious one, and Caddie was ready to go and meet it" (246). The very next day, she forgoes joining her brothers in the barn and remains in the house to partake in more feminine domestic tasks. When her sister Clara raves about a new quilting pattern that she has learned, the now-reformed tomboy decides to try. As she remarks, "'I guess if I can mend clocks, I ought to be able to quilt'" (249). Reinforcing essentialist views of gender, the young girl possesses an innate talent for quilting: "By noon she was quite as good as Clara or Annabelle and so pleased with herself that she thought quilting one of the greatest sports in the world" (249).

A parallel conversion scene occurs in the sixth novel of the *Little House* series, *The Long Winter*. At the end of the previous book—*By the Shores of Silver Lake*—fourteen-year-old Laura was at the height of her tomboyish powers. As Ann Romines has written: "she feels newly large and powerful, ready to reject conventional myths" (39). In fact, when no men are available to help Pa with the haying, Laura is given permission to do so herself, and she capably performs this strenuous male work. If *By the Shores of Silver Lake* is a narrative celebrating Laura's tomboyish prowess, *The Long Winter* is one about the need for such behaviors to be tamed. During the novel's brief seventh-month time span, Laura is made vividly aware that she will be required to abandon her former tomboyish freedom, independence and autonomy as she inches closer to adulthood. First, when the active tomboy instinctively leaps up to catch a ball at school, the other children chastise her behavior: "A great shout went up from the other boys, "'Hey, . . . Girls don't play ball!'" (78). Laura, who was formerly so proud of her tomboyish ability to bale hay, now reflects: "She did not know why she had done such a thing and she was *ashamed, fearful of what these girls might think of her*" [my italics] (78). These lessons are amplified during the long and nearly lethal winter that forms the centerpiece of novel. With seven months of harsh blizzards that leave the Ingalls family without adequate food, heat or shelter, Laura is confined to the house and domestic duties. During this time, the young girl goes from being independent, adventurous and confident to being quiet, obedient and almost utterly dependent on men. In the words of Romines once again, "Laura's growing awareness of her own limits and duties as a woman brings new weight and sobriety to the *Little House* series" (36).

The racialization of white tomboys in previous literary works likewise permeated those from the 1930s. In *Caddie Woodlawn* and the *Little House* series, the gender-bending central characters are repeatedly seen as existing outside the confines of whiteness, since they exist outside the confines of white womanhood. But, one key difference emerged: whereas previous tomboyish characters had acquired these traits largely through African American sources, ones in children's literature did so via American Indian ones. In *Little House on the Prairie* (1935), the tomboyish central character receives the stern admonishment: "'Dear me, Laura, must you yell like an Indian? I declare,' Ma said, 'if you girls aren't getting to look like Indians! Can I never teach you to keep your sunbonnets on?'" (122). Although sometimes uttered by her older sister Mary or younger sister Grace instead of her mother, similar passages appear in every subsequent book of the series: *On the Banks of Plum Creek* (1937), *By the Shores of Silver Lake* (1939), *The Long Winter* (1940), *Little Town on the Prairie* (1941) and even *These Happy Golden Years* (1943), in which Laura leaves home to marry Almanzo. In many of these examples, the young girl seemingly invites the connection between her white tomboyism and American Indian tribalism through her curiosity about the Osage Indians. In an oft-discussed scene near the end of *Little House on the Prairie*, for instance, Laura sees an Indian papoose and—in an act that combines cross-cultural identification with white racist entitlement—begs her father to give it to her.[9] Significantly, this incident takes place after the Ingalls family has moved from the Wisconsin woods—where the presence of American Indians was omitted and denied—to "Indian Territory" where it is repeatedly acknowledged and vividly experienced. In this new geographic terrain and more intercultural context, Mrs. Ingalls becomes fixated on the racial status of her family in general and tomboyish daughter in particular. Thus, she begins a campaign to preserve Laura's whiteness.

A similar theme permeates *Caddie Woodlawn*. The title character's closest friend outside of her two brothers is not another rough-and-tumble girl or—echoing the pattern of countless other novels that feature tomboyish characters—a sissy boy. Instead, it is Indian John, the leader of the local tribe. Moreover, the traveling circuit rider says of the gender-bending title character in one of the opening pages of the novel: "'When are you going to begin making a young lady out of this wild Indian, Mrs. Woodlawn?'" (14). In doing so, he connects Caddie with a longstanding phenomenon in U.S. culture whereby rambunctious white children of either gender are accused of behaving "like a bunch of wild Indians."

While these examples form another instance of the way in which white female gender rebellion is filtered through nonwhite peoples and cultures, a crucial difference exists between them. Blacks and Indians do share status as nonwhite minority groups, but they possess conflicting cultural positions. As Rachel Adams has noted, "Any comparison of the two must be sensitive to the distinctive histories of these groups within the United States, their very different significance to American anthropologists,

---

9. Upon seeing the infant, Laura erupts: "'Pa, . . . get me that little Indian baby!'" (308). When her mother admonishes her, she repeats her request more desperately: "'Oh, I want it! I want it! . . . Please, Pa, please!'" (308). As the papoose disappears into the distance with its mother, Mrs. Ingalls asks why she wants the infant and Laura is unable to articulate the exact kinship she feels with the American Indians: "'Its eyes are so black,' Laura sobbed. She could not say what she meant" (309).

and the various ways in which they were exploited by interested parties" (*Sideshow* 43). One of the most notable—and, for the purposes of this project, perhaps most crucial—differences between African Americans and American Indians is their racial histories. Unlike blacks, who have always been marked as racially Other, indigenous tribal peoples were initially seen as white. As Rebecca Blevins Faery, Alden T. Vaughn, and most recently Nancy Shoemaker have written, when European explorers first landed in North America, they described American Indians as "very little different in color from Englishmen" (Faery 160). Although acknowledging that the continent's indigenous peoples had skin tones that were more "olive," "bronze" or "copper," white Western explorers also asserted that this difference arose not from biological difference, but from a combination of their cultural practices (namely applying stains and pigments to the skin) and their geographic environment (that is, prolonged exposure to the sun). As Captain John Smith said of tribal peoples near Jamestown, they are "a colour brown when they are of any age, *but they are born white*" [my emphasis] (quoted in Vaughn 925).

As relations between the white settlers and indigenous tribal peoples shifted from relatively peaceful to openly hostile, American Indians ceased to be viewed as racially similar and became Other. Although this change occurred at different times in different regions, both Rebecca Blevins Faery and Alden T. Vaughn note that it was widely in place by the middle of the eighteenth century. During the 1700s, tribal peoples went from being associated with whiteness to being linked to a myriad of different forms of nonwhiteness: from "copper" and "bronze" to "tawny" and "red." For these reasons, while it is worthwhile to note the racialization of white tomboyism via American Indian tribalism in children's literature, it necessitates a separate study. Especially given the central role that the nation's indigenous tribal peoples have played in the construction of U.S. political and cultural identity—serving for centuries as a powerful symbol of the nation—it is a distinct phenomenon.

This issue aside, the boom in tomboyish children's literature during the 1930s offered important life lessons for adolescent girls growing up amidst the trials of the Great Depression. Paradoxically, though, none of these books was set during the 1930s or addressed the hardships of this era directly. Instead, all were historical novels that retreated to the past in general and to the late nineteenth century, when tomboyism experienced its first literary and cultural heyday, in particular. In *Caddie Woodlawn* and the first book in the *Little House* series, for instance, the central characters live in Wisconsin during the 1860s and 1870s, respectively. Likewise, in the Newbery-award winning *Roller Skates*, the tomboyish central character Lucinda frolics in New York during the 1890s. Even Carolyn Keene's Nancy Drew mystery books—which are not commonly considered historical novels—can be classified in this way. With her bobbed hair and trusty roadster, Nancy Drew is patterned after the flapper, even though all of the narratives take place in the period following the 1920s.

It would not be until the following decade that another national crisis—the outbreak of the Second World War—would locate tomboyism firmly back in the present era. From the women who donned such "mannish" attire as coveralls and steel-toed boots for their work in civilian munitions factories to those who risked their lives on the front lines of battle serving the military forces abroad, the upheavals of the war would practically mandate that American women engage in some form of tomboyism. The following chapter examines the seemingly ubiquitous nature of gender-bending female figures in the mid 1940s and early 1950s and the complicated and often conflicting societal responses that were precipitated by them. In light of the increased wartime participation in this code of conduct, tomboys achieved both a number and a notoriety never seen before in American history. As William Chafe has asserted, the changes in female gender roles during the Second World War made this era "a watershed in the history of American women" (136). Chapter seven will reveal how the same was true for tomboyism. During the mid-1940s and early 1950s, this code of conduct acquired an array of characteristics that would endure long beyond V-E and V-J days.

International Tomboy: Around the World in 80 Dames! from Dazzle Publishers, 1958. As even the models on this cover suggest, the magazine employs a very liberal or loose definition of tomboyism that reveals Cold War desires to re-associate this code of conduct with both femininity and heterosexuality. *(Photograph by Lisa Marie O'Quinn. From the collection of Michelle Ann Abate.)*

Produce bag from Tom*Boy Grocery Store. The name and accompanying logo were trademarked in 1937 and registered to the Associated Grocers' Company of St. Louis, Missouri. One location of the store still exists in St. Louis, called Le Grand's Tom Boy. The original Tom*Boy sign adorns the exterior of the store, while many objects and artifacts from the Tom*Boy franchise are on display inside the shop. *(Photograph by Lisa Marie O'Quinn. From the collection of Michelle Ann Abate.)*

Various issues of the L'il Tomboy comic book series. Published by Charlton from 1956 to 1959, the comics feature a title character much like a female Dennis the Menace. Yet, with her heavily starched skirt, shoulder-length hair and lacy underpants, she exemplifies a more feminine form of tomboyism. *(Photograph by Olivia Paige Body. From the collection of Michelle Ann Abate.)*

Draft pull for Tomboy Red Lager beer which was brewed and bottled by Local Color Brewing Company in Novi, Michigan beginning in January 1998. The label image of a muscular young woman with a large wrench and equally large chest is reminiscent of the promotional poster for Herb Freed's 1985 film *Tomboy*. Both images present a feminine and (hetero)sexually alluring form of this code of conduct. *(Photograph by Lisa Marie O'Quinn. From the collection of Michelle Ann Abate.)*

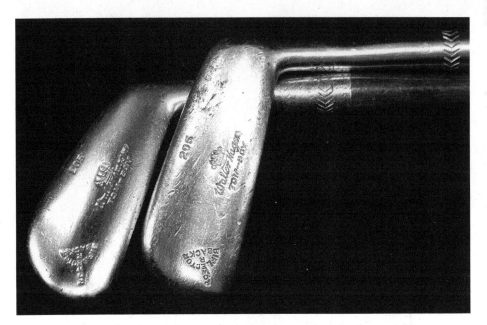

Tom-Boy Irons by Walter Hagen. The clubs were originally introduced in 1933 and sold through 1938, and were among the first sets designed for women. Note the baseball-like detail on the shaft. *(Photograph by Lisa Marie O'Quinn. From the collection of Michelle Ann Abate.)*

THE SECRET REMOTE CONTROL IS IN THE POCKET BOOK

Detail of lower left corner of box for the "Tumbling Tomboy" doll, revealing that the toy's "Secret Remote Control is in the Pocket Book." Although the doll may tumble, she is not too tomboyish for a purse. In fact, this feminine accessory ironically controls her tomboyish acrobatics. *(Photograph by Lisa Marie O'Quinn. From the collection of Michelle Ann Abate.)*

FACING PAGE: "Tumbling Tomboy" doll, manufactured by Remco Industries, circa 1969. Given the doll's form-fitting pants, sleeveless shirt and braided long hair, one wonders what is so tomboyish about her. Indeed, the toy is a good example of the expansion of tomboyism with the advent of second-wave feminism during the late 1960s and early 1970s, and also the way in which the new mass-marketed form of this code of conduct was feminized. *(Photograph by Lisa Marie O'Quinn. From the collection of Michelle Ann Abate.)*

Glass ashtray with the logo of the St. Louis-based Tom*Boy grocery store. Note the girl's stylized and almost minstrelized features. *(Photograph by Lisa Marie O'Quinn. From the collection of Michelle Ann Abate.)*

FACING PAGE: Cans for various flavors of Tomboy soda. Distributed by the Seven-Up Bottling Company of Indianapolis, Indiana. *(Photograph by Lisa Marie O'Quinn. From the collection of Michelle Ann Abate.)*

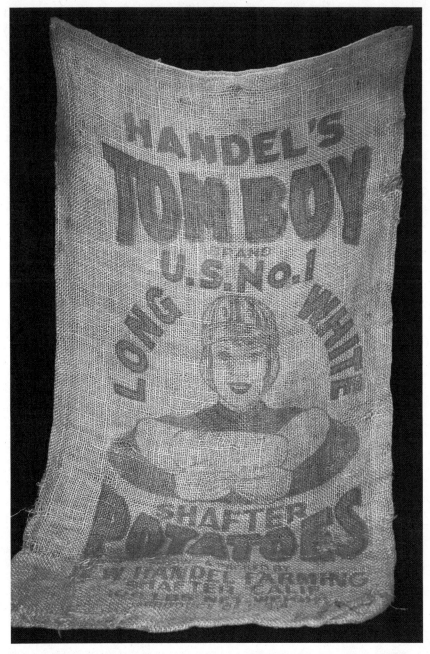

Burlap sack for "Tomboy" brand potatoes from F. W. Handel Farming in Shafter, California. The logo was initially created for, and registered to, the Richland Fruit Company in 1923 for a brand of their grapes, and was transferred to Handel's long white potatoes in 1935 or 1936. Tomboy potatoes were the company's top-selling national brand for decades. Handel Farms stopped making these burlap sacks in 1971. *(Photograph by Lisa Marie O'Quinn. From the collection of Michelle Ann Abate.)*

7

The Tomboy Turns Freakishly Queer and Queerly Freakish

Carson McCullers's The Member of the Wedding

E ven more than it did during the Civil War, tomboyism emerged as a valuable code of conduct during the Second World War. As William Chafe has written, the attack on Pearl Harbor and the deployment of millions of men for military positions overseas caused a labor crisis that "led to the employment of women on a scale previously unforeseen in U.S. history" (121). In order to keep the military forces supplied abroad and satisfy civilian needs at home, millions of women—young and old, married and single, black and white, urban and rural—joined the workforce between 1941 and 1945.

As a result, a paradigm shift occurred. Whereas the Depression era had insisted that a woman's place was as a feminine wife and mother in the home, the war years asserted that during this time of national crisis she served best as a tomboyish worker in a factory. As Karen Anderson has noted, "Government, industry, the media, women's clubs, and other voluntary organizations joined in urging women to do their patriotic duty by taking a job" (4). Together with obtaining employment in unprecedented numbers, they also held positions that were previously prohibited. While hundreds of thousands of women assumed stereotypically feminine jobs as secretaries and nurses, a significant number were employed in formerly male fields as welders, drill-press operators and, of course, riveters. Indeed, with a bandana tied around her head, a fierce look in her eye and a muscular arm punctuating her assertion "We Can Do It," wartime icon Rosie the Riveter is perhaps the most enduring image of the tomboyish toughness that was being asked of the nation's women.

The iconoclastic actions of adolescent girls and adult women during World War II went beyond simply helping to save the Union from the divisive forces of Southern secessionists, as it had done during the Civil War. Amidst this new global conflict, tomboyism had the potential to help save the world from the destructive powers of European fascists. As a result, whereas this code of conduct had previously formed a new national childrearing practice and form of U.S. female gender expression, it now represented a valuable means to protect Western democracy.

Echoing the cinematic legacy of the flapper, film played a major role in the dissemination of tomboyism during the mid-1940s and early 1950s. Whether produced as part of an official government propaganda campaign or as an independent effort to capture the spirit of the times, an array of movies featured strong, independent female figures. Many of these films, such as *Woman of the Year* (1942) and *Without Love* (1945), made a direct link between their tomboyish main characters and the war effort. Tess Harding in *Woman of the Year*, for instance, gives a rousing speech about women's wartime obligations: "Our place is no longer in the home. It is also in the first line of battle." Meanwhile, others, like *National Velvet* (1944) and *Home in Indiana* (1944), reflected the general tomboyish atmosphere permeating the era. Mirroring the many adolescent girls who were old enough to be aware of transformations to women's gender roles but too young to take a shift in a factory, these movies featured gender-bending figures who excelled at horse racing. In light of the sheer abundance of films that featured tomboys, Rebecca Bell-Metereau has argued that they constituted their own distinct cinematic category. Joining such popular genres as the screwball comedy, the movie musical and *film noir*, the "tomboy film" emerged as its own unique type during the mid 1940s and early 1950s (Bell-Metereau 96).

Rather than presenting tomboyish figures as anomalies brought about by wartime conditions, many films called attention to their historical antecedents. From the beloved Jo March in Mervyn LeRoy's *Little Women* (1949) and fifteenth-century martyr Joan of Arc in Victor Fleming's 1948 film by the same name to the celebrated markswoman Annie Oakley in George Sidney's *Annie Get Your Gun* (1950) and the rootin'-tootin' frontierswoman in David Butler's *Calamity Jane* (1953), the central characters in these movies demonstrated that gender-bending female figures have played an important role in Western nations for generations. Adolescent girls and young women during the war years may have been asked to engage in tomboyishness, but there had been many other times in history when they had been called upon to do the same.

Whether films featuring tomboys were set in the present day or the historical past, they existed at the heart of the era's entertainment industry.

Receiving both critical acclaim and box office success, these movies featured some of the most popular and well-respected actresses in the tomboy role. Screen icon Doris Day plays baseball-playing Majorie Winfield in *On Moonlight Bay* (1951) and the rootin'-tootin' title character in *Calamity Jane* (1953). A shortly shorn Ingrid Bergman stars as the cross-dressing Catholic messenger in *Joan of Arc* (1948). A young Elizabeth Taylor is steeplechase champion Velvet Brown in *National Velvet* (1945). Child star Margaret O'Brien occupies the role of the delightfully mischievous Tootie in *Meet Me in St. Louis* (1944), for which she received a special Academy Award. Finally, Hollywood legend June Allyson plays the beloved Jo March in Mervin LeRoy's *Little Women* (1949).

Of the numerous actresses who played tomboyish figures during the mid-1940s and early 1950s, however, perhaps none was more visible or, arguably, more influential than Katharine Hepburn. Infamous for her fierce independence, penchant to wear pants, and "eccentric brand of sassy feminism" (Sarris "Ain't" 450), her name become synonymous with a type of tough New England tomboyism both on and off the screen. Born in 1907 to progressive parents who were supporters of not only women's rights but the physical culture movement, the future actress was raised as a tomboy. Her 1991 autobiography, *Me: Stories of My Life*, contains repeated references to the premium that her suffragette mother and physician father placed on athleticism. With their constant encouragement to swim, dive, run, jump, swing, climb, sled and generally explore, Hepburn recalled, "They brought us up with a feeling of freedom. There were NO RULES. . . . Do it? Yes, do it! And tell me about it" [her emphasis] (Hepburn 27, 34).[1] This adventurous spirit and athletic interest persisted throughout her adult life. Although Hepburn had a special affection for golf, she confessed candidly in her autobiography, "Hell—I love all sports" (43). In fact, the actress proudly noted that even at the age of eighty she remained fit and limber. In a comment that recalls a remark by a fellow devotee of the physical culture movement, Chartlotte Perkins Gilman—who, incidentally, was a one-time visitor to the actress's childhood home—Hepburn boasted that she could not only do a handstand, but "stay up for a count of three or four minutes" (Hepburn 25).

---

1. Hepburn's interest in such gender-bending activities frequently made her wish that she had been born a boy and even inspired her to create a male alter ego. As she notes in her autobiography, "I was freckled—wore my hair like a boy's. In fact, with one brother Tom older and my two younger, Dick and Bob, being a girl was a torment. I'd always wanted to be a boy. Jimmy was my name, if you want to know" (Hepburn 39). Years later, while Hepburn was a student at Bryn Mawr, she continued this interest in co-opting masculine dress, habits and activities; the aspiring actress frequently played male roles in campus plays. Several pictures from Hepburn's college days in her autobiography show her dressed in men's attire and playing male parts (71).

Given Hepburn's tomboyish upbringing, it seems appropriate that one of her earliest screen appearances was as Jo March in George Cukor's *Little Women* (1933).[2] Although the actress couldn't have known it at the time, this role was prophetic, for she would go on to embody an array of gender-bending female figures in the years to come, including a pioneering female pilot in the film *Christopher Strong* (1933), an untamed mountain girl in *Spitfire* (1933), and a cross-dressing grifter in *Sylvia Scarlett* (1936). While the portrayal of autonomous and even iconoclastic women would remain a staple of Hepburn's career, they assumed an added significance during the war era. Labeled "box-office poison" and virtually banished from Hollywood during the late 1930s, the actress rekindled her career, at least in part, through her portrayal of tomboyish characters. For her wartime appearances as Tess Harding in *Woman of the Year* (1942) and Jamie Rowan in *Without Love* (1945), as well as her postwar roles as New York attorney Amanda Bonner in *Adam's Rib* (1948) and sports champion Pat in *Pat and Mike* (1952), Hepburn was lavished with both critical and popular acclaim. For these reasons, while film historians commonly refer to the 1940s and early 1950s as Hepburn's "MGM period," it could also be deemed her tomboy one.

The growing national importance of tomboys during the Second World War caused these figures to appear in both established and unexpected areas of society. As in previous historical eras, popular books aimed at a largely female readership became a common place to model this code of conduct and encourage young women to adopt it. Perhaps the most powerful among these was the Cherry Ames series. Written by Helen Wells and debuting in 1943 with the publication of *Cherry Ames, Student Nurse*, it chronicled the experiences of a young woman from Illinois who volunteers to serve as a field nurse for the United States Army. With her long hair, attractive dresses and conventional good looks, Cherry is more of a feminine tomboy than a gender-bending one. Nonetheless, akin to her counterparts during the Civil War, the young nurse's performance of an array of difficult and often even dangerous tasks causes her to be classified as a behavioral tomboy; she participates in this code of conduct as a result of cultural circumstance and wartime necessity if not innate inclination or genetic disposition. True to the propagandistic intent of the Cherry Ames books, the series made clear links between the title character's tomboyish

2. The same could be said for her early work in the theater. The stage performance which made Hepburn the talk of New York and also got her noticed by Hollywood directors was a 1932 Broadway production of *The Warrior's Husband*. Playing Antiope, the half-boy, half-woman, Hepburn recalled her dramatic, gender-bending stage entrance: "I leapt down the stairs, three or more steps at a time . . . rounded the corner . . . one jump for the last four stairs . . . threw the stag on the ground and landed on one knee, paying obeisance to Hippolyta, my sister, Queen of the Amazons. The audience, of course, burst into applause. They could hardly do anything else" (Hepburn 124).

war efforts and Allied victory, as in this passage from *Cherry Ames, Army Nurse* (1944): "As the war deepened, and there were more and greater battles, more and still more nurses were going to be needed . . . if thousands of men were to be healed and return to battle . . . *if we were to win*" [italics in original] (193).

The wartime need for tomboyish women was so great, in fact, that images of this code of conduct expanded to new cultural forms. In the burgeoning field of comic books, for example, a new superheroine called Wonder Woman made her debut. Conceived by psychologist William Moulton Marston, she appeared only one month after the attack on Pearl Harbor and was a direct product of wartime propaganda: Wonder Woman rescued an American pilot in the first issue, battled villains from Axis nations in many subsequent episodes, and always wore a costume that was red, white and blue. Acknowledging the influence that wartime changes to women's gender roles had on Wonder Woman's appearance and actions, in fact, creator Marston told his editor upon proposing the superheroine, "I fully believe that I am hitting a great movement now underway—the growth in the power of women, and I want you to let that theme alone—or drop the project" (quoted in Daniels 23).

While displays of tomboyish female strength and independence were a tremendous boon to the nation during the war, they were also a source of tremendous anxiety. As William H. Chafe has written, these actions had the potential to eradicate longstanding conceptions about women's proper place and natural abilities: "The fact that women were adept at using acety-lene torches as well as sewing machines called into question some of the more rigid distinctions that had been established between the type of labor performed by males and that by females" (124). Given the revolutionary potential of these revelations, the federal government and private industry soon agreed that wartime tomboyism needed to be carefully controlled and—in a word that would come to have profound significance during the Cold War era—culturally contained. As a consequence, wartime rhetoric soon began to stress that in the same way that it was women's patriotic duty to take a factory position, it was also their duty to "'not go berserk over the new opportunities for masculine clothing and mannish actions'" (Anderson 60). Radio announcements, posters and magazine ads presented more feminine reasons for women to join the war effort, urging them to "help," "care for" and "assist" the men overseas. Moreover, these venues encouraged female workers to maintain a "ladylike" appearance when they did so. Karen Anderson has documented that, as early as 1942, many facto-ries required women to wear not only safety goggles on the job, but lipstick as well. As a 1943 advertisement for Boeing Aircraft asserted: "Now, at day's end, her hands may be bruised, there's grease under her nails, her make-up is smudged and her curls are out of place. When she checks in the next morning at 6:30 a.m. her hands will be smooth, her nails polished, her makeup and curls in order, for Marguette is neither a drudge nor a slave but the heroine of a new order" (quoted in Anderson 61).

Analogous messages permeated the Cherry Ames series. In *Cherry Ames, Chief Nurse* (1944), the title character "made a rule that her nurses wear their feminine white uniforms on Sundays and curl their hair and powder their noses, come storms, heat or bombings—and it perked up everyone's morale" (69). Finally, even Wonder Woman largely conformed to stereotypical notions about women's appearance. As creator William Moulton Marston asserted, his new superheroine heeded societal desires for "'a character with the allure of an attractive woman but with the strength and power of a man. . . . I have given Wonder Woman this dominant force but have kept her loving, tender, maternal and feminine in every other way'" (quoted in Daniels 22). Such remarks prompted Charles Hannon to observe that the comic book's underlying message was that even though the nation's sisters, wives and mothers were being called upon to perform unconventional work during wartime, "that is no excuse for a woman to neglect her femininity" (110).

Closely related to the prerogative that women engage in more feminine forms of tomboyism was the one that their gender-bending behavior was a temporary condition of the war effort. This code of conduct was necessary during this time of national crisis, but it would not be a permanent identity. As a result, nearly all of the books and films released during this era emphasize prevailing beliefs in the situational nature of tomboyism and the accompanying importance of taming. In Clarence Brown's *National Velvet* (1944), for example, Mrs. Brown may allow her twelve-year-old daughter to enter her horse in England's most prestigious race, but she makes it clear that such tomboyish endeavors are temporary and circumstantial:

> I believe that everyone should have a chance at a breathtaking piece of folly. . . . Win or lose, it's all the same, it's how you take it that counts. It's knowing when to let go. Knowing when it's time to go on to the next thing. Things become suitable at the time, Velvet. Enjoy each thing and then forget it and go on to the next.

Such statements are even more surprising given Mrs. Brown's history. In one of the opening scenes of the film, viewers learn that Velvet's mother was the first woman to swim the English Channel.[3] In spite of Mrs. Brown's historic achievement, she still considers such tomboyish feats the product of a specific time and place rather than a lifelong mode of behavior. Connecting her accomplishment with her daughter's own tomboyish dream,

3. This real-life feat was accomplished by American Gertrude Ederle on August 6th, 1926. Ederle not only swam across the Channel safely, but she beat the best men's time for doing so by a full two hours.

she explains to Velvet: "I was twenty when they said that a woman couldn't swim the Channel. You're twelve. You think your horse can win the Grand National. Your dream has come early, but remember, Velvet, it will have to last you for the rest of your life."

Recalling the antebellum origins of tomboyism as a preparatory stage for marriage and motherhood—along with societal fears about lesbianism—one of the primary reasons that tomboyish cinematic figures abandoned their iconoclastic ways was the affections of a man. In *Home in Indiana* (1944), for example, harness racer Charlotte Bruce forgoes her gender-bending ways so that neighbor Sparke Thornton will see her as a love interest rather than a training buddy. Likewise, in *Woman of the Year* (1942), Tess Harding is so desperate to keep her husband that she offers to abandon her successful career and become a homemaker.

While the heteronormative purpose for tomboy taming remained the same, the rate at which this event was expected to occur was radically different. In previous historical eras, the process by which gender-bending female figures sloughed off their iconoclastic ways was slow and gradual, constituting the bulk of the plot in books like *Little Women* and *What Katy Did*. However, echoing wartime beliefs that females would abandon their tomboyish ways and return to more traditional gender roles the moment that hostilities ended, the process became sudden, abrupt and immediate. Roy Del Ruth's *On Moonlight Bay* (1951) provides a vivid example of this phenomenon. Set at the start of the First World War but clearly speaking to the gender-bending women who had just emerged from the Second, the film depicts the rapid transformation of tomboy Marjorie Winfield. Wearing a baseball jersey and helping the movers carry heavy furniture in the opening scene, the young woman suddenly and completely abandons these behaviors the moment that she sees new neighbor and future beau William Sherman. Asked out on a date by the college boy, she gleefully casts off her baseball jersey for what her mother says is her first party dress. Then, when the two kiss that evening, Marjorie knocks her baseball mitt and ball off a side table in an act that clearly symbolizes the abandonment of her tomboyish ways.[4]

---

4. A similar observation could be made about *Home in Indiana*. During one brief montage scene, Charlotte Bruce transforms from a rough-and-tumble harness racer who wears pants and delights in "besting boys" to a feminine, reserved and even passive young woman who is desperate to please her man. Echoing the belief that outward changes signal inward ones, Charlotte becomes progressively more feminine in each scene of the sequence. First, the young woman abandons her jeans for slacks. Then, she trades her slacks for skirts. Next, she swaps her skirts for dresses, and finally she abandons her dresses for a formal ball gown. By the end of the film, the once-gender-bending girl has lost all vestiges of tomboyism. Formerly strong-willed and opinionated, Charlotte is now demure and acquiescent. When her husband-to-be describes his plans for their future, her only response is the emotionless, "If you say so, Sparke."

Reinforcing this message, historical films like *Annie Get Your Gun* demonstrated that while strong, independent women have been an important part of the United States for generations, they also eventually sloughed off their tomboyish ways and embraced more normative identities. Rather than presenting Annie Oakley as an iconoclastic woman who expanded female gender roles, George Sidney's movie musical presents her as a traditional woman who actually conformed to stereotypical notions of them. The title character becomes so enamored with fellow sharpshooter Frank Butler that she is willing to become—as the title of one of her most famous musical numbers indicates—"Second Best" in order to keep him. After being reminded of the message of Annie's opening song, "You can't get a man with a gun," she decides to deliberately lose a shooting match to Butler so that she can successfully win him as a husband. Interestingly, although the 1950 film claims to bring the story of this legendary real-life markswoman to the silver screen, Shirl Kasper asserts that there is no historical basis for this event. As friends and colleagues said of the real Frank Butler, "The more applause Annie received, the happier Frank seemed to be, and the harder he worked to make a success of her act" (Kasper 77). Such discrepancies aver Rebecca Bell-Metereau's assertion in *Hollywood Androgyny* that historical films say more about the era in which they are made and released than the one they are purporting to depict (73).

Carson McCullers and the "Frankie Addams Phenomenon"

In the same way Hollywood films like *Annie Get Your Gun*, comic books like *Wonder Woman*, and series books like *Cherry Ames* formed important sites for the dissemination of tomboyism during the Second World War, so too did the fiction of Carson McCullers. Born Lula Carson Smith in Columbus, Georgia, in 1917, the future author repudiated the model of the Southern belle and instead tramped through the woods, rode horses, and climbed trees. As she later boasted, "'I was the best roller-skater for all the blocks around. . . . I was always coming home with scabbed knees or hurt arms'" (Savigneau 2). McCullers's tomboyish behavior was matched by her equally tomboyish appearance. Always longing to stand out from the crowd, she refused to conform to feminine conventions of dress. As biographer Virginia Spencer Carr noted, she cut her hair short and "wore dirty tennis shoes or brown Girl Scout Oxfords when the other girls were wearing hose and shoes with dainty heels" (29).

The tomboyish atmosphere during the war years allowed McCullers to expand on these traits. Although chronic ill health (exacerbated by chronic drinking) prevented her from engaging in much physical activity, it did not impede her from cultivating a gender-bending appearance. Upon meeting the parents of her future husband, Reeves McCullers, for instance, the bride-to-be stunned them with her unconventional attire. In the words of Virginia Spencer Carr, "They had never seen anything like the white tailored blouse with its elaborate embroidering on the long sleeves and the front of the bodice, which Carson wore with a man's tailored coat" (77). Several years later, while at Yaddo artists' colony, McCullers shocked fellow writers with her masculine attire. Given the author's penchant for men's attire coupled with her boyish figure, both Anais Nin in 1943 and psychologist Dr. Mary Mercer in 1953 later mistook her for a young man. As Nin wrote in her journal, "I saw a girl so tall and so lanky that I first thought it was a boy. Her hair was short, she wore a cyclist's cap, tennis shoes and pants" (quoted in Savigneau 73).

McCullers was as affected by the war as by the changes that it brought to female gender roles. As biographer Virginia Spencer Carr has written, the author and her husband Reeves were horrified when Hitler marched into Vienna and then invaded Poland. When France and Britain declared war against the Nazis, "Carson believed her country to be criminally negligent and immoral for not getting involved directly" (Carr 84). The newlyweds spoke out passionately about the events in Europe, and even considered adopting a refugee child (Carr 84). While the couple's sudden divorce in 1941 derailed this plan, they remained heavily involved in the war effort. Shortly after the attack on Pearl Harbor, Reeves, who had a successful career in the army prior to their marriage, reenlisted. With his previous military service, he was accepted into the elite corps of Army Rangers. Serving with the Second Battalion for the duration of the conflict, Reeves was part of the landing at Omaha and saw fighting throughout Europe. Wounded three times before being discharged in February 1945, he received multiple medals and commendations, including the Purple Heart (Carr 243).

Although McCullers was legally divorced from Reeves at the time, the two stayed in close contact. During her leisure hours, she read books on battle tactics, scanned newspapers for information about what was happening in Europe, and listened incessantly to radio programs for news about local soldiers who had been killed or were missing in action. Eager to do her part, McCullers volunteered to be a war correspondent but was turned down because of her ill health. Unable to participate in the war effort from abroad, she did so from home. In an April 1943 issue of *Mademoiselle*, McCullers published the tender personal essay "Love's Not Time's Fool" about the hardships of a wife whose husband is fighting overseas. Although Carson and Reeves remained separated, she nonetheless signed the piece "From a War Wife." The author may not have known it at the time, but the byline proved prophetic. Soon after Reeves returned from Europe, the two joined millions of other couples in what would become one of the biggest marriage booms in the nation's history and remarried.

McCullers's involvement with the Second World War and her participation in female gender iconoclasm merged in her fiction. Doing some of
her best writing during the war years, the Southern-born author released
multiple texts that showcased tomboyish figures as their main characters:
Mick Kelly in her first published novel *The Heart is a Lonely Hunter*
(1940), Amelia Evans in her gothic novella *The Ballad of the Sad Café*
(1943) and Frankie Addams in what is perhaps her most famous tomboy
text, *The Member of the Wedding*. In fact, with her crew cut, boy's shorts
and BVD t-shirt, twelve-year-old Frankie is arguably the most popular
literary tomboy after Jo March. At least in part because of the appeal of
this gender-bending character, *The Member of the Wedding* was critically
acclaimed and commercially successful upon its release in 1946. Moreover, the novel went on to be adapted as an award-winning Broadway play
in 1950 and then a popular motion picture in 1952. As a result, Klaus
Lubbers has observed, "For the general reading public, the name of Carson
McCullers has come to be associated with Frankie Addams" (33).

The Member of the Wedding does more than simply embed elements
of wartime tomboyism; it discusses the conflict directly. Written over a
five-year period that overlapped exactly with the U.S. involvement in the
war, the book's plot, setting and characters are inextricably connected
with it. Biographer Virginia Spencer Carr has written that broadcasts
of the war news played incessantly in the background while McCullers
was composing the narrative, and they do so in the book as well. In the
kitchen where Frankie, her six-year-old cousin John Henry and black
cook Berenice Sadie Brown spend their days, a radio with news about
the battle is on constantly: "[A] war voice crossed with the gabble of an
advertiser. . . . The radio had stayed on all the summer long" (8). Rather
than giving a calendar date for the action of the novel, Frankie uses the
timetable created by the war effort: "It was the summer when Patton was
chasing the Germans across France" (20). Like McCullers herself, the
tomboyish main character is personally affected by the war. Frankie's
brother is a corporal in the army and, echoing the desire many of the
nation's women, she wishes to join the fight. "She wanted to be a boy and
go to war as a Marine. She thought about flying aeroplanes and winning
gold medals for bravery" (21).

Focusing on this well-known tomboy text along with its World War II
context, this chapter explores the way in which the seemingly normal
and common phenomenon of tomboyism came to be cast as abnormal
and bizarre. Although this code of conduct permeated nearly all facets of
American literature and culture during the Second World War, anxiety
about its increasing power and presence caused it to be characterized as
unnatural and even abnormal. In Clarence Brown's *Velvet Brown*, for
example, the title character is presented as an oddity or anomaly after
winning the Grand National. In a comment that recalls the spectatorship

at circus sideshows, Velvet's father remarks, "When people see something new, something unusual, it is only natural that they want to stare."[5]

George Cukor's *Pat and Mike* takes such sentiments one step further. Rather than describing the championship-winning title character as an unusual figure, it characterizes her as a freakish one. As manager Mike Conovan explains to Pat's fiancé, "You see, athletes, they ain't like us, they're like what you call freaks. No one understands them. They can't even understand . . . themselves." While the accomplishments of Pat and Velvet are admittedly out of the ordinary, their achievements are not presented in a positive light as "exceptional" or "extraordinary." Instead, these films use derogatory terms like "oddity" and even "freak."

Carson McCullers did not simply have a passing interest in human freaks and oddities; as critics and biographers have frequently noted, they constituted a central preoccupation of her life and work. Biographer Virginia Spencer Carr has discussed how "As a ten year old in the deep South in 1927, Lula Carson Smith viewed . . . with terror and fascination the midway freaks who made their fall trek to her hometown, Columbus, Georgia" (1). In a compelling irony, more than simply staring at freakish figures, she was also categorized as one by neighbors and classmates. Because of her eccentric appearance and unusual habits, young girls would gather in "little clumps of femininity" and call the future author "freakish looking" (Carr 30–31).

McCullers' fascination with human oddities carried over into her adult life. The author spent hours poring over George Davis's collection of freak photographs while living in Brooklyn in the early 1940s, and she also frequently incorporated freakish figures into her writing. From a deaf-mute who urinates on buildings and is eventually sent to a sanitarium in *The Heart is a Lonely Hunter* to a woman who is six feet tall and in love with a hunchback dwarf in *The Ballad of the Sad Café*, most of her characters contain a physical or psychological trait that deems them abnormal. In fact, given the sheer number of unusual individuals, one critic remarked that in McCullers's narratives "not even the horse is normal" (Evans *Carson* 80).

This section takes up the long-familiar subject of freaks and oddities in the fiction of Carson McCullers and pushes it in a new direction by refracting it through the lens of wartime tomboyism. Throughout *The Member of the Wedding*, tomboy Frankie Addams becomes a symbol of the gendered, raced and sexualized anxieties that have emerged from the flux and instability of the war years. Given the massive transformations not only to female gender roles but also to national attitudes about race and

5. A similar phenomenon emerges in George Sidney's *Annie Get Your Gun*. When Annie Oakley bests championship marksman Frank Butler in a shooting contest, the manager for Buffalo Bill's Wild West Show immediately comments on her commercial appeal: "Yes, she'd be a novelty."

sexuality, carnal changes during the mid 1940s started to appear carnivalesque. Wartime tomboys were as much a product of these alterations as a reflection of them. Accordingly, McCullers's gender-bending female character is associated with an unusual gender, sexual and racial identity. In *The Member of the Wedding*, Frankie Addams demonstrates how the wartime tomboy turned freakishly queer and queerly freakish.

"Individuation Running Rampant Into Chaos": The Wartime Tomboy as Sideshow Freak

Although wartime changes to women's gender roles are perhaps the most oft-discussed aspects of the upheavals of the Second World War, they were not the only ones. In the same way that the societal status of middle- and upper-class white women changed during this time, so did that of two other minority groups: Africans Americans and gays and lesbians.

While the Second World War and its immediate aftermath was a time of tremendous hardship for black Americans—from the enforced segregation of the nation's armed forces to the institutionalized racism that initially forbade blacks from obtaining jobs in war factories—it was also a time of tremendous gains. On the battlefront, African Americans lobbied successfully for the creation of many new all-black military forces. Both the first squadron of black pilots—the Tuskegee Airmen—and the first black overseas unit of the Women's Army Corps—the historic 6888th—were founded during the Second World War. Likewise, on the homefront, African Americans won the right to obtain jobs along with union memberships in many formerly all-white workplaces when President Roosevelt issued Executive Order 8802: "There shall be no discrimination in the employment of workers in the defense industries or Government because of race, creed, color, or national origin."[6] In the wake of this directive, over one million blacks entered the war factories and "the wages of black families increased from 40 percent to 60 percent of that of white families" (Takaki 43). Taken collectively, these events made the Second World War, as the title of Ronald Takaki's recent history asserts, a "double victory" for African Americans. In helping to defeat European fascism, they also made major strides in combating U.S. racism.

The advances gained by African Americans during the Second World War were mirrored in many ways by homosexuals. As historians such as Lillian Faderman and Allan Bérubé have written, the conflict was a turning point for both the societal visibility and political power of gay men and lesbians in the United States. Although the government's official policy was to exclude

---

6. See Franklin D. Roosevelt, Executive Order 8802, in *The Federal Register*, vol. 6 (July 27, 1941).

homosexuals from military service, their unofficial one was increased tolerance of them. During this time of national crisis, when the nation needed
the help of every citizen, it could ill afford to turn away anyone who was
willing to serve in uniform, especially if the only impediment to inscrip-
tion was sexual orientation. In a powerful example of this phenomenon,
Faderman relays the experience of a WAC sergeant who was ordered by
General Eisenhower to expel all the lesbians in her unit. After she informed
the future U.S. president that his directive would seriously deplete the WAC
unit—including the sergeant herself—he responded with astounding new
instructions: "Forget the order" (Faderman "Odd Girls" 118).

This atmosphere of increased tolerance extended to gays and lesbians
in civilian life. Drawn, like many of their heterosexual counterparts, to the
lucrative jobs in urban munitions factories, homosexual men and women
began to gather in cities. Freed from their former sense of isolation, gay
men and lesbians developed a newfound identity, common culture and
even collective strength. Indeed, as Allan Bérubé has written, "They ate
meals together, went out to the gay bars together, and slept on each other's
sofas when it was too late or too expensive to take the subway home"
(Coming 246).

As with transformations in white women's gender roles, changes in the
status of African Americans and gays and lesbians benefited the war effort
while they threatened the status quo. The upheavals of the Second World
War were allowing formerly subordinated groups to gain cultural power.
Fears that these temporary changes during wartime would become permanent in peacetime sparked a backlash. Neil Wynn has written that some
factory executives defied Roosevelt's Executive Order by barring blacks
from holding jobs or joining unions. Meanwhile, white workers often organized protests or went on strike when compelled to work alongside African
Americans. As early as the spring of 1942, violent and often deadly race
riots erupted in cities around the nation (Wynn 68–73).

Gay men and lesbians fared little better. In spite of the increased tolerance for homosexuals in the armed forces, some received dishonorable
"blue discharges" if their sexual orientation became "too public" (Bérubé
Coming 246–249). Meanwhile, on the homefront, many were sent for
psychiatric treatment, subjected to shock therapy and even institutionalized when friends, co-workers or family members discovered their homosexuality and sought to "cure" them.

Although changes to the racial status of African Americans, the sexual
standing of gays and lesbians and the gender roles of white women are
commonly seen as three disparate entities during the Second World War,
they were intimately connected. In the minds of many citizens, millions of
men had been sent overseas to protect American culture and customs, but
this very way of life seemed to be crumbling as a result of the upheavals
brought about by the conflict.

The Member of the Wedding was written and released in the midst of this crisis. While critics have commonly seen the narrative's unusual characters as a commentary on the alienation and loneliness of the human condition,[7] a more material and contemporaneous explanation is possible. Frankie's freakishly queer and queerly freakish characteristics could be seen as emerging from the era's growing anxiety about the seemingly bizarre changes taking place in the nation's gender, sexual and racial codes. As Rosemarie Garland Thomson has written about the cultural logic underpinning sideshow spectacles in the United States, "Freaks embodied the threat of individuation running rampant into chaos" (*Extraordinary* 66). Whether their freakishness arose from a congenital condition (such as albinism or vitiligo) or a learned skill (like sword swallowing or snake charming), sideshow attractions became emblems of what happens when the human body experiences a loss of control or lack of order (Thomson *Extraordinary* 66).

The mid-1940s, when *The Member of the Wedding* was published, marked the decline of literal sideshows in the United States.[8] However, the nation was experiencing a heightened sense of figurative chaos. As Frankie Addams observes, the fighting across Europe had put everything in flux: "She thought of the world as huge and cracked and loose and turning a thousand miles an hour. The geography book at school was out of date; the countries of the world had changed" (McCullers *Member* 20). Coupled with shifting geo-political boundaries, the upheavals of the war were causing traditional notions about gender, race and sexuality to unravel. From women taking traditionally male jobs in factories, blacks making palpable progress in their quest for inclusion in white American society, and gay men and lesbians becoming valued members of military and civilian life, the world seemed—to evoke a phrase from a previous chapter—topsy-turvy. In this environment of increasing entropy, freakishness appeared to be taking hold. For many, it seemed only a matter of time before changes to the nation's gender, sexual and racial categories spun completely out of control and, in the words of Rosemarie Garland Thomson once again, there was "individuation running rampant into chaos."

---

7. For examples of this argument, see especially Virginia Spencer Carr's *Understanding Carson McCullers* (Columbia: University of South Carolina, 1990), Klaus Lubber's "The Necessary Order: A Study of Theme and Structure in Carson McCullers's Fiction" (in *Carson McCullers*, Ed. Harold Bloom, New York: Chelsea House, 1986: 33–52) and Ihan Hasaan's *Contemporary American Literature, 1945–1972* (New York: Frederick Ungar, 1973).

8. For more on the origins, heyday and decline of sideshows in the United States, see Robert Bogdan's *Freak Show: Presenting Human Oddities for Amusement and Profit* (Chicago: U of Chicago, 1988) and Rachel Adams's *Sideshow, U. S. A.: Freaks and the American Cultural Imagination* (Chicago: U of Chicago, 2001).

The tomboy had long existed on the border between masculinity and femininity, heterosexuality and homosexuality, whiteness and blackness. Thus, she became an apt symbol for the era's gendered, raced and sexualized concerns about the crumbling wartime distinctions between normality and abnormality, ordinariness and freakishness, moderation and excess. Previous discussions of Frankie Addams have cast her as a freak in terms of her unusual gender identity (as a boyish girl) and sexual interest (longing to merge with a married couple). But, an awareness of the hidden cultural history of tomboyism allows a new category to be added: racial difference. As with the gender-bending figures spotlighted in previous chapters, Frankie is an ostensibly Caucasian character who is associated with various forms of ambiguous nonwhiteness. From her "dark white" skin tone to her strong identificatory link with nonwhite peoples and cultures, Frankie defies notions of white racial "normalcy" as much as gender and sexual "normativity." For these reasons, the display of human oddities may have formerly been confined to the fringes of society via the sideshow stage, but *The Member of the Wedding* warns that such traits were now becoming part of mainstream American culture. In McCullers' 1946 novel, wartime tomboy Frankie Addams becomes a twentieth-century reconfiguration of the nineteenth-century freak.

The tomboyish main character in *The Member of the Wedding* is described as unnatural, unusual and even bizarre from the first time readers are introduced to her. Echoing Leslie Fiedler's influential argument that freaks function as outer physical manifestations of our inner psychological fears and desires, the twelve-year-old character "was afraid of all the Freaks, for it seemed to her that they had looked at her in a secret way and tried to connect their eyes with hers, as though to say: we know you" (18). In the wake of a summer growth spurt, the youth "was grown so tall that she was almost a big freak" (2). Frankie estimates that if she continues to grow at this rate she will be over nine feet tall by the time she is an adult. In a remark that belies the young girl's highly gendered notion of normalcy and abnormalcy, she muses, "And what would be a lady who is over nine feet tall? A Freak." (16–17).

Although all of the freaks at the Chattahoochee Exposition give Frankie a sense of the uncanny, her tomboyish gender identity causes her to have a special attraction to a particular one of them: the Half-Man Half-Woman. While Frankie makes passing reference to the other human oddities, she pauses to describe this figure in detail:

The last booth was always very crowded, for it was the booth of the Half-Man Half-Woman, a morphodite and a miracle of science. This Freak was divided completely in half—the left side was a man and the right side a woman. The costume on the left was a leopard skin and on the right side a brassiere and a spangled skirt. Half the face was dark bearded and the other half bright glazed with paint. (18)

Later in the novel, when Frankie models the dress she has purchased for her brother's wedding, her resemblance to this figure increases. Although Berenice never explicitly compares Frankie to the Half-Man Half-Woman, she calls attention to her divided gender appearance: "'You had all your hair shaved off like a convict, and now you tie a silver ribbon around this head without any hair. It just looks peculiar. . . . Here, you got on this grown woman's evening dress. Orange satin. And that brown crust on your elbows. The two things just don't mix'" (84).

Closely related to the gender freakishness of Frankie Addams is her anomalous sexual identity. The young girl exists outside the realm of heter-onormativity to become part of the emerging taxonomy of the queer. As the *Oxford English Dictionary* notes, the term "queer" first emerged in the sixteenth century as an adjective to refer to entities or events that were "Strange, odd, peculiar, eccentric" ("queer" 1014). In light of the growing homosexual community and its growing visibility in the United States, the term acquired a more particularized meaning during the 1920s. Together with referring to any strange or unusual behavior, it came to denote a specific type: nonheteronormative sexual activity, especially male homo-sexuality. As a result, as Rachel Adams has discussed, the categories of the queer and the freak overlapped. A 1936 article in *Current Psychology and Psychoanalysis*, for instance, objected to scientific pronouncements that Greenwich Village had been transformed into "a palace of 'Freak Exhibits'" since becoming home to a burgeoning homosexual community (quoted in Spencer 340). Likewise, Dr. George Henry in the glossary to his 1941 volume *Sex Variants* offered the following two-word definition of the 'freak': "a homosexual" (quoted in Katz *Gay/Lesbian* 577).

Carson McCullers was intimately connected with the co-joined discourse of the freak and the queer. As biographers Virginia Spencer Carr and Josyane Savigneau note, classmates called young Lula Carson Smith a "queer duck" and "a queer young girl who looked like a boy" (Carr 91; Savigneau 28). Years later, the famous February House in Brooklyn where the author lived in the early 1940s was, in the words of Virginia Spencer Carr, a "queer aggregate of artists" (117). Residents at the abode included stripper Gypsy Lee Rose and gay author W. H. Auden.

McCullers did more than simply associate with men and women who existed outside the realm of heteronormativity; she could also be counted among them. Although commonly remembered as a heterosexual writer because of her longstanding relationship with Reeves McCullers, she engaged in an array of emotional and erotic attachments that could be deemed "queer." First, the author had a series of infatuations with women, including a devastating crush on film star Greta Garbo (at whose hotel room door she showed up one night), an intense infatuation with fellow author Katherine Anne Porter, an obsession with a New York ballerina, and a passionate entanglement with Annemarie Clarac-Schwartzenbach.[9] In a decidedly queer detail, however, the seemingly highly sexual McCullers was paradoxically quite asexual. As Carr has written, when she asked someone to go to bed with her, she was more often looking for a sleeping partner than a sexual one (398). Moreover, when McCullers was sexually active, it was not as part of a traditional couple. Instead, the author preferred triangulated relationships. The most famous and oft-cited among these was with composer David Diamond. During the early 1940s, both Carson and Reeves were sexually involved with the talented young composer (see Carr 148–150). As even this brief discussion indicates, the terms "heterosexual," "homosexual" and "bisexual" do not accurately characterize Carson McCullers's sexual identity. Given the diverse range of her erotic relationships, the multivalent classification "queer" is more accurate.

The Member of the Wedding was written during this period when the author was both living amidst the "queer aggregate of artists" and engaging in the "queer" love triangle with David Diamond. Not surprisingly, it presents an array of queer emotional and erotic relationships. Coupled with such oft-mentioned details as John Henry's queer proclivity for cross-dressing and Berenice's story about the queer desires of transsexual Lily Mae Jenkins, the tomboyish main character possesses an array of characteristics that can also be viewed through this rubric. Combining the wartime rise in marriage rates with McCullers's own preference for triangulated relationships, the novel documents—as its title suggests—Frankie's interest in becoming a member of her brother's wedding. After a summer of feeling "left out of everything" (21), the adolescent girl had an epiphany: "She loved her brother and the bride and she was a member of the wedding. The three of them would go into the world and they would always be together" (43). Feeling an intense connection with the bridal couple, the twelve-year-old decides, "'We'll go to every place together. It's like I've known it all my life, that I belong to be with them. I love the two of them so much" (43). Identifying the couple as the "we of me," Frankie imagines joining her brother and soon-to-be sister-in-law in the ceremony, on their honeymoon, and in their daily lives thereafter. As neither a homosexual nor entirely heterosexual desire but something that exists on the interstice between the two, Frankie's wish can best be characterized as queer. Indeed, as Elizabeth Freeman has written of the arrangement, "[W]hat does it mean to be in love not with a person, but with a couple, with the scene

9. For more information on Carson McCullers's same-sex crushes and romances, see Virginia Spencer Carr's biography, *The Lonely Hunter* (Garden City, NJ: Doubleday & Co., 1975).

of couplehood and its pageantry? What does it mean to want to interrupt this scene without simply annihilating it?" (112). Both in the context of wartime emphasis on heteronormativity and especially given that one of the members of the wedding couple is her blood relative, Frankie's desire is decidedly non-normative.

The concept of queerness, however, is not externally imposed on *The Member of the Wedding*; as Rachel Adams has written, the word itself appears an "improbably frequent" number of times in the narrative ("Mixture" 561). The walls of the kitchen where the tomboyish girl, her cousin John Henry and cook Berenice spend the bulk of their time, for instance, are covered with "queer child drawings" (McCullers *Member* 4). Similarly, when Frankie is alone at night, she reports feeling "a queer tightness in her chest" (22). Finally, with the war raging across Europe, she remarks that the past few months have seemed like "a long queer season" (20). More sexually charged usages are also present. Frankie refers to her erotic experiments with neighbor Barney MacKean as a "queer sin" (23). Likewise, her sexual experience with the drunken sailor in the hotel room left her "feeling a little queer" (68).

Pushing past views of Frankie as a gender and sexual freak because of her tomboyish behavior and "queer" erotic attachments, she possesses a third locus of enfreakment: racial difference. The *Oxford English Dictionary* reveals that the term "freak" was originally defined as "to fleck or streak with color . . . to variegate" ("freak" 156). Anticipating associations of whiteness with "normality" and blackness with difference, the word "freak" emerged in the seventeenth century to denote a heterogeneous coloration. Reflecting this use of the term, the ostensibly Caucasian Frankie is also cast as bizarre because she possesses various nonwhite characteristics. Coupled with the young girl's face being described as a "dark ugly mug" (37), Thadious M. Davis notes that her most powerful identificatory moments are with nonwhite characters ("Erasing" 208). In one of the opening sequences of the novel, for instance, Frankie experiences a profound psychic connection with an elderly black man. In language that echoes the young girl's kinship with the freaks at the Chattahoochee Exposition, Frankie "looked at him, he looked at her, and to the outward appearance that was all. But in that glance, [she] felt between his eyes and her own eyes a new unnamable connection, as though they were known to each other" (50). The young girl shares a similar link with Berenice. When the black cook discusses how a close friend "'feel like he just can't breath no more. He feel like he got to break something or break himself'" (114), the twelve-year-old tomboy expresses a parallel sentiment: "'Sometimes I feel like I want to break something too. I feel like I could just tear up the whole town'" (114).

At times, Frankie's strong identificatory link with different peoples and cultures precipitates a longing for a biological bond with them. In a desire to help with the war effort, for example, "She decided to donate blood to the Red Cross; she wanted to donate a quart a week and her blood would be in the veins of Australians and Fighting French and Chinese, all over the whole world, and *it would be as though she were close kin to all of these people*" [italics mine] (21). In keeping with cultural logic of the one-drop rule, Frankie believes that mixing her blood with men and women around the world would give her a familial bond with them.[10] Recalling the etymological origins of the term "freak," Frankie wants her bloodline to be racially flecked and variegated.

Lusus Naturae: Tomboyish Wartime Freakishness as an Omen for Postwar Normalcy

Given the numerous forms of freakishness operating in *The Member of the Wedding*, critics such as Leslie Fiedler, Barbara A. White and most recently Rachel Adams have argued that the novel breaks down the rigid barriers between normalcy and abnormalcy, difference and sameness, likeness and Other. Drawing on Mikhail Bakhtin's observations about medieval carnivals, they argue that this carnivalesque text participates in "the defeat of power, of earthly kings, of the earthly upper classes, of all that oppresses and restricts" (Bakhtin *Rabelais* 92). As Adams has written, by revealing how no one is truly "normal," the 1946 novel provides "a place to begin imagining a community rooted in heterogeneity rather than sameness, desire rather than proscription, where each member can find in herself 'a mixture of delicious and freak'" (*Sideshow* 110).

Contrary to assertions that the freakishly queer and queerly freakish Frankie Addams breaks down the sharp divide between normalcy and abnormalcy, the opposite is true at the end of the text. Challenging Fiedler's argument that freaks are physical manifestations of our inner fears and desires, both Robert Bogdan and Rosemarie Garland Thomson have argued that the public spectacle of the extraordinary body has historically served the reverse function. Rather than eroding the distinctions between normalcy and abnormalcy, sideshows have served to reinforce them. In the words of Thomson:

> The immense popularity of the shows between the Jacksonian and Progressive eras suggests that the onlookers needed to constantly reaffirm the difference between 'them' and 'us' at a time when

---

10. Frankie's belief in the malleable nature of race not only applies to her own identity, but that of others. Near the end of the novel, for instance, she argues that Honey Brown could escape his troubles by leaving the South, relocating to the Caribbean and "chang[ing] into a Cuban" (125).

immigration, emancipation of the slaves, and female suffrage confounded previously reliable physical indices of status and privilege such as maleness and Western European features. (*Extraordinary* 65)

Especially for men and women who were on the fringes of society, the extraordinary body provided them with the opportunity to seem more "normal" or, at least, less different. "The extravagant and indisputable otherness of the freak's physiognomy reassured those whose bodies and costuming did not match the fully enfranchised and indubitably American ideal" (Thomson 65).

Frankie Addams participates in this process. Rather than announcing the wartime erosion of gender, race and sexuality, she ultimately reinscribes them. At the end of the novel, the young girl ceases to be a freak. In doing so, she demonstrates the historical reality that freakishness is not an innate identity but a performed one. As such, it can be voluntarily adopted and—perhaps more importantly—also cast off. In the words of Bogdan, "Every exhibit [at a sideshow] was, in the strict sense of the word, a fraud . . . every person exhibited was misrepresented to the public" (10). Freak shows commonly used artificial backdrops, fictional biographies, and coached behaviors. As Frankie herself discovers about a figure at the Chattahoochee Exposition, he "was not a genuine Wild Nigger, but a crazy colored man from Selma" (17).

Echoing this important facet of the freak show, Frankie occupies the role of freak, but she also abandons it. In a manner that recalls the historical legacy of tomboy taming as well as the wartime mandate that it be abrupt and immediate, the young girl suddenly sloughs off her gender freakishness, sexual queerness and racial difference at the end of *The Member of the Wedding* and embraces an identity that is more hegemonic. After being a tomboyish freak with a queer sexual identity and a strong identificatory link with nonwhite peoples, Frankie experiences an abrupt shift to behaviors that are stereotypically feminine, clearly heteronormative and unmistakably rooted in whiteness. The first and most obvious index of this phenomenon is the abandonment of her tomboyish nature. In the days following her brother's wedding, she forgoes her shorts and BVD t-shirts and reverts to her feminine given name, "Frances." Providing an outward manifestation of this inner change, Frankie makes her first female friend and decides to stop visiting the figure who she believes is her physical and psychic double: the Half-Man Half-Woman. Although the young girl still attends the Chattahoochee Fair, she avoids the Freak Pavilion, agreeing with her new gal pal Mary Littlejohn that "it was morbid to stare at freaks" (*Member* 150).

Closely related to Frankie's abandonment of tomboyism is her abandonment of queer sexual desires. Although the young girl is initially devastated when she is forsaken by her brother and his bride, she replaces this queer fantasy with more heteronormative ones. Akin to other giggly romantic teenagers, Frankie and Mary Littlejohn read Tennyson and dream of becoming famous artists. Moreover, echoing the imperialist ethos that underwrites much white Western tourism, Frankie now sees foreign cultures as sources of entertainment rather than opportunities for cultural exchange. Foregoing her previous desire to be "close kin" with the world, the young girl speaks of European countries as stepping stones that exist for her own bourgeois amusement: "'We will most likely pass through Luxembourg when we go around the world together'" (153).

Together with Frankie's embrace of the gender and sexual roles for white middle-class women is her embrace of their racial identity. Instead of forming close ties with racial and ethnic minority groups, she does so with a playmate who is the literal and figurative epitome of the "Fair Maiden." Mary Littlejohn not only has "braids of a woven mixture of corn-yellow and brown" (150), but is also so pale and wan that Berenice jokingly characterizes her as "marshmallow white" (150). In addition to befriending this figure who possesses a strong tie with corporeal whiteness, Frankie relocates to an area that has a strong infrastructural association with it. In the final pages of McCullers's narrative, the Addams family is preparing to move to the suburbs. Coupled with being a product of the postwar building boom, suburbia was a product of postwar efforts at racial consolidation. As Rosalind Rosenberg notes, "the Federal Housing Authority did not approve mortgage funds for integrated communities" (145). The racial exclusivity associated with the new subdevelopments was so strong, in fact, that historian Catharine Jurca titled her recent book about the postwar flight to the suburbs, "White Diaspora." Not coincidentally, McCullers's tomboy who formerly possessed a strong identificatory link with Berenice now asserts her privileged status as a white person by using a racial slur. On the ride home from her brother's wedding ceremony, Frankie "was sitting next to Berenice, back with the colored people, and when she thought of it she used the mean word she had never used before, nigger—for now she hated everyone and wanted only to spite and shame" (135).

Robert Bogdan, in his landmark study *Freak Show*, reveals that long before individuals with physical and mental deformities became sideshow attractions for entertainment and profit, they were seen as bearers of divine meaning. Classified as *lusus naturae* (literally, a freak or sport of nature), they were viewed as prophetic symbols of events to come. The gender, sexual and racial freakishness of Carson McCullers's tomboyish main character in *The Member of the Wedding* can be seen as returning to this original meaning of freaks. Rather than existing for amusement, Frankie becomes a foreboding index of what will happen if the gender, sexual and racial chaos of the war years is allowed to continue. As a vivid emblem of the sideshow dictum of "individuation running rampant into chaos," McCullers's tomboy is not a progressive symbol of women's wartime liberation or an example that we are all "freakish" in some way. In yet another reflection of the antebellum purpose of tomboyism as a means of maintaining the gender, sexual and racial status quo, she is a reactionary figure who will reinstate more normative codes during the postwar era.

The Cold War and The Case of the Disappearing Tomboy: Tomboyism Moves from Mainstream American Culture to Its Pulp Counterculture

Societal fears over the long-term effects of wartime changes to traditional gender and sexual roles received scientific confirmation in the years following the declaration of V-E and V-J day. In 1948, Alfred Kinsey published his now infamous *Sexual Behavior in the Human Male.* Interviewing thousands of men from various strata of society, he and his assistants asked the subjects about their sexual activity and erotic experiences. In addition to collecting data on taboo heterosexual behavior such as extra-marital affairs and anal intercourse, he also inquired about homosexual encounters, and found that the incidence of same-sex erotic activity was much higher than anyone had previously believed. An astounding 37% of the men Kinsey surveyed admitted to having had at least one sexual experience with another man, while 10% reported having erotic experiences with men exclusively (Kinsey *Male* 650). Because of its surprising findings about the rate of homosexual activity, The Kinsey Report, as it would come to be known, caught the attention of scientists and citizens alike. Within months after its release, *Sexual Behavior in the Human Male* became a bestseller.

Five years later, in 1953, Kinsey released the results of a companion study about female erotic experience. Appropriately titled *Sexual Behavior in the Human Female*, it found that while the incidence of homosexuality was lower in women—only 13% reported having had at least one same-sex encounter and only 6% identified as being exclusively homosexual (Kinsey *Female* 375)—it was still both statistically and socially significant. To a society that was already growing increasingly fearful of female gender iconoclasm, Kinsey's book was the spark that set off the powder keg. Whereas individuals had previously spoken hypothetically about the long-term impact that wartime upheavals to gender and sexual roles would have on the postwar nation, they now had scientific confirmation for such concerns. As in the *fin-de-siecle* when the "discovery" of female homosexuality led to the demonization of both the adult New Woman and the adolescent tomboy, the publication of the Kinsey Reports had an analogous impact on the postwar era. In a comment that recalled Richard von Krafft-Ebing's 1882 observation that "a bold and tomboyish style" was an adolescent symptom of adult sexual inversion, Harvey E. Kaye asserted in a 1967 paper to the Society of Medical Psychoanalysts in New York that one of the key childhood indicators of adult lesbianism was "a tendency to see themselves as tomboys" (197).

The link between childhood tomboyism and adult homosexuality might seem to have eradicated this code of conduct from American literature and culture, but the late 1950s and the decade of the 1960s actually witnessed the release of a considerable number of tomboy-themed novels and films. Most notable among these in the nation's print culture were the reissue of Carolyn Keene's *Nancy Drew* mystery series, the appearance of Harper Lee's Pulitzer Prize-winning *To Kill a Mockingbird* (1960), and the publication of Louise Fitzhugh's *Harriet the Spy* (1964). Meanwhile, on the silver screen, some of the era's biggest female stars played tomboys, including Debbie Reynolds in *Tammy and the Bachelor* (1957), Sandra Dee in *Gidget* (1959), and Patty Duke in the movie musical *Billie* (1965).

Although tomboyism was not obliterated by the Cold War emphasis on femininity, it was radically transformed by it. Akin to previous historical eras when this code of conduct came under attack, mainstream presentations of it reverted to more conservative traits. The revisions to the Nancy Drew mystery series form a poignant and in many ways representative example. Initially released from 1930 to 1956, the novels were reissued beginning in 1959. In these new editions, an array of elements had been modified: the texts were condensed, the main character's age was changed from sixteen to eighteen, and most of the more overt instances of racism were excised. In an often overlooked alteration, however, the tomboyishness of the text's title character was also tamed. In the original 1930s series, Nancy Drew is an autonomous and adventurous figure who is capable, confident, and courageous. Indeed, as Deborah Siegel has written of her, "There is nothing this girl cannot or will not do. . . . Nancy fixes motorboats in darkness, changes tires in thunderstorms, rides horses, sleeps outside" (172). In the first novel, *The Secret of the Old Clock* (1930) alone, for example, Nancy is introduced to readers as a "pretty girl" who "enjoyed sports of all kinds" (12). In addition, frequent mention is made of her exceptional driving skills. When running an errand for her father, for instance, Nancy selects "the shortest route to her destination" and "deftly" shifts gears, even along muddy roads (26). She shows the same knack for solving mysteries. While searching for Josiah Crowley's missing second will, Nancy interviews all of the witnesses herself, does all of her own research, and pieces together her own clues, often placing herself in physical danger. In addition, Nancy frequently circumvents the authorities in order to solve a case, even withholding evidence from the police at one point. Although the amateur sleuth does discuss the case with her father—noted local lawyer Carson Drew—he is more of a passive observer than active participant.

In the revised editions of the Nancy Drew series though, many of these elements were changed. In the 1959 version of *The Secret of the Old Clock*, for example, no mention is made of Nancy's interest in athletics. In addition, while out running the errand for her father, the young woman foregoes the more direct but treacherous backroads and instead selects the safer "recently constructed highway" (34). Likewise, Nancy asks her father to interview key witnesses and help gather clues (48–53). Then, instead of circumventing the police, she obediently turns over all her evidence to the invariably male officers. Finally, rather than relying on her own intelligence and famous sense of intuition, Nancy often defers to masculine judgment and patriarchal authority.

This pattern continues throughout all subsequent volumes of the series. In the second novel—*The Hidden Staircase* (1930)—Nancy takes a long and vigorous hike in the opening pages of the story, goes to a haunted old mansion alone to investigate the mystery, is given a revolver by her father to take with her when she does so, and even rescues Carson Drew when he is captured by the villain. To be sure, Nancy and her father experience a type of gendered role reversal in this scene, with the weakened male lawyer assuming the role of the "damsel in distress" while his strong and daring tomboyish daughter embodies the proverbial "knight in shining armor": "'I'll be all right,' Carson Drew forced a wan smile. 'Couldn't have stood it much longer, though. If you hadn't come just when you did'" (Keene *Hidden* 195). Once again, though, none of these elements are present in the 1959 revised edition: Nancy's long and vigorous hike is removed, Helen accompanies her to the haunted mansion, the young sleuth is never given a firearm, and Carson Drew is rescued by the male police captain. Both men also play an important role in "helping" Nancy solve the case.

Even Nancy's boyish cousin, George Fayne, is not exempt from this phenomenon. In the opening pages of *The Secret at Shadow Ranch* (1931), the young woman makes a decidedly tomboyish entrance into the series:

> "Alice is as pretty as a picture," George supplied. "Not homely like me."
>
> "Why, you're not a bit homely," Nancy assured her promptly. "I think you're quite distinctive looking myself."
>
> "You base flatterer! Look at this straight hair and pug nose! And everyone says I'm irresponsible and terribly boyish."
>
> "Well, you sort of pride yourself on being boyish, don't you? Your personality fits in with your name, you will admit."
>
> "I do like my name" George admitted, "but I get tired of explaining to folks that it isn't short for Georgia." (Keene *Shadow* 3–4)

Needless to say, this exchange, along with many of George's other overtly boyish actions and attitudes, is excised from the revised edition. Given these changes, Carolyn Heilbrun has commented that the new Nancy Drew is "more of a Barbie doll conforming to that ideal of femininity dear to the radical right" whose ideology dominated the postwar period (16). Editors ostensibly revised classic Nancy Drew texts like *The Secret at Shadow Ranch* and *The Hidden Staircase* to eliminate elements of racism, update technological references, and make the texts more concise. But, given the title character's changing gender role, a more accurate title for the rewritten versions may have been "The Case of the Disappearing Tomboy."

Alterations to the Nancy Drew mystery series to make its formerly gender-bending title character more ladylike were emblematic of the type of tomboyism presented in countless other novels and films, and especially those that had a predominantly young audience. In Harper Lee's *To Kill a Mockingbird* (1960), for example, Jean Louise "Scout" Finch may wear overalls and play sports with her older brother Jem, but she also willingly dons a dress, asks for a baton, and tells the friends of her aunt that she does not want to be lawyer like her father when she grows up but simply "a lady" (Lee 230). Indeed, Scout allows her playmate Dill to repeatedly kiss her and even looks forward to marrying him someday. Moreover, the tomboyish girl has a range of reactions to the Missionary Society Ladies meeting hosted by her aunt near the end of the novel. Wearing tomboyish britches under her "pink Sunday dress" (228), she is alternatively repulsed by the artificiality of the women gathered and attracted to their refinement. "Ladies in bunches always filled me with vague apprehension and a firm desire to be elsewhere" (Lee 229), Scout notes. But, she also acknowledges, "They smelled heavenly" (Lee 229).

Scout may waver in her attitudes about femininity, but—in keeping with rigid postwar attitudes about gender—she also realizes, "There was no doubt about it, I must soon enter this world" (Lee 233). As a result, the young girl begins her negotiation of what will likely be a lifelong dual or split existence: she will physically enter the world of women as society requires, but will psychologically remain more aligned with that of men. In a passage that says much about Scout's current state of mind and even more about her future condition of being, she reflects on the reason driving this division:

> Ladies seemed to live in faint horror of men, seemed unwilling to approve wholeheartedly of them. But I liked them. There was something about them, no matter of much they cussed and drank and gambled and chewed; no matter how undelectable they were, there was something about them that I instinctively liked . . . they weren't—
>
> "Hypocrites, Mrs. Perkins, born hypocrites," Mrs. Meriweather was saying. (Lee 234)

Given Scout's observation that men "did not trap you with innocent questions to make fun of you; even Jem was not highly critical unless you said something stupid" (Lee 234), her seeming social gender conformity will be little more—to borrow a phrase from Judith Butler—than a superficial gender performance.

As a consequence, in the same way that the Cold War era was politically bifurcated by U.S. democracy and Soviet communism, tomboy culture was split into mainstream and countercultural forms. Together with this code of conduct's appearance in socially innocuous children's books and feel-good Hollywood movies, it inhabited the subversive world of lesbian pulp fiction. Whereas mainstream representations of this code of conduct repudiated the connection between gender and sexual iconoclasm, inexpensive paperback novels embraced it. Marking a shift in this project's focus from what Lawrence Levine would characterize as highbrow canonical literature to lowbrow forms of popular culture, the next chapter reveals the rich life that tomboyism enjoyed in lesbian pulp fiction during the Cold War era. As societal intolerance for gender nonconformity made it unacceptable to depict tough and transgressive female figures in mainstream forms of visual and print media, these images went underground to more subversive forms. In the wake of growing societal fears about female gender and sexual nonconformity, this new type of bold and butchy tomboy became—in the words of one popular paperback novel—the "odd girl out."

8

The Tomboy Becomes
the "Odd Girl Out"

Ann Bannon's Women in the Shadows

While the 1950s are commonly considered a period of moral wholesomeness and sexual repression, they were also a time of dissident desires and alternative value systems. Not far beneath the era's surface of smiling conformity lurked a subversive underbelly. Forming a powerful counterpart to the throngs of housewives populating the nation's suburbs, lesbian communities emerged in many of its urban areas. Initially formed during the Second World War, they remained in cities like New York and San Francisco after the end of the conflict and became the locus of not only the nation's nascent homosexual population but also its fight for social and political rights. For these reasons, while the 1950s were a time of intense oppression against individuals with alternative gender and sexual identities, it was also the period that gave birth to the modern gay and lesbian movement. The first homophile organizations in the United States—the Mattachine Society and Daughters of Bilitis—were each founded during the 1950s. Fueled by the increased acceptance that gays and lesbians enjoyed during World War II, as well as the findings of Alfred Kinsey that homosexuality among Americans was much more common than previously believed, they made a case for the public recognition of same-sex romance in the United States.

The continued visibility of gays and lesbians elicited a combination of fear and fascination from mainstream American society. On one hand, homosexuality was socially demonized and scientifically pathologized. Whereas gay men and lesbians during the Second World War had been valued members of the nation's military and civilian population, the postwar era reversed this message. As Lillian Faderman has written, the 1950s witnessed the heyday of beliefs in the homosexual "sicko" (*Odd* 130). Sparked by the postwar popularity of neo-Freudian theory, the profound sexual repression that permeated the Cold War era, and the paranoia that surrounded any form of nonconformity, gay men and lesbians were seen as suffering from a physical disease or at least a psychological disorder. In fact, when the American Psychiatric Association issued its first official catalogue of psychological maladies, *The Diagnostic and Statistical Manual of Mental Disorders* (DSM-I), in 1952, homosexuality was categorized as a sociopathic personality disturbance. As John D'Emilio has documented, these attitudes caused gay men and lesbians to be rooted out from government jobs at a rate that exceeded those of suspected communists, dishonorably discharged by the thousands from all branches of the military, and sent to doctors all over the country to receive "procedures ranging from the relatively benign, such as psycho-therapy and hypnosis, to castration, hysterectomy, electroshock, aversion therapy and the administration of untested drugs" (18).

Even though American society publicly disparaged homosexuality during the 1950s and early 1960s, it was also privately curious about it. Heterosexual men and women may not have been comfortable living near or working beside a gay man or a lesbian, but they were eager to read about them in the burgeoning new genre of paperback fiction. Although the Cold War appetite for inexpensive paperback novels is commonly thought to have been satiated with such innocuous fare as westerns and detective fiction, titles with more subversive themes were also popular. As Kenneth Davis notes, during the 1950s and 1960s, "schlock [was] turned out to appease a gluttonous mass appetite for sex and sensationalism" (xi). Lesbian-themed narratives were not only produced by nearly every major press, they quickly became one of the industry's most lucrative genres. As Suzanna Danuta Walters notes, "In 1957, Reed Marr's *Women without Men* was one of the top selling paperbacks of the year" (84). Likewise, in 1952, when Vin Packer's *Spring Fire* was published, "it sold 1,463,917 copies in its first printing, more than *The Postman Always Rings Twice* by James Cain and more than *My Cousin Rachel* by Daphne du Maurier sold in that same year" (Packer *Spring* viii).

Although the life span of lesbian pulp fiction encompassed less than two decades, the genre compensated with quantity for what it lacked in longevity. As the Selected Tomboy Bibliography at the end of this project attests, hundreds of titles were released during the 1950s and early 1960s. While most of these books were written by heterosexual men and intended to titillate a male audience, some were penned (often under a pseudonym) by women and directed at the burgeoning postwar lesbian community. Titles like Vin Packer's aforementioned *Spring Fire* (1952), Patricia High-smith's *The Price of Salt* (1952) and Valerie Taylor's *The Girls in 3-B* (1959) became important sources of identity for this nascent group. As Roberta Yushba has written, urban and especially rural women "could read them and see that they were not the only lesbians in the world" (30).

Lesbian pulp fiction may have flourished during the 1950s and 1960s, but its representation of same-sex romance was not free from prevailing cultural stereotypes and legal constrictions, even by authors who were themselves homosexual. In the same way that the Hays Code imposed strict guidelines about the depiction of "sexual perversion" in film, the Comstock Act did so in print media. While modified several times since its introduction in 1873, the statute forbade the distribution of materials that could be considered "immoral" or "obscene."[1] For these reasons, pulp novels provided new voice and visibility to same-sex romance, but they were forbidden from presenting it as enjoyable, healthy or rewarding.[2] The sheer number of novels with such pejorative words as "odd," "warped" or "strange" in the title illustrates the way in which the genre echoed prevailing attitudes about the aberrant nature of same-sex love while simultaneously giving legitimacy to those desires.

In an often overlooked facet of lesbian pulp fiction, these books also provided a new cultural home for tomboyism. Paperback novels had an adult rather than a child audience and were largely a populist form that existed outside of bourgeois literary conventions. Thus, they were able to depict more radical modes of female behavior than their mainstream counterparts like Paul Wendkos' movie musical *Gidget* (1959), Harper Lee's novel *To Kill a Mockingbird* (1960), or the Nancy Drew mystery series, which was revised and released beginning in 1959. In contrast to Nancy Drew's stylish dresses, girlish bob and feminine physique, for example, the athletic main character Susan Mitchell in Vin Packer's *Spring Fire* is described by her classmates as a "muscle-bound Amazon" who is "built like a barn" (Packer 4, 58). Meanwhile, unlike Scout Finch's willingness to wear a dress in Harper Lee's Pulitzer Prize-winning *To Kill a Mockingbird* (1960), the central figure in Paula Christian's *The Other Side of Desire* shocks her neighbors by donning "boy's shirts and slacks" (17). Finally, unlike the comely girl surfer Gidget who falls so deeply for a hunky male love interest that she compares it to being "hit by a sledgehammer," the figures in lesbian pulp novels reflected postwar beliefs that a boyish type of childhood tomboyism would lead to a

1. For the text of the original Comstock Act, see the American Memory Project from the Library of Congress: http://memory.loc.gov/cgibin/ampage?collId=llsb&fileName=042/llsb042.db&recNum=4628. For a discussion about the history and evolution of the statute and others like it, see Frederick F. Schauer's *The Law of Obscenity* (Washington, D.C.: Bureau of National Affairs, 1976).

2. Vin Packer, in the introduction to the recently reissued edition of *Spring Fire*, provides a vivid example of this phenomenon. As an editor informed her when she presented the manuscript, "'You cannot make homosexuality attractive. No happy ending. . . . [Y]our main character can't decided she's not strong enough to live that life. . . . She has to reject it knowing that it's wrong'" (Packer vi). As the editor went on to explain, this suggestion was not a matter of editorial direction, but legal limitation: "'You see our books go through the mails. They have to pass inspection. . . . If your book appears to proselytize for homosexuality, all the books sent with it to the distributors are returned'" (Packer vi). As a result of such restrictions, Packer crafted a tragic conclusion for her narrative: "at the end one young woman goes mad, while the other realizes that she had never really loved her in the first place" (Packer vii).

mannish form of adult lesbianism. In the code of postwar pulps, any female character who was even remotely tomboyish was also ultimately a homosexual. In Patricia Highsmith's *The Price of Salt*, the sexually aggressive Abby is described as having behaved "like a tomboy" when she was young (173). Likewise, in Tereska Torres' *Women's Barracks* (1950), all of the female figures who have gender-bending qualities also engage in same-sex affairs. The narrative's most notorious female flirt, Mickey, for instance, has a "slim, boyish, somewhat gawky figure" and is "broad-shouldered, with narrow hips, long muscular legs, and diminutive pointed breasts" (13). Similarly, her love-interest, Ann, is characterized as "a strapping large girl with a boyish haircut" who had a "heavy, almost masculine voice . . . and a friendly, easy way of being helpful—like a big brother" (14).

Of all the writers who presented tomboyish characters in lesbian-themed paperback novels during the postwar, Ann Bannon was perhaps the most famous. In 1957, at the age of twenty-two, she released her first pulp novel about same-sex love: *Odd Girl Out*. The book was an immediate success and went on to become the second best-selling paperback of that year (Bannon *Odd* vii). Over the next half decade, the steady commercial sales and ongoing readerly interest in Bannon's work would prompt her to pen four more interrelated books about lesbian love: *I Am a Woman* (1959), *Women in the Shadows* (1959), *Journey to a Woman* (1960) and *Beebo Brinker* (1962). All of these narratives went through multiple press runs during the 1950s and 1960s. Given both the postwar popularity of Bannon's pulp novels along with their importance in the burgeoning canon of LGBTQ literature, they have been reprinted several times. In 1975, the Arno Press reissued *I Am a Woman* as part of its ongoing series on homosexuality. Then, during the early the 1980s, the lesbian press Naiad reissued all five of Bannon's books. Likewise, in 1995, the Quality Paperback Book Club published the novels in a single volume. Finally, beginning in 2001, the San Francisco-based publishing company Cleis began bringing her books back into print. With the Beebo Brinker series receiving more commercial success, critical attention, and cultural longevity than any other lesbian pulp novels, Christopher Nealon has aptly noted that Bannon's work "is now firmly ensconced as the premier fictional representation of lesbian life in the fifties and sixties" (748).

Although Bannon's books follow the experiences of a Midwestern girl named Laura Landon, they are not commonly remembered for, or even referred to by, this character. The series acquired its name from Betty Jean "Beebo" Brinker, who makes her appearance in the second novel and whose backstory is the subject of the final book in the series. With her short hair, penchant for wearing men's clothes and adoption of stereotypically masculine attitudes, Beebo is the epitome of pulp tomboyism. Indeed, as Bannon herself recently remarked about her character, "Her nickname was one of those too-cute tomboy variations on a boy's name" (*I Am* x).

In a compelling paradox, Bannon may have crafted the most famous and enduring tomboyish character in paperback fiction, but she could not be included in this category herself. Unlike all of the other writers spotlighted in this study, Bannon was neither especially tomboyish when she was young nor a gender-bending woman as an adult. As she noted, "I inhabited all the 'good girl' traditions, myths, and strictures of the years following World War II" (*Women* 200). Born Ann Thayer in Joliet, Illinois in 1932 (like many pulp authors, "Ann Bannon" was a pseudonym), she lived a double life. While acknowledging that "a big part of me was an iconoclast, a venturesome and spirited person" (Bannon "Interview" 18), she was unable to thwart societal expectations about proper feminine dress and deportment. In a remark that foreshadowed late-twentieth-century observations about the performative nature of femininity, she once reflected about her youthful gender identity:

> I always felt like a visitor from another planet, successfully disguised as a young girl. It became sort of a game; I would dress, talk, gesture, and move like the other little girls, but I would keep the secret that I was different somehow and didn't really belong in their company. That way, no one would bother me, my mother would be happy, and I would live the rest of my life in my fantasies.[3]

Bannon continued this facade in her adult life. When the future author was in her early twenties, she got married, moved to the suburbs and began having children. From the standpoint of public appearances, she was a typical middle-class wife and mother. As she once noted, " . . . this was 1956. I was twenty-two and while I had a college education, it was ornamental" (Bannon *Odd* xiii). But, Bannon lived a double life as an author of lesbian pulp fiction. When her husband was away on business, she took secret trips to Greenwich Village, recalling: "I made the most of every moment. I visited every bar I could, and I got acquainted with some wonderful people. I walked the streets for hours, soaking it all up" (Bannon *Odd* vii). This disparity between Bannon's outer heteronormative life and inner homosexual one made her pulp career possible. As she recalled, "' . . . everyone in my daily life thought I was just a very nice, young conventional wife and mother. They really didn't know what was going on in my head or my emotions and that was sort of how I got away with it'" (quoted in Tilchen 10).

Examining this popular author from one of the most popular paperback genres of the 1950s and 1960s, this chapter reveals how tomboyism formed a key component to the construction of gender-bending female characters in lesbian pulp fiction. Contrary to attitudes about the impotent nature of

---

3. Quotation taken from an e-mail exchange that this author had with Bannon on September 21, 2004.

"trash" culture, figures like Bannon's Beebo Brinker represent an influential coordinate in the unwritten history of tomboyism in the United States. Throughout its residence in lesbian pulp narratives, this code of conduct underwent significant transformation and acquired an array of traits that would persist throughout the remainder of the twentieth century. As the following section discusses, in inexpensive paperback novels, tomboyism moved out of the realm of heteronormativity and was firmly yoked with homosexuality. In addition, it shifted from being linked with boyishness to being associated with a new form of female masculinity known as butchness. Also, in a radical break from its origins, it abandoned its previous aim of improving female health and instead was associated with more anti-social elements and even self-destructive behaviors. Finally, in a characteristic that was perhaps the most controversial, it went from signaling a transgressive code of conduct to a potential index of something that would come to be known in the wake of Christine Jorgensen's much-publicized sex-change operation in 1952 as transsexualism.

The Tomboyish Root of Pulp Butchness: Paperback Novels Put the "Tom" Back into Tomboyism

From Beebo Brinker's debut in Bannon's 1959 novel *I Am a Woman*, readers and critics have commonly seen her as participating in the postwar phenomenon of lesbian butchness. A complex code of personal style, sexual role play and physical and emotional self-presentation, butchness emerged among working-class lesbians in general and those involved in the urban bar scene in particular in the years following the end of World War II. As Suzanna Walters, Diana Hamer and Judith Halberstam have each discussed, butches embodied a highly stylized form of female masculinity. They were lesbians who not only wore men's clothes, but adopted stereotypically masculine behaviors: they lit cigarettes, opened car doors and brought flowers to their more feminine lady loves, called femmes.[4] In a gesture that typified butch behavior, Beebo uses the following suave strategy to charm Laura Landon:

> Beebo turned back to her and returned the smile. Then she reached into her pocket and pulled out a dime. She flipped it in the air and then dropped it insolently in front of Laura. "Here's a dime, sweetheart," she said. "Call me sometime." And with a little grin at Jack, she turned and left them. (Bannon *I Am* 71)

4. For more general information about the construction of butch/femme during the postwar and its influence on gender identities among queer women today, see Sally R. Munt's essay collection, *Butch/Femme: Inside Lesbian Gender* (London: Cassell, 1998).

Whether such actions were disparaged as mere imitations of heterosexual gender roles, as many lesbian feminists would later assert,[5] or championed as a daring subversion of these forms, as Joan Nestle has argued,[6] they were at the center of many working-class lesbian communities. Indeed, as Lillian Faderman has written of butch/femme culture during the Cold War, it was "the *sine qua non* of being a lesbian within that group" (168).

With her confident swagger, short haircut and men's clothing, Beebo Brinker epitomizes postwar lesbian butchness.[7] For femmes, she was the figure whom they fantasized about dating; for butches, she was the tough and transgressive character whom they fantasized about embodying. Indeed, when both Laura Landon in *I Am a Woman* and Beth Cullison in *Journey to a Woman* first see Beebo, they are instantly attracted to her. Laura can barely take her eyes off "the handsome boyish girl" across the room (*I Am* 69). Meanwhile, Beth notices the striking woman "wearing slacks and a man-cut jacket," and she is also acutely aware that she "wasn't the only one who turned to look at [Beebo] as she made her way up to the bar" (*Journey* 46). Far from being limited to merely these fictional characters, such sentiments extended to Beebo's factual creator and, of course, many members of the series' readership. As Bannon herself has said about the now nearly iconic status of Beebo: "Big, bold, handsome, the quintessential 1950s buccaneer butch, she was a heller and I adored her" (*I Am* v).

In an oft-overlooked facet of this character and, by extension, postwar pulp butchness, much of Beebo's behavior is actually a rich amalgamation or stylized amplification of more than one hundred years of tomboyish traits. Echoing one of the most foundational facets of this code of conduct, Beebo is motherless. As readers learn in the novel that bears her name, her mother died when she was young and she was subsequently raised by her father and elder brother (*Beebo* 50–52). More than simply possessing this general trait of tomboyism, Beebo possesses specific qualities that recall some of most famous tomboyish characters. For example, reflecting the

5. For a useful overview of the backlash against butch/femme identities both in the 1950s and especially during the 1970s and 1980s, see Lillian Faderman's *Odd Girls and Twilight Lovers: A History of Lesbian Life in Twentieth-Century America* (New York: Penguin, 1991).

6. For discussions of butch/femme as revolutionary, subversive and even libratory identities for homosexual women, see both Joan Nestle's *A Restricted Country* (Ithaca, NY: Firebrand, 1987) and Elizabeth Lapovsky Kennedy and Madeline B. Davis's *Boots of Leather, Slippers of Gold: A History of a Lesbian Community* (New York: Penguin, 1993).

7. For discussions of Beebo Brinker as the embodiment of postwar butchness, see Diane Hamer's "'I Am a Woman': Ann Bannon and the Writing of Lesbian Identity in the 1950s," in *Lesbian and Gay Writing: An Anthology of Critical Essays* (Philadelphia: Temple UP, 1990. 47–50) and Suzanna Danuta Walters's "As Her Hand Crept Slowly Up Her Thigh: Ann Bannon and the Politics of Pulp," *Social Text*, 23 (Fall-Winter 1989): 83–101.

description of Elizabeth Stuart Phelps's Gypsy Breynton as "a very pretty, piquant mistake; as if a mischievous boy had somehow stolen the plaid dress, red cheeks, quick wit, and little indescribable graces of a girl, and was playing off a continual joke on the world" (51), Beebo is presented as "more boy than girl" (*Beebo* 107). Likewise, recalling Jim Burden's complaint of his Bohemian neighbor Antonia: "She was too proud of her strength" (Cather *Antonia* 81), Beebo has "muscular angles," "broad shoulders and hardly a hint of a bosom" (*Beebo* 19, 29). Finally, in keeping with E. D. E. N. Southworth's "newsboy" Capitola Black, Bannon's character is partially crossdressed when first introduced to readers: "She wore a sporty jacket, the kind with a gold thread emblem on the breast pocket; a man's white shirt, open at the throat" (*Beebo* 15).

Given the powerful postwar conflation between gender identity and sexual object choice, Beebo's tomboyism is a signifier for her lesbianism. In the final novel of the series, which is actually a prequel to the other four, Jack Mann accurately ascertains the young woman's homosexuality based on her gender-bending attire and actions: "Jack, watching Beebo who was watching the waitress, saw her wide blue eyes glide up and down the plump pink-uniformed body with curious interest" (*Beebo* 12). By the time Laura encounters Beebo several years later, she is a bona fide lesbian Casanova, with a reputation for sexual prowess and an impressive list of past lovers. As a swaggering Beebo boasts the first time she meets Laura in a lesbian bar: "'I know most of the girls in here . . . I've probably slept with half of them'" (*I Am* 85). Such passages reveal that as this code of conduct marked its one-hundredth anniversary in American literature and culture, lesbian pulp fiction put the "tom" back into tomboyism. Recalling the use of this prefix to signify a sexually assertive male who aggressively pursues females, tomboyishly tough female figures in pulp fiction severed any connection with heterosexuality and were instead firmly associated with homosexuality.

Helping to construct this link between gender nonconformity and sexual iconoclasm was a shift from previous wartime viewpoints about the voluntary nature of tomboyism. The postwar period asserted that an individual's gender and, by extension, sexual identity emerged from a combination of biological and psychological sources. Throughout the Beebo Brinker series, the tomboyish title character argues that her iconoclastic nature has been present since she was a child. As she explains to a friend in the final novel of the series, "'. . . . long before I knew anything about sex I knew I wanted to be tall and strong and ride horses and have a career . . . and never marry a man or learn to cook or have babies" (Bannon *Beebo* 50). This biologically based explanation for her identity is coupled with a psychologically rooted one: her upbringing. Given both the historical view of motherlessness as an environmental cause for tomboyism and the popularity of 1950s neo-Freudian beliefs which identified dysfunctional parenting strategies as a cause for female homosexuality,[8] the issue looms large. When Beebo tells Jack Mann about her childhood experiences in the final novel of the series, for instance, she makes frequent reference to the way in which her father and elder brother largely raised her "as a boy" (Bannon *Beebo* 50–52).

The presence of these involuntary causes for tomboyism once again necessitated the eradication of one of this code of conduct's most pervasive traits, especially during the Second World War: taming. In spite of the 1950s faith in the psychoanalytic "talking cure," attempts to reform tomboyish pulp female figures repeatedly prove futile. In *Beebo Brinker*, the title character recounts numerous failed attempts by family members, teachers and friends to feminize her. Even in the face of physical threats from her brother, cruel taunts from her classmates and a humiliating expulsion from school after being caught wearing men's clothes, she is unable to abandon her tomboyish ways or the lesbianism with which they are associated. At one point, Beebo echoes Nan Prince's justifications in *A Country Doctor*, making the emphatic assertion: "'And so help me God, I'm not ashamed of being what I can't *help* being" [italics in original] (*Beebo* 163).

Although characters in lesbian pulp fiction may have embodied some of the most historically well-known traits of tomboyism, there was one that they largely rejected: the eugenic concern for women's health. Given that this code of conduct was now part of the nation's subversive counterculture rather than its mainstream dominant culture, it was less invested in serving larger societal aims. In most postwar pulp novels, gender-bending female characters engaged in an array of unhealthy, anti-social and even self-destructive behaviors. In a detail that satisfied the era's legal requirements that lesbians be presented as unhappy while it simultaneously reflected the centrality of bar life in urban lesbian culture, the most common among these was excessive drinking. Throughout each novel of Bannon's series, Beebo struggles with alcohol. She is a frequent patron at the Greenwich Village bar "The Cellar," and she imbibes at home just as frequently. In fact, by the middle novel of the series—*Women in the Shadows* (1959)—Beebo's liquor habit is so strong that Laura tells her, "'You were drunk the night I met you and you've been more or less drunk ever since'" (13). In light of these details, Diane Hamer unhesitatingly characterized the tomboyishly butch character as an alcoholic (58).

Tomboyish characters in lesbian pulp fiction added new traits to this code of conduct while they reacted to ones that were already well estab-lished. Arguably the most influential among these concerned gender iden-tity. Echoing the *fin-de-siecle* inversion model of homosexuality which

8. For more on neo-Freudian explanations for homosexuality during the postwar era, see Neil Miller's *Out of the Past: Gay and Lesbian History from 1860 to the Present* (New York: Vintage, 1995): 247–257.

argued that lesbians were really men trapped in women's bodies, pulp novels depicted butch figures who displayed a type of gender dysphoria. Going far beyond the sentiments of previous tomboyish characters like Jo March, who lamented being born a girl because she enjoyed boy's games, activities and freedoms much more, these women repeatedly cast themselves as more male than female. In *Women in the Shadows*, for instance, Beebo and Jack have the following exchange:

"'You know, it comes as a shock to me now and then that you're female,' he said. 'Yeah. Comes as a shock to me too.' He saw tears starting in her eyes again and put a kind hand on her arm" (19). Given the frequency and sincerity of such comments, Christopher Nealon has written that the protagonists of Bannon's novels "are depicted as beautifully mis-embodied, women in boy-men's bodies" and that the "anguish of this mis-embodied position serves as the emotional crux" for the text (755).

Significantly, although the postwar era revived *fin-de-siecle* beliefs in the inversion model of homosexuality, it did not use the term "invert" to describe such figures. Instead, a new word emerged to take its place: "transsexual." First appearing in medical journals during the late 1940s, and entering the mainstream lexicon in 1952 when news of Christine Jorgensen's sex change operation made national headlines and sparked a media frenzy,[9] the term had a slightly different meaning than it does today. As the *Oxford English Dictionary* notes, together with referring to individuals who had sexual reassignment surgery like Jorgensen, "transsexual" also referred more generally to men and women "having the physical characteristics of one sex and the psychological characteristics of the other" ("transsexual" 426–427). This viewpoint overlapped with the postwar belief in the inversion model of homosexuality. Ironically, according to such logic, homosexuality may have been pathologized as a sexual "perversion," but it was simultaneously cast as a variation of heterosexuality. If lesbians were really "men trapped in women's bodies," then their seemingly same-sex desire was actually a displaced form of attraction between members of the opposite sex.

This paradox aside, such thinking caused tomboyishly butch figures in pulp fiction to go from having a merely transgressive gender identity to a proto-transsexual one. Because they desired the love object commonly associated with the opposite gender, the social and scientific community during the 1950s asserted that they must also desire to belong to the opposite sex. In a powerful illustration of such sentiments, Beebo remarks about her psyche and thus her body: "'there's a boy inside it'" (*Beebo* 50).

9. For more information on transsexualism in the 1950s in general and Christine Jorgensen in particular, see especially Joanne Meyerowitz's *How Sex Changed: A History of Transsexuality in the United States* (Cambridge: Harvard UP, 2002).

* * *

The pulp association of tomboyism with a transsexual gender identity combined with the era's strong belief in the biological origins for human behavior allowed paperback novels like the Beebo Brinker series to do more than simply provide a haven for representations of tomboyish female figures during this period of heightened gender and sexual conformity. These books also became a refuge for the continued association of these ostensibly Caucasian figures with various forms of nonwhiteness. Written against the backdrop of the growing popularity of such black-inspired cultural phenomena as rock 'n' roll and the emergence of Norman Mailer's concept of "White Negro," lesbian pulp fiction participated in what W. T. Lhamon, Jr., has characterized as the "deliberate speed" of white society toward black culture during this era. Far from occupying the figurative dark underbelly of American society, white tomboyish figures went on to inhabit an array of social and cultural positions of literal blackness.

"Women in the Shadows": Beebo Brinker and the Dark Passage of White Tomboys Through Pulp Fiction

While the postwar boom in pulp fiction and the emergence of an urban lesbian subculture were noteworthy events during the 1950s, they were not the only cultural phenomena occurring in the United States. As Wini Breines has noted, "Central to the story of the fifties is the powerful influence of black culture" (61). After the Second World War, intensified codes of segregation caused African Americans to have a decreased presence in American social, political and economic life. Nearly all of the characteristics commonly associated with the 1950s—from the attainment of a white-collar job and the purchase of a suburban home to the achievement of a standard of living that allowed one to have both material luxuries such as a television and domestic accoutrements such as a nonworking spouse—were predicated on having white skin. Between social practices that relegated blacks to low-paying positions and civic laws that forbade them from purchasing homes in the new all-white suburbs, the 1950s conception of the American Dream was out of reach for countless minority families. In the words of Wini Breines once again, from the standpoint of economic access and socio-political agency, African Americans were an "invisible border culture" (62).

Although blacks may have been largely absent from the nation's economic, social and political life, they were paradoxically at the center of its cultural imagination. Forming another instance of what Toni Morrison has identified as the centrality of black culture in white American society, many Caucasians began to identify with and even appropriate various forms of blackness during the 1950s. Disillusioned by the sterility and boredom of the suburbs, sickened by the nation's false "Leave It to Beaver" façade and frightened by postwar fears over nuclear holocaust, these largely middle-class individuals "began to see themselves positioned like blacks, as victims and dupes of the status quo" (Lhamon *Deliberate* 39). Sharing the doubt, despair and feelings of powerlessness that African Americans had long known, they romanticized what they saw as their "latent blackness" (Lhamon *Deliberate* 40).

As a result, what Norman Mailer characterized as the "White Negro" was born. Throughout the 1950s and early 1960s, predominantly white counterculture groups such as the Beat Generation and bohemian avant-garde used black culture to articulate their disaffection and fill the void in their lives. Instead of listening to white singers and songwriters, for instance, these men and women became devotees of black musicians like Charlie Parker, Thelonious Monk and Miles Davis.[10] Some took this affiliation even further and began to naïvely insist that they were figuratively or psychologically African American. Although they did not possess dark skin, they argued that they had a black soul. In a representative example of this sentiment, in Jack Kerouac's *On the Road* (1957), main character Sal Paradise asserts: "I walked . . . wishing I were a Negro, feeling that the best the white world had offered was not enough ecstasy for me, not enough life, joy, kicks, darkness, music, not enough night" (148). As a possible extension of this phenomenon, the color black—which had long been associated with various forms of literal and figurative darkness— became popular. Wini Breines has observed that throughout both the urban bohemian underground and the suburban sock hop, black turtle-necks, black leather jackets, even black berets and sunglasses became fashion staples (69). Going far beyond simply signaling an affinity with a certain social crowd, such actions came to be seen as the essence of cool. As Norman Mailer famously asserted in 1957, "the source of [white] Hip is the Negro." For these reasons, the 1950s may have been a time of intensified codes of social segregation, but they were simultaneously a time of cultural miscegenation.

Although lesbian pulp fiction emerged during the height of white envy for black culture, it is not commonly associated with this phenomenon. In fact, the opposite has historically been true. Few pulp narratives feature characters who hail from racial or ethnic minority groups, and even fewer are written by authors who are nonwhite.[11] Lisa Walker has noted that the vast

10. See, for example, William Lawlor's *Beat Culture: Lifestyles, Icons, and Impact* (Santa Barbara, CA: A-B-C Clio, 2005).

11. Ann Allen Shockley's 1974 novel *Loving Her* is commonly seen as the first paperback that was not only written by a black author but featured a black lesbian as its main character. By the time Shockley's text was written and released, however, the heyday of lesbian pulps had passed.

majority of these books presented "race and class as a 'neutral background' against which to dramatize their emergent [white] lesbianism" (105).

This detail, however, ought not to imply that lesbian pulp fiction existed outside of the white fascination with black culture during the 1950s. On the contrary, together with being a product of the era's paperback appetite for sex and sensationalism, books like Bannon's *Women in the Shadows* (1959) were also the product of the nascent fight for gay and lesbian rights which participated in the phenomenon. As Neil Miller, John D'Emilio and Greta Schiller have demonstrated, homophile organizations such as the Daughters of Bilitis and the Mattachine Society largely embraced scientific assertions that gays and lesbians were biologically different from heterosexuals, seeing them as a platform on which to claim their rights. If men and women were born gay or lesbian, then their behavior was innate rather than something they had chosen or could control. Thus, they argued, it was unjust that gay men and lesbians were discriminated against and denied social acceptance.

While this argument could have drawn comparisons with an array of other biologically based characteristics—from eye color to shoe size—race was by far the most common. In an act that ignored the presence of racial and ethnic minorities within their community, as well as collapsed the vast differences between race and sexuality, the homophile movement frequently argued that being a (white) homosexual was parallel to being a member of a racial minority group. As Lisa Walker has written, advocates often asserted that gay men and lesbians faced similar types of personal prejudice, societal stigma and social exclusion.[12] In light of such perceived similarities between homophobia and racism, the homophile movement adopted a tactic employed by antebellum white feminists more than a century ago: they co-opted many of the rhetorical strategies used by proponents of black civil rights in their advocacy for homosexual rights. As Steve Hogan and Lee Hudson have written, one of the movement's first rallying cries, the 1966 mantra "Gay is Good," was self-consciously modeled after a popular mantra from the burgeoning fight for African American civil rights: "Black is Beautiful" (235).

Because pulp paperbacks like *Women in the Shadows* were as much a product of the burgeoning homophile movement as its paperback one, they were infused with the cultural logic and rhetorical strategies of these organizations. Coupled with associating its gender-bending main character with various forms of dark whiteness and making repeated links between (white) homosexuality and the black race, Bannon's 1959 novel incorporates another powerful link. Throughout *Women in the Shadows*, Beebo

12. For a useful overview of the historical connections between the largely white homophile movement and the black civil rights one, see especially the Introduction to Walker's *Looking Like What You Are: Sexual Style, Race and Lesbian Identity* (New York: NYU, 2001).

exists at the center of intersecting forms of gender, sexual and racial passing. Appearing only a few years after the *Brown v. Board of Education* decision, the lynching of Emmett Till, and the Montgomery bus boycott, Bannon's tomboyishly butch character reflects the imbricated nature of masculinity and femininity, homosexuality and heterosexuality and—perhaps most importantly—blackness and whiteness during the 1950s.

• • •

Akin to nearly all of the gender-bending female figures highlighted in this study, from the moment that readers are introduced to Bannon's ostensibly Caucasian Beebo Brinker, she is associated with various forms of nonwhiteness. Throughout *Women in the Shadows*, along with the other three novels in which she appears—*I Am a Woman*, *Journey to a Woman*, and *Beebo Brinker*—Beebo is presented with skin tones and physical traits that call into question her purported racial identity. When Laura first meets the tomboyishly butch figure in *I Am a Woman*, for instance, her hair is so dark that the curls look "blue-black" in the dim light of the Greenwich bar (82). As both Janet Gabler-Hover and Jennifer DeVere Brody have written, this designation places her in dialogue with a historical tactic by which white authors identified black characters. In many narratives from the nineteenth and early twentieth centuries, possession of "blue-black hair" was a type of shorthand that announced an individual as African American and especially someone of mixed race ancestry (Gabler-Hover 39–40). Indeed, the combination of Beebo's distinct physical appearance and her non-Anglo-American nickname causes one character to assume she is a member of a nonwhite minority group. Upon first meeting her, the young woman remarks that the tomboyish figure seems more Asian Indian than Caucasian (Bannon *Shadows* 47).

Perhaps even more important than Beebo's association with various forms of figurative blackness is her connection with literal manifestations of it. Echoing a common rhetorical strategy of the homophile movement, *Women in the Shadows* makes frequent comparisons between white homosexuality and racial blackness. At one point, for instance, Beebo's girlfriend Laura has a conversation with an African American character during which she draws a direct comparison between her sexual identity and his racial one. Asking Milo why he is both heterosexual and black, he responds, "'I was born that way'" (176). When Laura explains her same-sex desires, she insists on a parallel situation. Ignoring the discrepancies between racial and sexual difference, she also asserts, "'I was made this way'" (176). After enumerating an array of factors that have contributed to her sexual orientation—"My father. A girl named Beth. Myself"—she ends with one that is decidedly non-voluntary: "'Fate'" (176).

However faulty, limited and even naïve, such remarks establish a kinship between white homosexuality and racial blackness, thereby facilitating a whole host of other racialized connections. Coupled with being linked with various physical suggestions of nonwhiteness, for instance, Bannon's tomboyishly butch Brinker is associated with another form of American Africanism: passing. Amidst heated debates over slavery and the growing number of blacks who were escaping bondage during the mid-nineteenth century, the word acquired a new meaning. For the first time in history, it began to refer to identity change in general and the phenomenon of African Americans masquerading as white Europeans in particular. As the *Oxford English Dictionary* asserts, "'Passing' is the word used to describe Negroes merging indistinguishably into a white community in America" (307). Violating beliefs about the fixed nature of identity, and calling into question essentialist beliefs about race, passing men and women sparked intense cultural anxiety. As Elaine K. Ginsberg has written on the subject, "As the term metaphorically implies, such an individual crossed or passed through a racial line or boundary—indeed *trespassed*—to assume a new identity, escaping the subordination and oppression accompanying one identity and accessing the privileges and status of the other" [italics in original] (3).

While historians commonly discuss the racial implications of passing, few address the way in which this phenomenon was often interconnected with other common markers of identity. In an effort to confound potential captors, many runaway slaves changed their perceived gender and sexual identity along with their racial one: many men became women, women became men, husbands became wives, sons became daughters, and so on. In *Incidents in the Life of a Slave Girl* (1861), for instance, Harriet Jacobs notes how she escaped an abusive master by disguising herself as not simply a white person but a male sailor. Describing this dual gender and racial transformation, she recalls: "Betty brought me a suit of sailor's clothes,—jacket, trousers, and tarpaulin hat. She gave me a small bundle, saying I might need it where I was going. . . . 'Put your hands in your pockets, and walk rickety, like de sailors.' I performed to her satisfaction" (111–112). Similarly, in an oft-recounted episode that illustrates the transformative power of racial masquerade, sexual subterfuge, and gender transvestism, Ellen Craft and her husband William escaped to freedom through a clever combined manipulation of their gender, racial and sexual identities. As William Craft recounts in *Running a Thousand Miles to Freedom* (1860): "[I]t occurred to me that, as my wife was nearly white, I might get her to disguise herself as an invalid gentleman, and assume to be my master, while I could attend as his slave, and that in this manner we might effect our escape" (29).

Although *Women in the Shadows* was written and released nearly one hundred years after these events, it appeared during a time when passing was both culturally powerful and socially pervasive once again. However, the 1850s trope of black people moving into white culture was reversed during the 1950s. Adopting various facets of blackness and black culture, whites attempted to literally or at least figuratively "pass" into black culture. First published in 1959 during what may be seen as the heyday of this phenomenon, *Women in the Shadows* and its tomboyishly butch character Beebo Brinker participate in overlapping forms of gender, racial and sexual passing. More than simply mutually co-existing, these elements recall the historical actualities of passing and are mutually constructed.

One of the first and perhaps most powerful instances of passing in Bannon's novel is Beebo's desire to be seen as a man. The tomboyishly butch character both privately thinks of herself and often even publicly lives as one. As Laura discovers, Beebo does not simply work as an elevator boy at a local business office, her boss and co-workers actually think she is one: "The manager took her for 'one of those queers, but perfectly harmless.' But he meant a *male* homosexual" [italics in original] (Bannon *Shadows* 9). Echoing such sentiments, Beebo contemplates her relationship with Laura one evening, and laments, "'I'd sell my soul to be an honest-to-God male. I could marry Laura! I could marry her. Give her my name. Give her kids . . . oh, wouldn't that be so lovely! So lovely. . . . '" (Bannon *Shadows* 27).

In the same way that this ostensibly female Beebo passes for male, so too does another female figure, dancer Patsy Robinson, pass for a different sexual and racial identity. Although the beautiful young woman is both African American and married, she masquerades as an Asian Indian named Tris Robischon who is erotically involved with both men and women. The young dancer's embrace of a nonwhite identity reveals the way in which racial passing is not always confined to the black/white binary but can broaden to include other racial and ethnic categories. Similarly, her presentation as a type of "bisexual lesbian" reveals how sexual passing often defies the heterosexual/homosexual dyad to embrace configurations that can be more accurately characterized as queer.

Beebo and Laura first encounter Tris Robischon and the co-joined nature of her sexual and racial passing while shopping at a department store. In an effort to convincingly present herself as Asian Indian, Tris has marked her forehead with "a tiny red dot" (30) to resemble the Hindu bindi and has also altered the sound of her voice. As Laura notes, the young woman speaks in "dainty English. . . . It was a strange accent, like none Laura had ever heard, very precise, and softly spoken, but not noticeably British or anything else" (40). Tris crafts her physical space as carefully as her appearance. In keeping with her adopted identity, the young dancer has filled her studio with an array of items from Southeast Asia. "The room was fitted up Indian fashion with rich red silk drapes on the bed. The bed itself was actually more of a low couch, very capacious, and covered with tumbled silk curtains" (44).

Tris's racial masquerade is interconnected with her sexual one. Almost immediately upon meeting Laura, Tris begins to flirt with her.

"Do you like me, Laura?" she said, her green eyes too close and her sweet skin redolent of jasmine.

"Yes, Tris," Laura said, saying her name for the first time and feeling the fine shivering return to her limbs.

"Good," Tris grinned at her. "That is payment enough." Laura felt suddenly like she had better sit down or she would fall down. (Bannon *Shadows* 43–44)

Lest Laura have any lingering doubts about the young dancer's sexual interest in women, Tris announces it a few moments later. When Laura sees a picture of one of the young woman's beautiful male dancing partners, she asks if the handsome blonde man is also her husband, or at least, fiancé. Amused by the thought, Tris responds, "'Engaged! . . . He is a homosexual, Laura. . . . Can you imagine two homosexuals getting married? Could anything be sillier? What would they do with each other?'" (45). Soon after this remark, the young dancer substitutes this verbal discussion about her homosexuality with a physical display of it: "Tris leaned down and kissed [Laura's] forehead very softly. . . . Tris kissed her cheeks, so lightly that Laura could hardly feel it. . . . And Tris kissed her lips. Laura lay beneath her, too thrilled to move, only letting the lovely shock flow through her body" (49).

In spite of these seemingly unambiguous passages, Tris's sexuality is neither simple nor straightforward. Arising from a combination of both her genuine erotic interest in men as well as her enjoyment of the societal privileges that it affords, Tris has a bisexual or what may more be accurately characterized as a queer sexual identity. Even though the young woman kisses Laura passionately, she insists that she is not gay:

"You know, Laura, I must tell you something. You are a homosexual. Yes?"

Laura swallowed. "Yes," she said.

"You should know then . . . I am not. Not like you. I like the company of girls, yes. My dance pupils. Friends. But I love men. I love them. Do you understand?" (Bannon *Shadows* 71)

Tris quickly contradicts this declaration, though, by aggressively pursuing Laura. Only a few moments after making the above-quoted statement, the pair "stopped dancing and just clung together and kissed, swaying slightly" (Bannon *Shadows* 72). Within moments, such affections lead to lovemaking: "By eight o'clock they were lying on the big red silk couch in the bedroom, murmuring inanities to each other, discovering one another's bodies and emotions" (Bannon *Shadows* 72).

Tris Robischon's passing for a queer Asian Indian and Beebo Brinker's passing for a man are interrelated in *Women in the Shadows*; the mysterious young dancer is the other/Other woman in Beebo's longstanding relationship with Laura. As Laura writes in her journal soon after meeting Tris, "*I am in love. I'm sure of it. The more I'm with Beebo the more I want Tris. Oh, God, how much I love her!*" [italics in original] (Bannon *Shadows* 75). Echoing the white envy for blackness during this era, Laura's attraction to the mysterious young dancer arises in large part from her fetishization of the dark Other. The Caucasian woman is drawn to Tris largely because of her non-Western background and nonwhite skin tone. Characterizing Tris's complexion "three parts cream and one part coffee," Laura has "a brief vision of all that creamy tan skin unveiled and undulating to the rhythm of muffled gongs and bells and wailing reeds" (30, 31). When Laura sees the exotic young woman performing in her dance studio, she is thrilled that Tris is "the same luscious tan from waist to bottom" (40). Later, as they lie in bed together, Laura tells Tris, "'Your skin is beautiful. . . . You're the prettiest color I ever saw'" (102). The young dancer, however, feels differently. Unconvinced that dark skin could ever be considered beautiful, she warns Laura not to get too close lest the color rubs off. Illustrating what Wini Breines has characterized as the "white identification with and objectification and appropriation of black culture" and blackness (54), Laura hopes this will happen. "'What a queer idea!' Laura said. 'You'd have to touch me everywhere then, every corner of me, till we were both the same color. Then you'd be almost white and I'd be almost tan—and yet we'd be the same'" (Bannon *Shadows* 102–103).

Earlier, Tris offered her own provocative analogy about homosexuality and race. Building on the association of Beebo's tomboyish white butchness with various forms of literal and figurative blackness, the young dancer equates whiteness with heterosexuality and blackness with homosexuality. When confronted about her oscillating sexuality, Tris tells Laura: "'If you force me to choose between black and white, I'm white,' she explained, and Laura later thought she heard a double emphasis on the word 'white.' 'I like men. More than women'" (46). To the young dancer who is transgressing both racial and sexual categories, whiteness becomes a stand-in for heterosexuality while blackness becomes a stand-in for lesbianism. Her comments reinforce 1950s beliefs in the oppositional nature of whiteness and blackness along with heterosexuality and homosexuality, and, in doing so, call attention to the possibility that these categories function as parallels. Echoing an argument by the era's homophile movement, white homosexuality can be substituted for, or interchanged with, racial blackness.

Using the "Woman in the Shadow" to Engender the "Angel in the House": Butchness and Blackness Facilitate Whiteness and Heteronormativity

Akin to previous instances when white tomboys affiliated themselves with various forms of blackness and black culture, such moments of "playing in the dark" in *Women in the Shadows* are ultimately in the service of whiteness. In spite of the efforts by both Beebo and Tris to live as members of a different racial, gender and even sexual group, their masquerade is ultimately unveiled. Reflecting many other individuals who are caught "passing," this discovery has disastrous consequences. For Beebo, it takes the form of a physical attack. Laura returns home one evening to find her lover lying on their bed with her clothes torn, her dog brutally murdered, and her face bruised and bloodied. In yet another example of the overlapping nature of gender, racial and sexual passing in Bannon's novel, the incident occurs while Laura is visiting Tris in her dance studio for the first time.

In a surprising revelation that indicates the soap operatic nature of pulp novels in general and Bannon's series in particular, Beebo faked the incident in a desperate attempt to resuscitate her relationship with Laura. A mutual friend informs Laura about Beebo's cuts, bruises and scrapes, "'She did that to herself. . . . I don't know why she did it, but I guess she did it out of frustrated love'" (Bannon *Shadows* 159). Together with feeling betrayed by the fraud, Laura sees it as another instance of Beebo's failed attempt to embrace stereotypically masculine characteristics. As she announces to her friend Jack, "'The more mannish a woman is, the more sense you think she's got!'" (161). Laura views the stunt as further proof that Beebo is just another "'damn silly female'" (161). Outraged, she decides to finally end their relationship.

During the same time that Beebo's gender passing is crumbling, so too is the racial and sexual passing of her narrative counterpart, Tris. Even during Laura's initial encounter with the young dancer, she suspects that Tris is neither Asian Indian nor committed to an erotic life with other women. First, Laura notices that Tris's accent waxes and wanes. At some points, the dancer has a British inflection, while at other moments "Tris spoke without any accent at all. It sounded clear and plain, like Laura's own English" (49). Adding to her skepticism, when Laura asks Tris for more information about her family heritage, she is nervous and becomes defensive. "'Laura, stop it! Why do you ask me such things? . . . I refuse to be quizzed like a criminal'" (99–100).

Tris's fluctuating accent and evasive answers about India mirror her fluctuating sexual identity and evasive stance about her erotic interest in women. When Laura goes away with Tris for a romantic weekend on Long Island, the co-joined nature of the young dancer's sexual and racial masquerade is unveiled. During their second night at the beach house, Tris's husband Milo arrives and discloses his wife's background. As Laura tells later tells Jack, "'He's a Negro. And so is she. . . . She's from New York, Jack. She was born right here and her name is Patsy Robinson. She's only seventeen but they've been married two years'" (108). Although Laura is still fascinated with the beautiful young dancer, she is disturbed by Tris's unhealthy relationship with both her racial identity and sexual orientation and thus decides to break off the relationship.

Laura's decision to end her romantic involvement with Beebo and Tris does not signal the cessation of gender, racial and sexual passing in *Women in the Shadows*. Rather than eliminating the love triangle between the three women, these events merely cause it to morph into a different form. Laura learns that Tris may have initiated a sexual liaison with her, but it was the tomboyishly butch Beebo who was Tris's real erotic interest. As a mutual friend informs her, "'Tris was nuts for [Beebo]. That time she burst in on you and Beebo got so mad—yes, she told me about it—she came to see Beebo, not you. She didn't care a damn if it got you in trouble. The only thing she cared about was seeing Beebo'" (154).

This unexpected news prompts Laura to contemplate her attraction to both women, and her assessment highlights the centrality of gender and racial difference in the construction of lesbian sexuality once again. Given Laura's awareness that it was "the big ones, the butches who acted like men and expected to be treated as such . . . who excited [her] the most" (127), she wonders why she was enamored with the feminine Tris. Although the dancer did not possess the tomboyish butchness, she did have "that marvelous fragrant tan skin" (128). This remark forms the novel's third comment about the role of race in the construction of lesbian gender and sexual identity. As Lisa Walker has written, it "suggests that Laura was only drawn to Tris because she has mistakenly replaced one form of difference—gender difference between lesbians—with another: racial difference" (113); Tris's blackness served as a substitute for Beebo's butchness.

The final twist to Bannon's novel also constitutes its final instance of passing. Laura's discovery that her masquerading former lovers are now lovers themselves compels her to engage in a masquerade of her own identity. In a gesture that combines Beebo's previous gender passing with Tris's racial and sexual one, she accepts the longstanding marriage proposal from gay friend and confidant Jack Mann, and masquerades as an upper-middle class feminine wife and mother on the Upper East Side of Manhattan. After years of economic hardship and personal unhappiness, Laura is enticed by the promise of financial stability, loving companionship and sexual freedom, for the pair agrees that they will not consummate the marriage and will instead maintain their same-sex affairs. In an even more shocking detail, Laura consents not only to marry Jack but also to bear his child through artificial insemination. More than simply playing the role of a doting wife, Laura begins to genuinely embody it. In the days following their nuptials, "Laura went to pains to please [Jack], to show him that she cared and that she was working to make things right as she had promised him" (116).

As Diane Hamer has pointed out, far from being presented as a foolish and ultimately doomed lark, the sham marriage between Laura and Jack is cast as the most positive, promising and healthy relationship in the book (52). Indeed, Laura says of their union: "they were, all things considered, happy" (116). Unlike nearly all of the other couples presented in *Women in the Shadows*, their union is practically devoid of domestic violence, sexual betrayal, and self-loathing. Even when the couple encounters obstacles—most notably when Jack's former lover appears and wants to whisk him away to California—their bond is strengthened. Jack realizes that his lesbian wife is paradoxically much healthier for him than his gay boyfriend. Reuniting with Laura, the couple "lay in each other's arms and talked and made plans. They talked about Beebo and Terry, about themselves, about their baby, about life and how good it was when you were brave enough to face it" (194). By offering a way for gay characters to attain public social approval while retaining their private sexual freedom, the union between Jack and Laura permits *Women in the Shadows* to end on a note of hopeful optimism. Moreover, in a novel that is saturated with failed attempts at sexual, gender and racial passing, it is the only masquerade that is not unveiled. On the contrary, Laura and Jack's marriage is held up as an exemplar. In an almost fairy-tale ending, the last line of the novel reports about the pair: "And they fell asleep together with the sigh of relief and hope that only the lost, who have found themselves, can feel" (195).

Laura's nuptials with Jack Mann, however, accomplish much more than simply providing Bannon a way to satisfy the censors while retaining some semblance of a "happy" (albeit troublesome and problematic) ending for her gay characters. The arrangement also allows the novel's ostensible main character to reconnect with whiteness and the privileges that it affords. Through the actions of the tomboyish "woman in the shadows" Beebo, Laura becomes the postwar version of Coventry Patmore's oft-mentioned Victorian concept of the "angel in the house." Her decision to pass as an upper-middle-class white wife and mother allows her to claim a position in the nation's ruling class. As a stay-at-home spouse of a successful engineer, she enjoys all the material comforts and social privileges that accompany her fraudulent marital status and posh Upper East Side address, which "was newly renovated, lustrous with new paint, elegant with a new elevator, and bustling with chic tenants" (110). Whereas Laura had previously existed outside of mainstream postwar culture, she has now been folded back into it. A few weeks after their nuptials, in fact, "it occurred to her that Jack was a man who was taking care of his woman. And she relaxed. . . . The apartment was quiet and pretty, and Laura, who was lazy as a cat for the first time in her life, felt like a princess" (116). Given this outcome, Bannon's pulp novel does not challenge the gender, sexual and racial norms of the 1950s. Akin to previous texts that contained tomboyish characters, it reinforces them. Echoing the antebellum purpose of white tomboyism, the overlapping forms of passing with which Beebo is associated reinscribe upper-middle-class white heteronormativity for the book's ostensible central character. In this way, tomboyish figures in lesbian pulp fiction may have severed their connection to eugenics, but this shift did not mean that they abandoned this code of conduct's longstanding aim of strengthening whiteness. The pulp tomboy served as merely the conduit for these benefits rather than the direct recipient of them, but she was an instrument of these changes nonetheless.

From Exploitation "Sinema" to Family Film: The Tomboy Returns to the Silver Screen

While this chapter has focused on the representation of tomboyish characters in postwar pulp fiction, inexpensive paperback novels were not the only medium in which they could be found during the 1950s and 1960s. Recalling the predominance of gender-bending female figures in films from the war era, they also appeared on the silver screen, but with a significant modification: these figures populated the underground world of what came to be known as schlock or exploitation "sinema."

While movies that present lurid subject matter have existed almost since the birth of commercial motion pictures, both Eric Schaefer and Robert M. Payne have written that they crystallized into a distinct cinematic form in the early 1930s with the introduction of the Motion Picture Production Code. Although the long list of forbidden subject matter generated by the Hays Office was intended to eliminate inappropriate material from film, it quickly gave rise a new genre of scandalous cinema that existed outside of the studio system.[13] Whatever the Production Code forbade major studios from depicting—drug use, gang violence, rape, miscegenation, venereal disease, nudity, abortion, unwed motherhood—exploitation films took as their main subject and, as the name of the genre suggests, exploited audience curiosity about it for maximum profits.[14] Using saturation advertising techniques and hype marketing tactics, filmmakers such as Roger

13. Akin to pulp novels which showed a seedy underground world but could be found in almost every drug store rack and airport newsstand during the 1950s and early 1960s, exploitation films were also not relegated to secret, back-alley theaters but were shown at neighborhood cinemas. The independent producers of exploitation cinema either leased their film to local theaters for a predetermined period of time (usually a couple of weeks) or, in a practice known as "four-walling," purchased all the seats and sold tickets to their movie directly.

14. In the same way that pulp fiction was able to circumvent prevailing obscenity laws and discuss forbidden subject matter by presenting a largely negative image of lesbian life, so too did exploitation film. These illicit movies were able to evade the Hays Code through what has often been deemed their "compulsory conservativism." As Gary Johnson has written, "These movies typically began with a scrolling text that warned audiences about a social problem (drug addiction, prostitution, venereal disease, etc.). Or they began with a lecturer who warned the audience about the dangers of the vices depicted in the film"

Corman, Doris Wishman and David Friedman attracted large crowds to their meagerly funded, hastily written and quickly produced pictures.[15]

While topics like drug use, abortion and venereal disease were among the most popular for exploitation films, female gender and sexual iconoclasm was also a frequently addressed issue. For example, drawing on public anxiety about the rising postwar rate of juvenile delinquency, a sub-category of the exploitation genre specialized in the presentation of tomboyish female gangs. In films such as William Morgan's *The Violent Years* (1956), Robert C. Derteno's *Girl Gang* (1956) and Sande N. Johnsen's *Teenage Gang Debs* (1966), young women defied their conventional gender roles by donning leather jackets, wearing denim jeans and engaging in illegal activities like drug trafficking, gun play and even murder. The young women in *The Violent Years* (1956) even adopt boyish nicknames: Pauline becomes Paul, Georgia is known as George, and Phyllis goes by Phil. Moreover, in keeping with the strong association between tomboyism and homosexuality in pulp fiction, movies like Joseph P. Mawra's *Chained Women* (1965) and Peter Woodcock's *Daughters of Lesbos* (1968) featured tough women who also loved women. Reflecting the era's medico-scientific approaches to sexual deviance, many aped the rhetorical style of sociologists and psychiatrists. At the start of the pseudo-documentary *Daughters of Lesbos*, a male voice-over asks: "Do you know the difference between the Bull Dyke, the Stomping Butch and the Baby Butch?"

Over time, a combination of the continued success of pulp fiction, the popularity of exploitation films, and the steady erosion of the Hays Code caused formerly forbidden sexual subject matter to begin appearing in more mainstream cinema, including Nicholas Ray's *Johnny Guitar* (1954), William Wyler's *The Children's Hour* (1961) and Edward Dmytryk's *Walk on the Wild Side* (1962). In *Johnny Guitar*, for instance, Joan Crawford's character, Vienna, may operate a saloon in the West, but she can be connected with the postwar codes of urban lesbianism. As Judith Halberstam has written, Vienna dons the era's butch uniform of dark pants and button-down shirts, and also possesses an unmistakable erotic tension with another gender-bending female character in the film played by Mercedes McCambridge (*Female* 194–195). Similarly, *Walk on the Wild Side* (1962) takes place in a New Orleans brothel that is run by a tough lesbian madam who possesses the tomboyishly significant

---

(par. 5). Known collectively as the "square-up," these tactics allowed exploitation films to justify showing almost anything on screen.

15. Providing an indication of the popularity these films, Felicia Feaster and Bret Wood have noted, "The crowds that queued up along the sidewalks to see these films more closely resembled the throngs of jobless men or women in the breadlines of Depression-stricken New York" than those awaiting entrance to what would come to be dubbed "schlock sinema" (8).

name "Jo." Finally, *The Children's Hour* (1961), about two teachers who are falsely accused of being lesbians, contains an array of elements culled from both pulp fiction and exploitation sinema: the film takes place at an all-girls' boarding school, the teachers are charged with "having had sinful sexual knowledge of one another," and one of them commits suicide at the end.

Tomboyish figures may have inhabited the seedy worlds of exploitation film and pulp fiction during the 1950s and 1960s, but they were not destined to remain in these venues. In the coming decades, events such as the rebirth of white feminism, changes in national childrearing practices, and the inauguration of the gay and lesbian liberation movement catapulted this character back into the mainstream. In recurring roles by young stars such as Jodie Foster, Tatum O'Neal and Kristy McNichol, tomboyhood returned to Hollywood during the 1970s and 1980s. In the following chapter, I examine how this code of conduct made this dramatic shift, the social and cultural factors that precipitated it, and the elements that carried over from its residence in pulp fiction and schlock sinema.

9

The Tomboy Returns to Hollywood

Tatum O'Neal in Peter Bogdanovich's Paper Moon

Although the cinematic depiction of tomboyish characters crystallized into a distinct category during the 1940s, critics like Judith Halberstam have argued that it did not reach its heyday until several decades later. Beginning in the 1970s and lasting until the early 1980s, the tomboy film emerged as a box-office staple. Major Hollywood studios such as United Artists, Disney and Paramount released an array of feature-length movies that showcased spunky female heroines. From *Paper Moon* (1973) and *The Bad News Bears* (1976) to *Candleshoe* (1978) and *Times Square* (1980), these films, as Halberstam has noted, "tended to imagine girlhood as tomboyhood" (*Female* 188).

This chapter charts the return of tomboyhood to Hollywood during the 1970s and 1980s and the changes that resulted from its residence in this popular visual medium once again. After decades of being relegated to the liminal counterculture of pulp fiction, tomboyism regained its former status as a fixture in the nation's mass culture. As the discussion that follows will demonstrate, although the 1970s and 1980s are commonly associated with the Watergate scandal and the Mideast oil crisis, they could also be remembered for the return of the tomboy. In the same way that a constellation of political and economic factors precipitated the resignation of President Nixon and the rise of domestic gas prices, events such as the rebirth of white feminism, changes in national childrearing practices and the inauguration of the gay and lesbian liberation movement sparked a renewed national interest in this gender-bending code of female conduct.

Pretty as Well as Punk: Tradition and Transgression in Cinematic Tomboyism during the 1970s and 1980s

While the publication of Betty Friedan's *The Feminine Mystique* may have reignited national interest in women's rights during the mid-1960s, the second-wave feminist movement did not reach a critical mass in many ways until the early 1970s. As William H. Chafe and, more recently, Jane F. Gerhard have written, after nearly a decade of increasing levels of social and political organization, the fight for women's rights began to have a visible presence and palpable impact on American life during this period. In historic steps like the 1972 passage of Title IX that mandated equal allocation of funds for female athletics and the Supreme Court ruling that same year which required states to allow unmarried women access to birth control, women were winning increased political, social and economic freedoms during this era.[1]

Although the efforts of the second-wave feminist movement are commonly associated with such adult matters as sexual freedom and economic parity, they also had a profound impact on issues relevant to children. As Judith Halberstam has noted, growing skepticism about the "naturalness" of conventional gender roles caused millions of parents to rethink their childrearing practices in general and approach to raising young girls in particular. In contrast to the 1950s' emphasis on the more feminine traits of conformity, submissiveness and obedience, parents began to encourage their daughters to adopt the more feminist ones of confidence, individuality and independence (Halberstam *Female* 188). Within this environment of more experimental approaches to parenting, iconoclastic codes of conduct such as tomboyism began to increase in popularity.

In a powerful index of this phenomenon, a study conducted by Janet S. Hyde, B. G. Rosenberg and Jo Ann Behrman and published in a 1977 issue of *Psychology of Women Quarterly* reported that 51% of adult women, 63% of girls entering junior high and 78% of undergraduate females would characterize themselves as childhood tomboys (73). These statistics contradicted the assumption, which the researchers cite in the opening sentence of their study, that "the meager research on tomboyism is based on the

---

1. For more information on the second-wave feminist movement and its impact on American women's social and sexual life, see William H. Chafe's *The Paradox of Change: American Women in the 20th Century* (New York: Oxford UP, 1991) and Jane Gerhard's *Desiring Revolution: Second-Wave Feminism and the Rewriting of Twentieth-Century American Sexual Thought* (New York: Columbia UP, 2001).

assumption that it is rare and abnormal" (73). As the findings of Hyde, Rosenberg and Behrman indicate, the growth of the second-wave feminist movement and alterations to national childrearing practices had transformed this code of conduct from a "rare" and even "abnormal" identity to more common and normative one.

The re-emergence of tomboyism during the 1970s and early 1980s arose from constructive influences like the reinvigoration of white feminism, but it was also shaped by some destructive ones, namely the dissolution of American family life through separation and divorce. "Between 1960 and 1967 the divorce rate increased from 2.2 per 1,000 population to 2.7, but this gradual increase began to accelerate rapidly, so that by 1974 it stood at 4.6 per 1,000" ("Modern World" 42). Reflecting this change, in films such as *Little Darlings* (1980), *Candleshoe* (1978), *The Bad News Bears* (1976) and especially *Foxes* (1980), the tomboyish central characters come from "broken homes." Each of these girls either has only one parent or, in the case of orphans Casey Brown in *Candleshoe* and Sarah Brown in *International Velvet*, none at all.

For young girls living in such unstable, uncertain and even chaotic environments, tomboyism represented not simply a feminist statement but a survival tactic. Hailing from homes in which they had been abandoned emotionally and/or physically by their parents, they did not have the luxury of being femininely passive, delicate and naïve. Akin to antebellum figure Capitola Black, they must be strong, independent and, perhaps most importantly, self-sufficient. In *Candleshoe*, for instance, rough-and-tumble Casey Brown agrees to pose as the long-lost granddaughter of a wealthy British woman not because she is cruel or even criminal, but because she is poor and lonely. By participating in the scam, the orphaned fourteen-year-old girl hopes to gain both economic security and familial stability.[2] Similarly, throughout Adrian Lyne's *Foxes*, Jeanie serves as the guardian for not only herself, but also her schoolmates and divorced parents. The young woman is the one who saves her troubled friend from the destructive influences of "Hollyweird" Boulevard, helps Madge clean up after a disastrous party at her boyfriend's house, and comforts Brad after Annie dies in a car accident. In addition, she helps her mother study for an upcoming test, and expresses concern that her father—who is a successful concert organizer—is not getting sufficient rest. Putting her own needs and interests

2. Amanda Whurlitzer from Michael Ritchie's popular film *The Bad News Bears* can also be seen in this way. Raised by a struggling single mom, the eleven-year-old girl is selling star maps on the side of the road when she is first introduced. The pint-sized pitcher agrees to join the team, at least in part, out of desire for a father figure: Morris Buttermaker, the coach of the Bears, used to date Amanda's mother, and she secretly hopes her involvement with the league will spark a reconciliation. When the season is nearly over, the young girl is afraid of losing him from her life: she anxiously asks Buttermaker if he will take her to the movies sometime, or her and her mother to a ballgame.

aside, Jeanie is much more of a responsible adult than any of the ostensible parental figures in her life.

Some tomboyish characters became so disaffected by the vacuity, broken promises and artificiality of middle-class suburban life that they engaged in not simply an isolated rebellion against selected facets, but a wholesale rejection of it. For these figures, the punk movement beckoned. As Judith Halberstam has argued, this combined music and fashion movement "allowed for a different trajectory of rebellion than feminism did" (Halberstam "Bondage" 153). With its interest in shock and emphasis on ugliness, it represented a radical new way for young women to reject femininity. By sporting Mohawks, wearing black lipstick and piercing their ears with safety pins, punk allowed girls, in the words of Halberstam once again, to be "unpretty" ("Bondage" 154).

Allan Moyle's 1980 film *Times Square* is set in a grungy, pre-Disneyfied Times Square, and it showcases the centrality of punk in the gender rebellion of two young girls. While the Ramones's anthem "I Wanna Be Sedated" blares on the soundtrack, Pammy and Nicky frolic through the gritty streets of New York and dream of becoming rock stars. Robin Johnson's character, Nicky, is an especially strong punk figure and, at the same time, also an acutely tomboyish one. During the course of the film, she eats the petals off a bouquet of roses, plays the most cacophonous music on her electric guitar, writes a song in which she equates herself to a "damn dog," makes the flip prophecy that she doesn't expect to live past the age of twenty-one, and warns Pammy not to take the sedatives that the doctor has given them because they make you lose your fight and "fight's all ya' got."

The birth of the punk movement, transformations to American family life, and rise of second-wave feminism were not the only social phenomena fueling the increased visibility of tomboyism during the 1970s and 1980s. Together with the impact of these events were the ones precipitated by advancements in the fight for gay and lesbian rights. After decades of homosexuals existing on the margins of society, the Stonewall Rebellion on June 28, 1969, marked their movement into the mainstream. As Martin B. Duberman and more recently David Carter have discussed, it signaled the end of the largely accomodationist homophile movement and the commencement of the more activistic fight for gay and lesbian liberation. In the aftermath of the Stonewall riots, gay bars and even bath houses that had operated clandestinely now did so openly. Moreover, as Lillian Faderman has written, being a lesbian almost became a prerequisite for being a feminist during the 1970s. With heterosexuality seen as perpetuating the subjugation of women, homosexuality represented an attractive alternative—and even necessary next step—for many female advocates of women's rights. Throughout the country, women began living on single-sex communes, replacing history with "herstory," and reviving goddess-based religions. Because lesbianism could now be claimed as a political identity rather than merely a sexual one, Faderman estimates "There were probably more lesbians in America during the 1970s than any other time in history" (*Odd* 207).

As a result of such events, national sentiments about homosexuality began to change. In perhaps one of the most powerful indices of this phenomenon, the 1973 edition of the American Psychiatric Association's *Diagnostic and Statistical Manual of Mental Disorders* removed homosexuality from its list of ailments. Admittedly, this change was a controversial one that was met with acute resistance by some of the organization's members. Ronald Bayer has documented that initial discussions of the removal prompted heated debate, while its eventual implementation ignited a virtual schism in the APA.[3] Nonetheless, in spite of the controversy, the alteration was adopted and it marked a milestone for LGBTQ peoples in the United States. As Lillian Faderman has written, gay men and lesbians had insisted for decades that they did not suffer from a mental illness and, in a landmark decision that reversed the opinions of generations of scientists, the psychiatric community now officially agreed with them (*Odd* 214).

Fueled by this increased social visibility of, and scientific acceptance for, homosexuality, many Hollywood films from the 1970s and 1980s featured gender-bending female figures who possessed homoerotic traits. Throughout *Times Square*, for instance, the relationship between Nicky and Pammy goes beyond mere friendship. At various points, the tough street girl seems enamored with her upper-class accomplice, and vice versa. When the two first meet in the psychiatric hospital, for instance, Pammy writes a tender poem about her rebellious roommate. "Poem, for Nicky Marotta. Tiny fossil bones, translucent skin. . . . Dinosaur, you don't belong here. They'll kill you for your tiny tusks. But your ribs are my ladder, Nicky. I am so amazed. I am so amazed." After the duo escapes from the institution and takes up residence in an abandoned warehouse, Pammy and Nicky spoon in bed one morning. Later, Nicky becomes incensed when Johnny LaGuardia, a male radio host with whom they have developed a relationship, visits Pammy. Acting like a jealous lover, she explodes in a rage, yelling and throwing household items at the pair. Afterward, she burns various mementoes of her time with Pammy and then—in a gesture that recalls the endings of lesbian pulp narratives—attempts suicide by jumping in the river. Appearing on LaGuardia's radio show later that night, Nicky performs a song whose lyrics are a raw and barely coded confession of her love for Pammy: "I never told you everything. / I never said the stuff I should. / I was chicken to tell you. / I never thought I could."

---

3. For more information about the heated discussion, controversial debate and even open dissention surrounding the removal of homosexuality from the *DSM*, see Ronald Bayer's *Homosexuality and American Psychiatry* (Basic Books, 1981).

A similar theme permeates *Little Darlings*. Recalling the postwar association of adolescent tomboyism with adult lesbianism, the central female characters are accused of being "lezzies" in one of the opening scenes of the movie. While the feminine Ferris is quick to deny the charge, the tomboyish Angel engages in an act that seems to confirm the allegation: she playfully attempts to grab the breast of her accuser.[4] Although *Little Darlings* quickly degenerates into a contest over which one of the girls can be the first to lose their virginity to a guy, a homoerotic undertone remains. Akin to the triangulation that Eve Kosofsky Sedgwick has identified between two men who are competing over a woman, a lesbian-charged one emerges between these two young women who are in competition over men. Unable to have sex with each other, Angel and Ferris displace this desire onto the competitive quest for heterosexual intimacy. As one of their fellow campers remarks on the sexual tension between them: "Two little virgins, how quaint. No wonder you're always fighting, it's all that unreleased energy."

Although many Hollywood films from the 1970s and 1980s presented tomboyish characters who defied heteronormative sexual roles, nearly all depicted them conforming to traditional gender ones. Unlike the butchness that permeated postwar pulp fiction, tomboyish characters from the 1970s and 1980s largely distanced themselves from more masculine forms of this code of conduct.[5] While some of these figures engaged in traditionally male activities (such as baseball in *The Bad News Bears*) and often even acquired boyish names (like Nicky in *Times Square*), they were far more feminine than their antecedents in pulp fiction. In *Foxes*, for instance, Jeanie has long hair, wears skirts and often even dons high-heeled shoes. Likewise, the opening scene of *Little Darlings* shows the tough and tomboyish Angel Bright kicking a boy in the groin, but it also shows her sporting long hair, wearing girl's clothes and retaining her very feminine first name. Finally, in

---

4. A parallel scene occurs in *Foxes*. When Jeanie and her friends repudiate the sexual advances of a group of young men outside of a rock concert, the guys instantly begin shouting, "Dykes! Dykes!" at them. Instead of refuting this accusation or even becoming offended by it, the mischievous girls embrace it: they begin hugging and kissing each other in an exaggerated display.

5. This trait was not merely limited to adolescent tomboys from this era; it also extended to include a figure who is perhaps their most famous adult counterpart: the title character from Woody Allen's 1977 film *Annie Hall*. This "kooky" cinematic character may have worn men's shirts and ties, but, as Angela McRobbie has noted, her image "was not even vaguely menacing" (43). Unlike the sexual style of the butch lesbian, she softened or feminized her look. Selecting ties and vests that drew attention to her hips and chest, tucking in men's shirts to make them more form-fitting and accenting the entire ensemble with a floppy feminine hat, her seemingly gender-bending style emphasized the traditional womanly figure. As a result, Annie Hall's outfits may have been comprised of male clothing, but they never "conferred on girls and women a true androgyny" (McRobbie 44). On the contrary, in the words of Angela McRobbie, her ensembles simply "alerted others to the feminine potential of the male wardrobe" (44).

The Bad News Bears, Amanda Whurlitzer does agree to pitch for the all-boys baseball team, but only after she has been assured that throwing fastballs will not interfere with her body's development of feminine characteristics. When Coach Buttermaker first approaches the young girl about pitching for the Bears, in fact, her response recalls negative *fin-de-siecle* attitudes about women and athletics: "My mom said you almost ruined me with that sports stuff. . . . I'm through with all that tomboy stuff." Although Morris asserts that baseball is not "tomboy stuff" but the national pastime, Amanda goes on to explain, "I'm almost twelve and I'll be getting a bra soon . . . I can't be playing no dumb baseball." Wearing a long skirt, costume jewelry and a halter top when first introduced to viewers, the talented female pitcher does not seem very tomboyish. On the contrary, Amanda uses her gender-bending talent for baseball as a means to facilitate her more gender appropriate desire to study dance: she agrees to join the team only after Buttermaker promises to pay for a series of ballet lessons.[6]

The appearance of the new psychiatric condition, "Gender Identity Disorder of Childhood," in the 1980 edition of the *Diagnostic and Statistical Manual of Mental Disorders* suggests that the increased emphasis on more feminine forms of tomboyism may have had its root in a scientific rather than merely social cause. Although the American Psychiatric Association asserted that this new childhood psychological condition was "not merely the rejection of stereotypical sex role behavior as, for example, 'tomboyishness' in girls" (264), it nonetheless described this illness in language that was eerily reminiscent of this code of conduct. According to the *DSM-III,* girls with Gender Identity Disorder "regularly have male peer groups, an avid interest in sports and rough-and-tumble play, and a lack of interest in playing with dolls or playing 'house' (unless playing the father or another male role)" (264). Only more rarely, the description went on to assert, did a girl suffering from GID express more pronounced disavowals of their gender through "claims that she will grow up to become a man (not merely in role), that she is biologically unable to become pregnant, that she will not develop breasts, or that she has, or will grow, a penis" (*DSM-III* 264). Indeed, the APA noted, "Some of these children, particularly girls, show no other signs of psychopathology" than the tomboyish traits described above (*DSM-III* 264–265).

---

6. A similar observation could be made about a movie that is not commonly grouped with the tomboy films from the 1970s and early 1980s but could be in many ways: Herb Freed's 1985 romantic comedy *Tomboy.* Although the title character, Tomasina "Tommy" Boyd, is a gifted car mechanic who rides a dirt bike to work and enjoys shooting hoops with the guys, she is nonetheless an acutely feminine figure: Tommy has long hair and is always wearing tight-fitting jeans and shirts. For these reasons, while *Tomboy* is ostensibly about a gender-bending young woman, its underlying message is that even this seemingly iconoclastic figure is nothing more than another sex object for men. Indeed, Freed's romantic comedy is a weak imitation of Adrian Lyne's popular 1983 film *Flashdance.*

Tomboyism and Gender Identity Disorder also had similar origins and social trajectories. Recalling the historical view that the lack of a strong maternal influence could be a cause for tomboyism, the *DSM-III* asserted that girls who develop GID often "have mothers who were apparently unavailable to them at a very early age, either psychologically or physically, because of illness or abandonment; the girl seems to make a compensatory identification with the father, which leads to the adoption of a male gender identity" (265). Likewise, echoing the longstanding tradition of tomboy taming, the *DSM-III* offered the following prognosis for GID: "For females the age at onset is also early, but most begin to acquiesce to social pressures during late childhood or adolescence and give up an exaggerated insistence on male activities and attire" (265).

Akin to previous historical eras, when more masculine forms of female gender expression were pathologized, concern about GID in girls was rooted in fears that childhood gender nonconformity would lead to adult sexual nonconformity. In the words of Shannon Minter, "Much of this research was touted as a means to identify 'prehomosexual' and 'pretrans-sexual' children and to prevent them from growing up to be gay or trans-sexual" (11–12). In light of these details, homosexuality may have been officially removed from the American Psychiatric Association's *Diagnostic and Statistical Manual* in 1973, but it resurfaced via Gender Identity Disorder of childhood in the very next edition. As Matthew Rottnek has noted, "Here, homosexuality-as-pathology is simply reconfigured as a childhood disorder" (1).[7]

Coupled with constituting a clear backlash against the advances made by the gay and lesbian liberation movement, the reconfiguration of adult homosexuality as a form of childhood gender dysphoria also impacted the cinematic presentation of tomboyish characters. Allan Moyle's *Times Square* contains homoerotic elements, but neither main character is explicitly presented as a lesbian. In commentary on the recent DVD edition of the film, the director reveals that all of the overt lesbian content in the original script and initial cut of *Times Square* was removed during later editing, even though some of these deletions jeopardized the logic of movie's basic plot and its narrative continuity. Likewise, all of the other films that contained homoerotic overtones discounted the potential lesbian identity of their characters by calling attention to their hyper-heterosexuality. In *Little Darlings*, Angel Bright and Ferris Whitley may have a crush on each other, but neither of them ever directly vocalizes let alone acts on it. Instead, as mentioned

7. For more information on the origins, history and evolution of Gender Identity Disorder—as well as the suggestive echoes between it and homosexuality—see Matthew Rottnek's *Sissies and Tonboys: Gender Nonconformity and Homosexuality in Childhood* (New York: NYU, 1999) along with Eve Kosofsky Sedgwick's "How to Bring Your Kids Up Gay," *Social Text*, 29, (1990): 18–27.

before, the movie quickly devolves into a contest over which girl can be the first to have sex with a guy. Likewise, in *Foxes*, Jeanie may joke about how she and her friends are "dykes," but she also mentions repeatedly that she lost her virginity when she was only twelve years old and has slept with multiple boys since then.

The End of the Age of Innocence: *Paper Moon* and the Transformation of U.S. Childhood and Its Tomboyhood

Although an array of motion pictures during the 1970s and early 1980s featured tomboyish young girls, Peter Bogdanovich's *Paper Moon* came to epitomize this trend. The central character of the 1973 film is a nine-year-old girl who possesses many signature elements of this code of conduct. Echoing the family circumstances of numerous tomboyish figures, for instance, the youth is motherless and alone when first introduced to viewers. The film begins at the sparsely attended funeral of Addie's mother, barroom dancer Essie May Loggins. With her mother deceased and her father unknown, one of the mourners laments, "The child's got nowhere to go."

Together with exemplifying the typical family history and even prepubescent age coordinates of many U.S. tomboys, Addie embodies their classic physical appearance and psychological identity. Although the young girl is wearing a dress at the funeral, she is far more boyish than girlish. The opening shot of *Paper Moon*, in fact, presents a close-up of Addie's face. The young girl's hair is shorn so short that she looks like a boy. Moreover, her locks are so uneven that it appears as if she cut them herself.

Addie's tomboyish haircut is matched by her equally tomboyish attire throughout the remainder of the film. Reflecting a common feature of many gender-bending female figures, the youth prefers a boyish pair of dark denim overalls to a girlish dress. Moses Pray, an itinerant con man who attends the funeral of his former flame and is subsequently conscripted to drive her orphaned daughter to relatives in St. Joseph, Missouri, quickly realizes that Addie does not seem to own anything other than the overalls. Although the young girl was wearing a dress at her mother's funeral, it was either borrowed for the occasion or left behind in Kansas, for she never pulls the garment from her suitcase.

Addie's boyish external appearance perfectly suits her internal psychological identity. Defying stereotypes about the pleasant personality of little girls, she is nearly always scowling. As Jon Landau commented in his review of *Paper Moon*, "Addie looks like a dour, surly tomboy" (66). The youth's perpetual pout intensifies near the middle of the film when Moses participates in yet another signature facet of tomboyism: he attempts to tame Addie, putting a feminine ribbon in her hair. In a shot that embodies the quintessential image of a tomboy in many ways, the camera begins in tight focus on the pretty item and then pulls back to reveal a grimacing Addie who has her hands thrust defiantly in the pockets of her denim overalls. Although the young girl does not actually voice her disapproval, her dislike is plain.

The combination of Addie's boyish clothes, short haircut and gruff manner precipitate a final common hallmark facet of tomboyish characters: she is frequently mistaken for a boy. When Moses finishes having a shave, the barber turns to Addie and says, "All right, boy, you're next." Earlier, Moses had taken her shopping in town, and a store clerk remarked, "First off, I didn't know if she were a boy or a girl."

In large part because of the appeal of O'Neal's tomboyish character, *Paper Moon* became a commercial as well as critical success. The film ranked among the top ten highest grossing movies of 1973,[8] and it also received no fewer than four Oscar nominations.[9] Moreover, *Paper Moon*'s one win—Tatum O'Neal for Best Actress in a Supporting Role—made motion picture history. The youth's debut performance as the tomboyish grifter Addie Loggins rendered her the youngest person to win an Academy Award in a competitive category: Tatum was nine when the film was released and ten at the time of the Oscar ceremony. Reflecting her own iconoclastic personality—and also undoubtedly attempting to evoke the character that she portrayed in the movie—O'Neal slicked her short hair back and wore a tuxedo instead of a dress to the Academy Awards. In the wake of the critical and commercial success of *Paper Moon*, it was adapted as an episodic television series during the following broadcasting season. Although O'Neal did not reprise her role for the small screen, none other than her fellow tomboy star Jodie Foster was cast as Addie.

Whether or not Tatum O'Neal realized it at the time, she would be linked with tomboyism in general and the pint-sized grifter Addie Loggins in particular thereafter. For nearly a decade following the release of *Paper Moon*, she portrayed gender-bending characters almost exclusively. In fact, O'Neal appeared in several of the other well-known tomboy films from the era, including *The Bad News Bears* (1976), in which she played central character Amanda Whurlitzer, and *International Velvet* (1978), where she appeared as main character Sarah Brown. Exemplifying the tremendous influence that Tatum O'Neal's tomboyish role in *Paper Moon* had on both her professional career and her personal life, she titled her recent autobiography *A Paper Life* (2004).

8. *Paper Moon* earned 16.5 million dollars at the box office, ranking it number seven on the list of top-grossing films from 1973. For more information on the box-office draw of *Paper Moon*, see Marc Sigoloff's *The Films of the Seventies: A Filmography of American, British and Canadian Films, 1970–1979* (Jefferson, NC: MacFarland, 1984) along with the article "The Top Grossing Films of 1973" in the May 8th, 1974 issue of *Variety*.

9. *Paper Moon* earned two nominations for Best Supporting Actress, one for Best Sound and one for Best Adapted Screenplay.

In this section, I explore the elements that made Peter Bogdanovich's 1973 film so commercially popular, critically praised and ultimately historically resonant. *Paper Moon* reflected not simply transformations to the cultural construction of tomboyhood, but also conceptions of childhood. As Anne Higonnet has persuasively written, Enlightenment era views of childhood as a time of innocence began to erode during the later decades of the twentieth century. Beginning in the 1960s and 1970s, U.S. culture began to present children as sexually aware and socially savvy rather than naïvely angelic. In everything from films and books to advertisements and television shows, young girls and boys were engaging in such adult actions as drinking, smoking, having sex and talking knowledgably about everything from racism and political corruption to social injustice and war atrocities. As a result, childhood was no longer seen as a time of purity. Instead, in a return to pre-Enlightenment views that boys and girls were sinful "little adults," American culture began to view them in a manner that Higonnet characterizes as "Knowing Children" (12).

Paper Moon reflects this shift. As a nine-year-old girl who not only swears and smokes but steals and swindles, Addie Loggins possesses a maturity beyond her years. Indeed, as O'Neal herself has noted in her autobiography, one critic asserted that her performance "rewrote the book on movie moppets" by embodying a new type of child star "for a hip, cynical age" (4). O'Neal's portrayal of Addie Loggins transformed the more-than-century-long phenomenon of tomboyism from a healthful childrearing practice and feminist gender expression into a disturbing form of pre-adult precociousness.

The way in which Addie's tomboyhood reflects shifting cultural attitudes about childhood emerges from the opening scene of Bogdanovich's film. Contrary to stereotypes about the emotional nature of women in general and girls in particular, the youth does not cry at her mother's funeral. Instead, the newly orphaned girl demonstrates exceptional self-control: she stands by the graveside in a manner that is not merely solemn but stoic. Addie's expressionless demeanor suggests that her tomboyish toughness is as much a product of her circumstance as it is her innate personality. Although the youth is only nine years old, her life has been riddled with hardship. Addie is not only the illegitimate daughter of a barroom dancer (and likely prostitute), but she is also being raised amidst a national economic crisis: *Paper Moon* is set in the mid-1930s, during the most crushing years of the Great Depression. As John T. Dunlop and Walter Galenson have written, unemployment rates remained among the highest in the nation's history between 1933, the year that the song "It's Only a Paper Moon" from which the film draws its title was originally recorded by Paul Whiteman and His Orchestra, and 1936, the year that many critics identify as the precise timeframe for the film.[10]

---

10. After peaking at 24.9% in 1933, unemployment in the United States dropped only slightly to 21.7% in 1934, 20.1% in 1935 and 17% in 1936 (Dunlop and Galenson 27).

Exacerbating Addie's lack of material comfort is her lack of familial connection. The youth has never known her father, and she has also been estranged from her mother's family: her maternal relatives have all but disowned the loose-living Essie May Loggins and her illegitimate daughter. As a result, akin to many children in the 1970s and early 1980s whose lives were torn apart by physical divorce or emotional abandonment, Addie was forced to grow up fast. The stereotypical childhood traits of innocence, dependency and even naïveté are unknown luxuries to her. In light of her difficult family circumstances and trying historical era, Addie has needed to be independent and self-reliant from a young age. In fact, throughout *Paper Moon*, the nine-year-old character is so intellectually astute and emotionally unflappable that she does not seem like a child. As one film critic observed, Addie's "movements and feelings are as controlled and repressed as those of any normal adult" (Landau 66). She never cries or whimpers, never seems uncertain or rattled and, perhaps most importantly, never gets confused or scared. On the contrary, the street smart and crafty youth remains in-the-know about her guardian's latest scam and is often one step ahead of him. In the opening minutes of Bogdanovich's film, for example, Moses drives to the office of the man whose brother was responsible for killing Addie's mother in a drunk driving accident. While there, he extorts two hundred dollars from the gentleman by threatening to file a more costly wrongful death lawsuit in the name of securing, as he asserts, what the orphaned little girl is "rightly owed." Although Addie was ushered out of the room during this conversation, she has been listening through the door and is aware of her claim to the settlement. In a further indication of her street smarts and craftiness, she waits until the most opportune moment to make this known: after Moses has spent the bulk of the money to first purchase himself a new car and then to buy her a "child's price" train ticket with the intention of sending her to Missouri alone. As they sit in a trackside luncheonette waiting for her departure time, Addie announces in a stern tone: "I want my two hundred dollars." The clever young girl tells him that it would be different if he were her "Pa," but since he repeatedly insists that they are not related, he should give her the cash. In a tone that grows steadily louder and more insistent, she tells him: "It's my money you got, and I want it. I want my money, you took my two hundred dollars! I heard you through the door. It's my money you got, and I want it!" The stubborn young girl remains unconvinced by any of his elaborate rationales. Finally, when the now-exasperated con man points out that he doesn't have the full two hundred dollars anymore and she knows it, she growls at him, "Then *GIT* it." As Tom Milne has written, Addie's insistence in this scene demonstrates "that the sweetly awful child is going to be more than a match for him as far as wits are concerned" (13).

This issue of Moses owing Addie two hundred dollars becomes a recurring topic and, at times, even a running joke throughout the remainder of the film. To avoid an embarrassing public scene at the luncheonette, Moses temporarily refrains from sending the young girl to St. Joe until he is able to repay her. In keeping with Addie's stubbornness and self-sufficiency, the youth repeatedly reminds him of the amount outstanding on the debt. In one especially amusing scene, Moses tells Addie after a profitable day of grifting and scamming, "I now owe you one hundred and three dollars and seventy-two cents." But the young girl, who has been keeping a meticulous mental record of the debt, corrects him. Out of the dark, Addie slowly and matter-of-factly clarifies the number of pennies remaining: "Seventy-four." The fact that the young girl is not only able to keep track of the amount, but do so in her head, is astounding. Indeed, as Jon Landau remarked of this scene, Addie demonstrates a "facility with cash unprecedented in the history of childhood" (66).

Although the partnership between Moses and Addie was intended to be a temporary arrangement, it becomes indefinite when the con man realizes that the tomboyish young girl is an even better scam artist than himself. Moses sets out to earn back Addie's two hundred dollars through his most reliable con: reading the death notices in the newspaper and then selling Bibles to new widows by fraudulently claiming that their husbands had placed the order as a surprise gift for them before they died. When he knocks on the door of his first "customer," however, a sheriff unexpectedly appears. The officer, who has been visiting with the widow, is rightly skeptical of Moses' claims. Addie sees that Moses is in danger of not only losing the sale but also of possibly being arrested, and intervenes. She gets out of the car, walks up to the house and in her most cute, innocent and sweet voice says, "Daddy, can we go now? I want to get to church and pray for Momma." Addie's words erase the duo's distrust of Moses. In fact, the formerly suspicious sheriff now offers to purchase the purportedly pre-ordered Bible for the grieving widow. When he asks about the balance remaining on the account, the sly tomboy once again takes the lead. Whereas Moses routinely asks for eight dollars, Addie sees the officer's eagerness and thus tells him that twelve dollars is due. To Moses' astonishment, the sheriff unquestioningly pays it.

Although the traveling con man is alarmed by Addie's boldness and daring, he also realizes, as Tom Milne has written, "that she is an indispensable partner" (13). Acutely aware of the potential to make even more money by teaming up with the young girl, Moses asks her a question that is more befitting another adult: "How'd you like to do some business with me?" Together with conducting Moses' longtime confidence game of selling Bibles to new widows, the duo devises new cons that are possible only because they are working in tandem. First, the pair swindles money from an elderly store clerk by distracting her while she is making change. Then, they extort an even larger sum from a merchant at a second general store by having Addie lie about the bill denomination that she used to pay for her purchase, and then whimper and sniffle until the manager refunds the fraudulent (and always greater) amount of change owed.

The only time that the precocious tomboy acts like a child in general and sweet little girl in particular is when she is doing so deliberately as part of a carefully wrought plan. As Thomas Harris has observed, Addie "understands perfectly well what possibilities are open to her in her privileged status as a minor" (144–145). At repeated points, she utilizes her cuteness to maximize profits. For example, each time a new widow answers the door and Moses begins his spiel about the pre-ordered Bible, she dons her sweetest little girl face. At the same time though, she systematically scans the inside of the home to get a sense of the widow's level of wealth. By doing so, Addie is able to extract an unprecedented twenty-four dollars for a Bible from an affluent older woman. Moreover, she is given an additional five dollars, as the wealthy new widow says, for simply coming to her door.[11]

Given the way in which Addie masterminds various scams, a series of role reversals occur between her and Moses. These inversions encompass not only their gender identities—with the female character frequently occupying the traditional male role of assertiveness, and the male character often taking the stereotypical female stance of passivity—but also their age expectations: the nine-year-old Addie assumes more of an adult nature throughout the film, while the adult Moses often acts more like a child. As Jon Landau has written, akin to an impulsive youngster, the grown con man spends money almost as quickly as he "earns" it, and has no plans for the future beyond the pleasures of today (66). Conversely, in keeping with a mature adult, Addie is a meticulous accountant who remains focused on saving for tomorrow. She is the one who is entrusted with keeping track of their earnings, in fact, storing them in a cigar box.

A key element accentuating Addie's adult nature is Tatum O'Neal's spunky personality in general and the distinctive sound of her voice in particular. The young girl's tone is not the light, sweet and soft one that is stereotypically associated with little girls. Instead, O'Neal's unexpected voice is a low, raspy and gruff. Polly Platt, in fact, described it as a "whiskey voice" while director Peter Bogdanovich characterized it variously as a "deep voice" and "'a marvelous husky voice'" (Wade 28). However the young girl's tone is classified, it gives all of her comments a maturity far beyond her age, but especially those that are already precocious, like her unexpected announcement to Moses in the sheriff's office: "Daddy, I have to go to the shithouse."

11. This accomplishment pales in comparison, however, to Addie's complicated plan to oust the dancer/prostitute Trixie Delight. Although the steps are so carefully choreographed that they would pose a challenge for an adult to successfully execute, the nine-year-old child performs them with skill, confidence and precision.

The characterization of O'Neal as having a "whiskey voice" may be apt but it is also ironic, for although her character engages in an array of adult activities, drinking is not one of them. A more accurate description of Addie's tone might be a smoker's voice, given how often the young girl lights up. In scenes that are shocking to contemporary viewers but also, undoubtedly, to those from the 1970s, Addie puffs away throughout *Paper Moon*.[12] In a vivid illustration of her smoking experience and even prowess, the nine-year-old girl lights a match single-handedly at one point, striking it off her finger rather than from the matchbook. Smoking embodies such an important facet of Addie's character that it is featured on the promotional poster for the movie. The image, which imitates a souvenir photograph taken at a carnival, shows Addie and Moses sitting in a large paper moon, with Tatum clutching her radio and holding a cigarette. Lest viewers think that the object is merely a prop, smoke curls up from the tip.

For these reasons, Tatum O'Neal may have been compared to Shirley Temple for her possession of a seemingly innate acting ability, and *Paper Moon* may have been likened to Temple's film *Little Miss Marker* (1934) for its portrayal of savvy orphan girl, but this is where the similarities cease. As Richard Hatch has rightly noted, O'Neal's presentation of Addie Loggins "would have shocked the ribbons out of Miss Temple's golden hair" (764). In the words of Andrew Sarris, "O'Neal's devilish daughter emerges as the dialectical antithesis of Shirley Temple. Imagine a character played by little Shirley in the good old days acknowledging cheerfully that her mother was a tart, that she herself was a bastard, and that the swindling of widows was a pleasant pastime" ("Little" 83).

In a final index of the way in which cinematic tomboyhood from the 1970s and early 1980s belied shifting cultural attitudes about childhood, the precocity associated with *Paper Moon*'s Addie Loggins was mirrored by the media treatment of Tatum O'Neal herself. Numerous articles sexualized and what may even be called "adulterated" the ten-year-old actress, talking about her as if she were a coy young woman instead of prepubescent girl. In an interview with O'Neal that appeared in the July 19th, 1973, issue of *Rolling Stone*, staff writer Valerie Wade began her article by noting that the young actress had "the sexiest voice since Monroe" (28). Likewise, director Peter Bogdanovich quipped of his pint-sized star, "'She is ten going on 30'" (Wade 28, 29). Even O'Neal's father, Ryan, who co-stars with her in the film,

---

12. Bogdanovich's account of how he was able to get young Tatum to smoke is equally alarming. In a story that seems like nothing short of child abuse or at least child exploitation, he tells a journalist at *Rolling Stone*: "'On the first day of rehearsals, I told Tatum that she was going to have to start smoking, and, of course she said she didn't want to. We got her some cigarettes and it was tough; she was coughing since she could not fake it and had to inhale. Finally, the prop man found these lettuce cigarettes, literally shredded lettuce, made in Texas. By the end of the picture she was smoking all the time. She got hooked, but she stopped a month after the picture was over'" (Wade 28).

inculcated this opinion. A notorious Hollywood playboy, Ryan routinely took his pre-pubescent daughter with him to parties where she made age-inappropriate friends like Cher and Stanley Kubrick and also witnessed such age-inappropriate activities as people drinking, doing drugs and having sex. By the time Tatum was barely a teenager, she was notorious for engaging in such behaviors herself. Looking back on these years in her autobiography, O'Neal lamented how her childhood was "adultized" (106).

• • •

Although O'Neal's portrayal of tomboy Addie embodies one of the most vivid examples of the changing nature of childhood, it was not the only one. An array of female characters in other tomboy films, along with narratives written for young readers, reflected this shift as well. One of the team members in *The Bad News Bears*, for instance, is convinced that the ball club is destined for failure because, as he asserts in a comment that would be shocking to hear from an adult but especially from a young child, his teammates are nothing but "a bunch of Jews, spics, niggers, [and] pansies." A similar phenomenon occurs in *Times Square*. Near the middle of the film, runaway Pammy composes a song for her politician father that is comprised of all the derogatory slurs that she has heard him utter and her accompanying affinity with these oppressed groups. As she asserts in the chorus to the tune, "Spic, nigger, faggot, bum—your daughter is one."

For many tomboyish characters during the 1970s and early 1980s, their youthful precocity also included promiscuous sexual activity. The numerous erotic experiences among Jeanie and her friends in *Foxes* prompt the youth's mother to remark that although her daughter and accompanying group of friends look like children, they don't act like them. Similarly, and perhaps even more shockingly, although Amanda Whurlitzer from *The Bad News Bears* is only eleven years old, she is sexually aware if not sexually active. After losing a bet with local "bad boy" Kelly Dean, the pretty tomboy has to go out on a date with him. When a surprised Coach Buttermaker remarks that girls her age don't go out on dates, she cynically retorts: "Of course they do, where ya' been. I know an eleven-year-old girl who's on the pill."

A variation on this phenomenon appeared in many children's books published during this era. From groundbreaking earlier novels like Louise Fitzhugh's *Harriet the Spy* (1964) to more contemporary works like M. E. Kerr's *Dinky Hocker Shoots Smack!* (1972) and Katherine Paterson's *The Great Gilly Hopkins* (1978), the female protagonists in these new and historically important narratives were tomboyish girls. Paterson's Gilly, for example, demonstrates her prowess on the basketball court and revels in fighting six boys at one time. Likewise, Harriet resists taking dance lessons, enjoys wearing a pair of old jeans, and delights in playing the traditionally male role—as the title of Fitzhugh's novel suggests—of a spy.

Even more importantly though, the presentation of tomboyism in these novels reflected the powerful shift in attitude about American childhood in general and girlhood in particular. Although the main characters in *Harriet the Spy* and *The Great Gilly Hopkins* are only eleven years old, they face an array of decidedly adult issues and mature problems: Gilly has been given up by her birth mother and has spent the past few years bouncing around different foster homes; meanwhile, Harriet's mother and father are physically present but emotionally or psychically absent. Mr. and Mrs. Welsch are too preoccupied with their high-pressure careers and high-profile Manhattan cocktail parties to pay more than passing attention to their daughter. During the first section of book, in fact, Harriet rarely sees her parents and they—in a detail that is even more telling—rarely see her, even when they are home. Instead, Mr. and Mrs. Welsch have hired Ole Golly, a nanny, to look after her. As even these brief examples indicate, Harriet and especially Gilly live in environments that do not allow them to be children or have childhoods in the traditional sense. Instead of enjoying carefree lives marked by peer play, parental love and personal innocence, these figures are acutely aware of the loneliness, injustice and disappointment that can pervade adult life.

In the same way that characters like Gilly and Harriet are not protected from adult concerns, they do not respond to these problems in child-like ways. Instead of turning to the support, wisdom and protection of adult authority figures—as boys and especially girls in novels for children had done in the past—these young girls reject them, proving themselves more capable, mature and responsible than many grown men and women. Akin to Addie in *Paper Moon*, the title character in *The Great Gilly Hopkins* does not have the luxury of being a passive "little girl"; rather, her situation dictates that she must be tomboyishly strong and self-reliant. In stark contrast to many of the frail and feminine orphaned girls who permeated previous works of children's literature, the eleven-year-old is a master at manipulating her caseworker, exploiting the weaknesses of her teachers, and preying on the good intentions as well as character foibles of her foster parents to gain power and assume control. Indeed, in a comment that is as clever and confident as it is cold and calculating, Gilly muses soon after arriving at the home of Mrs. Trotter:

> She could stand anything, she thought—a gross guardian, a freaky kid, an ugly, dirty house—as long as she was in charge.
> She was well on the way. (7)

Abandoned by her own parents and then rejected by various foster ones, Gilly has learned that adults are not a source of stability, protection or love. On the contrary, as Anne Scott MacLeod has noted, the grownups in many contemporary novels for young people behave more like children, shirking responsibility, avoiding leadership roles and acting immature. Mrs. Trotter, Gilly's new foster mother, for example, cries easily and keeps a dirty house like a child who has either never learned to properly clean their room or is simply too lazy to do it thoroughly. As a result, Gilly realizes that she must take care of herself. Akin to Tatum O'Neal's Addie, she has adopted a stance of self-protection and self-preservation, routinely lying, stealing and swearing to get what she wants. The young girl's age notwithstanding, she is more like a precocious young adult than a pre-adolescent child.

A different version of this theme runs through *Harriet the Spy*. Although Harriet's parents are wealthy and well educated, they routinely overreact, throw temper tantrums, and even change their minds capriciously like children. When Mr. Welsch is confronted by a problem with his daughter one evening, for example, he whines: "'I just can't cope with this kind of thing. I come home from the office and I want some peace and quiet and a martini'" (247).[13] Not surprisingly given these conditions, Harriet has acquired a maturity beyond her years. Instead of admiring and even idolizing adults, she sees the faults, flaws and weaknesses that are present in everyone, a fact that is vividly clear in the often cruel comments that Harriet makes about friends, neighbors and classmates in her spy notebook:

"IF MARION HAWTHORNE DOESN'T WATCH OUT SHE'S GOING TO GROW UP TO INTO A LADY HITLER" (184).

Harriet's observations, however, routinely contain more than simply the blunt honesty and unmitigated truth often expressed by children; instead, many possess a wisdom, self-reflection and insight more indicative of adults. After spying on Ole Golly during her date with Mr. Waldenstein, for instance, the eleven-year-old wonders:

"LIFE IS A GREAT MYSTERY. IS EVERYBODY A DIFERENT PERSON WHEN THEY ARE WITH SOMEONE ELSE?" (97).

Then, after her nanny gets married and moves away to Montreal, she muses:

"I WONDER IF WHEN YOU DREAM ABOUT SOMEBODY THEY DREAM ABOUT YOU" (142).

When Harriet's classmates find her notebook and read the harsh remarks that she has written about them, Fitzhugh's title character learns an even more unexpected adult lesson. In a letter to help Harriet handle the ridicule, retribution and ostracization that she has been experiencing in the wake of this event, Ole Golly tells her former charge, "You have to apologize," as one might expect (278). But, she goes on to offer a second,

---

13. The familial circumstances of Simon "Sport" Rocque, Harriet's best friend, are even more extreme; the eleven-year-old boy cooks, cleans and even keeps the checkbook for his struggling writer father. As he resentfully tells Harriet, if he didn't perform these duties, his irresponsible divorced father would let the house get filthy, not prepare meals for himself or his son, and frivolously spend even their food money, probably on alcohol.

more shocking piece of advice: "You have to lie" (278). Publicly initiating Harriet into an adult world that she has privately long known to be duplicitous, Ole Golly offers the following rationalization or justification for this course of action: "Otherwise you are going to lose a friend. Little lies that make people feel better are not bad . . . but to yourself you must always tell the truth" (278). In the words of MacLeod, Fitzhugh precipitated a profound change in literature for young people with this passage:

> First, she was repudiating a long-observed adult responsibility to be a role model and a keeper of the moral universe for children's literature. And second, she was letting a child, an unambiguous, preadolescent, eleven-year-old child, in on one of the untidy realities of the adult world, with no moral judgment attached. (199)

In children's books like *Harriet the Spy* and *The Great Gilly Hopkins*, "The old relationship between child and adult had begun to shift" (MacLeod 199), and this shift was presented through the actions of a tough, and often troubled, tomboyish character.

Both Change and Stasis: *Paper Moon* and the Transformation of Racialized White Tomboyism

The return of white feminism and the emergence of gay and lesbian liberation were not the only social or political movements to have a palpable impact on the literary and cinematic portrayal of tomboys during the 1970s and early 1980s. Together with the increasing societal power of these groups, the fight for African American civil rights that had dominated the previous two decades also exerted an influence. From the accomplishments of Martin Luther King, Jr. and the passage of the Civil Rights Act to the coining of the phrase "Black is Beautiful" and the changes wrought by the Black Power Movement, the era witnessed many palpable changes as a result of ongoing efforts to confront and dismantle prejudice.

In the wake of these transformations, it became increasingly unacceptable to present gender-bending white characters with such blatant elements of blackness. Rather than eradicating the longstanding association of tomboyish figures with various elements of nonwhiteness, these changes merely caused it to morph into a different form. Cinematic tomboys may have shared the same broad racial characteristics during this era—namely, that they were still overwhelmingly Caucasian—but they did not possess the same physical ones. Unlike previous decades, tomboyish girls on the silver screen were not all brunettes. While some, such as Robin Johnson and Kristy McNichol, had brown hair and dark features, others, namely Jodie Foster and Tatum O'Neal, had fair skin and dirty-blonde locks. These characteristics pointed to a shift in both the history of white tomboyism in United States and its hidden history as a racialized construct. Ostensibly Caucasian characters continued to "fade to black" in feature films from the 1970s and 1980s, but the process by which they did so changed. No longer linked with physical cues of blackness or at least nonwhiteness, cinematic tomboys acquired these traits from their surroundings. In many Hollywood films from this period, gender-bending female characters inhabited environments that teemed with racially charged people, places, and events. In this way, tomboy stars like Jodie Foster and Tatum O'Neal may have ostensibly seemed more like literal "Fair Maidens," but they still embodied the figurative "Dark Lady" in many ways.

The tomboyish main character in *Paper Moon* inhabits a racially charged environment that complicates her connection with nonwhiteness. From the overall aesthetic appearance of the film and the popularity of blackface minstrelsy during the era in which it is set, to the multiple racialized elements with which Moses Pray can be associated and Addie's friendship with Trixie's black maid Imogene, Bogdanovich's film reveals how this ostensible change in the cinematic presentation of white tomboys was really nothing more than a form of stasis.

The immersion of tomboy Addie Loggins in a racialized environment is announced in many ways by the visual style of the movie. *Paper Moon* is set in the Depression Era and is filmed in a grainy black and white. As Laszlo Kovacs, the film's director of photography, notes on the recently released DVD of *Paper Moon*, in fact, he shot the film through intense red filters to intensify the stark contrast between lights and darks.

Echoing the visual appearance of Bogdanovich's film is the presentation of grifter Moses Pray. Although the name of Addie's guardian most obviously evokes the Biblical figure who brought the Jews out of Egypt, this sacred connotation is coupled by several secular ones. The young man's traffic in cons and scams, for instance, recalls the life and career of Moses Kimball. Although a figure who is not well remembered today, Kimball was the close friend and occasional business partner of the self-proclaimed "king of humbuggery," P. T. Barnum. Recalling Addie's remark that when Moze "was wound up right, he could sell doodle bugs for doorknobs," Barnum and Kimball "mastered the rhetoric of moral elevation, scientific instruction, and cultural refinement in presenting their attractions" (Dennett 6). Even though the pair denied involvement in the so-called Moon Hoax of 1835,[14] they were repeatedly credited with this scam that echoes the title

14. The hoax began on August 25, 1835, when an article appeared in the *New York Sun* proclaiming that life had been discovered on the moon. Receiving national attention and igniting a media sensation, five more features quickly followed. Each article was falsely attributed to Sir John Herschel who was among the most respected astronomers of his day, and all provided extensive information about the myriad kinds of fantastical animals living

of Bogdanovich's film. In addition, P. T. Barnum got his start in puffery by selling Bibles door-to-door, and he also had a removable gold cap tooth which he put in or took out according to the situation, just like Moses Pray. Finally, reflecting the entertainment form for which Barnum is primarily associated, Bogdanovich's sly grifter meets his sweetheart, Miss Trixie Delight, at a carnival. In light of Moses' various links to humbuggery, it seems fitting that a line from the opening song of *Paper Moon* asserts, "It's a Barnum and Bailey world." Likewise, the tagline for the film proclaims, "As P. T. Barnum put it, 'There's a sucker born every minute.'"

Before P. T. Barnum became involved with the circuses with which he is commonly connected, he was associated with a more racially charged entertainment mode that was experiencing a renaissance during the era in which *Paper Moon* is set: blackface minstrelsy. Sparked in many ways by the release of Alan Crosland's film *The Jazz Singer* (1927), minstrelsy experienced a level of popularity that it had not enjoyed since the middle of the nineteenth century. From Shirley Temple in *The Littlest Rebel* (1935) and Fred Astaire in *Swing Time* (1936) to Martha Raye in *College Holiday* (1936) and Mickey Rooney in *Babes in Arms* (1939), an array of white performers blacked up during the 1930s.

Although seldom discussed in theatrical histories about minstrelsy, this performance mode made its debut in such venues as Barnum's museum of curiosities in New York City. According to *P. T. Barnum: America's Greatest Showman*, the self-proclaimed "king of humbuggery" featured a blackface troupe at his Manhattan American Museum as early as October 1836 (Kunhardt, Kunhardt and Kunhardt 25). Then, during the 1840s, Dan Rice, one of the originators of blackface, was on the showman's payroll. By the 1850s, his museum debuted Conway's wildly popular version of *Uncle Tom's Cabin*.[15] So influential was Barnum in the success of this pro-Southern version of Harriet Beecher Stowe's novel that when the production opened at the National Theatre years later, it tipped its hat to the showman's museum. In a line added to the script, a character asks Topsy, "Did you ever hear of Barnum?" (Dennett *Weird* 136).

P. T. Barnum did more than simply provide a venue for blackface; he was one of its earliest participants. As Henry W. Root notes in *The Unknown Barnum*, whenever a performer was ill or absent, the showman "blacked

---

on the moon. While historians commonly attribute authorship of the articles to Richard Adams Locke, a staff reporter for the *New York Sun*, it has never been definitely proven. For more information on the Moon Hoax of 1835, see *Sins against Science: The Scientific Media Hoaxes of Poe, Twain and Others*, edited by Lynda Walsh and James P. Zappen (Albany, NY: SUNY, 2007).

15. Echoing this trend, Robert Toll notes in *Blacking Up* that all four of the men who are commonly credited with introducing minstrelsy to the American stage—Billy Whitlock, Frank Pelham, Dan Emmett, and Frank Bower—"had experience as blackface entertainers with circuses" (30).

up and sang the songs himself" (70). As early as 1837, such appearances earned Barnum the reputation for being an "acceptable blackface singer" in his own right (Kunhardt et al. 25). When P. T. Barnum left the dime museum business for the traveling circus in the late 1860s, he maintained a connection to minstrelsy. One of the showman's most famous sideshow curiosities—African-American William Henry Johnson who was billed as the great "What Is It?" or the "Man-Monkey!" and touted as the missing link between apes and humans—was nicknamed "Zip" by Barnum after the popular minstrel figure Zip Coon.

Reflecting this history, the racialized infused nature of Moses Pray in *Paper Moon* can be extended to his nickname "Moze" which evokes a popular blackface character.[16] As David Roediger has written: "A low-comedy representative of young urban maleness—a fighter and a lover—Mose was typically an unemployed or apprentice artisan and a member of the volunteer fire department whose disorderly behavior provoked the wrath of city fathers before the Civil War" (99). By 1852, minstrel troupes throughout the country began performing a number titled "Wake Up Mose." In a detail that brings this character and his connection to P. T. Barnum full circle, Eric Lott notes there was even a "bit part in Conway's *Uncle Tom's Cabin* for a slave called Little Mose" (228).[17]

The connections between the film character Moze and the minstrel figure Mose go beyond the mere shared pronunciation of their names. Throughout Bogdanovich's film, Moses Pray possesses an array of characteristics that echo this popular figure from the minstrel stage. Although the clever con man is not a fireman, he expresses repeated concern about the fire hazard posed by Addie's smoking. Likewise, the traveling Bible salesman may repeatedly deny that he is Addie's Pa, but he nevertheless becomes a father figure for the young girl. Enjoying her company and sulking when they quarrel, the relationship goes beyond a mere business arrangement. Finally, Moses may roam the rural Midwest, but he is also a type of urban dandy. Always impeccably dressed in stylish seersucker suits with slicked hair, he is frequently fussing with his appearance.

While the minstrel Mose was originally conceptualized as a white character, performance troupes soon began presenting him in blackface. "White Mose enjoyed a striking, but relatively brief, popularity. . . . But Mose in blackface proved quite durable, incarnated as both an urban dandy and as a fatherly Southern Black" (Roediger 100). By the early twentieth century,

16. Giving further credence to this reading, Moses does not possess this nickname in the novel on which the film is based, Joe David Brown's bestselling *Addie Pray* (1971). In the book, the traveling Bible salesman is called "Long Boy" because he is so tall.

17. For more information about both the various theatrical productions of and social meanings attached to Mose on the minstrel stage, see Richard M. Dorson's "Mose the Far-Famed and World-Renowned" in *American Literature*, vol. 15 (Nov. 1943): 288–300.

the figure had transformed once again, now surfacing in the nation's material culture. As David Roediger notes, Mose "became Aunt Jemima's husband in the rag doll and salt-n-pepper shaker families of the twentieth century" (100).

Once again, this detail can be connected to Bogdanovich's film. The ostensible destination of Addie and Moses' car trip is St. Joseph, Missouri. Together with being the locale where Addie's relatives reside, it is also the locale in which the blackface character Aunt Jemima became a pancake mix icon. As M. M. Manring notes, in 1889, Missouri entrepreneur Chris Rutt was looking for a spokesperson for his new self-rising pancake flour. After seeing the Aunt Jemima character at a minstrel performance in St. Joseph, Rutt knew he "had found his trade name, and Aunt Jemima, as we know her today had met her maker" (Manring 61).

Even though the Bible salesman never blacks up in *Paper Moon*, his actions have a type of minstrelized effect on Addie. After becoming romantically involved with Trixie, for instance, Moze has his tomboyish companion sit in the back seat with the carnival dancer's black maid, Imogene. With her unruly braids and penchant for making embarrassing outbursts about Trixie's colored past ("Tell him about the time that man almost hit you over the head with a bottle, Miss Trixie. . . . Tell him about the time you almost got thrown in jail, Miss Trixie"), the African American girl's actions and appearance recall Topsy from Stowe's *Uncle Tom's Cabin*, a figure who was infamously described as "rather funny specimen in the Jim Crow line" (258). Moreover, echoing the relationship between Jo and Topsy discussed in Chapter 2, Addie and Imogene are presented as twinned characters. The pair shares similar backgrounds: both are without family of their own and must fend for themselves. At various points, the figurative connection between these two characters is made literal. As Addie and Imogene sit beside each other on the hotel staircase, they have the same facial expression and body posture. Later, the two girls do not simply commiserate, but conspire. Given that both are eager to embarrass the carnival dancer Trixie Delight and foil her relationship with Mose, they join forces. Addie offers Imogene enough money for her to leave her unpaid servitude with Trixie and take the train back to her family. In exchange, the young black maid agrees to assist in the elaborate scam that the tomboy has been formulating to separate Moze and the carnival dancer.

Akin to the way in which racialized white tomboys from previous historical eras ultimately reinforced their own privileged whiteness and, by extension, white racial control, Addie's teamwork with the black maid Imogene does not break down rigid social distinctions. On the contrary, her efforts reinstitute a traditional—and racially homogenous—nuclear white family. For all of Addie's independence and precocity, she wants nothing more than to be part of a loving family relationship. To that end, the young girl uses the two hundred dollar settlement that Moses obtained on her behalf as a means to enforce this relationship. As Jon Landau has noted, she "holds the debt over his head whenever he suggests getting rid of her" (66). Addie wants to have her picture taken with the sly grifter in the carnival paper moon, in fact, to codify their fragile father-daughter bond. When Moze declines because he is more interested in seeing Trixie, his refusal reinforces the fact that they are not family. The lyrics to the popular 1930s song, "It's Only a Paper Moon," from which Bogdanovich took the title for his film, reflect Addie's deep need for parental love, support and approval:

> *It's only a paper moon,*
> *sailing over a cardboard sea,*
> *but it wouldn't be make-believe*
> *if you believed in me.*
> —Whiteman

The orphaned nine-year-old girl is so hungry for a father figure that she even looks to the nation's president, Franklin Delano Roosevelt, whom she affectionately calls "Frankie." At repeated points throughout the film, she irritates Moze by prefacing some pat platitude with the justification, "Frankie Roosevelt says. . . ."

After Addie ousts Trixie, she and Moses quickly return to doing what the young girl enjoys most: living, working and traveling together as a team. When they steal cases of bootleg whiskey and then sell them back to their original owner for an exorbitant profit, they pose as father and daughter. Indeed, this event forms one of few times that Moses acts in an overtly paternal way toward Addie: he holds her hand and calls her by terms of endearment. Likewise, a few scenes later, Moses tells a rural family that he wants to trade his new car for their old jalopy because the sheriff is unjustly trying to take away his "little girl." Once the swap has been made and Addie and Moze have successfully crossed the state line into St. Joseph, Missouri, they begin planning their next con. As Moses boasts about how much money they will make from it, Addie asks hopefully if they can use the profits to buy a house and even a piano. Whereas Moze enjoys the rootless life of an itinerant con man, the tomboyish young girl wants nothing more than to be folded into a stable and loving family.

Unfortunately, this dream never becomes a reality. Before long, the Kansas sheriff finds Moze, his henchmen rough him up, and they steal all his money. Completely broke and both literally and figuratively beaten, Moses decides that the time has come to perform his original objective: dropping Addie off at her aunt's house in St. Joseph. Although welcomed cordially by her mother's sister, Addie is repulsed by the sterility, formality and coldness of her relative's home. Realizing that this environment is not conducive to forming a loving family connection, the scrappy tomboy runs away, catching up with Moze whose jalopy has stalled not far down the road. When the surprised con man angrily says that he does not want her riding with him anymore, Addie cites her fail-safe reason for their continued association: she reminds him that he still owes her two hundred dollars. Although Moses protests, it is short lived and merely symbolic, for his truck, whose brakes are faulty, starts rolling down the hill and the two chase after it. The film ends with Moses and Addie hopping in the vehicle and heading down a seemingly endless white chalk road.

In this way, although the method for racializing white tomboys during the 1970s and early 1980s may have changed, the end result was the same. Gender-bending female characters may have no longer been directly linked with various facets of blackness or at least nonwhiteness, but they still acquired these traits from secondary sites and environmental sources. More-over, these tomboyish figures continued to use these seemingly nonwhite traits as a paradoxical means to buttress whiteness and white hegemony. It would not be until the 1990s—with the heightened awareness about the unmarked nature of both feminism and the LGBTQ movement, along with emergence of whiteness studies—that this phenomenon would undergo a more palpable and permanent transformation.

Queering the Sequel: From Tomboy Film to New Lesbian Cinema

In the era that followed, the societal presence and cultural power of tomboy films only increased. Fueled by the unisex fashions of the grunge move-ment, the growing participation of girls in athletics, and the widespread popularity of "Girl Power" during the 1990s, gender-bending female characters appeared in movies that were as numerous as they were diverse, from light comedies aimed at largely young audiences such as *Don't Tell Mom the Babysitter's Dead* (1991) and *The Mighty Ducks* (1992) to more serious adult fare like *The Man in the Moon* (1991) and *A League of Their Own* (1992).

Perhaps the biggest growth in the cinematic depiction of tomboyism, however, occurred in the burgeoning genre of films with explicitly lesbian content. Prompted by the massive advances in the LGBTQ movement during the 1990s, these movies routinely featured tomboys not as ancillary characters, but as main protagonists. While film critics commonly bifur-cate these productions into those made by major Hollywood studios, like *Bound* (1996) or *Set It Off* (1996), and those created by smaller indepen-dent venues, such as *Go Fish* (1994) and *The Incredibly True Adventure of Two Girls in Love* (1995), they nonetheless demonstrated that the tomboy film had morphed into a multifaceted type of new lesbian cinema.

The following epilogue spotlights the massive increase in lesbian-themed films during the 1990s and the gender-bending female figures who appeared in them. These movies simultaneously reflected a surge in the production of a specific type of white tomboyism while they paradoxically rang the death knell for the more-than-century-long tradition of associating these figures with various forms of nonwhiteness. What began as a movement away from racialization in tomboy films from the 1970s and 1980s would become a full-fledged renunciation of it in lesbian movies during the following decade. The 1990s would witness the long-overdue return of whiteness to white tomboyism.

Epilogue: The Tomboy "Comes Into the Light"

Transformations to White Feminism,
the Emergence of Whiteness Studies and
the End of Racialized White Tomboyism

The racialization of white tomboyism may have found a continued life in Hollywood film from the 1970s and early 1980s, but this resurgence would not last. While the 1990s witnessed an increase in the presence of tomboyish figures in American literature and culture, it also signaled the end of their association with various forms of nonwhiteness. In contrast to this more-than-century-long phenomenon, gender-bending female figures during this era did not possess signifiers of African American culture. Instead, they were presented in ways that called attention to their Caucasian heritage.

Focusing on the numerous lesbian-themed films released during the 1990s that teemed with tomboyish characters, this epilogue chronicles the ways in which the emergence of whiteness studies, along with a heightened awareness about the unmarked whiteness of both mainstream U.S. feminism and the LGBTQ movement, brought a close to the more-than-century-long phenomenon of racialized white tomboyism in the nation's literature and culture. In a pointed irony, this period of tomboy boom was also the time of its ultimate bust.

One Step Forward, Two Steps Back: The Girlishness of Girl Power and the Advent of "Pretty Tomboyism"

Not since the era of the Second World War, perhaps, had tomboyism been as seemingly powerful and pervasive in the United States as during the 1990s. Increasing gains by the feminist movement allowed adolescent girls and young women to challenge traditional gender roles. As both Rita James Simon and Jere Longman have written, one of the most visible indices of this phenomenon was the first generation of girls raised under Title IX participating in competitive sports in record numbers. No longer merely relegated to the feminine activities of cheerleading, swimming or gymnastics, they were involved in ones that were more iconoclastic. From forming female rugby and lacrosse teams to winning the legal right to compete in formerly all-male sports like college football and baseball,[1] women in athletics had a new and more powerful presence.

Together with participating in a larger variety of sports during the 1990s, American girls were competing at higher levels. For the first time in the nation's history, professional women's athletic leagues such as the WNBA were formed and became overnight sensations. In fact, when the U.S. women's national soccer team played in the World Cup final on July 10, 1999, more than 90,000 spectators, including President Clinton, attended the event while another 40 million watched it on television. As a result of this phenomenon, women athletes like soccer star Mia Hamm and basketball sensation Sheryl Swoopes became household names. Television ads, product endorsements and sports highlight shows now routinely recognized the accomplishments of women, rather than spotlighting an occasional female athlete. Indeed, as Jere Longman aptly noted, by the mid-1990s women's sports in the United States had reached "a critical mass of public and corporate interest" (4).

As a result of these changes, a phrase that recalled mantras from feminist consciousness-raising groups during the 1970s—"Girl Power"— entered the mainstream. Serving as the title for Hilary Carlip's popular 1995 book as well as the catch phrase for the popular British musical group The Spice Girls, the concept celebrated female autonomy. As Natalie G. Adams has observed, by the middle of the decade, t-shirts with phrases like "Girls Rule" emblazoned across the chest began adorning hip teenagers in New York City and, later, ten-year-olds at suburban malls (102–103). A tomboyish sensibility seemed to be sweeping the nation.

---

1. Liz Heaston became the first woman to play in a college football game on October 18, 1997 when she kicked in two points for Willamette University. For more information, see *The Chronicle of Higher Education,* http://chronicle.com/errors.dir/noauthorization. php3?page=/che-data/articles.dir/art-44.dir/issue-10.dir/10a05503.htm. Similarly, Ila Borders became the first woman to pitch in a college baseball game on February 15, 1994. In addition, she was the first woman pitcher to start a professional baseball game, on July 9, 1998. For more information, see http://static.highbeam.com/n/newsweek/august101998/ throwingacurveballpitcherilabordersoftheduluthduk/

Finally, and perhaps most famously, Heather Sue Mercer filed a filed a sexual discrimination case against Duke University in 1999 after she was cut from their football team, and won a $2 million verdict. To read the case, go to http://lw.bna.com/lw/19990803/991014.htm.

This growth in gender-bending actions among American girls was accompanied by a growth in their gender-bending appearance. During the 1990s, the influence of grunge rock and growing concern for the natural environment sparked a new clothing style for girls. Carpenter (or work-men's) jeans, flannel shirts, and "all-terrain" shoes became fashionable for women. To accentuate this new unisex look, girls eschewed the traditional string of pearls or daub of lipstick. As Marianna Torgovnick discusses in *Primitive Passions*, tattooing and body piercing grew in popularity. A product of the era's fascination with "tribal" cultures (or, at least, Western interpretations of tribal cultures), these practices moved out of the fringe and into the mainstream. Throughout the nation, middle- and upper-class white young women began adorning their bodies with symbols that were modeled—however liberally and loosely—after the cultural practices of tribal peoples in Africa, the Pacific Rim and the Americas.

Such heightened interest in tomboyish activities in the nation's mate-rial culture was mirrored in its popular entertainment. Sherrie Inness has written that the 1990s "witnessed an explosion of tough women in the popular media" (*Action* 1). Mainstream television shows like *Buffy the Vampire Slayer* (1997–2003), *Xena: Warrior Princess* (1995–2001) and *La Femme Nikita* (1997–2001) were centered around strong and assertive female figures. Likewise, a growing number of action and adventure movies spotlighted a personally feisty and physically fit female protagonist, from Sarah Connor in *Terminator 2: Judgment Day* (1991) and Gail Hartman in *The River Wild* (1994) to Lt. Jordan O'Neil in *G. I. Jane* (1997) and Trinity in *The Matrix* (1999). Moreover, in the world of women's health and body image, a trimmer and tougher look was becoming popular. Celebrities like Madonna, Sarah Jessica Parker and Janet Jackson sported six-pack abs and visible arm muscles. In the wake of this shift, women began "taking up boxing and other sports typically considered in previous years to be just for men" (Inness *Action* 3). Indeed, both a kickboxing craze and a Tae Bo one swept the nation.

Although American society appeared to be engaged in the wholesale advocacy of tomboyish behavior during the 1990s, it was not the utopia for tomboys that it appeared. Akin to the simultaneous proliferation of and paranoia about gender-bending female figures during the Second World War, the 1990s did not sanction a wide swath of iconoclastic behavior for girls but only a narrow range of it: what Judith Halberstam has termed "feminine tomboyism." Epitomized in many ways by a young girl who plays softball instead of baseball and whose hair is pulled back in a long pony tail rather than cropped in a short crew cut, this form of gender expres-sion remained tied to femininity and, perhaps even more importantly, heterosexuality.

The gender conformity of seemingly gender-bending tomboyism during the 1990s was perhaps most vividly evidenced in Girl Power, which ostensibly made a comprehensive case for female empowerment but actually advocated a limited and socially innocuous form of it. As Pamela J. Bettis and Natalie G. Adams have observed, "although Girl Power ... positions girls in supposedly more liberatory spaces, it is still driven by dominant conceptions of ideal femininity" (xiii). Rather than addressing actual forms of female gender oppression and offering means by which these obstacles could be eliminated, the movement merely offered a snappy catch phrase that could be printed on t-shirts and stamped on lunch boxes. As Nicole Seymour has remarked, "In reality, this concept of 'girl power' is a cheerful badge for the privileged teen or young woman to wear; it doesn't seem to care either about concrete empowerment, or the ugly reality of the forces that work against it" (par. 8).

Similar observations could be made about the seemingly iconoclastic activities of tattooing and body piercing. Body modification may have become popular among young women during the 1990s, but it remained a highly gendered (and even highly heteronormative) endeavor. As Marianna Torgovnick has noted, for each sex, specific sites on the body were coded as "appropriate" places to be inked and/or pierced (*Passions* 191–195). While men focused on masculine areas such as their chest and biceps, women concentrated on feminine regions like the hip and the small of the back. Even such seemingly rebellious activities as bellybutton and tongue piercing were seen as the height of feminine sexiness: the former because it accentuated a shapely, flat stomach and the latter because of its ability to heighten the pleasure of oral sex on men. In this way, purportedly iconoclastic behavior was actually in the service of traditional gender stereotypes as well as the longstanding sexualization of women.

Echoing this trend, many seemingly tomboyish cultural trends were often nothing more than repackaged forms of femininity. For example, Sherrie Inness has commented that although it was "praiseworthy for [women] to be more muscular and aggressive than in the past," this seemingly "whole new aesthetic" was more superficial than substantive (*Action* 5). In Hollywood films as in real life, "The stereotypical female heroine [could] be muscular but not so much that she presents a threat to the males with whom she stars. Her muscularity might be impressive for 'a girl,' but she is no challenge for the 'boys'" (Inness *Action* 12). These figures remained feminine in spite of being fierce and girlish in spite of being tomboyish. Thus, they were appealing to men: they wore tight-fitting clothes, had long hair and repeatedly demonstrated that they were not lesbians.[2] For these reasons, beautiful women may have fought villains, but as Sherrie

---

2. A vivid example of this phenomenon can be found in Ridley Scott's *G.I. Jane* (1997). Repeated emphasis is placed on the heterosexuality of Lt. Jordan O'Neil. In the opening scene of the movie, for instance, she must promise that she does not "play for the other side" before being approved her as the first female candidate for SEAL training.

Inness has aptly noted, "their fundamental purpose [was] to function as eye candy" (*Action* 14).

In light of this aesthetic, gender-bending behavior among adolescent girls and young women during the 1990s went beyond merely embodying the feminine form of tomboyism that Judith Halberstam has identified; it could be seen as seen as reflecting the name of a new business that was founded in 1997: "Pretty Tomboy"-ism. The website for the "Pretty Tomboy" clothing company contained the following mission statement: "Pretty Tomboy Clothing's mission is to incorporate feminine colors and a female twist to comfortable active wear" (par. 2). In keeping with this objective, the final vowel in the word "tomboy" was sometimes formed by a soccer ball or basketball on their t-shirts and sweatshirts, but more often by a pair of bright red lips. Many of the tomboy-themed songs released during this era embedded a similar message. For example, folk musician Tret Fure decided to title her tune "Tomboy Girl" rather than simply "Tomboy," thereby calling added attention to this figure's feminine or at least female status. Likewise, the title track from Sally Taylor's 1998 album, *Tomboy Bride*, describes a girl who may have "wild ways" and "picks up a fight," but also possesses "long hair" and a "waist [that] is slight."

Recalling the WWII era, movies during the 1990s featured tomboyish women from history who had either successfully tamed their iconoclastic ways or been severely punished for refusing to do so. Even more astounding, they spotlighted many of the exact same figures as during the mid 1940s and early 1950s, namely Jo March, who appeared Gillian Armstrong's 1994 remake of *Little Women*, and Joan of Arc, who was spotlighted in Luc Besson's 1999 biopic *The Messenger*. Epitomizing the cultural message being sent about tomboyism by these films, the third feature-length adaptation of Alcott's girls' novel starred the pixie-like actress Winona Rider as the topsy-turvy main character. As many critics noted, her portrayal of Jo lacked the robust nature of a rough-and-tumble tomboy. At no point does Ryder slide down banisters or leap over fences like in Katharine Hepburn's spirited 1933 performance. Likewise, almost all of the lines from Alcott's original text about Jo longing to be born a boy, disparaging the conventions of women's traditional gender role and insisting on being called the "son Jo" are excised from the script. As one critic noted, these changes made Ryder "sexier and more vulnerable than the tomboy Jos we're used to" (Ansen 57). At the same time, they made the 1994 version of Alcott's character scarcely tomboyish enough to be tamed.

Given the way in which the cinematic portrayal of tomboyism in the 1990s echoed both the figures and the messages from the mid-1940s and early 1950s, it is not surprising that one of the era's most popular films was

---

Then, later, she adamantly denies accusations of lesbianism that have been levied by male superiors who wish to get her expelled from the program.

Penny Marshall's *A League of Their Own* (1992). Presenting a fictional-ized account of the formation of the All-American Girls' Professional Base-ball League (AAGPBL) in 1943, the production represented an ostensible wholesale endorsement of tomboyism. Showing women batting, fielding and even sliding, *League* seemed to combine the "We Can Do It" slogan of the 1940s with the "Girl Power" spirit of the 1990s. Yet, reflecting the simultaneous celebration and condemnation of tomboyism during the war years, the portrayal of gender-bending women in *A League of Their Own* was as complicated as it was conflicted. Although the female team members engage in the seemingly tomboyish act of playing professional baseball, they do so within a set of rigid restrictions: players must wear short skirts during games, travel with a female chaperone and take lessons at charm and beauty school. As manager Ira Lowenstein asserts, "Every girl in this league is going to be a lady." Prospective players are selected as much on the basis of their physical appearance as their athletic ability, sometimes more so. For example, Marla Hooch, who is an exceptional slugger but is not exceptionally pretty, is only allowed to attend tryouts after her father pleads with the scout not to punish the motherless girl for his "mistake" of raising her like a boy. Then, during a montage scene, images of women running, batting and fielding are accompanied by a voiceover from a female radio commentator about the "masculinization" of women during wartime:

> When our boys come home from war, what kind of girls will they be coming home to? And now the most disgusting example of this sexual confusion: Mr. Walter Harvey of Harvey Bars is presenting us with women's baseball. Right here in Chicago, young girls plucked from their families are gathered at Harvey Field to see which one of them can be the most masculine.

Later, in a comment that recalls Charles Hannon's observation about how Wonder Woman's battle to save the world was "no excuse for a woman to neglect her femininity" (110), an announcer asserts that for the players of the AAGPBL, "legging out a triple is no reason to let your nose get shiny." In *When Women Played Hardball*, Susan E. Johnson attests to the historical accuracy of such assertions. According to the League's manual: "Every effort is made to select girls of *ability*, real or potential, and to develop that ability to its fullest power. But no less emphasis is placed on femininity" [italics in original] (qtd in S. E. Johnson xxi). Given these guidelines, Johnson goes on to discuss how players were, in fact, required to wear makeup, keep their hair long, play in short dresses, receive lessons in charm and beauty, and travel with a female chaperone, as Marshall's film indicates.

This heightened emphasis on the feminine gender identity of tomboyism was coupled with an equally strong stress on its heternormative sexual nature. In *A League of Their Own*, for instance, there is no indication that any of the tomboyish figures are homosexual in spite of the massive growth in lesbian visibility during the Second World War and Susan E. Johnson's discussion about the relative "open secret" of homosexuality among League members. While homosexual players were officially forbidden from the AAGPBL, akin to their status in the military, they were unofficially tolerated and, at times, even accepted as long as their sexual orientation and accompanying romantic liaisons did not become "too obvious" (S. E. Johnson 116). In spite of this historical reality, repeated mention is made throughout *A League of Their Own* of husbands and boyfriends who are either fighting overseas or waiting for them at home. Moreover, all of the single girls on the team are boy-crazy. Led by Madonna's mischievous character "All-the-Way" May, they defy, dupe and—when necessary—drug their female chaperone so they can sneak out to meet men. Even the film's most likely lesbian character, the somewhat butch-looking slugger Marla Hooch (played by out lesbian actress Megan Cavanagh), is presented as irrefutably heterosexual. During her first visit to a bar with her teammates, she meets a man, falls in love, and leaves the League to get married. This sequence combines the heightened emphasis on tomboy taming during the Second World War with the antebellum origins of this code of conduct as a preparatory stage for marriage and motherhood. At the same time, it further affirms Rebecca Bell-Metereux's assertion that historical films routinely say more about the era in which they are made and released than the one they are purporting to depict. *A League of Their Own* is as least as much about the nation's conflicted feelings regarding tomboyish transformations to female gender roles during the 1990s as it is an account about the anxieties about them during the 1940s.

In a final index of the heterosexualization of tomboyism during the 1990s, gender-bending female figures began appearing in the unlikely genre of romance novels. In books like Mary Lou Rich's *The Tomboy* (1996) or Leanna Wilson's *His Tomboy Bride* (1998), authors did not simply fold a tomboyish character into their steamy stories of boy-meets-girl love, they made her the centerpiece. *His Tomboy Bride* (1998), for instance, concerns the romance between tomboy Billie Rae Gunther and her longtime friend Nick Latham. A passage from one of the opening pages of the novel reveals the erotic appeal of the healthy, vibrant, and spirited tomboyish woman:

> Even though she tried to hide the facts under an oversize [sic] plaid shirt, the evidence was clear—she was all woman. Her faded jeans hugged her slim hips as intimately as a man longed to hold a woman. . . . With each step, she exuded confidence. He couldn't decide which way he liked her best—rough and ordinary as a cowhand or elegant as any New York model. Or which wreaked more havoc on his libido. (Wilson 31)

A similar sentiment pervades Mary Lou Rich's *The Tomboy* (1996). In this narrative, the best friend of the twenty-year-old Atalanta "Allie" Daltry begins to see her as not simply a riding partner but a potential romantic one: "Hal had said she'd filled out in all the places. . . . She'd been so shocked when he said it, she'd danged near fell off her horse. . . . Once he'd held her so long, she thought he might kiss her" (Rich 79).

"Tales of Dyke Derring-Do": The Emergence of New Queer Cinema and the Counterpoint of the Lesbian Tomboy

While the joint heterosexualization and feminization of tomboyism embodied important characteristics during the 1990s, it only presented part of the picture. Although this code of conduct was shaped by what some critics have called a "postfeminist" national climate, it was also influenced by another phenomenon: the LGBTQ movement.

During the 1990s, the fight for homosexual rights made unprecedented strides in the United States. Out of the tragedy of the AIDS crisis came a level of organization, urgency, and activism that was unprecedented in the nation's history. Advocacy groups like ACT-UP (AIDS Coalition To Unleash Power), GLAAD (Gay and Lesbian Alliance Against Defamation), the Lesbian Avengers, and Queer Nation were either founded during this decade or gained increased prominence during it.[3] In the words of Lauren Berlant and Elizabeth Freeman, the organizations did not make a polite case for homosexual rights, they "refused closeting strategies of assimilation and [went] for the broadest and most explicit assertion of presence" (156). Adopting in-your-face tactics like public kiss-ins, the forced outings of closeted officials and—in a self-conscious inversion of the 1950s paradigm—queer invasions of straight bars,[4] gay men and lesbians were no longer willing to quietly wait for recognition. In the wake of the AIDS epidemic, they could no longer afford to do so. Given the decimation of

3. ACT-UP was founded in 1987 by Larry Kramer and several hundred other activists in New York City; GLAAD was founded in 1985, also in New York City, largely as a means to protest the *New York Post*'s sensationalized and inaccurate coverage of the AIDS epidemic; the first Lesbian Avengers meeting was held in New York City in 1992; finally, the manifesto for Queer Nation was distributed at the Pride Parade in New York City in 1990. For a helpful but concise digest of the past origins as well as present history of these organizations, see Steve Hogan and Lee Hudson's *Completely Queer: The Gay and Lesbian Encyclopedia* (New York: Henry Holt, 1998).

4. For both specific examples of this phenomenon and their broader political significance, see not only Lauren Berlant and Elizabeth Freeman's chapter "Queer Nationality" in *National Identities and Post-Americanist Narratives* (Ed. by Donald E. Pease. Durham: Duke UP, 1994) but also the Epilogue to Lillian Faderman's *Odd Girls and Twilight Lovers: A History of Lesbian Identity in Twentieth-Century America* (New York: Penguin, 1991).

the LGBTQ community by HIV while the Reagan Administration largely stood by, many realized—as one popular slogan of the era put it—that their silence would equal their death.

Although the aggressive efforts of groups such as ACT-UP and Queer Nation alienated some and frightened others, they were effective. During the 1990s, landmark gains were made in the fight for LGBTQ rights. Many state governments along with private companies amended their policies of nondiscrimination to include sexual orientation, while an array of major cities passed legislation that recognized domestic partnerships between cohabitating unmarried couples, whether heterosexual or homosexual.[5] In addition, the field of gay and lesbian studies emerged as a new academic discipline. Throughout the decade, numerous books and articles—including the bulk of the ones cited throughout these chapters—were published on queer literature, politics and history.

With homosexuality more visible and widely accepted, coming out of the closet became feasible for many gay men and lesbians. In a powerful indicator of this climate of increased acceptance, even some celebrities in the notoriously closeted fields of acting and music decided to make their sexual orientations public during the 1990s. Most notable among these perhaps were musicians Melissa Etheridge, whose 1993 album was matter-of-factly called *Yes I Am*, and k. d. lang, who appeared in a now infamous photo on the August 1993 cover of *Vanity Fair* wearing a suit, sitting in a barber's chair and getting a shave from sexy supermodel Cindy Crawford. Moreover, in a landmark moment in 1997, comedian Ellen DeGeneres made television history when her small screen alter ego uttered a disclosure that would later—in a slightly modified form—adorn the cover of *Time* magazine: "Yep, I'm Gay" (Handy).

The appearance of lesbian characters on television and performers in the music industry, however, paled in comparison to the presence of homosexual women on the silver screen. During the 1990s, movies that featured lesbian or, at least, bisexual female characters began to flood theaters. As Harry M. Benshoff and Sean Griffin have written, for a brief period lesbianism became chic in Hollywood films, with productions like *Three of Hearts* (1993), *Bound* (1996) and *Set It Off* (1996) capitalizing on the newfound popularity of—and growing commercial market for—same-sex subject matter. Arguably even more important than these mainstream movies were ones that formed part of what film critic B. Ruby Rich famously dubbed the New Queer Cinema.[6] Made by smaller independent studios, films from this genre were generally directed by lesbian filmmakers, featured lesbian

---

5. For more information on specific organizations who adopted such statutes and also the precise dates when they did so, see http://library.findlaw.com.

6. See Rich's "New Queer Cinema," *Sight & Sound*, Volume 2, Issue 5 (September 1992): 30–34.

performers and were intended—unlike *Bound* or *Three of Hearts*—for a queer female audience. Productions like *Salmonberries* (1992), *Go Fish* (1994), *Bar Girls* (1995), *The Incredibly True Adventure of Two Girls in Love* (1995), *When Night is Falling* (1995), *Tank Girl* (1995) and *The Watermelon Woman* (1996) constituted a mere handful of titles within New Queer Cinema, and thus reveal both its size and scope. With most of these films optioned by major distributors, they appeared in movie theaters or at least video rental stores throughout the nation.

In light of both the sheer number of lesbian-themed films and their widespread availability, Shameem Kabir, among other film critics, has noted that the 1990s was the period when lesbian cinema emerged as an indisputable force in the United States. The commercial success of, and critical esteem for, these films moved the cinematic representation of female homosexuality "from the margins to the mainstream, where lesbian desire [was] no longer unspeakable but spoken, no longer killed off but celebrated, no longer about pathologization but about oppositional choices and healthy preferences" (Kabir 3). As one popular lapel pin of the era put it, "We Are Everywhere"; in light of the strong presence of lesbians on the silver screen alone, it seemed that they were.

The lesbian-themed films released during the 1990s also became a home for an alternative form of tomboyism. Whereas gender-bending female figures in cultural movements like Girl Power or movies like *A League of Their Own* were feminine and boy-crazy, the figures in this venue were boyish and lesbian. In fact, given the pseudo-rebellious nature of many ostensibly tomboyish behaviors during the 1990s, gender-bending characters in New Queer Cinema emerged as the antithesis of, or even antidote to, their more feminine and heterosexual counterparts. Unafraid of rejecting conventional notions of femininity and embracing a boyish identity, gender-bending figures in movies such as *Go Fish* (1994), *The Incredibly True Adventure of Two Girls in Love* (1995) and *Salmonberries* (1992) were true iconoclasts. Their participation in this code of female conduct was not tempered by the era's feminizing efforts and accompanying desire to be seen as either a "pretty tomboy" or a "tomboy girl." On the contrary, with their hair cropped short, tough attitude, and involvement in an array of traditionally masculine activities, they were decidedly unpretty and unmistakably tom*boy*ish.[7]

7. In *The Incredibly True Adventure of Two Girls in Love*, for instance, central character Randy Dean has short hair, wears baggy men's clothes and is a competent mechanic. Likewise, in *Go Fish* (1994), the main character, Max, is almost always shown wearing sporty overalls and a backwards-facing baseball cap. Finally, in Percy Adlon's *Salmonberries*, the tough and stoic Kotz, played by lesbian crooner k.d. lang, embodies something of a return to postwar butchness. With her short haircut and strong demeanor, she is often mistaken for a young man instead of a young woman.

Although the presence of masculine and homosexual tomboys in New Queer Cinema seemed to indicate societal acceptance for gender and sexual nonconformity, the opposite was true in some ways. Akin to previous historical eras, a social and scientific backlash emerged. The new classification of childhood mental conditions—Gender Identity Disorder—that made its debut in the 1980 edition of the American Psychiatric Association's *Diagnostic and Statistical Manual of Mental Disorders* acquired increased importance in the years following its emergence. The 1987 revision to the *DSM-III* broadened the scope of this condition and increased the number of tomboyish girls to whom it could apply. For example, GID in girls could now be diagnosed by the presence of one of two traits: either the formerly listed "persistent repudiation of female anatomic structures" or the newly added "persistent marked aversion to normative feminine clothing and insistence on wearing stereotypical masculine clothing" (*DSM-III-R* 73). This modification may account for why the cautionary assertion that GID was "not merely a child's nonconformity to stereotypic sex-role behavior as, for example, 'tombyishness' in girls" was moved to a parenthetical aside. Although this comment was still included, it no longer applied.

The fourth edition of the *Diagnostic and Statistical Manual*, published in 1994, continued this trend. It instituted additional alterations that revealed the heightened societal interest in Gender Identity Disorder and also continued its ever-growing similarity to tomboyism. Before readers even examined the changes to GID in the *DSM-IV*, they likely noticed the increased attention devoted to it. Whereas the discussion of this condition occupied around three pages of text in the *DSM-III* and *DSM-III-R*, it received more than six pages in the *DSM-IV*. Moreover, this new, longer description further eroded the already crumbling distinction between GID and tomboyism, for it could have been describing a stereotypical tomboy:

> Girls with Gender Identity Disorder display intense negative reactions to parental expectations or attempts to have them wear dresses or other feminine attire. Some may refuse to attend school or social events where such clothes may be required. They prefer boy's clothing and short hair and are often misidentified as boys, and may ask to be called by a boy's name. Their fantasy heroes are most often powerful male figures, such as Batman or Superman. These girls prefer boys as playmates, with whom they share interests in contact sports, rough-and-tumble play, and traditional boyhood games. They show little interest in dolls or any form of feminine dress up or role-play activity. (*DSM-IV* 533)

This scientific blurring between childhood tomboyism, Gender Identity Disorder, and adult lesbianism raised anxiety among many parents. A segment that appeared on the April 14, 1995, broadcast of the popular television newsmagazine *Dateline NBC* and was tellingly titled "Sugar and Spice" demonstrated the way in which changing scientific attitudes about female gender nonconformity were rapidly changing national attitudes about active girlhoods. As anchor Jane Pauley asserts in the lead-in to the piece, a new research project being conducted by scientists at Northwestern University "is the first long-term study of its kind to determine if there's a link between tomboyish behavior and sexual preference." While viewers watch a group of young girls engage in various forms of rough-and-tumble play, the reporting journalist gives ominous statistics about the incidence of homosexuality among the general population and the projected rate among tomboys: "Right now, 1 percent of the general population is thought to be lesbian. The scientists at Northwestern think 10 percent of the tomboy population will be gay." After hearing these statistics, the mother of one of the young girls participating in the study changes her attitude about her daughter's tomboyism: "No, I didn't like it," she remarks, and then later and even more anxiously, "Yes, I was alarmed."

As even this brief discussion indicates, the bifurcation of this code of conduct into competing and even contradictory forms was perhaps never more apparent than during the final decade of the twentieth century. In 1995, for example, Lynne Yamaguchi and Karen Barber equated tomboyism with lesbianism in the title of their collection, *Tomboys!: Tales of Dyke Derring-Do*. Meanwhile, four years later, Jan Secrist in her *Tomboy Tales: The Adventures of Midlife Mavericks* limited her investigation of former childhood tomboys to only those who are, as she asserts at both the beginning and end of her discussion, "happily heterosexual" (12, 205). As the nation was poised on the brink of a new millennium, tomboyism was similarly poised between a conservative throwback to its antebellum origins and a progressive reinvention that embraced more radical gender and sexual characteristics.

"Legally Blonde": The Return of Whiteness to White Tomboyism

Together with changes in many of the gender traits and sexual characteristics of white tomboyism during the 1990s, this code of conduct experienced a shift in three of its foundational elements: the concept of whiteness, the construction of the white feminist movement, and the fight for LGBTQ rights. Over the course of the decade, these modifications did more than simply alter the way in which gender-bending female characters became associated with various forms of nonwhiteness; they eliminated this phenomenon altogether.

After centuries in which Caucasians were largely excluded from discussions about race, they were folded into them as the end of the twentieth century approached. Cultural historians and literary critics like David

Roediger, Shelley Fisher Fishkin and Ruth Frankenberg made a case for eliminating the unmarked nature of whiteness. In the words of Richard Dyer, "as long as white people are not racially seen and named, they/we function as a human norm" (Dyer 10). Hence, these individuals attempted to dislodge this group from its privileged—and protected—position of power. As the editors to a collection of essays asserted, they were interested in "prying [whiteness] open and wedging it off its unexamined center" (Fine, Weis, Wong and Powell vii).

Whiteness studies impacted academic fields that were already in existence while constituting a new area of intellectual inquiry itself. For example, throughout the late 1980s and early 1990s, bell hooks, Patricia Hill Collins and Hazel Carby exposed not simply the racial blindness of mainstream white feminism but its often racist practices. As Collins asserted in *Black Feminist Thought*, "Even though Black women intellectuals have long expressed a unique feminist consciousness about the intersection of race and class in structuring gender, historically we have not been full participants in white feminist organizations" (7). All too often, the fight for gender equality did not include racial equality, and a keen awareness about male sexism did not embed a similar cognizance of white racism or, at least, white privilege. In the words of Collins once again, "Theories advanced as being universally applicable to women as a group on closer examination . . . promote the notion of a generic woman who is white and middle class" (7–8). Although such arguments came as a shock to many white feminists who had always considered themselves egalitarian, they made an impact. Ruth Frankenberg has written that in the wake of such remarks, the movement began to address the "particularism of white feminism" and unpack the ways in which both femininity and feminism were racially marked and even exclusive (4).

Heavily influenced by—and historically closely connected to—the feminist movement, the LGBTQ one had a similar history. As John D'Emilio, Jonathan Ned Katz and Greta Schiller have each discussed, from its origins during the 1950s, homophile efforts in the United States had long been connected with whiteness. Not only were the Mattachine Society and the Daughters of Bilitis all-white organizations, but they also shied away from or, at least, did not actively recruit the membership of racial and ethnic minorities. Unaware of the way in which various forms of prejudice interlock and overlap, leaders of these organizations often argued that they did not want to "distract" from the fight for homosexual rights with the one for black civil rights.[8]

---

8. For more information on the racial composition of early homophile organizations, see Jonathan Ned Katz's *Gay American History* (New York: Meridian, 1976), Greta Schiller's film *Before Stonewall* (1984), and, more recently, Elizabeth Armstrong's *Forging*

Akin to their white feminist counterparts, this pattern changed during the 1990s. In publications like Allan Bérubé's "How Gay Stays White and What Kind of White It Stays," LGBTQ scholars began to interrogate the unmarked whiteness of their movement and its relationship to various minority groups. As Bérubé asserted, white homosexuals could no longer think, act or write as if their community was neither comprised of, nor buttressed by, people of color. Moreover, they could no longer afford to overlook the fact that similar strategies of discrimination were used to deny minority groups—whether black, working-class, female or homosexual—their civil rights.

Changes in thinking about these three fundamental components to white tomboyism disrupted the basis on which ostensibly Caucasian figures had historically been racialized. As a result, the 1990s rang the death-knell for the phenomenon. After more than 150 years of associating white tomboys with various forms of nonwhiteness, films during the 1990s participated in the opposite phenomenon: they called attention to their Caucasian heritage. More than simply presenting an isolated tomboy character who has light hair and fair features as in Hollywood films during the 1970s and 1980s, these works made certain that their spunky female figures were physically as well as culturally "whitewashed." The presentation of Amelia Evans in Merchant and Ivory's 1991 cinematic version of *The Ballad of the Sad Café* forms a poignant example. Contrary to repeated associations of this character with various forms of dark whiteness in McCullers's 1943 novella, Vanessa Redgrave's Amelia has hair so blonde that it is almost white. As Jennifer DeVere Brody has discussed, hair tone, texture and especially color have long been viewed as signifiers of race: "The use of the blond wigs, and the dying of one's hair, expressed a need to artificially construct whiteness in an effort to emphasize difference—to make the whiteness of whiteness hypervisible" (88).

This "bleaching" or "whitewashing" of Carson McCullers's formerly brunette character was indicative of a new paradigm for the cinematic presentation of Caucasian tomboyism. In films throughout the 1990s, many gender-bending female characters sported blonde hair, including Watts in Howard Deutch's *Some Kind of Wonderful* (1987), the butch Tracey from Marita Giovanni's movie *Bar Girls* (1995), the hard-hitting title character from Rachel Talalay's *Tank Girl* (1995), and Randall "Randy" Dean from Maria Maggenti's *The Incredibly True Adventure of Two Girls in Love* (1995). Whether their locks were artificially lightened or naturally blonde, they called attention to rather than obfuscated their whiteness. After more than a century and a half, tomboys no longer positioned themselves as the literal antithesis of the "Fair Maiden."

Gay Identities: Organizing Sexuality in San Francisco, 1950–1994 (University of Chicago, 2002).

In the same way that the physical appearance of Caucasian tomboys changed during the 1990s, so did the meaning of their characterization. With their bleached hair and "fair" features, this new type of tomboy explored what it meant to be Caucasian in the United States. Although this phenomenon was evidenced in numerous sites and sources during the 1990s, it was perhaps most vividly illustrated by the differences between Fannie Flagg's 1987 novel *Fried Green Tomatoes at the Whistle Stop Café* and Jon Avnet's 1991 popular film adaptation of it.[9] In Flagg's text, the tomboyish Imagene "Idgie" Threadgoode is associated with various forms of American Africanism. When the young woman installs a radio at the café, for instance, she invites her neighbors to listen to her favorite program: the minstrel-based *Amos 'n' Andy* (Flagg 45). Similarly, in the rigidly segregated Alabama of the 1930s, in which the novel is set, Idgie repeatedly engages in the daring and even dangerous task of criticizing white racism and defending black people. At one point, the tomboyish young woman tells the sheriff how ridiculous she finds the KKK parades: "'I think a bunch of grown men getting liquored up and putting sheets on their heads is pretty damn funny'" (Flagg 54). A few moments later, Idgie insists on serving blacks at her café. Justifying this decision, she jokes that white men are "'terrified to sit next to a nigger and have a meal, but they'll eat eggs that came right out of a chicken's ass'" (Flagg 55).

In Jon Avnet's film adaptation of Flagg's text, however, many of these details are changed. Although Idgie remains a staunch advocate for the black community in general and the African Americans who work at her café in particular, she is not connected with either blackness or black culture. Instead, the movie emphasizes Idgie's status as a white person and her place in the white community. No mention is made, for instance, of her affection for minstrelized radio programs. Similarly, the comment about white people's refusal to dine with blacks but their comfort with eating chicken eggs comes not from Idgie but from her black employee, Sipsey.

The differences between Fannie Flagg's novel and Jon Avnet's film do not end here. In the book, Idgie frequents Troutville and, later, Slagtown, both all-black enclaves, where she plays cards, drinks whiskey and communes as if she were one of the locals. As the narrator notes, the young woman "had as many friends over in Troutville as she did in Whistle Stop. She was always over there preaching at some funeral if a friend of hers died. She

9. In an indication of the contemporaneous popularity of both works, Avnet's film earned $82 million at the box office upon its release in late 1991, making it the eleventh top-grossing film of that year. In addition, it was nominated for two Academy Awards: Jessica Tandy for Best Actress in a Supporting Role, and Fannie Flagg and Carol Sobieski for Best Adapted Screenplay. Meanwhile, Flagg's novel received a major commercial boost by the popularity of the film, causing the formerly modest-selling narrative to spend 39 weeks on *The New York Times* Best Sellers paperback list in 1992.

told me one time that she preferred them to some of the whites she knew'"
(Flagg 284). Akin to the tomboyish characters profiled in previous chapters,
Idgie's adoption of masculine breeches allows her to breach the colorline.
Once again, in Jon Avnet's film version, these details have been changed.
Although black men and women inhabit the gambling and drinking estab-
lishment in which Idgie is a regular, it is not an all-black environment. In
fact, when Ruth storms into the River Club to bring Idgie back home, there
are more white faces in the establishment than black ones.

Idgie does more than simply place herself in the frequent company
of blacks in Flagg's novel; she also actively aids them. Empathetic to the
widespread poverty among African Americans during the Depression, the
tomboyish young woman disguises herself as a male hobo, hops government trains, and throws off parcels of food when passing through black
communities. "'I suddenly figured out why I'd seen her and Old Grady
Kilgore, the railroad detective, always whispering. He'd been the one who
was tipping her off about the train schedules . . . it had been my Aunt Idgie
jumping them trains all along'" (Flagg 332). In an action that recalls blackface performers, the young woman smears herself with coal to disguise her
identity when assuming the role of "Railroad Bill": "I heard them talking
and pretty soon they came out, and Aunt Idgie was drying her hands and
face. When I got in there, the sink was still full of coal dust" (Flagg 332).

In the 1991 film version, however, Idgie neither disguises herself as
Railroad Bill nor does she distribute food to blacks alone. Hopping a railroad car, the fair-skinned young woman with blonde hair dispenses food
to a shanty town that is populated by both blacks and whites. Even during
instances when the tomboyish young woman associates with African American characters—such as her friendships with Big George and Sipsey—her
interaction says more about her whiteness than it does about forging a
connection with blackness. As Ann Pellegrini has noted, the way in which
Caucasians treat African Americans in Avnet's film becomes a type of
litmus test for whether they are admirable characters. Ruth's ex-husband,
Frank Bennett, for instance, is disparaged both because he hits women
and also because he is a member of the Klan. His racism "becomes a way
of making distinctions within the category of whiteness between 'good'
white people and 'bad' white people" (Pellegrini 91). In this way, rather
than establishing a link between Idgie and African American culture, her
empathy for blacks establishes her as an admirable white character. In the
words of Pellegrini once again, "*blackness* demarcates differences within
whiteness" [italics in original] (90).

Significantly, the added emphasis on Idgie's racial whiteness in Avnet's
film is at the expense of her lesbian identity. Although the relationship
between Idgie and Ruth is tender, loving and even sensual in Flagg's text,
these elements are largely eliminated or, at least, obfuscated in Avnet's film.
In fact, Judith Halberstam has written,

Fried Green Tomatoes (1991) won a GLAAD media award for its positive depiction of a lesbian relationship, but the erotic nature of the relationship between the two women in the film was actually so submerged that many heterosexual audiences were able to categorize what they saw as a strong friendship between two women rather than a dyke drama. (*Female* 220–221)

Together with demonstrating the broad cultural anxiety about homosexual forms of tomboyism during the 1990s, these details bring Avnet's film in dialogue with the postwar pulp equation of whiteness with heterosexuality and blackness with homosexuality. In distancing Idgie from black racial difference, the film distances her from queer sexual difference, and vice versa. Interestingly, Flagg co-wrote the screenplay that was based on her novel. Even more significantly, her work earned her a nomination for Best Adapted Screenplay at the 1992 Academy Awards.

By disassociating Idgie from both literal and figurative associations with blackness, Jon Avnet's film changes the racial dynamics present in Flagg's novel in general and its tomboyish main character in particular. Whereas the 1987 text frequently places Idgie on the interstice between blackness and whiteness, the 1991 movie locates her on the Caucasian side of the colorline. Unlike the gender-bending female figures profiled in previous chapters, Idgie is an unequivocally white character. Phrased in a different way, she is a white tomboy who has renewed her association with her whiteness.

Although Avnet's *Fried Green Tomatoes* forms one of the most vivid examples of the end of racialized white tomboyism during the 1990s, it was not the only film to do so. Maria Maggenti's *The Incredibly True Adventure of Two Girls in Love* can also be seen in this way, and it demonstrates how this phenomenon was not limited to Hollywood representations of tomboys but included those in the purportedly more progressive New Queer Cinema. The presentation of tomboy Randall "Randy" Dean in *True Adventure* calls into question an array of assumptions about racial categorization. In contrast to stereotypes about the Caucasian family as suburban, nuclear and solidly middle class, the blonde-haired Randy hails from a blue-collar home that is headed by a lesbian aunt. Working at a gas station and living with an array of extended family members and guests, Randy and her family may be politely categorized as working class, but they are more commonly and crassly deemed "white trash." Matt Wray and Annalee Newitz have argued that this designation is as much a racist as a classist slur: "white trash is, for whites, the most visible and clearly marked form of whiteness" (4). Whereas American society frequently seeks to obfuscate whiteness, the term "white trash" calls attention to it. The portrait of working-class lesbian Randy Dean in *The Incredibly True Adventure of Two Girls in Love* functions in this way. Because the tomboyish character defies conventional understandings of whiteness, she repeatedly reminds viewers of this racial classification.

Randy's African American girlfriend Evie extends this issue. Reversing the former historical practice of associating white tomboys with various elements of blackness, the feminine Evie is a black character who is linked with stereotypical markers of whiteness: the young woman lives in an upscale suburban neighborhood, drives a luxury car, and takes piano lessons. By inverting common racial stereotypes, the coupling of these two young women serves to call attention to rather than obfuscate the issue of race. The film forces viewers to examine the way in which the categories of black and white are historically produced and culturally perpetuated.

Echoing this trend, many other feature-length films from the 1990s depicted an interracial lesbian couple as a way to interrogate the meanings of—rather than blur the boundaries between—whiteness and blackness. These included *Work* (1996) along with three movies that were all released in 1995: *Bar Girls*, *When Night Is Falling*, and *Boys on the Side*.[10] Commenting on this phenomenon, Ann Pellegrini has noted, "So many of such feature-length films have come out, and in such a relatively compressed period of time, that this interracial couple has become virtually the cinematic face of lesbianism during the 1990s" (88). Such couplings can also be seen as arising from the era's growing anxiety about the place of race in feminist studies and queer theory. Displacing differences of gender onto differences of race, these films about ostensible same-sex romance become ones about interracial coupling. The union between two women is eclipsed by the one between blackness and whiteness.

* * *

In the opening pages of Toni Morrison's *The Bluest Eye* (1970), the narrator observes, "There is really nothing more to say—except *why*. But since *why* is difficult to handle, one must take refuge in *how*" [italics in original] (34). Positioned as a prefatory comment to a scene in which the protagonist gives birth to her father's baby, the remark makes a distinction between the process by which an event occurs and the reason for that event. Tracing a trajectory of the ways in which white tomboyism has often been predicated on various forms of nonwhiteness, this project challenges Morrison's assertion. Rather than viewing the "why" as independent from the "how," it positions them as interdependent, for the various ways in which ostensibly white tomboys became associated with nonwhite peoples and cultures cannot be separated from the motivations behind this

10. Of course, Herbert Ross's 1995 film, *Boys on the Side,* inverts the paradigm. In this film, the tomboyish lesbian (played by Whoopi Goldberg) is black, while her feminine and formerly heterosexual lover (played by *Fried Green Tomatoes* alum Mary-Louise Parker) is white.

phenomenon. By illuminating a further aspect of the interlocking nature of race, gender and sexuality in the United States, this project contributes to ongoing destabilization of the supposed naturalness of female gender roles, the presumed biological normalcy of heterosexuality, and the purported monolithic nature of whiteness.

In what has become an oft-quoted statement, Naomi Wolf once pointed out that illuminating the racisms of the past is one of the comforting things "well-meaning white people" often do without necessarily working to dismantle present forms of racism. More than simply outlining the way in which white tomboyism has historically fetishized people of color, the larger aim of this project is to construct this legacy so that it may be dismantled or deconstructed. By exploring the literary and cultural history of white tomboyism—and, in doing so, uncovering its hidden history as a racially charged construct—it is my hope that these pages offer the first step toward imagining a form of white female gender rebellion that is not predicated on the appropriation of nonwhite peoples and cultures.

Selected Bibliography[1]

ADULT AND CHILDREN'S LITERATURE[2] (CHRONOLOGICAL)

James Fenimore Cooper, *The Last of the Mohicans* (1826)
Catharine Maria Sedgwick, *Hope Leslie* (1827)
Catharine Maria Sedgwick, *The Linwoods* (1835)
E. D. E. N. Southworth, *The Deserted Wife* (1849)
Susan Warner, *The Wide, Wide World* (1850)
Alice Cary, *Hagar* (1852)
E. D. E. N. Southworth, *The Discarded Daughter* (1852)
Harriet Beecher Stowe, *Uncle Tom's Cabin* (1852)
E. D. E. N. Southworth, "Eveline Murray; or The Fine Figure" (1854)
Caroline Chesebro', *Susan, The Fisherman's Daughter; or, Getting Along* (1855)
Mary J. Holmes, *'Lena Rivers* (1856)
Harriet Beecher Stowe, *Dred* (1856)

---

1. As the title of this section suggests, this list is meant to be neither exhaustive nor all-inclusive. Instead of providing a definitive account of tomboyism, it is meant to provide a useful overview of the phenomenon in American print and visual culture in general and a handy reference guide for my discussion in the previous chapters in particular. In addition to adding materials to each of the categories, this list could also be expanded to include novels and films that appeared after the end point of this project in the 1990s. Moreover, it could also be broadened to encompass additional genres, such as comic books like the *Li'l Tomboy* series (1956–1959) or television programs such as *Father Knows Best* (1954–1960), *The Facts of Life* (1979–1988) and *Who's The Boss* (1984–1992). Although rich and worthy fields of inquiry, these areas were simply beyond the scope of my project.

2. While I considered dividing this section into narratives written for children and those primarily intended for adults, the number of texts that were crosswritten—or ones that appealed equally to both audiences—made this task virtually impossible. Especially during the nineteenth and early twentieth centuries, many of these titles enjoyed a dual readership, and I did not want to obscure or even erase this important historical detail.

E. D. E. N. Southworth, *Vivia; or, The Secret of Power* (1857)

E. D. E. N. Southworth, *The Three Beauties* (1858)

E. D. E. N. Southworth, *The Hidden Hand* (1859 first serialization, 1888 first book publication)

Harriet Wilson, *Our Nig* (1859)

Elizabeth Barstow Stoddard, *The Morgesons* (1862)

E. D. E. N. Southworth, *The Fatal Marriage* (1863)

Louisa May Alcott, *Moods* (1864)

Elizabeth Stuart Phelps, *Gypsy Breynton* (1866)

Elizabeth Stuart Phelps, *Gypsy's Cousin Joy* (1866)

Elizabeth Stuart Phelps, *Gypsy's Sowing and Reaping* (1866)

Elizabeth Stuart Phelps, *Gypsy's Year at the Golden Crescent* (1867)

Martha Finley, *Elsie Dinsmore* (1867)

Louisa May Alcott, *Little Women* (1868)

E. D. E. N. Southworth, *How He Won Her* (1869)

Sarah Orne Jewett, "The Girl with the Cannon Dress" (1870)

Louisa May Alcott, *Little Men* (1871)

Harriet Beecher Stowe, *My Wife and I; or, Harry Henderson's History* (1871)

Susan Coolidge, *What Katy Did* (1872)

George M. Baker, *Running to Waste: The Story of a Tomboy* (1874)

Lillie Devereux Blake, *Fettered for Life* (1874)

Susan Coolidge, *What Katy Did at School* (1874)

Sarah Orne Jewett, *Deephaven* (1877)

Sarah Orne Jewett, "The Best China Saucer" (1878)

Henry James, *Watch and Ward* (1878)

Sarah Orne Jewett, "The Water Dolly" (1878)

Louisa May Alcott, *Jack and Jill: A Village Story* (1880)

William Dean Howells, *Dr. Breen's Practice* (1881)

E. D. E. N. Southworth, *A Leap in the Dark* (1881)

Elizabeth Stuart Phelps, *Doctor Zay* (1882)

John Hay, *The Bread-Winners* (1883)

Sarah Orne Jewett, *A Country Doctor* (1884)

Sarah Orne Jewett, "Tom's Husband" (1884)

Oliver Wendell Holmes, *A Modern Antipathy* (1885)

Louisa May Alcott, *Jo's Boys* (1886)

Charlotte Perkins Gilman, "Why Women Do Not Reform Their Dress" (1886) [nonfiction]

Henry James, *The Bostonians* (1886)

Sarah Orne Jewett, "Farmer Finch" (1886)

Izola L. Forrester, "Tom Junior—Tomboy" (1886/7)

Susan Coolidge, *What Katy Did Next* (1887)

Sarah Orne Jewett, "A Christmas Guest" (1887)

Martha Finley, *Elsie's Widowhood* (1889)

Mary Wilkins Freeman, "Louisa," in *New England Nun* (1891)

Wenona Gilman, *Val, the Tomboy* (1891)

Annie Nathan Meyer, *Helen Brent, M.D.: A Social Study* (1892)

Sarah Orne Jewett, "The Hilton's Holiday" (1895)

Annie Fellows Johnston, *The Little Colonel* series (1895–1907)

Willa Cather, "Tommy, the Unsentimental" (1896)

Lily F. Wesselhoeft, *Torpeanuts the Tomboy* (1897)

Mark Twain, "Hellfire Hotchkiss" (written 1897, published 1967)

Gertrude Altherton, *The Californians* (1898)

Willa Cather, "The Way of the World" (1898)

Charlotte Perkins Gilman, *Women and Economics* (1898) [nonfiction]

Kate Chopin, "Charlie" (written 1900, published 1969)
Jeanette L. Gilder, *The Autobiography of a Tomboy* (1900)
Charlotte Perkins Gilman, "A Protest" (1900) [poetry]
Amy E. Blanchard, *A Little Tomboy* (1903)
Kate Douglas Wiggin, *Rebecca of Sunnybrook Farm* (1903)
L. Frank Baum, *The Land of Oz* (1904)
Jeanette L. Gilder, *The Tom-Boy at Work* (1904)
Beaulah Marie Dix, *Merrylips* (1906)
Charlotte Perkins Gilman, "When I Was a Witch" (1910)
Charlotte Perkins Gilman, "Big Hats—Women's—at Base Ball!" (approx. 1910)[3] [poetry]
Charlotte Perkins Gilman, "Her Hat Still With Us" (approx. 1910) [poetry]
Charlotte Perkins Gilman, "The Cripple" (1910) [poetry]
W. C. Metcalfe, *Ice-Gripped; or, The Tomboy of Boston* (1910)
Anna Fuller, "The Tomboy," *Later Pratt Portraits* (1911)
Charlotte Perkins Gilman, "Old Water" (1911)
Charlotte Perkins Gilman, "Mrs. Noah" (1911) [poetry]
Charlotte Perkins Gilman, *The Man-Made World* (1911) [nonfiction]
Sui Sin Far, "A Chinese Boy-Girl," in *Mrs. Spring Fragrance* (1912)
Sui Sin Far, "The Smuggling of Tie Co," in *Mrs. Spring Fragrance* (1912)
Sui Sin Far, "Tian Shan's Kindred Spirit," in *Mrs. Spring Fragrance* (1912)
Charlotte Perkins Gilman, "Her Memories" (1912)
H. B. Marriott Watson, *The Tomboy, and Others* (1912)
Willa Cather, *O Pioneers!* (1913)
Charlotte Perkins Gilman, *Moving the Mountain* (1913)
Mary Johnston, *Hagar* (1913)
Mary E. Mumford, *A Regular Tomboy* (1913)
Charlotte Perkins Gilman, *Benigna Machiavelli* (1914)
Charlotte Perkins Gilman, "This Is a Lady's Hat" (1914) [poetry]
Charlotte Perkins Gilman, "If I Were a Man" (1914)
Charlotte Perkins Gilman, "Spoken To" (1915)
Charlotte Perkins Gilman, *Herland* (1915)
Charlotte Perkins Gilman, "The Unnatural Mother" (1916)
Charlotte Perkins Gilman, "Joan's Defender" (1916)
Charlotte Perkins Gilman, "The Vintage" (1916)
Katherine Dunlap Cather, "Tomboy of Bordeaux," in *Boyhood Stories of Famous Men* (1917)
Willa Cather, *My Antonia* (1918)
F. Scott Fitzgerald, *This Side of Paradise* (1920)
F. Scott Fitzgerald, "Bernice Bobs Her Hair" (1920)
F. Scott Fitzgerald, The Offshore Pirate" (1920)
Zitkala-Sa, "A Warrior's Daughter," in *American Indian Stories* (1921)
F. Scott Fitzgerald, *The Beautiful and Damned* (1922)
F. Scott Fitzgerald, "Winter Dreams" (1922)
Zelda Fitzgerald, "Eulogy on the Flapper" (1922) [nonfiction]
Zelda Fitzgerald, "Friend Husband's Latest" (1922) [nonfiction]
Gertrude Atherton, *Black Oxen* (1923)
Warner Fabian, *Flaming Youth* (1923)
Lilian Garis, *Gloria at Boarding School* (1923)

---

3. The precise date of composition for this poem, along with "Her Hat Still With Us" listed below it, is unknown. As Denise D. Knight notes in *The Later Poetry of Charlotte Perkins Gilman*—where these verses were published for the first time—"Gilman added a handwritten note that this poem was written 'about 1910'" (181).

Percy Marks, *The Plastic Age* (1924)

Twenty Authors, *Bobbed Hair* (1925)

F. Scott Fitzgerald, *The Great Gatsby* (1925)

Zelda Fitzgerald, "What Became of the Flappers?" (1925) [nonfiction]

Anita Loos, *Gentlemen Prefer Blondes* (1925)

Helen Woodbury, *The Misty Flats* (1925)

Ernest Hemingway, *The Sun Also Rises* (1926)

Caroline Dale Snedeker, *Downright Dencey* (1927)

Armine von Tempski, *Hula* (1927)

Phyllis Duganne & Harriet Gersman, "Tomboy!" in *The American Girl* (1928)

Zelda Fitzgerald, "Paint and Powder" (1929) [nonfiction]

Zelda Fitzgerald, "The Original Follies Girl" (1929)

Lilian Garis, *A Girl Called Ted* (1929)

Lilian Garis, *Tony and Ted: Two Girls of Today* (1929)

Zelda Fitzgerald, "The Girl wWith Talent" (1930)

Zelda Fitzgerald, "A Millionaire's Girl" (1930)

Zelda Fitzgerald, "Other Names for Roses" (written 1930; published 1991)

Dinah Stevens, *Tomboy* (1930)

Carolyn Keene, *The Nancy Drew Mystery* series (1930–1956)

William Faulkner, *Light in August* (1932)

Zelda Fitzgerald, *Save Me the Waltz* (1932)

Bess Moyer, *The Girl Flyers on Adventure Island* (1932)

Laura Ingalls Wilder, *Little House in the Big Woods* (1932)

Ellis Parker Butler & Louise Andrews Kent, *Jo Ann, Tomboy* (1933)

Nathaniel West, *Miss Lonelyhearts* (1933)

Laura Ingalls Wilder, *Farmer Boy* (1933)

Patrick Cassidy, "Honolulu Tomboy," in *The Sun and the Rain* (1934)

F. Scott Fitzgerald, *Tender Is the Night* (1934)

Josephine W. Johnson, *Now in November* (1934)

Carol Ryrie Brink, *Caddie Woodlawn* (1935)

Anne Pence Davis, *Mimi at Camp: The Adventures of a Tomboy* (1935)

Anne Pence Davis, *Mimi at Sheridan School* (1935)

Kate Seredy, *The Good Master* (1935)

Laura Ingalls Wilder, *Little House on the Prairie* (1935)

Ruth Sawyer, *Roller Skates* (1936)

Carson McCullers, "Like That" (written 1935–1936; first published 1971)

Clair Blank, *The Adventure Girls in the Air* (1936)

Anne Pence Davis, *Mimi's House Party* (1936)

Sara Haardt, "Tomboy," in *Southern Album* (1936)

Winifred Van Etten, *I Am the Fox* (1936)

Laura Ingalls Wilder, *On the Banks of Plum Creek* (1937)

Elizabeth Enright, *Thimble Summer* (1938)

William Faulkner, *The Unvanquished* (1938)

Laura Ingalls Wilder, *By the Shores of Silver Lake* (1939)

Ruth Sawyer, *The Year of Jubilo* (1940)

Carson McCullers, *The Heart Is a Lonely Hunter* (1940)

Laura Ingalls Wilder, *The Long Winter* (1940)

Sally Benson, *Meet Me in St. Louis* (1941)

Laura Ingalls Wilder, *Little Town on the Prairie* (1941)

Carson McCullers, *The Ballad of the Sad Café* (1943, 1951)

Laura Ingalls Wilder, *These Happy Golden Years* (1943)

Peggy Goodin, *Clementine* (1946)

William Hand, *Fair City—The Tomboy* (1946)

Carson McCullers, *The Member of the Wedding* (1946)
T. H. White, *Mistress Masham's Repose* (1946)
Berta Ruck, *Tomboy in Lace* (1947)
Marian M. Schoolland, *Tomboy Janie* (1947)
Marian M. Schoolland, *Tomboy Janie's Cousin Prue* (1949)
Hal Ellson, *Tomboy* (1950)
Lois Lenski, *Texas Tomboy* (1950)
Allyn Allen, *Lone Star Tomboy* (1951)
Ruth Langland Holberg, *Tomboy Row* (1952)
Ruth Seid, *The Changelings* (1955)
Beverly Cleary, *Beezus and Ramona* (1955)
Pamela Moore, *Chocolates for Breakfast* (1956)
Marian M. Schoolland, *Tomboy Janie's Adventures with Peek* (1956)
Carolyn Keene, *The Nancy Drew Mystery Series* (revised and reissued beginning in 1959)
Paula Marshall, *Brown Girl, Brownstones* (1959)
Esphyr Slobodkina, *Billie* (1959)
Harper Lee, *To Kill a Mockingbird* (1960)
Miriam Parker Betts, *Tomboy Teacher* (1961)
Barbara Clayton, *Tomboy* (1961)
Louise Fitzhugh, *Harriet the Spy* (1964)
Shirley Sargent, *Yosemite Tomboy* (1967)
S. E. Hinton, *The Outsiders* (1967)
[no author], *Kansas Tomboy* (1968)
Elizabeth Burleson, *Middl'un* (1968)
Beverly Cleary, *Ramona the Pest* (1968)
Harriet Fish Backus, *Tomboy Bride* (1969)
Beverly Cleary, *Ramona and Her Father* (1969)
Isabel Miller, *A Place for Us* (1969; retitled *Patience and Sarah* in 1972)
Charlotte Steiner, *Tomboy's Doll* (1969)
Joe David Brown, *Addie Pray* (1971)
Laura Ingalls Wilder, *The First Four Years* (1971)
M. E. Kerr, *Dinky Hocker Shoots Smack!* (1972)
Jane Langton, *The Boyhood of Grace Jones* (1972)
Rita Mae Brown, *Rubyfruit Jungle* (1973)
M. E. Kerr, *The Son of Someone Famous* (1974)
B. Miles, *The Real Me* (1974)
Maxine Hong Kingston, *The Woman Warrior* (1975)
Beverly Cleary, *Ramona the Brave* (1975)
Katherine Paterson, *Bridge to Terabithia* (1977)
Norma Klein, *Tomboy* (1978)
Katherine Paterson, *The Great Gilly Hopkins* (1978)
Beverly Cleary, *Ramona and Her Mother* (1979)
M. E. Kerr, *Little Little* (1981)
Alice Willsey, *Tomboy Ranch* (1981)
Beverly Cleary, *Ramona Quimby, Age 8* (1981)
Cynthia Voight, *Homecoming* (1981)
Nancy Garden, *Annie on My Mind* (1982)
Edith Summer Kelly, *Weeds* (1982)
Robin McKinley, *The Blue Sword* (1982)
Sandra Cisneros, *The House on Mango Street* (1984)
Robin McKinley, *The Hero and the Crown* (1984)
Beverly Cleary, *Ramona Forever* (1984)
Toni Morrison, *The Bluest Eye* (1984)

Dusty Richards, *Marshall Lockhart the Tomboy* (1984)
Jerry Spinelli, *Who Put that Hair in my Toothbrush?* (1984)
Jamaica Kincaid, *Annie John* (1985)
Cynthia Voight, *Jackaroo* (1985)
Jennifer Cole, *Three's a Crowd* (1986)
Jennifer Cole, *Too Late for Love* (1986)
Ernest Hemingway, *The Garden of Eden* (written 1946–1961; published 1986)
Mary DeLapp, *Minnesota Tomboy* (1987)
Fannie Flagg, *Fried Green Tomatoes at the Whistle Stop Café* (1987)
Toni Morrison, *Sula* (1987)
Larry McMurtry, *Buffalo Girls* (1990)
Linda Lewis, *The Tomboy Terror in Bunk 109* (1991)
Jamaica Kincaid, *At the Bottom of the River* (1992)
Leslie Feinberg, *Stone Butch Blues* (1993)
M. E. Kerr, *Deliver Us from Evie* (1994)
Mary Lou Rich, *The Tomboy* (1996)
Pam Muñoz Ryan, *Riding Freedom* (1998)
Leanna Wilson, *His Tomboy Bride* (1998)
Sharon Dennis Wyeth, *Tomboy Trouble* (1998)
Beverly Cleary, *Ramona's World* (1999)
Polly Smrcka, *Hatch Hollow Tomboy* (1999)
Jennifer L. Holm, *Our Only May Amelia* (1999)

DIME WESTERN, DETECTIVE AND ADVENTURE NOVELS[4] (CHRONOLOGICAL)

Frederick Whittaker, *The Mustang-Hunters; or, The Beautiful Amazon of the Hidden Valley* (1871)
Edward L. Wheeler, *Hurricane Nell, the Girl Dead-Shot; or, The Queen of the Saddle and Lasso* (1877)
Edward L. Wheeler, *Deadwood Dick, The Prince of the Road* (October 1877)
Albert W. Aiken, *The Two Detectives; or, the Fortunes of a Bowery Girl* (November 1877)
Edward L. Wheeler, *The Double Daggers; or, Deadwood Dick's Defiance* (December 1877)
Edward L. Wheeler, *Buffalo Ben, the Prince of the Pistol; or, Deadwood Dick in Disguise* (February 1878)
Edward L. Wheeler, *Bob Woolf, the Border Ruffian; or, The Girl Dead-Shot* (March 1878)
Edward L. Wheeler, *Wild Ivan, the Boy Claude Duval; or, The Brotherhood of Death* (March 1878)
Edward L. Wheeler, *The Phantom Miner; or, Deadwood Dick's Bonanza* (May 1878)
Edward L. Wheeler, *Old Avalanche; the Great Annihilator; or, Wild Edna, the Girl Brigand* (June 1878)
Edward L. Wheeler, *Omaha Oll, the Masked Terror; or, Deadwood Dick in Danger* (July 1878)

---

4. Given the sheer number of dime western, detective and adventure narratives published during this era—and also given that many of these books were never archived in library catalogues or, if they were, are now lost, missing or stolen—this section is perhaps the most incomplete. Although I address the history of tomboyish women on the frontier in general and in Western novels in particular in the prologue to chapter five, the subject deserves its own full-length study.

Coupled with the limited nature of this section, I should also note its equally limited range. My list of novels is largely culled from the catalogue of Beadle and Adams Company, a popular, prolific and successful publisher that was home to Edward Wheeler along with other well-known dime novelists such as Edward Ellis and Prentiss Ingraham. In light of the sheer number of texts that these authors released—often several in the same year—I have indicated, whenever possible, the month along with the year of publication.

Edward L. Wheeler, *Deadwood Dick's Eagles; or, The Pards of Flood Bar* (August 1878)

Edward L. Wheeler, *Deadwood Dick on Deck; or, Calamity Jane, the Heroine of Whoop-Up* (December 1878)

Edward L. Wheeler, *Corduroy Charlie, the Boy Bravo; or, Deadwood Dick's Last Act* (January 1879)

Capt. J. F. C. Adams, *Lightening Jo, the Terror of the Prairie* (February 1879)

Edward L. Wheeler, *Idyl, the Girl Minor; or, Rosebud Rob on Hand* (March 1879)

Capt. J. F. C. Adams, *Buck Buckram; or, Bess, the Female Trapper* (March 1879)

George Waldo Browne, *The Tiger of Taos; or, Wild Kate, Dandy Rock's Angel* (1879)

Edward L. Wheeler, *Deadwood Dick in Leadville; or, A Strange Stroke for Liberty* (June 1879)

Edward L. Wheeler, *Deadwood Dick's Device; or, The Sign of the Double Cross* (June 1879)

Edward L. Wheeler, *Deadwood Dick as Detective. A Story of the Great Carbonate Region* (August 1879)

Edward L. Wheeler, *Cinnamon Chip, the Girl Sport; or, The Golden Idol of Mt. Rosa* (Nov. 1879)

Edward L. Wheeler, *Bonanza Bill, Miner; or, Madam Mystery, the Female Forger* (Dec. 1879)

Edward L. Wheeler, *Deadwood Dick's Double; or, The Ghost of Gordon's Gultch* (January 1880)

Joseph E. Badger, *Night-Hawk Kit; or, The Daughter of the Ranch* (March 1880)

Edward L. Wheeler, *Blond Bill; or, Deadwood Dick's Home Base* (March 1880)

Edward L. Wheeler, *A Game of Gold; or, Deadwood Dick's Big Stride* (June 1880)

T. C. Harbaugh, *Gold Digger, the Sport; or, The Girl Avengers* (July 1880)

Edward L. Wheeler, *Deadwood Dick of Deadwood; or, The Picked Party* (July 1880)

Edward L. Wheeler, *New York Nell, the Boy-Girl Detective; or, Old Blakesly Money* (August 1880)

Phillip S. Warne, *Captain Mask, the Lady Road-Agent; or, Patent-Leather Joe's Defeat* (April 1881)

Edward L. Wheeler, *Deadwood Dick's Dream; or, The Rivals of the Road* (April 1881)

Prentiss Ingraham, *Little Grit, the Wild Rider; or, Bessie, the Stock Tender's Daughter* (May 1881)

Edward L. Wheeler, *The Black Hills Jezebel; or, Deadwood Dick's Ward* (May 1881)

Edward L. Wheeler, *Deadwood Dick's Doom; or, Calamity Jane's Last Adventure, a Tale of Death Notch* (June 1881)[5]

Edward L. Wheeler, *Fritz, the Bound-Boy Detective; or, Dot Leetle Game mit Rebecca* (July1881)

Edward L. Wheeler, *Captain Crack-Shot, the Girl Brigand; or, Gipsy Jack from Jimtown.* (Sept. 1881)

Edward L. Wheeler, *Sugar-Coated Sam; or, The Black Gown of Grim Gultch* (October 1881)

Prentiss Ingraham, *Grit, the Bravo Sport; or, The Woman Trailer* (October 1881)

Prentiss Ingraham, *Crimson Kate, the Girl Trailer; or, The Cowboy's Triumph* (December 1881)

T. C. Harbaugh, *Plucky Phil of the Mountain Trail; or, Rosa, the Red Jezebel* (December 1881)

---

5. In spite of the title, this novel is not, in fact, Calamity Jane's last adventure. She appears in Wheeler's next installment of the Deadwood Dick series, *Captain Crack-Shot, the Girl Brigand* (September 1881), along with an array of subsequent narratives. In a possible ironic explanation for the title, *Calamity Jane's Last Adventure* is the novel in which this tomboyish figure and Deadwood Dick are married.

Edward L. Wheeler, *Gold-Dust Dick. A Romance of Roughs and Toughs* (January 1882)
Edward L. Wheeler, *Apollo Bill, the Trail Tornado; or, Rowdy Kate from Right-Bower* (January 1882)
Edward L. Wheeler, *Sierra Sam, the Frontier Ferret; or, A Sister's Devotion* (March 1882)
Edward L. Wheeler, *Deadwood Dick's Divide; or, The Spirit of Swamp Lake* (August 1882)
Edward L. Wheeler, *Deadwood Dick's Death Trail; or, From Ocean to Ocean* (September 1882)
Edward L. Wheeler, *Denver Doll, the Detective Queen; or, Yankee's Eisler's Big Surround* (November 1882)
Edward L. Wheeler, *'Liza Jane, the Girl Miner; or, The Iron-Nerved Sport* (May 1883)
Edward L. Wheeler, *Deadwood Dick's Big Deal; or, The Gold Brick of Oregon* (June 1883)[6]
Edward L. Wheeler, *Deadwood Dick's Dozen; or, The Fakir of Phantom Flats* (September 1883)
Edward L. Wheeler, *Little Quick-Shot, the Scarlet Scout; or, The Dead Face of Daggersville* (November 1883)
Edward L. Wheeler, *Deadwood Dick's Ducats; or, Rainy Days in the Diggings* (March 1884)
Edward L. Wheeler, *Deadwood Dick Sentenced; or, The Terrible Vendetta* (April 1884)
Edward L. Wheeler, *Deadwood Dick's Claim; or, The Fairy Face of Faro Flats* (July 1884)[7]
Edward L. Wheeler, *Deadwood Dick in Dead City* (April 1885)
Edward L. Wheeler, *Deadwood Dick's Diamonds; or, The Mystery of Joan Porter* (June 1885)
Edward L. Wheeler, *Deadwood Dick in New York; or, "A Cute Case"* (August 1885)
Edward L. Wheeler, *Deadwood Dick's Dust; or, The Chained Hand* (October 1885)[8]
Edward L. Wheeler, *Deadwood Dick, Jr. Series* (1885—1897)[9]

LESBIAN PULP FICTION[10] (CHRONOLOGICAL)

Gale Wilhelm, *We Too are Drifting* (1935)
Gale Wilhelm, *Torchlight to Valhalla* (1936)

Diana Fredericks, *Diana: The Story of a Strange Love* (1939)
Felice Swados, *House of Fury* (1941)

---

6. In this novel, the son of Calamity Jane and Deadwood Dick—named simply Deadwood Dick, Jr.—is born. When Wheeler finally ended his Deadwood Dick series by killing off the title character for the final time in the thirty-third installment (see footnote 8), the Beadle and Adams Company promptly began one about his son. Commencing in 1885 and ending in 1897, the Deadwood Dick, Jr., series was comprised of ninety-seven novels, nearly three times the number of texts than the original sequence from which it emerged. The majority of these texts were written after Edward Wheeler's death, which critics and biographer estimate was around 1885, but the precise date is unknown (Brown 269). Nonetheless, all of the novels in the Deadwood Dick, Jr., series were published under Wheeler's name.

7. Calamity Jane, who by this point in the series is now Dick's arch nemesis rather than loving wife and faithful sidekick, dies in this narrative. Similar to the narrative liberties taken in many dime novels—and for which they are often disparaged and discredited—however, she is quickly resurrected, appearing without explanation in *Deadwood Dick's Diamonds; or, The Mystery of Joan Porter* (June 1885).

8. After thirty-three installments about this beloved Western road agent, Wheeler finally drew his Deadwood Dick series to a close by permanently and conclusively killing off his central character. Although Calamity Jane dies with Dick in this book, she once again does not remain deceased. Similar to her previous resurrections, this tomboyish figure makes passim appearances in many of the ninety-seven narratives about their son, Deadwood Dick, Jr.

9. During this twelve-year span, an astounding ninety-seven novels about the son of Calamity Jane and Deadwood Dick were published, making it the longest-running series about a single character in Beadle and Adams' history (Johannsen, par. 6).

10. A note on selection: Contrary to a common tactic of contemporary LGBT scholarship, I have elected to include pulp novels that were written either by men or by men who had adopted female pseudonyms. While these narratives are commonly seen as contributing to heterosexual titillation rather than the burgeoning lesbian community, they formed part of the climate of era and also undoubtedly made their way into the hands of some lesbian women.

Anna Elisabet Weirauch, *The Scorpion* (1948) [1932 in Germany]

Tereska Torres, *Women's Barracks* (1950)

Lucie Marchal, *The Mesh* (1951) [1949 in France]

Janet Pritchard, *Warped Women* (1951)

Lilyan Brock, *Queer Patterns* (1952)

Vincent E. Burns, *Female Convict* (1952)

Claire Morgan, *The Price of Salt* (1952)

Nancy Morgan, *City of Women* (1952)

Vin Packer, *Spring Fire* (1952)

J. C. Priest, *Forbidden* (1952)

Joan Henry, *Women in Prison* (1953)

Florence Stonebraker, *Strange Passions* (1953)

Gale Wilhelm, *The Strange Path* (1953)

Flora Fletcher, *Strange Sisters* (1954)

Sara Harris, *The Wayward Ones* (1954)

Ann Aldrich, *We Walk Alone* (1955)

R. V. Cassill, *Dormitory Women* (1955)

Agnete Holk, *Strange Friends* (1955)

Edwina Mark, *My Sister, My Beloved* (1955)

Michael Norday, *Warped* (1955)

Anonymous, *Adam and Two Eves* (1956)

Guy des Cars, *The Damned One* (1956)

Jordan Park, *Sorority House* (1956)

Ann Bannon, *Odd Girl Out* (1957)

Carol Emery, *Queer Affair* (1957)

Carol Emery, *Queer Affair* (1957)

Reed Marr, *Women Without Men* (1957)

Valerie Taylor, *Whisper Their Love* (1957)

Ann Aldrich, *We, Too, Must Love* (1958)

Ann Aldrich, *We Walk Alone* (1958)

Wenzell Brown, *Prison Girl* (1958)

March Hastings, *Three Women* (1958)

Orrie Hitt, *Girls' Dormitory* (1958)

Tereska Torres, *The Dangerous Games* (1958)

Vin Packer, *The Evil Friendship* (1958)

Kay Addams, *Queer Patterns* (1959)

Ann Bannon, *I Am A Woman* (1959)

Ann Bannon, *Women in the Shadows* (1959)

Sloane Britain, *First Person, 3rd Sex* (1959)

Vincent G. Burns, *Female Convict* (1959)

Paula Christian, *Edge of Twilight* (1959)

Ralph Dean, *One Kind of Woman* (1959)

Lesley Evans, *Strange Are the Ways of Love* (1959)

Don Holliday, *Sin School* (1959)

Don King, *Bitter Love* (1959)

Edwina Mark, *The Odd Ones* (1959)

Lee Morell, *Mimi* (1959)

J. C. Priest, *Private School* (1959)

Randy Salem, *Chris* (1959)

Valerie Taylor, *The Girls in 3-B* (1959)

Kay Addams, *Warped Desire* (1960)

Ann Aldrich (editor), *Carol in a Thousand Cities* (1960) [short story collection]

Ann Bannon, *Journey to A Woman* (1960)

Ann Bannon, *The Marriage* (1960)

Norman Bligh, *The Sisters* (1960)

Sloane Britain, *Meet Marilyn* (1960)

Sloan Britton, *Unnatural* (1960)

Arline McNamee Hammond, *Tomboy* (1960)

Marjorie Lee, *The Lion House* (1960)

Kay Martin, *The Whispered Sex* (1960)

Evans McKnight, *She Made Her Bed* (1960)

Lee Morell, *Nurses' Quarters* (1960)

Ray Morrison, *Reformatory Girls* (1960)

Valerie Taylor, *Stranger on Lesbos* (1960)

Shirley Verel, *The Other Side of Venus* (1960)

Harry Whittington, *Rebel Woman* (1960)

Arthur Adlon, *By Love Depraved* (1961)

Paula Christian, *Love Is Where You Find It* (1961)

March Hastings, *The 3rd Theme* (1961)

Jan Hudson, *Satan's Daughter* (1961)

Sheldon Lord, *Of Shame and Joy* (1961)

Martha Marsden, *Intimate* (1961)

Peggy Swenson, *The Unloved* (1961)

Jay Warren, *The Path Between* (1961)

Alain Abby, *Libido Beach* (1962)

Arthur Adlon, *The One Between* (1962)

Arthur Adlon, *Strange Seduction* (1962)

Arthur Adlon, *The Odd Kind* (1962)

Ann Bannon, *Beebo Brinker* (1962)

Loren Beauchamp, *Strange Delights* (1962)

Sloane Britain, *Ladder of Flesh* (1962)

Creighton Brown Burnham, *Born Innocent* (1962)

Joan Ellis, *Gay Girl* (1962)

Joan Ellis, *Gay Scene* (1962)

Edie Fisher, *Prisoner of My Past* (1962)

Miriam Gardner, *The Strange Women* (1962)

Paul Gregory, *The Price was Perversity* (1962)

James Harvey, *Degraded Women* (1962)

March Hastings, *The Third Sex Syndrome* (1962)

Jason Hytes, *The Doctor and the Dike* [sic] (1962)

Kimberly Kemp, *Operation: Sex* (1962)
Kimberly Kemp, *Perfume and Pain* (1962)
Kimberly Kemp, *Lap of Luxury* (1962)
Lester Lake, *Lady Lovers* (1962)
Sheldon Lord, *21 Gay Street* (1962)
Jack Lynn, *3 Passionate Sisters* (1962)
Dallas Mayo, *Voluptuous Voyage* (1962)
Randy Salem, *The Sex Between* (1962)
Randy Salem, *Tender Torment* (1962)
Andrew Shaw, *Reform School Girls* (1962)
Robert Turner, *Strange Sisters* (1962)
Richard Villanova, *Her Woman* (1962)
Anonymous, *Deviate Wife* (1963)
Barbara Brooks, *Just the Two of Us* (1963)
Paula Christian, *This Side of Love* (1963)
Jessie Dumont, *I Prefer Girls* (1963)
Tom Foran, *The Twisted Ones* (1963)
March Hastings, *Imitation Lovers* (1963)
March Hastings, *The Heat of Day* (1963)
Orrie Hitt, *Torrid Wench* (1963)
Kel Holland, *The Strange Young Wife* (1963)
Jason Hytes, *The Wild Week* (1963)
Sheldon Lord, *Marta* (1963)
Sheldon Lord, *The Sisterhood* (1963)
J. Malcolm Maxwell, *The Other Side of Love* (1963)
Jack Noble, *Unnatural Lovers* (1963)
Michael Norday, *Strange Thirsts* (1963)
Celia L. Powers, *Lesbo Wife* (1963)
Jo Ann Radcliff, *They Call Me Lez* (1963)
Herb Roberts, *The Narrow Line* (1963)
Peggy Swenson, *Pajama Party* (1963)
Valerie Taylor, *A World Without Men* (1963)
Valerie Taylor, *Return to Lesbos* (1963)
Lee Thomas, *Mask of Lesbos* (1963)
Richard Villanova, *The Other Kind* (1963)
Anonymous, *The Beds of Lesbos* (1964)
Kay Addams (as told to Orrie Hitt), *My Lesbians Loves* (1964)
D. W. Craig, *Only in Secret* (1964)
Miriam Gardner, *Twilight Lovers* (1964)
Kay Johnson, *Her Raging Needs* (1964)
Sheldon Lord, *The Third Way* (1964)
Kirby MacLane, *For Women Only* (1964)

Rea Michaels, *Two-Way Street* (1964)
Helen Morgan, *Killer Dyke* (1964)
Jane Rule, *Desert of the Heart* (1964)
Danni Sherwood, *So Strange a Love* (1964)
Peggy Swenson, *Queer Beach* (1964)
Peggy Swenson, *Lesbian Lure* (1964)
Peggy Swenson, *The Gay Partners* (1964)
Peggy Swenson, *Suzy and Vera* (1964)
Valerie Taylor, *Journey to Fulfillment* (1964)
Tom Vail, *This Too Is Love* (1964)
Edwin West, *Young and Innocent* (1964)
Sloan Britain, *Finders Keepers* (1965)
Paula Christian, *The Other Side of Desire* (1965)
Paula Christian, *Amanda* (1965)
Jill Emerson, *Enough of Sorrow* (1965)
March Hastings, *Abnormal Wife* (1965)
Kimberly Kemp, *Coming Out Party* (1965)
Kimberly Kemp, *Private Party* (1965)
Emory Paine, *The Beauty Game* (1965)
Paul V. Russo, *Into the Fire* (1965)
Randy Salem, *Sex in the Shadows* (1965)
Peggy Swenson, *Pamela's Secret Agony* (1965)
Sloane Britain, *Strumpets' Jungle* (1966)
Fred Haley, *Satan was a Lesbian* (1966)
Monica Roberts, *Woman of Darkness* (1966)
Julie Rowe, *By Appointment Only: Sex Salon* (1966)
Pauline Cooper, *The Olive Branch* (1967)
Stacey Clubb, *Left of Sex* (1967)
March Hastings, *Anybody's Girl* (1967)
Sheldon Lord, *69 Barrow Street* (1967)
Rhoda Rollins, *The Strange Trio* (1967)
March Hastings, *The Unashamed* (1968)
Eve Linkletter, *Lesbian Orgies* (1968)
Anonymous, *Tomboy: Revelation of a Girls' Reformatory* (1969)
Steve Harragin, *The Queer Sisters* [no date]
Nelson Edge, *Passion Fruit* [no date]
Fletcher Bennett, *Moment of Desire* [no date]

FILM (CHRONOLOGICAL)

Dir. Lewin Fitzhamon, *Tilly, The Tomboy, Buys Linoleum* (1910) [UK]
Dir. Lewin Fitzhamon, *Tilly, The Tomboy, Goes Boating* (1910) [UK]

Dir. Lewin Fitzhamon, *Tilly, The Tomboy, Plays Truant* (1910) [UK]
Dir. Lewin Fitzhamon, *Tilly, The Tomboy, Visits the Poor* (1910) [UK]

Dir. J. Stuart Blackto, *Uncle Tom's Cabin* (1910)

Dir. Unknown, *The Tomboy* (1911)

Dir. Unknown, *Dolly the Tomboy* (1912)

Dir. William Robert Dal, *Uncle Tom's Cabin* (1914)

Dir. Sidney Drew, *A Florida Enchantment* (1914)

Dir. Wilfred North, *Miss Tomboy and Freckles* (1914)

Dir. Harry Myers, *My Tomboy Girl* (1915)

Dir. Harry A. Pollar, *Miss Jackie of the Navy* (1916)

Dir. William Desmond Taylor, *Her Father's Son* (1916)

Dir. Alexander Butler, *Little Women* (1917)

Dir. Sherwood MacDonald, *Sunny Jane* (1917)

Dir. Marshall Neilan, *Rebecca of Sunnybrook Farm* (1917)

Dir. J. Searle Dawley, *Uncle Tom's Cabin* (1918)

Dir. Harley Knoles, *Little Women* (1918)

Dir. Oscar Apfel, *Phil-for-Short* (1919)

Dir. Frank Wilson, *The Irresistible Flapper* (1919)

Dir. Alan Crosland, *The Flapper* (1920)

Dir. David Kirkland, *In Search of a Sinner* (1920)

Dir. Wayne Mack, *Bubbles* (1920)

Dir. Roy William Neill, *Dangerous Business* (1920)

Dir. Dallas M. Fitzgerald, *The Off-Shore Pirate* (1921)

Dir. Carl Harbaugh, *The Tomboy* (1921)

Dir. Elmer Clifton, *Down to the Sea in Ships* (1922)

Dir. William C. de Mille, *Nice People* (1922)

Dir. Thomas N. Heffron, *Bobbed Hair* (1922)

Dir. F. Richard Jones, *The Country Flapper* (1922) [originally titled *The Cynic Effect* (1920)]

Dir. Stuart Paton, *The Married Flapper* (1922)

Dir. William A. Seiter, *The Beautiful and the Damned* (1922)

Dir. John Francis Dillon, *Flaming Youth* (1923)

Dir. Sidney Franklin, *Brass* (1923)

Dir. Robert Z. Leonard, *Jazzmania* (1923)

Dir. Frank Lloyd, *Black Oxen* (1923)

Dir. Jerome Storm, *Children of Jazz* (1923)

Dir. Sam Wood, *His Children's Children* (1923)

Dir. Sam Wood, *Prodigal Daughters* (1923)

Dir. Clarence G. Badger, *Painted People* (1924)

Dir. William Beaudine, *Daring Youth* (1924)

Dir. William Beaudine, *Daughters of Pleasure* (1924)

Dir. John Francis Dillon, *The Perfect Flapper* (1924)

Dir. Louis J. Gasnier, *Wine* (1924)

Dir. John Gorman, *The Painted Flapper* (1924)

Dir. Ward Hayes, *Flapper Fever* (1924)

Dir. David Kirkland, *The Tomboy* (1924)

Dir. Ernst Lubitsch, *The Marriage Circle* (1924)

Dir. Ernst Lubitsch, *Three Women* (1924)

Dir. Edward Ludwig, *Some Tomboy* (1924)

Dir. Justin H. McCloskey and Jane Murfin, *Flapper Wives* (1924)

Dir. Phil Rosen, *Being Respectable* (1924)

Dir. Frank Tuttle, *Dangerous Money* (1924)

Dir. Millard Webb, *The Dark Swan* (1924)

Dir. William Beaudine, *Little Annie Rooney* (1925)

Dir. Alan Crosland, *Bobbed Hair* (1925)

Dir. Roy Del Ruth, *Eve's Lover* (1925)

Dir. John Francis Dillon, *We Moderns* (1925)

Dir. Dallas M. Fitzgerald, *My Lady of Whims* (1925)

Dir. Charles Giblyn, *The Adventurous Sex* (1925)

Dir. Wesley Riggles, *The Plastic Age* (1925)

Dir. A. Edward Sutherland, *Wild, Wild Susan* (1925)

Dir. Clarence G. Badger, *The Campus Flirt* (1926)

Dir. Herbert Brenon, *Dancing Mothers* (1926)

Dir. Herbert Brenon, *The Great Gatsby* (1926)

Dir. Victor Fleming, *Mantrap* (1926)

Dir. Malcolm St. Clair, *The Show Off* (1926)

Dir. Josef von Sternberg, *Blonde Venus* (1926)

Dir. Dorothy Arzner, *Get Your Man* (1927)

Dir. Clarence G. Badger and (uncredited) Josef von Sternberg, *It* (1927)

Dir. Clarence G. Badger, *She's a Sheik* (1927)

Dir. Clarence G. Badger, *Swim, Girl, Swim* (1927)

Dir. Victor Fleming, *Hula* (1927)

Dir. Frank Lloyd, *Children of Divorce* (1927)

Dir. Harry A. Pollard, *Uncle Tom's Cabin* (1927)

Dir. Frank R. Strayer, *Rough House Rosie* (1927)

Dir. Millard Webb, *Naughty But Nice* (1927)

Dir. Lois Weber, *Sensation Seekers* (1927)

Dir. William A. Wellman, *Wings* (1927)

Dir. Clarence G. Badger, *Hot News* (1928)

Dir. Clarence G. Badger, *Red Hair* (1928)

Dir. Harry Beaumont, *Our Dancing Daughters* (1928)

Dir. Alan James, *The Cowboy and the Flapper* (1928)

Dir. Erle C. Kenton, *Bare Knees* (1928)

Dir. Malcolm St. Clair, *The Fleet's In* (1928)

Dir. F. Harmon Weight, *Jazz Mad* (1928)

Dir. William A. Wellman, *Beggars of Life* (1928)

Dir. Dorothy Arzner, *The Wild Party* (1929)

Dir. Jack Conway, *Our Modern Maidens* (1929)

Dir. Henry King, *She Goes to War* (1929)

Dir. Lothar Mendes, *Dangerous Curves* (1929)

Dir. William A. Seiter, *Synthetic Sin* (1929)

Dir. William A. Seiter, *Why Be Good?* (1929)

Dir. A. Edward Sutherland, *The Saturday Night Kid* (1929)

Dir. Sam Taylor, *Coquette* (1929)

Dir. James Tinling, *The Exalted Flapper* (1929)

Dir. Lewis Milestone, *The Front Page* (1931)

Dir. John Francis Dillon, *Call Her Savage* (1932)

Dir. Alfred Santell, *Rebecca of Sunnybrook Farm* (1932)

Dir. Dorothy Arzner, *Christopher Strong* (1933)

Dir. George Cukor, *Little Women* (1933)

Dir. Rouben Mamoulian, *Queen Christina* (1933)

Dir. David Butler, *The Little Colonel* (1935)

Dir. George Stevens, *Annie Oakley* (1935)

Dir. Cecil B. DeMille, *The Plainsman* (1936)

Dir. Allan Dwan, *Rebecca of Sunnybrook Farm* (1938)

Dir. Lambert Hillyer, *Women in Prison* (1938)

Dir. Lew Landers, *Condemned Women* (1938)

Dir. Howard Hawks, *His Girl Friday* (1940)

Dir. Robert F. McGowan, *Tomboy* (1940)

Dir. Harold D. Schuster, *A Very Young Lady* (1941)

Dir. George Stevens, *Woman of the Year* (1942)

Dir. John English, *Raiders of Sunset Pass* (1943)

Dir. Clarence Brown, *National Velvet* (1944)

Dir. Henry Hathaway, *Home in Indiana* (1944)

Dir. Vincente Minnelli, *Meet Me in St. Louis* (1944)

Dir. Harold S. Bucquet, *Without Love* (1945)

Dir. George Marshall, *Incendiary Blonde* (1945)

Dir. Charles Vidor, *A Song to Remember* (1945)

Dir. Victor Fleming, *Joan of Arc* (1948)

Dir. Ralph Murphy, *Mickey* (1948)

Dir. William Wellman, *Yellow Sky* (1948)

Dir. George Cukor, *Adam's Rib* (1949)

Dir. Lew Landers, *Stagecoach Kid* (1949)

Dir. Mervyn LeRoy, *Little Women* (1949)

Dir. Elliott Nugent, *The Great Gatsby* (1949)

Dir. John Cromwell, *Caged* (1950)

Dir. George Sidney, *Annie Get Your Gun* (1950)

Dir. Roy Del Ruth, *On Moonlight Bay* (1951)

Dir. Charles Lamont, *Flame of Araby* (a.k.a. *Flame of the Desert*) (1951)

Dir. George Cukor, *Pat and Mike* (1952)

Dir. Norman Z. McLeod, *Never Wave at a WAC* (1952)

Dir. Fred Zinnemann, *The Member of the Wedding* (1952)

Dir. David Butler, *Calamity Jane* (1953)

Dir. Alan Dwan, *Passion* (1954)

Dir. Nicholas Ray, *Johnny Guitar* (1954)

Dir. Don Weis, *The Adventures of Hajji Baba* (1954)

Dir. Lewis Seiler, *Women's Prison* (1955)

Dir. Edward L. Cahn, *Girls in Prison* (1956)

Dir. Robert C. Derteno, *Girl Gang* (1956)

Dir. William M. Morgan, *The Violent Years* (1956)

Dir. Walter Lang, *Desk Set* (1957)

Dir. Joseph Pevney, *Tammy and the Bachelor* (1957)

Dir. Orson Welles, *A Touch of Evil* (1958)

Dir. Paul Wendkos, *Gidget* (1959)

Dir. Francis D. Lyon, *Tomboy and the Champ* (1961)

Dir. Robert Wise, *West Side Story* (1961)

Dir. William Wyler, *The Children's Hour* (1961)

Dir. Edward Dmytryk, *Walk on the Wild Side* (1962)

Dir. Robert Mulligan, *To Kill a Mockingbird* (1962)

Dir. Melville Shavelson, *A New Kind of Love* (1963)

Dir. Norman Taurog, *Palm Springs Weekend* (1963)

Dir. John Ford, *Seven Women* (1965)

Dir. Joseph P. Mawra, *Chained Girls* (1965)

Dir. Robert Mulligan, *Inside Daisy Clover* (1965)

Dir. Don Weis, *Billie* (1965)

Dir. Doris Wishman, *Bad Girls Go to Hell* (1965)

Dir. Sande N. Johnsen, *Teenage Gang Debs* (1966)

Dir. John Huston, *Reflections in a Golden Eye* (1967)

Dir. Robert Aldrich, *The Killing of Sister George* (1968)[13]

Dir. Peter Woodcock, *Daughters of Lesbos* (1968)

Dir. Henry Hathaway, *True Grit* (1969)

Dir. Tom DeSimone, *Prison Girls* (1972)

Dir. Peter Bogdanovich, *Paper Moon* (1973)[14]

Dir. Jack Clayton, *The Great Gatsby* (1974)

Dir. Jonathan Demme, *Caged Heat* (1974)

Dir. Martin Scorsese, *Alice Doesn't Live Here Anymore* (1974)

Dir. Billy Wilder, *The Front Page* (1974)

Dir. Jack Hill, *Switchblade Sisters* (1975)

Dir. John G. Avildsen, *Rocky* (1976)

Dir. Michael Ritchie, *The Bad News Bears* (1976)

Dir. Woody Allen, *Annie Hall* (1977)

Dir. Michael Pressman, *The Bad News Bears in Breaking Training* (1977)

Dir. John Waters, *Desperate Living* (1977)

Dir. John Berry, *The Bad News Bears Go to Japan* (1978)[15]

Dir. Bryan Forbes, *International Velvet* (1978)

Dir. Randal Kleiser, *Grease* (1978)

Dir. Norman Tokar, *Candleshoe* (1978)

Dir. Adrian Lyne, *Foxes* (1980)

Dir. Ronald F. Maxwell, *Little Darlings* (1980)

Dir. Allan Moyle, *Times Square* (1980)

Dir. Howard Zieff, *Private Benjamin* (1980)

Dir. Glenn Jordan, *Only When I Laugh* (1981)

Dir. Blake Edwards, *Victor/Victoria* (1982)

Dir. Robert Towne, *Personal Best* (1982)

Dir. Slava Tsukerman, *Liquid Sky* (1982)

Dir. Susan Seidelman, *Smithereens* (1982)

Dir. John Sayles, *Lianna* (1983)

Dir. Barbra Streisand, *Yentl* (1983)

Dir. Herb Freed, *Tomboy* (1985)

Dir. Jeremy Paul Kagan, *The Journey of Natty Gann* (1985)

---

13. Although this film is a British production, it was released in the United States (in a slightly modified form so that it would receive an R-rating instead of the X-rating it had been assigned in England) and enjoyed wide critical attention and commercial viewership.

14. A short-lived television series based on the film aired during the 1974–1975 season. Interestingly, the role of Addie Loggins was not played by Tatum O'Neal but by another well-known tomboy star from this era: Jodie Foster.

15. In addition to the three films made about the Bad News Bears, a television series also debuted. Airing just one season—from 1979 to 1980—it followed Amanda Whurlitzer, Coach Buttermaker and the ragtag team of ballplayers. With low ratings and even lower critical reviews, the series was cancelled after only 23 episodes.

Dir. Tim Kincaid, *Bad Girls Dormitory* (1985)

Dir. James Cameron, *Aliens* (1986)

Dir. Donna Deitch, *Desert Hearts* (1986)

Dir. Penny Marshall, *Jumpin' Jack Flash* (1986)

Dir. Paul Schneider, *Something Special* (1986)

Dir. Paul Schneider, *Willy/Milly* (1986)

Dir. Howard Deutch, *Some Kind of Wonderful* (1987)

Dir. Sheila McLaughlin, *She Must Be Seeing Things* (1987)

Dir. Daniel Goldberg, *Feds* (1988)

Dir. Ted Kotcheff, *Switching Channels* (1988)

Dir. Jon Avnet, *Fried Green Tomatoes* (1991)

Dir. Simon Callow, *The Ballad of the Sad Café* (1991)

Dir. Jonathan Demme, *The Silence of the Lambs* (1991)

Dir. Stephen Herek, *Don't Tell Mom the Babysitter's Dead* (1991)

Dir. Robert Mulligan, *The Man in The Moon* (1991)

Dir. Percy Adlon, *Salmonberries* (1992)

Dir. Nicole Conn, *Claire of the Moon* (1992)

Dir. Stephen Herek, *The Mighty Ducks* (1992)

Dir. Penny Marshall, *A League of Their Own* (1992)

Dir. Yurek Bogayevicz, *Three of Hearts* (1993)

Dir. Maggie Greenwald, *The Ballad of Little Jo* (1993)

Dir. Gillian Armstrong, *Little Women* (1994)[16]

Dir. Jonathan Kaplan, *Bad Girls* (1994)

Dir. Ana Kokkinos, *Only the Brave* (1994)

Dir. Dawn Lodgson, *Tomboy!* (1994)

Dir. Rose Troche, *Go Fish* (1994)

Dir. Marita Giovanni, *Bar Girls* (1995)

Dir. Maria Maggenti, *The Incredibly True Adventure of Two Girls in Love* (1995)

Dir. Patricia Rozema, *When Night Is Falling* (1995)[17]

Dir. Rachel Talalay, *Tank Girl* (1995)[18]

Dir. Cheryl Dunye, *The Watermelon Woman* (1996)

Dir. Julie Dyer, *Late Bloomers* (1996)

Dir. F. Gary Gray, *Set It Off* (1996)

Dir. Mary Harron, *I Shot Andy Warhol* (1996)

Dir. Annette Haywood-Carter, *Foxfire* (1996)

Dir. J. Michael McClary, *Annie O* (1996)

Dir. Sharon Pollack, *Everything Relative* (1996)

Dir. Larry and Andy Wachowski, *Bound* (1996)

Dir. Heidi Arnesen, *Some Prefer Cake* (1997)

Dir. Fielder Cook, *The Member of the Wedding* (1997)

Dir. Alessandro De Gaetano, *Butch Camp* (1997)

Dir. Kelli Herd, *It's in the Water* (1997)

Dir. Ridley Scott, *G. I. Jane* (1997)

Dir. Alex Sichel, *All Over Me* (1997)

Dir. Jeanette L. Buck, *Out of Season* (1998)

Dir. Lisa Cholodenko, *High Art* (1998)

Dir. Michael Cristofer, *Gia* (1998)

Dir. Lukas Moodysson, *Show Me Love* (1998)

Dir. Jamie Babbit, *But I'm a Cheerleader* (1999)

Dir. Luc Besson, *The Messenger* (1999)

Dir. Max Färberböck, *Aimée and Jaguar* (1999)

Dir. Francine Rzeznik, *Equinox Knocks* (1999)

Dir. Anne Wheeler, *Better than Chocolate* (1999)

---

16. It should be noted that in addition to the three feature-length films made of *Little Women* (in 1933, 1949, and 1994) and the two silent versions of the book (in 1917 and 1918), Louisa May Alcott's narrative has also been brought to the small screen many times. In 1946, 1958, 1978 and 2001, *Little Women* appeared as a made-for-television movie. In addition, in 1970, an adaptation of the novel was presented as a television mini-series. Finally, in 2004, Louisa May Alcott's narrative was adapted as a musical for the Broadway stage.

17. This film is actually a Canadian rather than an American production. But, because *When Night Is Falling* had a wide release in the United States and a strong audience reception I decided to include it.

18. Once again, although *Tank Girl* is based on a British and not an American comic book, I have included this film because of its widespread distribution and commercial popularity in the United States.

PLAYS AND MUSICALS (CHRONOLOGICAL)

George M. Baker, *Our Folks: A Play in Three Acts* (1879) [Dramatized version of *Running to Waste: The Story of a Tomboy* (1874) by the same author]

Elizabeth Frances Guptill, *Brave Little Tomboy: A Play of the Revolution* (1912)

Charles O. Locke, *Tomboy, A Musical Comedy in Two Acts* (1925)

Zelda Fitzgerald, *Scandalabra* (written 1932; performed 1933; published 1980)

Lillian Hellman, *The Children's Hour* (1934)

Boyce Loving, *Tomboy: A Comedy in Three Acts* (1935)

Charles George, *My Tomboy Girl: A Musical Comedy in Three Acts* (1936)

Irving Berlin, *Annie Get Your Gun* (1946)

Carson McCullers, *The Member of the Wedding, A Play* (1951)

Arthur Laurents, *West Side Story* (1957)

William Walden, *Tomboy Wonder, A Comedy in Three Acts* (1958)

Edward Albee, *The Ballad of the Sad Café* (1963)

Jim Jacobs & Warren Casey, *Grease* (1972)

MUSIC (CHRONOLOGICAL)

Red Norvo, "Tomboy" (1934)

Gail Davis, "Tomboy" (for Annie Oakley television show, 1954–1957)

Perry Como, "Tomboy" (1958)

Ezell Helen Ingle, *Snips and Snails: Twelve Piano Solos for Boys and Tomboys* (1965)

Steve Allen, "Tomboy," vol 1., *Beautiful Songs by Steve Allen, 1964–1993*

The Beach Boys, "Hey Little Tomboy," *M. I. U. Album* (1978)

The Romantics, "Tomboy," *National Breakout* (1980)

Tomboy, *Back to the Beat* (1987)

Crosby, Stills and Nash, "Tomboy," *Live It Up* (1990)

Sally Taylor, "Tomboy Bride," *Tomboy Bride* (1998)

Tret Fure (with Cris Williamson), "Tomboy Girl," *Radio Quiet* (1999)

Works Cited

Adam's Rib. Dir. George Cukor. Perf. Katharine Hepburn, Spencer Tracy, Judy Holliday. MGM, 1948.

Adams, Natalie G. "Fighters and Cheerleaders: Disrupting the Discourse of the 'Girl Power' in the New Millennium." *Geographies of Girlhood: Identities In-Between.* Eds. Pamela J. Bettis and Natalie Adams. Mahwah, NJ: Lawrence Erlbaum Associates, 2005. 101–113.

Adams, Rachel. "'Mixture of Delicious and Freak': The Queer Fiction of Carson McCullers." *American Literature.* 71.3 (September 1999): 551–583.

———. *Sideshow, U. S. A.: Freaks and the American Cultural Imagination.* Chicago: U of Chicago P, 2001.

"adolescence." *The Oxford English Dictionary.* 2nd ed. 1989.

Alberghene, Janice M. "Autobiography and the Boundaries of Interpretation: On Reading *Little Women* and *The Living Is Easy.*" *Little Women and the Feminist Imagination: Criticism, Controversy, Personal Essays.* Ed. Janice M. Alberghene and Beverly Lyon Clark. New York: Garland, 1999. 347–376.

Alcott, Bronson. *The Journals of Bronson Alcott.* Ed. Odell Shepard. Boston: Little, Brown and Co., 1938.

Alcott, Louisa May. "Cupid and Chow-Chow." *Aunt Jo's Scrap Bag.* Vol. 3: *Cupid and Chow-Chow.* 1873. Boston: Roberts Brothers, 1880. 1–40.

———. "Hospital Sketches." 1863. *Alternative Alcott.* Ed. Elaine Showalter. New Brunswick: Rutgers UP, 1988. 1–73.

———. "How They Ran Away." *Lulu's Library.* Vol. 1. 1885. Boston: Roberts Brothers, 1886. 128–155.

———. *Jack and Jill.* 1880. Boston: Little, Brown and Company, 1928.

———. *Jo's Boys.* 1886. New York: Bantam, 1995.

———. *The Journals of Louisa May Alcott.* Ed. Joel Myerson and Daniel Shealy. Boston: Little, Brown and Co., 1989.

———. *Little Men.* 1871. New York: Penguin, 1986.

————. *Little Women*. 1868. Ed. Elaine Showalter. New York: Penguin, 1989.

————. *Louisa May Alcott: Her Life, Letters and Journals*. Ed. Ednah Cheney. Boston: Roberts Brothers, 1892.

————. "My Boys." *Aunt Jo's Scrap Bag*. Vol. 1: *My Boys*. 1871. Boston: Roberts Brothers, 1872. 1–34.

————. *The Selected Letters of Louisa May Alcott*. Eds. Joel Myerson and Daniel Shealy. Boston: Little, Brown and Co., 1987.

————. "Water-Lilies." *A Garland for Girls*. 1887. Boston: Little, Brown and Company, 1905. 96–131.

Aldridge, Janet. The Meadow-Brook Girls series. Akron, OH: Saalfield Pub. Co., 1913–1914.

Allen, Allyn. *Lone Star Tomboy*. New York: Franklin Watts, Inc., 1951.

Allen, Frederick Lewis. *Only Yesterday: An Informal History of the 1920s*. New York: Harper and Row, 1931.

Allen, Paula Wynn. *Building Domestic Liberty: Charlotte Perkins Gilman's Architectural Feminism*. Amherst: U of Massachusetts P, 1988.

An Alpine Flapper. Animated Short Comedy. Aesop's Fables Studio/Pathé Exchange, 1926.

American Psychiatric Association. *Diagnostic and Statistical Manual for Mental Disorders*. 1ˢᵗ ed. 1952. Washington, D. C.: American Psychiatric Association, 1965.

————. *Diagnostic and Statistical Manual for Mental Disorders—II*. 2ⁿᵈ ed. Washington, D. C.: American Psychiatric Association, 1968.

————. *Diagnostic and Statistical Manual for Mental Disorders—III*. Draft Revision to 3ʳᵈ ed. Washington, D. C.: American Psychiatric Association, 1978.

————. *Diagnostic and Statistical Manual for Mental Disorders—III*. 3ʳᵈ ed. Washington, D. C.: American Psychiatric Association America, 1980.

————. *Diagnostic and Statistical Manual for Mental Disorders—III-R*. Revisions to 3ʳᵈ ed. Washington, D. C.: American Psychiatric Association America, 1987.

————. *Diagnostic and Statistical Manual for Mental Disorders—IV*. 4ᵗʰ ed. Washington, D. C.: American Psychiatric Association, 1994.

————. *Diagnostic and Statistical Manual for Mental Disorders—IV-R*. Revision to 4ᵗʰ ed. Washington, D. C.: American Psychiatric Association, 2000.

Ammons, Elizabeth. *Conflicting Stories: American Women Writers at the Turn of the Twentieth Century*. New York: Oxford UP, 1991.

————. "Material Culture, Empire, and Jewett's *Country of the Pointed Firs*." *New Essays on* The Country of the Pointed Firs. Ed. June Howard. Cambridge: Cambridge UP, 1994. 81–99.

————. "*My Antonia* and African American Art." *New Essays on* My Antonia. Ed. Sharon O'Brien. Cambridge: Cambridge UP, 1999. 57–83.

Anderson, Karen. *Wartime Women: Sex Roles, Family Relations and the Status of Women During World War II*. Westport, CT: Greenwood Press, 1981.

Annals of Congress. Vol. 1: *Abridgements of the Debates of Congress, 1789–1856*. New York: D. Appleton and Co., 1857.

Annie Get Your Gun. Dir. George Sidney. Perf. Betty Hutton, Howard Keel, Louis Calhern. Warner Brothers, 1950.

Annie Hall. Dir. Woody Allen. Perf. Woody Allen, Diane Keaton, Tony Roberts, Carol Kane. MGM, 1977.

Ansen, David. Review of *Little Women*. *Newsweek*. 9 January 1994: 57.

Archdeacon, Thomas J. *Becoming American: An Ethnic History*. New York: The Free Press, 1983.

Ariès, Philippe. *Centuries of Childhood: A Social History of Family Life*. Trans. Robert Baldick. New York: Vintage, 1962.

Arthur, T. S. *Advice to Young Ladies on Their Duties and Conduct in Life*. Boston: G. W. Cottrell, 1851.

Babes in Arms. Dir. Busby Berkeley. Dir. Mickey Rooney, Judy Garland, Charles Winninger. MGM, 1939.

The Bad News Bears. Dir. Michael Ritchie. Perf. Walter Matthau, Tatum O'Neal, Vic Morrow, Joyce Van Patten. Paramount, 1976.

Baker, George M. *Running to Waste: The Story of a Tomboy.* 1874. Boston: Lee and Shepard, 1902.

Bakhtin, Mikhail. *Rabelais and His World.* Trans. Hélène Iswolsky. Bloomington: Indiana UP, 1984.

———. *Speech Genres and Other Late Essays.* Ed. Caryl Emerson and Michael Holquist. Trans. Vern W. McGee. Austin: U of Texas P, 1986.

The Ballad of the Sad Café. Dir. Simon Callow. Perf. Vanessa Redgrave, Keith Carradine, Cork Hubbert. Merchant Ivory, 1991.

Balme, Christopher. "Selling the Bird: Richard Walton Tully's *The Bird of Paradise* and the Dynamics of Theatrical Commodification." *Theatre Journal.* 57 (2005): 1–20.

Banner, Lois. *American Beauty.* Chicago: U of Chicago P, 1983.

Bannon, Ann. *Beebo Brinker.* 1962. San Francisco: Cleis, 2002.

———. *I Am a Woman.* 1959. San Francisco: Cleis, 2002.

———. Interview with Diane Anderson-Minshall. *Girlfriends.* July 1994: 18+.

———. *Journey to a Woman.* 1960. San Francisco: Cleis, 2002.

———. *The Marriage.* Greenwich, CT: Fawcett Gold Medal, 1960.

———. *Odd Girl Out.* 1957. San Francisco: Cleis, 2002.

———. *Women in the Shadows.* 1959. San Francisco: Cleis, 2002.

Banta, Martha. *Imaging American Women: Idea and Ideals in Cultural History.* New York: Columbia UP, 1987.

Bar Girls. Dir. Marita Giovanni. Perf. Nancy Allison Wolfe, Liza D'Agostino, Camilla Griggs, Justine Slater, Lisa Parker. Orion, 1995.

Bardes, Barbara, and Suzanne Gossett, eds. *Declarations of Independence: Women and Political Power in Nineteenth-Century American Fiction.* New Brunswick, NJ: Rutgers UP, 1990.

Barkan, Elazar, and Ronald Bush, eds. *Prehistories of the Future: The Primitivist Project and the Culture of Modernism.* Stanford: Stanford UP, 1995.

Baym, Nina. *Woman's Fiction: A Guide to Novels by and about Women, 1820–1870.* Ithaca, NY: Cornell UP, 1978.

Beauvoir, Simone de. *Memoirs of a Dutiful Daughter.* Trans. James Kirkup. Cleveland: World Pub. Co., 1959.

Bedell, Madelon. *The Alcotts: Biography of a Family.* New York: Clarkson N. Potter, 1980.

———. "Introduction." *Little Women.* By Louisa May Alcott. New York: The Modern Library, 1983. ix–xlix.

Bederman, Gail. *Manliness and Civilization: A Cultural History of Gender and Race in the United States, 1880–1917.* Chicago: U of Chicago P, 1995.

Bell-Metereau, Rebecca. *Hollywood Androgyny.* New York: Columbia UP, 1993.

Benshoff, Harry M., and Sean Griffin. *Queer Images: A History of Gay and Lesbian Film in America.* Lanham: Rowman & Littlefield, 2006.

Berlant, Lauren, and Elizabeth Freeman. "Queer Nationality." *National Identities and Post-Americanist Narratives.* Ed. Donald E. Pease. Durham, NC: DukeUP, 1994. 149–172.

Berman, Ruth. "No Jo Marches!" *Children's Literature in Education.* 29.4 (December 1998): 237–247.

Bernstein, Susan Naomi. "Writing and *Little Women*: Alcott's Rhetorical Subversion." *American Transcendental Quarterly.* 7 (1993): 29–45.

Bérubé, Allan. *Coming Out Under Fire: The History of Gay Men and Women in World War Two.* New York: Macmillan, 1990.

———. "How Gay Stays White and What Kind of White It Stays." *The Making and Unmaking of Whiteness.* Eds. Birgit Brander Rasmussen, Eric Klinenberg, Irene J. Nexica, and Matt Wray. Durham, NC: Duke UP, 2001. 234–265.

Bettis, Pamela J., and Natalie Adams, eds. *Geographies of Girlhood: Identities In-Between.* Mahwah, NJ: Lawrence Erlbaum Associates, 2005.

Betts, Miriam Parker. *Tomboy Teacher.* New York: Julian Messner, 1961.

Billie. Dir. Don Weis. Perf. Patty Duke, Jim Backus, Jane Greer. MGM, 1965.

Bishop, Ferman. "Sarah Orne Jewett's Ideas of Race." *The New England Quarterly.* 30.2 (June 1957): 243–249.

Blackwood, Evelyn. "*Tombois* in West Sumatra: Constructing Masculinity and Erotic Desire." *Cultural Anthropology.* 13.4 (1998): 491–521.

Blanchard, Amy E. *A Little Tomboy.* New York: Hurst and Company, 1903.

Blanchard, Paula. *Sarah Orne Jewett: Her World and Her Work.* Reading, MA: Addison-Wesley, 1994.

Bogdan, Robert. *Freak Show: Presenting Human Oddities for Amusement and Profit.* Chicago: U of Chicago P, 1988.

Bound. Dir. Larry and Andy Wachowski. Perf. Jennifer Tilly, Gina Gershon, Joe Pantoliano, John Ryan, Christopher Meloni, Richard C. Sarafin. Gramercy, 1996.

"The Boyette: Seaside Girls Who Dress Like Boys." *Daily Mail.* April 19, 1927. 7+.

Boyle, Regis Louise. *Mrs. E. D. E. N. Southworth, Novelist.* Washington, D.C.: Catholic U of America P, 1939.

Boys on the Side. Dir. Herbert Ross. Perf. Whoopi Goldberg, Mary-Louise Parker, Drew Barrymore. Warner Brothers, 1995.

Brantlinger, Patrick. "Victorians and Africans: The Genealogy of the Myth of the Dark Continent." *"Race," Writing and Difference.* Ed. Henry Louis Gates, Jr. Chicago: U of Chicago P, 1986. 185–222.

Breines, Wini. "Postwar White Girls' Dark Others." *The "Other" Fifties: Interrogating Mid-century American Icons.* Ed. Joel Foreman. Urbana: U of Illinois P, 1997. 53–77.

Brink, Carol Ryrie. *Caddie Woodlawn.* 1935. New York: Collier Books, 1970.

Brodhead, Richard. *Cultures of Letters: Scenes of Reading and Writing in Nineteenth-Century America.* Chicago: U of Chicago P, 1993.

Brody, Jennifer DeVere. *Impossible Purities: Blackness, Femininity, and Victorian Culture.* Durham, NC: Duke UP, 1998.

Brown, Bill, ed. *Reading the West: An Anthology of Dime Westerns.* Boston: Bedford, 1997.

Brown, Joe David. *Addie Pray.* New York: Signet, 1971.

Brown, Rita Mae. *Rubyfruit Jungle.* New York: Bantam, 1973.

Buck, Elizabeth. *Paradise Remade: The Politics of Culture and History in Hawai'i.* Philadelphia: Temple UP, 1993.

Buell, Lawrence. *New England Literary Culture: From Revolution Through Renaissance.* Cambridge: Cambridge UP, 1986.

Burn, Shawn Meghan, A. Kathleen O'Neil and Shirley Nederend. "Childhood Tomboyism and Adult Androgyny." *Sex Roles.* 34.5/6 (1996): 419–428.

Burroughs, Edgar Rice. *Jungle Tales of Tarzan.* 1915. New York: Ballantine, 1963.

———. *The Return of Tarzan.* 1913. New York: Ballantine, 1963.

———. *The Son of Tarzan.* 1915. New York: Ballantine, 1963.

———. *Tarzan and the Jewels of Opar.* 1916. New York: Ballantine, 1963.

———. *Tarzan of the Apes.* 1912. New York: Ballantine, 1963.

———. *Tarzan, Lord of the Jungle.* 1927. New York: Ballantine, 1963.

———. *Tarzan the Invincible.* 1930. New York: Ballantine, 1964.

———. *Tarzan Triumphant.* 1931. New York: Ballantine, 1964.

Butler, Judith. *Gender Trouble: Feminism and the Subversion of Identity.* New York: Routledge, 1990.

Cadogan, Mary, and Patricia Craig. *You're a Brick, Angela!: A New Look at Girls' Fiction from 1839 to 1975*. London: Victor Gollancz Ltd., 1976.

Calamity Jane. Dir. David Butler. Perf. Doris Day, Howard Keel and Allyn McLerie. Warner Brothers, 1953.

Call Her Savage. Dir. John Francis Dillon. Perf. Clara Bow, Monroe Owsley, Gilbert Roland, Thelma Todd. Fox Film, 1932.

The Cambridge Guide to Children's Books in English. Ed. Victor Watson. Cambridge: Cambridge UP, 2001.

Cameron, Julia. "Tomboys: Can 'Bad' Girls Be 'Good' Women?" *Mademoiselle*. 90 (May 1984): 168–169+.

Canby, Vincent. "For the Girls of Summer, Pop Flies and Charm School." *The New York Times*. 1 July 1992. late ed.: C13+.

Candleshoe. Dir. Norman Tokar. Perf. David Niven, Jodie Foster, Helen Hayes and Leo McKern. Disney, 1978.

Cane, Aleta. "Charlotte Perkins Gilman's *Herland* as a Feminist Response to Male Quest Romance." *Jack London Journal*, vol 2 (1995): 25–38.

Carby, Hazel. *Reconstructing Womanhood: The Emergence of the Afro-American Woman Novelist*. New York: Oxford UP, 1987.

Carden, Mary Paniccia. "Creative Fertility and the National Romance in Willa Cather's *O Pioneers!* and *My Antonia*." *Modern Fiction Studies*. 45.2 (Summer 1999): 275–302.

Carlip, Hillary. *Girl Power: Young Women Speak Out*. New York: Warner Books, 1995.

Carr, Virginia Spencer. *The Lonely Hunter: A Biography of Carson McCullers*. Garden City, NJ: Doubleday & Co., 1975.

Carter, David. *Stonewall: The Riots that Sparked the Gay Revolution*. New York: St. Martin's Press, 2005.

Cary, Richard. Introduction. *Sarah Orne Jewett Letters*. Rev. ed. Waterville, ME: Colby College Press, 1967.

———. "The Literary Rubrics of Sarah Orne Jewett." *Critical Essays on Sarah Orne Jewett*. Ed. Gwen L. Nagel. Boston: Hall, 1984. 198–211.

———. *Sarah Orne Jewett*. New Haven, CT: College and University Press, 1962.

Cather, Willa. *My Antonia*. 1918. Boston: Houghton Mifflin, 1988.

———. "The Namesake." *April Twilights*. 1903. Lincoln: U of Nebraska P, 1962. 25–26.

———. "The Novel Démeublé." *Willa Cather: Stories, Poems, and Other Writings*. New York: Library of America, 1992. 834–837.

———. *One of Ours*. 1922. New York: Vintage Classics, 1991.

———. *O Pioneers!* 1913. New York: Penguin, 1989.

———. *Sapphira and the Slave Girl*. 1940. New York: Vintage, 1968.

———. "Tommy, The Unsentimental." 1896. *Jo's Girls: Tomboy Tales of High Adventure, True Grit and Real Life*. Ed. Christian McEwan. Boston: Beacon, 1997. 174–181.

———. "The Way of the World." 1898. *Collected Short Fiction, 1892–1912*. Lincoln: U of Nebraska P, 1965. 395–404.

———. *Willa Cather in Person: Interviews, Speeches, Letters*. Ed. L. Brent Bohlke. Lincoln: U of Nebraska P, 1986.

"Caucasian." *The Oxford English Dictionary*. 2nd ed. 1989.

CBS News. "'Nancy Drew' Creator Dies: Mildred Wirt Benson, Original Author of Girl Detective Series, Dead at 96." 29 May 2002. <www.cbsnews.com/stories/2002/05/29/print> (accessed 22 Aug. 2007).

Chafe, William H. *The Paradox of Change: American Women in the 20th Century*. New York: Oxford UP, 1991.

Chained Girls. 1965. Dir. Joseph P. Mawra. Perf. Joel Holt (narrator), June Roberts (uncredited). Something Weird Video, 2003.

Chopin, Kate. "Charlie." *The Complete Works of Kate Chopin*. Ed. Per Seyersted. vol II. Baton Rouge: Louisiana State UP, 1969. 638–670.

Christian, Barbara. *Black Women Novelists: The Development of a Tradition, 1892–1976*. Westport, CT: Greenwood, 1980.

Christian, Paula. *The Other Side of Desire*. New York: Paperback Library, 1965.

Christopher Strong. Dir. Dorothy Arzner. Perf. Katharine Hepburn, Colin Clive.Turner, 1933.

Church, Joseph. "Fathers, Daughters, Slaves: The Haunted Scene of Writing in Jewett's 'In Dark New England Days.'" *American Transcendental Quarterly*. 5.3 (September 1993): 205–224.

Cisneros, Sandra. *The House on Mango Street*. New York: Vintage, 1984.

Clarke, Edward H. *Sex in Education; or, A Fair Chance for the Girls*. Boston: J. R. Osgood and Co., 1878.

Clayton, Barbara. *Tomboy*. New York: Funk and Wagnalls, 1961.

Clinton, Catherine. *The Other Civil War: American Women in the Nineteenth Century*. New York: Hill and Wang, 1984.

Clinton, Catherine, and Nina Silber, eds. *Divided Houses: Gender and the Civil War*. New York: Oxford UP, 1992.

Cogan, Frances B. *All-American Girl: The Ideal of Real Womanhood in Mid-Nineteenth Century America*. Athens, GA: U of Georgia P, 1989.

Cole, Jennifer. *Three's a Crowd*. New York: Fawcett Girls Only, 1986.

———. *Too Late for Love*. New York: Fawcett Girls Only, 1986.

Coleman, Dorothy S., Elizabeth A. Coleman and Evelyn J. Coleman. *The Collector's Encyclopedia of Dolls*. Vol. 2. New York: Crown Publishers Inc., 1986.

College Holiday. Dir. Frank Tuttle. Perf. Jack Benny, George Burns, Gracie Allen. Paramount, 1936.

Collins, Patricia Hill. *Black Feminist Thought: Knowledge, Consciousness and the Politics of Empowerment*. Boston: Unwin Hyman, 1990.

Como, Perry. *Tomboy*. LP. RCA-Victor, 1958.

Coolidge, Susan. *What Katy Did*. 1872. Boston: Little, Brown, and Co., 1938.

Corrigan, Lesa Carnes. "The Member of the Wedding." 2004. *The New Georgia Encyclopedia*. 22 December 2005. <http://www.georgiaencyclopedia.org/nge/ArticlePrintable.jsp?id=h-1239>

Coultrap-McQuinn, Susan. *Doing Literary Business: American Women Writers in the Nineteenth Century*. Chapel Hill: U of North Carolina P, 1990.

The Country Flapper. Dir. F. Richard Jones. Perf. Dorothy Gish, Glenn Hunter, Tom Douglas. Dorothy Gish Productions, 1922.

The Cowboy and the Flapper. Dir. Alan James. Perf. William Fairbanks, Dorothy Revier, Jack Richardson. Phil Goldstone Productions, 1924.

Craft, William. *Running a Thousand Miles to Freedom; or, The Escape of William and Ellen Craft from Slavery*. 1860. Miami: Mnemosyne, 1969.

Creed, Barbara. "Lesbian Bodies: Tribades, Tomboys and Tarts." *Sexy Bodies: The Strange Carnalities of Feminism*. Ed. Elizabeth Grosz and Elspeth Probyn. London: Routledge, 1995. 86–103.

Crèvecoeur, Hector St. John de. "Letters from an American Farmer." *The Heath Anthology of American Literature*. Ed. Paul Lauter. Boston: Houghton Mifflin, 1998. 851–881.

Crowley, John W. "*Little Women* and the Boy-Book." *The New England Quarterly*. 58.3 (September 1985): 384–399.

Curtis, L. Perry. *Ape and Angels: The Irishman in Victorian Caricature*. Washington, D.C.: Smithsonian Institution, 1971.

Daniels, Les. *Wonder Woman: The Complete History*. San Francisco: Chronicle Books, 2000.

Darwin, Charles. The Descent of Man. New York: D. Appleton & Co., 1871.

———. *The Origin of Species*. 1859. New York: Oxford UP, 1996.

Daughters of Lesbos. 1968. Dir. Peter Woodcock. Perf. Geri Miller, Linda Boyce, Jackie Richards. Something Weird Video, 2003.

Davis, Anne Pence. *Mimi at Camp: The Adventures of a Tomboy*. Chicago: Goldsmith, 1935.

———. *Mimi at Sheridan School*. Chicago: Goldsmith, 1935.

———. *Mimi's House Party*. Chicago: Goldsmith, 1936.

Davis, Kenneth C. *Two-Bit Culture: The Paperbacking of America*. Boston: Houghton Mifflin, 1984.

Davis, Thadious. "Erasing the 'We of Me' and Rewriting the Racial Script: Carson McCullers' Two *Member(s) of the Wedding*." *Critical Essays on Carson McCullers*. Ed. Beverly Lyon Clark and Melvin J. Friedman. New York: G. K. Hall & Co., 1996. 206–219.

D'Emilio, John. *Sexual Politics, Sexual Communities: The Making of a Homosexual Minority in the United States, 1940–1970*. 2nd ed. Chicago: U of Chicago P, 1998.

Deloria, Philip J. *Playing Indian*. New Haven: Yale UP, 1998.

Dennett, Andrea Stulman. *Weird and Wonderful: The Dime Museum in America*. New York: New York UP, 1997.

Denning, Michael. *Mechanic Accents: Dime Novels and Working-Class Culture in America*. London, New York: Verso, 1987.

Desert Hearts. Dir. Donna Deitch. Perf. Helen Shaver, Patricia Charbonneau, Audra Lindley, Andrea Akers, Dean Butler. Samuel Goldwyn, 1986.

Dirks, Tim. "Sexual or Erotic Films." http://www.filmsite.org/sexualfilms.html (accessed 6 June 2004).

Doan, Laura. *Fashioning Sapphism: The Origins of a Modern English Lesbian Subculture*. New York: Columbia, 2001.

Dobson, Joanne. "Introduction." *The Hidden Hand*. By E. D. E. N. Southworth. 1859. New Brunswick, NJ: Rutgers UP, 1988. xi–xli.

Donovan, Josephine. *Sarah Orne Jewett*. New York: Ungar, 1980.

Don't Tell Mom the Babysitter's Dead. Dir. Stephen Herek. Perf. Christina Applegate, Joanna Cassidy, John Getz. Cinema Plus, 1991.

Dorson, Richard M. "Mose the Far-Famed and World-Renowned." *American Literature*. 15 (November 1943): 288–300.

Doskow, Minna. "Introduction." *Charlotte Perkins Gilman's Utopian Novels: Moving the Mountain, Herland, With Her in Ourland*. Madison: Fairleigh Dickson UP, 1999. 9–29.

Douglas, Ann. *The Feminization of American Culture*. New York: Knopf, 1978.

———. *Terrible Honesty: Mongrel Manhattan in the 1920s*. New York: Farrar, Straus, and Giroux, 1995.

Down to the Sea in Ships. Dir. Elmer Clifton. Perf. Marguerite Courtot, Raymond McKee, Clara Bow. Whaling Film Corp., 1922.

Duberman, Martin B. *Stonewall*. New York: Penguin, 1994.

Duganne, Phyllis and Harriet Gersman. "Tomboy." *The American Girl*. 11.5 (May 1928): 7–9, 45–49.

Dunlop, John T. and Walter Galenson, eds. *Labor in the Twentieth Century*. New York: Academic Press, 1978.

Dyer, Richard. *White*. London: Routledge, 1997.

Elbert, Sarah. *A Hunger for Home: Louisa May Alcott and* Little Women. Philadelphia: Temple UP, 1984.

———. "Introduction." *Louisa May Alcott: On Race, Sex, and Slavery*. Boston: Northeastern UP, 1997. ix–lix.

Elliott, Mary. "The Closet of the Heart: Legacies of Domesticity in Tomboy Narratives and Lesbian Pulp Fiction, 1850–1965." Diss. U of Wisconsin-Milwaukee, 1999.

———. "When Girls Will Be Boys: 'Bad' Endings and Subversive Middles in Nineteenth-Century Tomboy Narratives and Twentieth-Century Lesbian Pulp Novels." *Legacy*. 15.1 (1998): 92–97.

Ellison, Ralph. "Change the Joke and Slip the Yoke." *Shadow and Act*. New York: Vintage International, 1995. 45–59.

Ellson, Hal. *Tomboy*. New York: Bantam Books, 1950.

Erens, Patricia. "The Flapper: Hollywood's First Liberated Woman." *Dancing Fools and Weary Blues: The Great Escape of the Twenties*. Ed. Lawrence R. Broer and John D. Walther. Bowling Green, OH: Bowling Green UP, 1990. 130–139.

"eugenic." *The Oxford English Dictionary*. 2nd ed. 1989.

Evans, Oliver. *Carson McCullers: Her Life and Work*. London: Peter Owen, 1965.

"Everything is Hot-tentotsy Now!" *Life*. July 15, 1926: cover image. Illustration by L. J. Holton.

The Exhalted Flapper. Dir. James Tinling. Perf. Sue Carol, Barry Norton, Irene Rich, Albert Conti. Fox Film, 1929.

Faderman, Lillian. *Odd Girls and Twilight Lovers: A History of Lesbian Life in Twentieth-Century America*. New York: Columbia UP, 1991.

———. *Surpassing the Love of Men: Romantic Friendships and Love Between Women from the Renaissance to the Present*. New York: Morrow, 1981.

Faery, Rebecca Blevins. *Cartographies of Desire: Captivity, Race and Sex in the Shaping of an American Nation*. Norman: University of Oklahoma P, 1999.

Fanon, Frantz. *Black Skin, White Masks*. Trans. Charles Marmann. New York: Grove, 1967.

Fans and Flappers. Dir. Unknown. Perf. Hal Stephens. Carnival Comedies, 1922.

Far, Sui Sin. "A Chinese Boy-Girl." *Mrs. Spring Fragrance and other Stories*. 1912. Urbana: U of Illinois, 1995. 155–59.

———. "The Smuggling of Tie Co." *Mrs. Spring Fragrance and other Stories*. 1912. Urbana: U of Illinois, 1995. 104–8.

———. "Tian Shan's Kindred Spirit." *Mrs. Spring Fragrance and other Stories*. 1912. Urbana: U of Illinois, 1995. 119–24.

Fass, Paula S. *The Damned and the Beautiful: American Youth in the 1920s*. Oxford: Oxford UP, 1977.

Faulkner, Anne Shaw. "Does Jazz Put the Sin in Syncopation?" *Ladies' Home Journal*. August 1921: 16, 34.

Feaster, Felicia, and Bret Wood. *Forbidden Fruit: The Golden Age of the Exploitation Film*. Baltimore, MD: Luminary Press, 1999.

Feinberg, Leslie. *Transgender Warriors: Making History from Joan of Arc to Dennis Rodman*. Boston: Beacon, 1996.

Felski, Rita. *The Gender of Modernity*. Cambridge: Harvard UP, 1995.

Fern, Fanny. *Caper-Sauce: A Volume of Chit-Chat about Men, Women, and Things*. New York: Carleton, 1872.

Fetterley, Judith. "Impersonating 'Little Women': The Radicalism of Alcott's *Behind a Mask*." *Women's Studies*. 10 (1983): 1–14.

———. "*Little Women*: Alcott's Civil War." *Feminist Studies*. 5 (1979): 369–383.

———. "Reading *Deephaven* as a Lesbian Text." *Sexual Practice, Textual Theory: Lesbian Cultural Criticism*. Eds. Susan J. Wolfe and Julia Penelope. Cambridge, MA: Blackwell, 1993. 164–183.

Fiedler, Leslie. "Adolescence and Maturity in the American Novel." *An End to Innocence: Essays on Culture and Politics*. 2nd ed. New York: Stein and Day, 1972. 191–210.

———. *Freaks: Myths and Images of the Secret Self*. New York: Doubleday, 1993.

———. "No!" In *Thunder: Essays on Myth and Literature*. London: Eyre and Spottiswoode, 1960.

Fine, Michelle, Lois Weis, L. Mun Wong and Linda C. Powell, eds. *Off White: Readings on Race, Power and Society*. New York: Taylor and Francis, 1996.

Fischer, Mike. "Pastoralism and Its Discontents: Willa Cather and the Burden of Imperialism." *Mosaic*. 23.1 (Winter 1990): 31–44.

Fish, Cheryl. *Black and White Women's Travel Narratives: Antebellum Explorations.* Gainesville: U of Florida P, 2004.

———. "Going Mobile: The Body at Work in Black and White Women's Travel Narratives, 1841–1857." Diss. CUNY, 1996.

———. "Voices of Restless (Dis)Continuity." *Women's Studies: An Interdisciplinary Journal.* 26.5 (1997): 475–495.

Fishkin, Shelley Fisher. "Interrogating 'Whiteness,' Complicating 'Blackness': Remapping American Culture." *American Quarterly.* 47.3 (September 1993): 428–466.

Fitzgerald, F. Scott. *This Side of Paradise.* 1920. New York: Charles Scribner's Sons, 1986.

Fitzhugh, Louise. *Harriet the Spy.* New York: Random House, 1964.

Flagg, Fannie. *Fried Green Tomatoes at the Whistle Stop Café.* New York: Doubleday, 1987.

Flaming Flappers. Dir. Fred Guiol. Perf. Glen Tryon, Tyler Brooke and James Finlayson. Hal Roach Studios, 1925.

"flapper." *The Oxford English Dictionary.* 2nd ed. 1989.

The Flapper. Dir. Alan Crosland. Perf. Olive Thomas, Warren Cook, Theodore Westman, Jr. Selznick Pictures, 1920.

Flapper Fever. Dirs. Ward Hayes and Eddie Lyons. Perf. Bobby Dunn. Eddie Lyons Comedies, 1924.

Flapper Wives. Dirs. Justin H. McCloskey and Jane Murfin. Perf. Mary Allison, Rockliffe Fellowes, Vera Reynolds. Lawrence Trimble and Jane Murfin Productions, 1924.

Flashdance. Dir. Adrian Lyne. Perf. Jennifer Beals, Michael Nouri, Lila Skala, and Sunny Johnson. Paramount, 1983.

The Flip Flapper (released in some U.S. theaters under the title "*Risky Business*"). Dirs. Harry B. Harris and Rollin S. Sturgeon. Perf. Fred Andrews, John Gough, Lillian Lawrence. Universal Film, 1920.

Foster, Frances Smith. *Witnessing History: The Development of Ante-Bellum Slave Narratives.* Westport, CT: Greenwood, 1979.

———. *Written by Herself: Literary Production by African American Women, 1746–1892.* Bloomington: Indiana UP, 1993.

Foucault, Michel. *The History of Sexuality: An Introduction.* 1978. Trans. Robert Hurley. New York: Vintage, 1990.

Foxes. Dir. Adrian Lyne. Perf. Jodie Foster, Cherie Currie, Marilyn Kagan, Kandace Stroh, Scott Baio, Sally Kellerman. MGM, 1980.

Frankenberg, Ruth. *White Women, Race Matters: The Social Construction of Whiteness.* Minneapolis: U of Minnesota P, 1993.

"freak." *The Oxford English Dictionary.* 2nd ed. 1989.

Frederickson, George. *The Black Image in the White Mind: The Debate on Afro-American Character and Destiny, 1817–1914.* New York: Harper and Row, 1971.

Freeman, Elizabeth. "'The We of Me': *The Member of the Wedding*'s Novel Alliances." *Women and Performance: A Journal of Feminist Theory.* 8.2. (1996): 111–135.

The Freewoman: A Weekly Humanist Review. London: New International Publishing Company. Published weekly from November 23, 1911 to October 10, 1912.

Freud, Sigmund. *The Question of Lay Analysis: An Introduction to Psychoanalysis.* New York: Norton, 1950.

Fried Green Tomatoes. Dir. Jon Avnet. Perf. Kathy Bates, Jessica Tandy, Mary Stuart Masterson, Mary-Louise Parker, Cicely Tyson, Chris O'Donnell. Universal, 1991.

Friedan, Betty. *The Feminine Mystique.* New York: Norton, 1963.

Frost, John Eldridge. *Sarah Orne Jewett.* Kittery Point, ME: Gundalow Club, 1960.

Fulton, Valerie. "Rewriting the Necessary Woman: Marriage and Professionalism in James, Jewett and Phelps." *The Henry James Review.* 15.3 (Fall 1994): 242–256.

Gabler-Hover, Janet. *Dreaming Black/Writing White: The Hagar Myth in American Cultural History.* Lexington, KY: U of Kentucky P, 2000.

Ganobcsik-Williams, Lisa. "The Intellectualism of Charlotte Perkins Gilman: Evolutionary Perspectives on Race, Ethnicity and Class." *Charlotte Perkins Gilman: Optimist Reformer.* Eds. Jill Rudd and Val Gough. Iowa City, IA: U of Iowa P, 1999: 16–41.

Garber, Marjorie. *Vested Interests: Cross-Dressing and Cultural Anxiety.* New York: Routledge, 1992.

Garis, Lilian. *Ted and Tony: Two Girls of Today.* New York: Grosset & Dunlap, 1929.

Gates, Jr., Henry Louis. "Introduction: Writing 'Race' and the Difference It Makes." *"Race," Writing and Difference.* Ed. Henry Louis Gates, Jr. Chicago: U of Chicago P, 1986. 1–20.

———. *The Signifying Monkey: A Theory of Afro-American Literary Criticism.* New York: Oxford , 1988.

Gelfant, Blanche H. "Introduction." *O Pioneers!* By Willa Cather. 1913. New York: Penguin, 1994. ix–xxxvi.

George, Charles. *My Tomboy Girl: A Musical Comedy in Three Acts.* Boston: Baker's Plays, 1936.

Gerhard, Jane. *Desiring Revolution: Second-Wave Feminism and the Rewriting of Twentieth-Century American Sexual Thought.* New York: Columbia UP, 2001.

G. I. Jane. Dir. Ridley Scott. Perf. Demi Moore, Viggo Mortensen, Anne Bancroft. Caravan Pictures, 1997.

Gidget. Dir. Paul Wendkos. Perf. Sandra Dee, James Darren, Cliff Robertson. Columbia, 1959.

Gilbert, Sandra, and Susan Gubar.———. *No Man's Land: The Place of the Woman Writer in the Twentieth Century.* Vol. 2:*Sexchanges.* New Haven: Yale UP, 1989.

Gilman, Charlotte Perkins. *The Abridged Diaries of Charlotte Perkins Gilman.* Ed. Denise D. Knight. Charlottesville: U of Virginia P, 1998.

———. *Herland.* 1915. New York: Signet, 1992.

———. "Is America Too Hospitable?" 1913. *Charlotte Perkins Gilman: A Nonfiction Reader.* Ed. Larry Ceplair. New York: Columbia UP, 1991. 288–295.

———. "Joan's Defender." 1916. *Herland, The Yellow Wall-Paper, and Selected Writings.* By Charlotte Perkins Gilman. Ed. Denise D. Knight. New York: Penguin, 1999. 327–335.

———. *A Journey from Within: The Love Letters of Charlotte Perkins Gilman, 1897–1900.* Ed. Mary A. Hill. Lewisburg, PA: Bucknell UP, 1995.

———. *The Living of Charlotte Perkins Gilman: An Autobiography.* 1935. Madison: U of Wisconsin P, 1990.

———. *The Man-Made World; or, Our Androcentric Culture.* New York: Co-Operative Press, 1911.

———. "Race Pride." *The Forerunner.* 70 (April 1913): 89–90.

———. "A Suggestion on the Negro Problem." *American Journal of Sociology.* 14.1 (July 1908): 78–85.

———. "Why Women Do Not Reform Their Dress." 1886. *Charlotte Perkins Gilman: A Nonfiction Reader.* Ed. Larry Ceplair. New York: Columbia, 1991. 23—4.

———. *Women and Economics: A Study of the Economic Relation Between Men and Women as a Factor in Social Evolution.* 1898. Mineola, NY: Dover, 1998.

Gilman, Sander. "Black Bodies, White Bodies: Toward an Iconography of Female Sexuality in Late Nineteenth-Century Art, Medicine, and Literature." *"Race," Writing and Difference.* Ed. Henry Louis Gates, Jr. Chicago: U of Chicago P, 1986. 223–261.

———. *Difference and Pathology: Stereotypes of Sexuality, Race and Madness.* Ithaca: Cornell UP, 1985.

———. *The Jew's Body.* New York: Routledge, 1991.

———. "Sexology, Psychoanalysis, and Degeneration: From a Theory of Race to a Race to Theory." *Degeneration: The Dark Side of Progress.* Ed. J. Edward Chamberlain and Sander Gilman. New York: Columbia UP, 1985. 73–96.

Ginsberg, Elaine K. "Introduction: The Politics of Passing." *Passing and the Fictions of Identity*. Ed. Elaine K. Ginsberg. Durham: Duke UP, 1–18.

Go Fish. Dir. Rose Troche. Perf. V. S. Brodie, Guinevere Turner, T. Wendy McMillan, Anastasia Sharp. Samuel Goldwyn, 1994.

Golden, Catherine J., and Joanne Schneider Zangrando, eds. *The Mixed Legacy of Charlotte Perkins Gilman*. Newark: U of Delaware P, 2000.

Gordon, Ann D., and Mari Jo Buhle. "Sex and Class in Colonial and Nineteenth-Century America." *Liberating Women's History: Theoretical and Critical Essays*. Ed. Berenice A Carroll. Urbana: University of Illinois P, 1976.

Gossett, Thomas. Uncle Tom's Cabin *and American Culture*. Dallas: Southern Methodist UP, 1985.

Gould, Stephen Jay. *The Mismeasure of Man*. New York: W. W. Norton, 1981.

Graver, Lawrence. *Carson McCullers*. Minneapolis: U of Minnesota P, 1969.

Green, Richard. *The "Sissy Boy Syndrome" and the Development of Homosexuality*. New Haven: Yale UP, 1987.

Gubar, Susan. *Racechanges: White Skin, Black Face in American Culture*. New York: Oxford UP, 1997.

———. "*She* and *Herland*: Feminism as Fantasy." *Charlotte Perkins Gilman: The Woman and Her Work*. Ed. Sheryl L. Meyering. Ann Arbor: UMI, 1989. 191–202.

Habegger, Alfred. "Funny Tomboys." *Gender, Fantasy, and Realism in American Literature*. New York: Columbia UP, 1982. 172–183.

———. "A Well Hidden Hand." *Novel*. 14.3 (Spring 1981): 197–212.

Haggard, H. Rider. *She*. 1887. New York: Oxford UP, 1998.

"The Hair-Raiser." *Li'l Tomboy*. Vol. 14, no. 94. Derby, CT: Charlton Publication, 1956.

Halberstam, Judith. *Female Masculinity*. Durham, NC: Duke UP, 1998.

———. "Oh Bondage Up Yours!: Female Masculinity and the Tomboy." *Sissies and Tomboys: Gender Nonconformity and Homosexual Childhood*. Ed. Matthew Rottnek. New York: New York UP, 1999. 153–179.

Hall, Mordaunt. "Beauty and Banalities." *The New York Times*. 29 August 1927. *The New York Times Film Reviews, 1913–1968*. vol. 1: 1913–1931. New York: New York Times, 1970. 383–384.

Hamer, Diane. "'I Am a Woman': Ann Bannon and the Writing of Lesbian Identity in the 1950s." *Lesbian and Gay Writing: An Anthology of Critical Essays*. Ed. Mark Lilly. Philadelphia: Temple UP, 1990. 47–75.

Handy, Bruce. "Yep, I'm Gay." *Time*. 14 April 1997.

Hannon, Charles. "'The Ballad of the Sad Café' and Other Stories of Women's Wartime Labor." *Bodies of Writing, Bodies in Performance*. Ed. Thomas Foster, Carol Siegel, and Ellen E. Berry. New York: New York UP, 1996. 97–119.

Harris, Thomas J. *Bogdanovich's Picture Shows*. Metuchen, NJ: Scarecrow Press, 1990.

Hasaan, Ihab. *Radical Innocence: The Contemporary American Novel*. Princeton, NJ: Princeton UP, 1961.

Haskell, Molly. *From Reverence to Rape: The Treatment of Women in the Movies*. 2nd ed. Chicago: U of Chicago P, 1987.

Hatch, Richard. Review of *Paper Moon*. *The Nation*. 11 June 1973: 764–765.

Heilbrun, Carolyn. "Nancy Drew: A Moment in Feminist History." *Rediscovering Nancy Drew*. Ed. Carolyn Stewart Dyer and Nancy Tillman Romalov. Iowa: U of Iowa P, 1995. 11–21.

Hemingway, Ernest. *The Garden of Eden*. (written 1946—61.) New York: Scribner, 1986.

Hepburn, Katharine. *Me: Stories of My Life*. New York: Random House, 1992.

Higashi, Sumiko. *Virgins, Vamps, and Flappers: The American Silent Movie Heroine*. Montreal, Canada: Eden Press, 1978.

Highsmith, Patricia. *The Price of Salt*. 1952. New York: Norton, 1984.

Higonnet, Anne. *Pictures of Innocence: The History and Crisis of Ideal Childhood.* New York: Thames and Hudson, 1998.

Hill, Mary A. *Charlotte Perkins Gilman: The Making of a Radical Feminist, 1860–1896.* Philadelphia: Temple UP, 1980.

———. *A Journey from Within: The Love Letters of Charlotte Perkins Gilman, 1897–1900.* Lewisburg, PA: Bucknell UP, 1995.

Hilton, Thos. B. "Reminiscences." *The Women's Era.* August 1894: 4–5.

Hines, Melissa, Susan Golombok, John Rust, Katie J. Johnston, Jean Golding, and the Avon Longitudinal Study of Parents and Children Study Team. "Testosterone During Pregnancy and Gender Role Behavior of Preschool Children: A Longitudinal, Population Study." *Child Development.* 73.6 (November/December 2002): 1678–1687.

Hogan, Steve, and Lee Hudson. "Tomboy." *Completely Queer: The Gay and Lesbian Encyclopedia.* New York: Henry Holt Company, 1998. 542–543.

Holberg, Ruth Langland. *Tomboy Row.* Garden City, NY: Doubleday, 1952.

Holmes, Mary J. *'Lena Rivers.* New York: G. W. Dillingham Co., 1856.

Home in Indiana. Dir. Henry Hathaway. Perf. Walter Brennan, Jeanne Crain, June Haver, Charlotte Greenwood. 20th Century Fox, 1944.

hooks, bell. *Ain't I a Woman: Black Women and Feminism.* Boston: South End, 1981.

Hope, Laura Lee. The Outdoor Girls series. New York: Grosset & Dunlap, 1913–1933.

Horton, James Oliver. *Free People of Color: Inside the African American Community.* Washington , D.C.: Smithsonian Institution Press, 1993.

"hoyden." *The Oxford English Dictionary.* 2nd ed. 1989.

Hudock, Amy. "Challenging the Definition of Heroism in E. D. E. N. Southworth's *The Hidden Hand.*" *American Transcendental Quarterly.* 9.1 (March 1995): 5–20.

Hula. Dir. Victor Fleming. Perf. Clara Bow, Clive Brook, Arlette Marchal. Paramount, 1927.

Hunt, Peter, Ed. *Children's Literature An Illustrated History.* New York: Oxford UP, 1995.

Hyde, Janet S., B. G. Rosenberg and Jo Ann Behrman. "Tomboyism." *Psychology of Women Quarterly.* 2 (1977): 73–75.

The Incredibly True Adventure of Two Girls in Love. Dir. Maria Maggenti. Perf. Laurel Holloman, Nicole Parker, Maggie Moore, Kate Stafford, Sabrina Artel. Fine Line, 1995.

Ingraham, Prentiss. *Crimson Kate, the Girl Tailor.* New York: Beadle and Adams, 1881.

Inness, Sherrie A. "Introduction." *Action Chicks: New Images of Tough Women in Popular Culture.* Ed. by Sherrie Inness. New York: Palgrave Macmillan, 2004. 1–17.

———. "'It Is Pluck, But—Is It Sense?': Athletic Student Culture in Progressive-era Girls' College Fiction." *The Girl's Own: Cultural Histories of the Anglo-American Girl, 1830—1915.* Ed. Claudia Nelson and Lynne Vallone. Athens: U of Georgia P, 1994. 216–242.

———. *Tough Girls: Women Warriors and Wonder Women in Popular Culture.* Philadelphia: U of Pennsylvania P, 1999.

International Tomboy: Around the World in 80 Dames. San Francisco: Dazzle Publishers, 1958.

International Velvet. Dir. Bryan Forbes. Perf. Tatum O'Neal, Christopher Plummer, Anthony Hopkins and Nanette Newman. Warner Brothers, 1978.

"It." Dir. Clarence Badger and (uncredited) Josef von Sternberg. Perf. Clara Bow, Antonio Moreno, William Austen. Famous Players Lasky/Paramount, 1927.

Jacobs, Harriet. *Incidents in the Life of a Slave Girl.* 1861. New York: Penguin, 2000.

Jacobson, Matthew. *Whiteness of a Different Color: European Immigrants and the Alchemy of Race.* Cambridge: Harvard UP, 1998.

James, Henry. *Watch and Ward.* 1878. *Henry James: Novels, 1871–1880.* New York: Library of America, 1983. 1–162.

James, Judith Giblin. *Wunderkind: The Reputation of Carson McCullers, 1940–1990.* Columbia, SC: Camden House, 1995.

Janeway, Elizabeth. "Meg, Jo, Beth, Amy and Louisa." *Critical Essays on Louisa May Alcott*. Ed. Madeleine B. Stern. Boston: G. K. Hall, 1984. 97–98.

The Jazz Singer. Dir. Alan Crosland. Perf. Al Jolson, May McAvoy, Warner Oland, and Eugenie Besserer. MGM, 1937.

Jewett, Sarah Orne. *A Country Doctor*. 1884. *Novels and Stories*. New York: Library of America, 1994. 143–370.

———. "*Deephaven*." 1877. *Novels and Stories*. New York: Library of America, 1994. 1–142.

———. *Letters of Sarah Orne Jewett*. Ed. Annie Fields. Boston: Houghton Mifflin Company, 1911.

———. "Looking Back on Girlhood." *Youth's Companion*. 65. 7 January 1892.

———. *The Story of the Normans, Told Chiefly in Relation to Their Conquest of England*. G. P. Putnam's Sons, 1887.

———. *The Tory Lover*. Boston: Houghton, Mifflin and Co., 1901.

Joan of Arc. Dir. Victor Fleming. Perf. Ingrid Bergman, Francis L. Sullivan, J. Carroll Naish. Image Entertainment, 1948.

Johannsen, Albert. *The House of Beadle and Adams and Its Dime and Nickel Novels: The Story of a Vanished Literature*. Tulsa: University of Oklahoma P, 1950.

Johnny Guitar. Dir. Nicholas Ray. Perf. Joan Crawford, Sterling Hayden, Scott Brady, Mercedes McCambridge, Ward Bond, Ben Cooper. Republic, 1954.

Johnson, Gary. Review of *Forbidden Fruit: The Golden Age of Exploitation Film*. http://www.imagesjournal.com/issue08/reviews/forbiddenfruit/book.html (accessed 20 June 2004).

Johnson, Susan E. *When Women Played Hardball*. Seattle, WA: Seal, 1994.

Jones, Anne Goodwyn. "Displacing Dixie: The Southern Subtext in *My Antonia*." *New Essays on My Antonia*. Ed. Sharon O'Brien. Cambridge: Cambridge UP, 1999. 85–109.

Jones, Jacqueline. *Labor of Love, Labor of Sorrow: Black Women, Work, and the Family from Slavery to the Present*. New York: Basic Books, 1985.

Jurca, Catherine. *White Diaspora: The Suburb and the Twentieth Century American Novel*. Princeton, NJ: Princeton UP, 2001.

Kabir, Shameem. *Daughters of Desire: Lesbians Representations in Film*. London: Cassell, 1998.

Kansas Tomboy. Cracker Jack Miniature Books. Gold Premiums, 1968.

Kasper, Shirl. *Annie Oakley*. Norman: U of Oklahoma P, 1992.

Kasson, John F. *Houdini, Tarzan and the Perfect Man: The White Male Body and the Challenge of Modernity in America*. New York: Farrar, Straus and Giroux, 2001.

Katz, Jonathan Ned. *Gay American History: Lesbians and Gay Men in the U.S.A.* 1976. New York: Meridian, 1992.

———. *Gay/Lesbian Almanac*. New York: Harper and Row, 1983.

Kaye, Harvey E. "'Ten Definitely Did Not Want Their Homosexuality Cured.'" *Gay American History: Lesbians and Gay Men in the U.S.A.* 1976. New York: Meridian, 1992. 196–197.

Keene, Carolyn. *The Hidden Staircase*. 1930. Bedford, MA: Applewood, 1991.

———. *The Hidden Staircase*. 1959. New York: Grosset and Dunlap, 1987.

———. *The Secret at Shadow Ranch*. 1931. Bedford, MA: Applewood, 1994.

———. *The Secret of the Old Clock*. 1930. Bedford, MA: Applewood, 1991.

———. *The Secret of the Old Clock*. 1959. New York: Grosset and Dunlap, 1987.

Kempley, Rita. "*A League of Their Own*: The Women Make a Hit." *The Washington Post*. 1 July 1992. late ed.: C1+.

Kenschaft, Lori J. "Homoerotics and Human Connections: Reading Carson McCullers 'As a Lesbian.'" *Critical Essays on Carson McCullers*. Ed. Beverly Lyon Clark and Melvin J. Friedman. New York: G. K. Hall & Co., 1996. 220–233.

Kerouac, Jack. *On the Road.* 1957. New York: Penguin, 1972.

Kerr, M. E. *Dinky Hocker Shoots Smack!* 1972. New York: HarperCollins, 1989.

Kessler, Carol Farley. *Charlotte Perkins Gilman: Her Progress Toward Utopia With Selected Writings.* Syracuse, NY: Syracuse UP, 1995.

Keyser, Elizabeth Lennox. *Whispers in the Dark: The Fiction of Louisa May Alcott.* Knoxville: University of Tennessee, 1993.

Kincaid, Jamaica. *Annie John.* New York: Farrar, Straus and Giroux, 1983.

———. "Girl." *The New Yorker.* 26 June 1978. 29.

Kingston, Maxine Hong. *The Woman Warrior: Memoirs of a Girlhood Among Ghosts.* New York: Random House, 1975.

Kinsey, Alfred and the Staff of Institute for Sex Research, Indiana University. *Sexual Behavior in the Human Female.* Philadelphia: Saunders, 1953.

———. *Sexual Behavior in the Human Male.* Philadelphia: Saunders, 1948.

Klein, Norma. *Tomboy.* New York: Simon and Schuster, 1978.

Klimasmith, Betsy. "Slave, Master, Mistress, Slave: Genre and Interracial Desire in Louisa May Alcott's Fiction." *American Transcendental Quarterly.* 11.2 (June 1997): 115–135.

Knight, Denise D. *The Abridged Diaries of Charlotte Perkins Gilman.* Charlottesville: U of Virginia P, 1998.

Krafft-Ebing, Richard von. *Psychopathia Sexualis.* 1886. Trans. Franklin S. Klaf. New York: Stein and Day, 1978.

Kunhardt, Phillip B., Jr., Phillip B. Kunhardt III, & Peter W. Kunhardt. *P. T. Barnum: America's Oldest Showman.* New York: Knopf, 1995.

Lambert, Deborah. "The Defeat of a Hero: Autonomy and Sexuality in *My Antonia.*" *American Literature.* 53 (1982): 676–690.

Landau, Jon. "'Moon': Bogdanovich's Clearest Success." *Rolling Stone.* 7 July 1973: 66–67.

Lane, Ann J. "Introduction." *The Charlotte Perkins Gilman Reader: The Yellow Wallpaper, and Other Fiction.* Ed. Ann J. Lane. New York: Pantheon, 1980.

———. *To Herland and Beyond: The Life and Work of Charlotte Perkins Gilman.* New York: Pantheon, 1990.

A League of Their Own. Dir. Penny Marshall. Perf. Geena Davis, Tom Hanks, Lori Petty. Sony Pictures, 1992.

Lears, T. J. Jackson. *No Place of Grace: Antimodernism and the Transformation of American Culture, 1880–1920.* Chicago: U of Chicago P, 1981.

Lee, Harper. *To Kill a Mockingbird.* New York: Popular Library, 1960.

Lenski, Lois. *Texas Tomboy.* Philadelphia: J. B. Lippincott Co., 1950.

Lewis, Dio. *Our Girls.* New York: Harper and Brothers, 1871.

Lewis, Edith. *Willa Cather, Living.* New York: Alfred A. Knopf, 1953.

Lewis, Linda. *The Tomboy Terror in Bunk 109.* New York: Pocket Books, 1991.

Lhamon, W. T., Jr. *Deliberate Speed: The Origins of Cultural Style in the American 1950s.* Washington, D.C.: Smithsonian Institution Press, 1990.

———. *Raising Cain: Blackface Performance from Jim Crow to Hip Hop.* Cambridge: Harvard UP, 1998.

Li'l Tomboy. Published no. 92 (October 1956)–no. 108 (May 1959). Derby, CT: Charlton Comics Group, 1956–1959.

Lindemann, Marilee. *Willa Cather: Queering America.* New York: Columbia UP, 1999.

Lipsitz, George. "The Possessive Investment in Whiteness: Racialized Social Democracy and the 'White' Problem in American Studies." *American Quarterly.* 47.3 (September 1995): 369–387.

Little Annie Rooney. Dir. William Beaudine. Perf. Mary Pickford, William Haines, Walter James. Terra/Mary Pickford Company, 1925.

Little Darlings. Dir. Ronald F. Maxwell. Perf. Tatum O'Neal, Kristy McNichol, Armand Assante, Matt Dillon, Maggie Blye. Paramount, 1980.

Little Miss Marker. Dir. Alexander Hall. Perf. Shirley Temple, Adolphe Menjou, Dorothy Dell and Charles Bickford. Universal, 1934.

Little Women. Dir. Gillian Armstrong. Perf. Winona Ryder, Gabriel Bryne, Susan Sarandon. Sony Pictures, 1994.

Little Women. Dir. George Cukor. Perf. Katharine Hepburn, Joan Bennett, Paul Lukas. R. K. O., 1933.

Little Women. Dir. Mervyn LeRoy. Perf. June Allyson, Peter Lawford, Margaret O'Brien. Warner Brothers, 1949.

The Littlest Rebel. Dir. David Butler. Perf. Shirley Temple, John Boles, Jack Holt, and Karen Morley. Twentieth Century Fox, 1935.Longman, Jere. *The Girls of Summer: The U.S. Women's Soccer Team and How It Changed the World.* New York: Harper Collins, 2001.

Loos, Anita. *Gentlemen Prefer Blondes.* 1925. New York: Penguin, 1998.

López, Ian F. Haney. *White by Law: The Legal Construction of Race.* New York: New York UP, 1996.

Lott, Eric. *Love and Theft: Blackface and the American Working Class.* New York: Oxford UP, 1993.

Lowe, Lisa. *Immigrant Acts: On Asian American Cultural Politics.* Durham, NC: Duke UP, 1996.

Lubbers, Klaus. "The Necessary Order: A Study of Theme and Structure in Carson McCullers's Fiction." *Carson McCullers.* Ed. Harold Bloom. New York: Chelsea House, 1986. 33–52.

MacLeod, Anne Scott. *American Childhood: Essays on Children's Literature of the Nineteenth and Twentieth Centuries.* Athens,: U of Georgia P, 1994.

Mailer, Norman. *The White Negro.* San Francisco: City Lights, 1957.

The Man in the Moon. Dir. Robert Mulligan. Perf. Sam Waterson, Tess Harper, Gail Strickland, Reese Witherspoon. MGM, 1991.

Mannin, Ethel. *Confessions and Impressions.* London: Jarrolds, 1930.

Manring, M. M. *Slave in a Box: The Strange Career of Aunt Jemima.* Charlottesville: U of Virginia P, 1998.

Marks, Patricia. *Bicycles, Bangs, and Bloomers: The New Woman in the Popular Press.* Lexington, KY: U of Kentucky P, 1990.

Marks, Percy. *The Plastic Age.* New York: Grosset and Dunlap, 1924.

The Married Flapper. Dir. Stuart Paton. Perf. Marie Prevost, Kenneth Harlon, Frank Kingsley. Universal Film, 1922.

Mason, Bobbie Ann. *The Girl Sleuth: On the Trail of Nancy Drew, Judy Bolton, and Cherry Ames.* 1975. Athens: U of Georgia P, 1995.

The Matrix. Dirs. Andy Wachowski and Larry Wachowski. Perf. Keanu Reeves, Laurence Fishburne, Carrie-Ann Moss. Warner Brothers, 1999.

Matthews, Jean. *The Rise of the New Woman: The Women's Movement in America, 1875–1930.* Chicago: Ivan R. Dee, 2003.

Matthiessen, F. O. *Sarah Orne Jewett.* Gloucester, MA: Peter Smith, 1965.

McClintock, Anne. *Imperial Leather: Race, Gender and Sexuality in the Colonial Conquest.* New York: Routledge, 1995.

McCullers, Carson. *The Ballad of the Sad Café and Other Stories.* 1951. New York: Bantam, 1991.

———. *The Heart is a Lonely Hunter.* 1940. New York: Bantam, 1967.

———. (signed by "A War Wife"). "Love's Not Time's Fool." *Mademoiselle.* 16 (April 1943): 95, 166–168.

———. *The Member of the Wedding.* 1946. New York: Bantam, 1973.

McDonald, Joyce. *The Stuff of Our Forebears: Willa Cather's Southern Heritage.* Tuscaloosa: U of Alabama P, 1998.

McDowell, Margaret B. *Carson McCullers.* Boston: Twayne, 1980.

McEwan, Christian, ed. *Jo's Girls: Tomboy Tales of High Adventure, True Grit and Real Adventure*. Boston: Beacon, 1997.

McNeil, Legs, and Gillian McCain, eds. *Please Kill Me: The Uncensored History of Punk*. New York: Grove, 1996.

McPherson, James M. *Battle Cry of Freedom: The Civil War Era*. New York: Ballantine, 1988.

McRobbie, Angela. *In the Culture Society: Art, Fashion and Popular Music*. London: Routledge, 1999.

Meet Me in St. Louis. Dir. Vincente Minnelli. Perf. Judy Garland, Margaret O'Brien, Lucille Bremer, Tom Drake, Mary Astor. MGM, 1944.

The Member of the Wedding. Dir. Fielder Cook. Perf. Alfre Woodard, Anna Paquin, Corey Dunn. Hallmark, 1997.

The Member of the Wedding. Dir. Fred Zinnemann. Perf. Ethel Waters, Julie Harris, Brandon De Wilde. Columbia, 1952.

The Messenger: The Story of Joan of Arc. Dir. Luc Besson. Perf. Milla Jovovich, John Malkovich, Faye Dunaway. Columbia, 1999.

Meyering, Sheryl L. *Understanding* O Pioneers! *and* My Antonia: *A Student Casebook to Issues, Sources and Historical Documents*. Westport, CT: Greenwood Press, 2002.

Meyerowitz, Joanne. *How Sex Changed: A History of Transsexuality in the United States*. Cambridge: Harvard UP, 2002.

Michaels, Walter Benn. *Our America: Nativism, Modernism, and Pluralism*. Durham, NC: Duke UP, 1995.

The Mighty Ducks. Dir. Stephen Herek. Perf. Emilio Estevez, Joss Ackland, Lane Smith. Walt Disney, 1991.

Miller, Neil. *Out of the Past: Gay and Lesbian History from 1860 to the Present*. New York: Vintage, 1995.

Milne, Tom. Review of *Paper Moon*. *Monthly Film Bulletin*. January 1974: 12–13.

Minter, Shannon. "Diagnosis and Treatment of Gender Identity Disorder in Children." *Sissies and Tomboys: Gender Nonconformity and Homosexual Childhood*. Ed. Matthew Rottnek. New York: New York UP, 1999. 9–33.

Miss Tomboy and Freckles. Dir. Wilfrid North. Perf. William Bechtel. [Production Studio Unknown], 1914.

Mitchell, Sally. "To Be a Boy." *The New Girl: Girls' Culture in England, 1880–1915*. Ed. Sally Mitchell. New York: Columbia UP, 1995. 103–138.

"The Modern World." *The Greenwood Encyclopedia of Daily Life: A Tour Through History from Ancient Times to the Present*. 2004 ed.

Morrison, Toni. *The Bluest Eye*. 1970. New York: McGraw-Hill, 1984.

———. *Playing in the Dark: Whiteness and the Literary Imagination*. New York: Random House, 1992.

Morton, Patricia. *Disfigured Images: The Historical Assault on Afro-American Women*. Westport, CT: Praeger, 1991.

Mullenix, Elizabeth Reitz. *Wearing the Breeches: Gender on the Antebellum Stage*. New York: St. Martin's Press, 2000.

Mumford, Mary E. *A Regular Tomboy*. Penn Publishing Company, 1913.

Myers, Mitzi, and U.C. Knoepflmacher. "From the Editors: 'Cross-Writing' and the Reconceptualization of Children's Literary Studies." *Children's Literature*. 25. (1997): vii–xvii.

National Velvet. Dir. Clarence Brown. Perf. Mickey Rooney, Elizabeth Taylor, Donald Crisp, and Angela Lansbury. MGM, 1944.

Nealon, Christopher. "Invert History: The Ambivalence of Lesbian Pulp Fiction." *New Literary History*. 31.4 (Autumn 2000): 745–764.

The New Freewoman. London: New International Publishing Company. Published semimonthly from January 15, 1913 to December 15, 1913.

Norvo, Red. "Tomboy." 1934. *Red Norvo and His All Stars*. LP. Columbia, 1974.

Nott, J. C., and George R. Gliddon. *Types of Mankind; or, Ethnographical Researches [sic], Based Upon the Ancient Monuments, Paintings, Sculptures, and Crania of Races, and Upon Their Natural, Geographical, Philological, and Biblical History.* Philadelphia: J. B. Lippincott and Co., 1854.

O'Brien, Sharon. "Tomboyism and Adolescent Conflict: Three Nineteenth-Century Case Studies." *Woman's Being, Woman's Place: Female Identity and Vocation in American History.* Ed. Mary Kelley. Boston: G. K. Hall and Co., 1979, 351–372.

———. *Willa Cather: The Emerging Voice.* Oxford: Oxford UP, 1987.

Okker, Patricia, and Jeffrey R. Williams. "'Reassuring Sounds': Minstrelsy and *The Hidden Hand*." *American Transcendental Quarterly.* 12.2 (June 1998): 133–144.

Omi, Michael, and Howard Winant. *Racial Formation in the United States: From the 1960s to the 1980s.* 1986. 2nd ed. New York: Routledge, 1994.

On Moonlight Bay. Dir. Roy Del Ruth. Perf. Doris Day, Gordon MacRae, Jack Smith. Warner Brothers, 1951.

O'Neal, Tatum. *A Paper Life.* New York: Harper Entertainment, 2004.

O'Rourke, Meghan. "Nancy Drew's Father: The Fiction Factory of Edward Stratemeyer." *The New Yorker.* 8 Nov. 2004. <www.newyorker.com> (accessed 22 Aug 2007).

The Oxford Companion to Women's Writing. Eds. Cathy N. Davidson and Linda Wagner-Martin. New York: Oxford, 1995.

Packer, Vin. *Spring Fire.* 1952. New York: Fawcett, 2004.

The Painted Flapper. Dir. John Gorman. Perf. James Kirkwood, Pauline Garon, Crauford Kent. Chadwick Pictures Corporation, 1924.

Painter, Nell Irvin. "Sojourner Truth." *The Oxford Companion to Women's Writing in The United States.* Ed. Cathy N. Davidson and Linda Wagner-Martin. New York: Oxford UP, 1995. 888–889.

Paper Moon. Dir. Peter Bogdanovich. Perf. Ryan O'Neal, Tatum O'Neal, Madeline Kahn, John Hillerman, P. J. Johnson, Randy Quaid. Paramount, 1973.

Papashvily, Helen Waite. *All the Happy Endings: A Study of the Domestic Novel in America, the Women Who Wrote It, the Women Who Read It, in the Nineteenth Century.* New York: Harper, 1956.

Parry, Sally E. "'You are needed, desperately needed!': Cherry Ames in World War II." *Nancy Drew and Company: Culture, Gender and Girls' Series.* Ed. Sherrie A. Inness. Bowling Green, OH: Bowling Green State UP, 1997. 129–144.

"passing." *The Oxford English Dictionary.* 2nd. ed. 1989.

Pat and Mike. Dir. George Cukor. Perf. Spencer Tracy, Katharine Hepburn, Aldo Ray, and Carl Switzer. MGM, 1952.

Paterson, Katherine. *The Great Gilly Hopkins.* New York: HarperTrophy, 1978.

Patton, Cindy. *Sex and Germs: The Politics of AIDS.* Boston: South End, 1985.

Payne, Robert M. "Beyond the Pale: Nudism, Race, and Resistance in *The Unashamed*." *Film Quarterly.* 54.2 (Winter 2000): 27–40.

Peck, Demaree. "'Possession Granted By a Different Lease': Alexandra Bergson's Imaginative Conquest of Cather's Nebraska." *Modern Fiction Studies.* 36.1 (Spring 1990): 5–22.

Pellegrini, Ann. "Women on Top, Boys on the Wide, But Some of Us Are Brave: Blackness, Lesbianism and the Visible." *College Literature.* 24.1 (February 1997): 83–97.

The Pennsylvania Freeman. Philadelphia, PA: Eastern District Executive Committee of the Anti-Slavery Society of Pennsylvania. Published weekly from March 15, 1838 to June 29, 1854.

The Perfect Flapper. Dir. John Francis Dillon. Perf. Colleen Moore, Syd Chaplin, Phyllis Haver. Associated First National Pictures, 1924.

Peterson, Carla. *"Doers of the Word": African-American Women Speakers and Writers in the North, 1830–1880.* New York: Oxford UP, 1995.

Peyser, Thomas. *Utopia and Cosmopolis: Globalization in the Era of American Literary Realism*. Durham, NC: Duke UP, 1998.

Phelps, Elizabeth Stuart. *Doctor Zay: A Novel*. 1882. New York: Feminist Press, 1987.

———. *Gypsy Breynton*. 1866. New York: Dodd, Mead and Company, 1894.

———. *Gypsy's Sowing and Reaping*. 1866. New York: Dodd, Mead and Company, 1876.

Pretty Tomboy Clothing. Ed. Keisha McDaniel. http://www.prettytomboyclothing.com/ (accessed 18 June 2005).

Price-Herndl, Diane. *The Invalid Woman: Figuring Feminine Illness in American Fiction and Culture, 1840–1940*. Chapel Hill: U of North Carolina P, 1993.

Prince, Nancy. *A Black Woman's Odyssey through Russia and Jamaica: A Narrative of Nancy Prince*. Originally published as *A Narrative of the Life and Travels of Mrs. Nancy Prince*. 1850. Princeton: Markus Wiener Publishers, 1990.

———. *The West Indies, Being a Description of the Islands, Progress of Christianity, Education and Liberty Among the Colored Population Generally*. Boston: Dow and Jackson, 1841.

Pryse, Marjorie. "Sex, Class and 'Category Crisis': Reading Jewett's Transitivity." *American Literature*. 70.3 (September 1998): 517–549.

"queer." *The Oxford English Dictionary*. 2nd ed. 1989.

Rable, George. "'Missing in Action': Women of the Confederacy." *Divided Houses: Gender and the Civil War*. Eds. Catherine Clinton and Nina Silber. New York: Oxford UP, 1992.

Rebecca of Sunnybrook Farm. Dir. Marhsall Nielan. Perf. Milton Berle, Mary Pickford, Eugene O'Brien. Mary Pickford Company, 1917.

Renza, Louis A. *"A White Heron" and the Question of Minor Literature*. Madison: U of Wisconsin P, 1984.

Reynolds, David S. *Beneath the American Renaissance: The Subversive Imagination in Nineteenth-Century America*. New York: Oxford UP, 1992.

Reynolds, Guy. *Willa Cather in Context: Progress, Race, Empire*. New York: St. Martin's Press, 1996.

Rich, Adrienne. "Compulsory Heterosexuality and Lesbian Existence (1980)." 1978. *Blood, Bread and Poetry: Selected Prose, 1979–1985*. New York: Norton, 1986. 23–75.

Rich, Mary Lou. *The Tomboy*. New York: Jove Books, 1996.

Richardson, Angelique, and Chris Willis, eds. *The New Woman in Fiction and Fact: Fin-de-Siecle Feminisms*. New York: Palgrave, 2001.

The River Wild. Dir. Curtis Hanson. Perf. Meryl Streep, Kevin Bacon, John C. O'Reilly. Universal, 1994.

Robinson, Phyllis C. *Willa, the Life of Willa Cather*. Garden City, NY: Doubleday, 1983.

Roediger, David. *The Wages of Whiteness: Race and the Making of the American Working Class*. New York: Verso, 1991.

Rogin, Michael. *Blackface, White Noise: Jewish Immigrants and the Hollywood Melting Pot*. Berkeley: U of California P, 1995.

Roman, Margaret. *Sarah Orne Jewett: Reconstructing Gender*. Tuscaloosa: U of Alabama P, 1992.

Romines, Ann. *"The Long Winter*: An Introduction to Western Womanhood." *Great Plains Quarterly*. 10 (Winter 1990): 36–47.

Roosevelt, Franklin D. Executive Order 8802. *The Federal Register*. vol 6. 27 July 1941.

Root, Harvey W. *The Unknown Barnum*. New York: Harper & Brothers, 1927.

Rosen, Marjorie. *Popcorn Venus: Women, Movies and the American Dream*. New York: Avon, 1973.

Rosenberg, Rosalind. *Divided Lives: American Women in the Twentieth Century*. New York: Hill and Wang, 1992.

Rosowski, Susan. *Birthing a Nation: Gender, Creativity and the West in American Literature*. Lincoln: U of Nebraska P, 1999.

Ross, Edward Alsworth. *Changing America: Studies in Contemporary Society*. New York: Century, 1912.

Ross, Sara. "Banking the Flames of Youth: The Hollywood Flapper, 1920–1930." Diss. U of Wisconsin, Madison, 2000.

Rottnek, Matthew. Introduction. *Sissies and Tomboys: Gender Nonconformity and Homosexual Childhood*. Ed. Matthew Rottnek. New York: New York UP, 1999. 1–5.

Rule, Jane. *Desert of the Heart*. 1964. Tallahasee, FL: Naiad, 1984.

Ryan, Pam Muñoz. *Riding Freedom*. New York: Scholastic, 1998.

Salmonberries. Dir. Percy Adlon. Perf. k. d. lang, Rosel Zech, Church Connors. Wolfe, 1992.

Samuels, Shirley, ed. *The Culture of Sentiment: Race, Gender, and Sentimentality in Nineteenth-Century America*. New York: Oxford UP, 1992.

Sanchez-Eppler, Karen. *Touching Liberty: Abolition, Feminism, and the Politics of the Body*. Berkeley: U of California P, 1993.

Sargent, Shirley. *Yosemite Tomboy*. Mariposa, CA: Ponderosa Press, 1967.

Sarris, Andrew. "A Little Child Shall Bleed Them." (Films in Focus Review of Peter Bogdanovich's *Paper Moon*). *The Village Voice*. 21 June 1973:83–84.

Sarris, Andrew. *"You Ain't Heard Nothin' Yet": The American Talking Film History and Memory, 1927—1949*. NY: Oxford, 1998.

Satirsky, Michael. "Afterward." *Doctor Zay: A Novel*. 1882. By Elizabeth Stuart Phelps. New York: Feminist Press, 1987. 259–321.

Savage, John. *England's Dreaming: Sex Pistols and Punk Rock*. London: Faber, 1991.

Savigneau, Josyane. *Carson McCullers: A Life*. Trans. Joan Howard. New York: Houghton Mifflin, 2001.

Sawyer, Ruth. *Roller Skates*. 1936. New York: Puffin, 1986.

Saxton, Martha. *Louisa May: A Modern Biography of Louisa May Alcott*. Boston: Houghton Mifflin, 1977.

Schaefer, Eric. *Bold! Shocking! Daring! True!: A History of Exploitation Films, 1919–1959*. Durham, NC: Duke UP, 1999.

Schauer, Frederick F. *The Law of Obscenity*. Washington, D.C.: Bureau of National Affairs, 1976.

Schick, Frank L. *The Paperbound Book in America: The History of Paperbacks and Their European Background*. New York: R. R. Bowker Co., 1958.

Schrag, Mitzi. "'Whiteness' as Loss in Sarah Orne Jewett's 'The Foreigner.'" *Jewett and Her Contemporaries: Reshaping the Canon*. Gainesville, FL: U of Florida P, 1999. 185–206.

Schwind, Jean. "The Benda Illustrations to *My Antonia*: Cather's 'Silent' Supplement to Jim Burden's Narrative." *PMLA*. 100.1 (January 1985): 51–67.

Secrist, Jan. *Tomboy Tales: The Adventures of Midlife Mavericks*. Irving, TX: Fusion, 1999.

Sedgwick, Eve Kosofsky. *Between Men: English Literature and Male Homosocial Desire*. New York: Columbia UP, 1985.

———. "How to Bring Your Kids Up Gay." *Social Text*. 29. (1990): 18–27.

Segel, Elizabeth. "The *Gypsy Breynton* Series: Setting the Pattern for American Tomboy Heroines." *Children's Literature Association Quarterly*. 14.2 (Summer 1989): 67–71.

———. "Tomboy Taming and Gender Role Socialization: The Evidence of Children's Books." *Gender Roles Through the Life Span: A Multidisciplinary Perspective*. Ed. Michael R. Stevenson. Muncie, IN: Ball State UP, 1994. 47–61.

Seredy, Kate. *The Good Master*. 1935. New York: Puffin, 1963.

Set It Off. Dir. Gary Gray. Perf. Jada Pinkett, Queen Latifah, Vivica A. Fox, Kimberly Elise, Blair Underwood. New Line, 1996.

Seymour, Nicole. "Anti-male slogans miss the point." *The Daily Bruin*. http://www .dailybruin.ucla.edu/news/articles.asp?id=1607 (accessed 24 October 2000).

Sherman, Sarah Way. *Sarah Orne Jewett, An American Persephone*. Hanover: U of New England P, 1989.

Shockley, Ann Allen. *Loving Her*. 1974. Boston: Northeastern UP, 1997.

Shoemaker, Nancy. *A Strange Likeness: Becoming Red and White in Eighteenth-Century North America*. New York: Oxford UP, 2004.

Siegel, Deborah. "Nancy Drew as New Girl Wonder: Solving It All for the 1930s." *Nancy Drew and Company: Culture, Gender, and Girls' Series*. Ed. Sherrie A. Inness. Bowling Green, OH: Bowling Green U Popular Press, 1997. 159–182.

Sigoloff, Marc. *The Films of the Seventies: A Filmography of American, British and Canadian Films, 1970–1979*. Jefferson, NC: MacFarland, 1984.

Silva, Noenoe K. *Aloha Betrayed: Native Hawaiian Resistance to American Colonialism*. Durham, NC: Duke UP, 2004.

———. "*He Kanawai E Ho'opau I Na Hula Kuolo Hawai'i*: The Political Economy of Banning the Hula," in *The Hawaiian Journal of History*. 34. (2000): 29–48.

Silverthorne, Elizabeth. *Sarah Orne Jewett: A Writer's Life*. New York: Overlook Press, 1993.

Sim, F. L. "Alice Mitchell and the Murder of Freda Ward." *Gay American History: Lesbians and Gay Men in the U.S.A.* 1976. Ed. Jonathan Ned Katz. New York: Meridian, 1992. 53–58.

Simon, Rita J., ed. *Sporting Equality: Title IX Thirty Years Later*. Somerset, NJ: Transaction Publishers, 2005.

Sklar, Robert. *The Plastic Age, 1917–1930*. New York: George Braziller, 1970.

Slote, Bernice. *The Kingdom of Art: Willa Cather's First Principles and Critical Statements, 1893–1896*. Lincoln: U of Nebraska P, 1966.

Smith-Rosenberg, Carroll. *Disorderly Conduct: Visions of Gender in Victorian America*. New York: A. A. Knopf, 1985.

Smith-Rosenberg, Carroll, and Charles Rosenberg. "The Female Animal: Medical and Biological Views of Woman and Her Role in Nineteenth-Century America." *Journal of American History*. LX.2 (September 1973).

Snedeker, Caroline Dale. *Downright Dencey*. Garden City, NY: Doubleday, 1927.

Snow, Malinda. "'That One Talent': Vocation as Theme in Sarah Orne Jewett's *A Country Doctor*." *Colby Library Quarterly*. 16 (1980): 138–147.

Sollors, Werner. *Beyond Ethnicity: Consent and Descent in American Culture*. New York: Oxford UP, 1986.

———. *Neither Black, Nor White, Yet Both: Thematic Explorations of Interracial Literature*. Cambridge: Harvard UP, 1997.

Some Kind of Wonderful. Dir. Howard Deutch. Perf. Eric Stolz, Lea Thompson, Mary Stuart Masterson, Craig Sheffer, John Ashton. Paramount, 1987.

Somerville, Siobhan B. *Queering the Color Line: Race and the Invention of Homosexuality in American Culture*. Durham, NC: Duke UP, 2000.

Southworth, E. D. E. N. *The Deserted Wife*. 1849. Philadelphia: T. B. Peterson and Brothers, 1875.

———. *The Discarded Daughter*. Philadelphia: A. Hart, 1852.

———. *The Fatal Marriage*. Philadelphia: T. B. Peterson and Brothers, 1863.

———. *The Hidden Hand*. 1888. New Brunswick, NJ: Rutgers UP, 1988.

———. *The Lost Heiress*. Philadelphia: T. B. Peterson and Brothers, 1853.

———. *The Three Beauties*. Philadelphia: T. B. Peterson and Brothers, 1858.

———. *Vivia; or, The Secret of Power*. Philadelphia: T. B. Peterson and Brothers, 1857.

Spencer, Colin. *Homosexuality in History*. New York: Harcourt Brace, 1995.

Spinelli, Jerry. *Who Put That Hair in the My Toothbrush?* New York: Scholastic, 1984.

Spitfire. Dir. John Cromwell. Perf. Katharine Hepburn, Robert Young. Turner Home Entertainment, 1934.

St. Germain, Amos. "The Flowering of Mass Society: A Historical Overview of the 1920s." *Dancing Fools and Weary Blues: The Great Escape of the Twenties.* Ed. Lawrence R. Broer and John D. Walther. Bowling Green, OH: Bowling GreenUP, 1990. 13–44.

Stenn, David. *Clara Bow: Runnin' Wild.* New York: Doubleday, 1988.

Stepin, Nancy. "Biological Degeneration: Races and Proper Places." *Degeneration: The Dark Side of Progress.* Ed. J. Edward Chamberlain and Sander Gilman. New York: Columbia UP, 1985. 97–120.

Stern, Madeleine. "Introduction." *Louisa May Alcott Unmasked: Collected Thrillers.* Boston: Northeastern UP, 1995. xi–xxix.

Stoddard, Elizabeth. *The Morgesons.* 1862. New York: Penguin, 1984.

Stoddard, Lothrop. *The Rising Tide of Color Against White World Supremacy.* New York: Scribner, 1921.

Stowe, Harriet Beecher. *Uncle Tom's Cabin.* 1852. New York: Signet, 1966.

Streeby, Shelley. *American Sensations: Class, Empire and the Production of Popular Culture.* Berkeley: U of California P, 2002.

Some Tomboy. Dir. Edward Ludwig. Perf. Wanda Wiley and Harry McCoy. Century Film Corporation, 1924.

"Sugar and Spice." Narr. Victoria Corderi. *Dateline NBC.* 14 April 1995. Transcript.

"A Symposium of Eminent Doctors on How to Be Healthy at All Ages." *Strand Magazine.* XXXI. February 1906: 297–308.

Sundquist, Eric J. *To Wake the Nations: Race in the Making of American Literature.* Cambridge: Harvard UP, 1993.

Swing Time. Dir. George Stevens. Perf. Fred Astaire, Ginger Rogers, Victor Moore, and Helen Broderick. Turner Home Entertainment, 1936.

Sylvia Scarlett. Dir. George Cukor. Perf. Katharine Hepburn, Cary Grant, Brian Aherne. Turner Home Entertainment, 1936.

Tammy and the Bachelor. Dir. Joseph Pevney. Perf. Debbie Reynolds, Walter Brennan, Leslie Nielsen. MCA, 1957.

Takaki, Ronald. *Double Victory: A Multicultural History of America in World War II.* Boston: Little, Brown and Company, 2000.

Tank Girl. Dir. Rachel Talalay. Perf. Lori Petty, Malcolm McDowell, Ice-T. MGM, 1995.

Tellefsen, Blythe. "Blood in the Wheat: Willa Cather's *My Antonia.*" *Studies in American Fiction.* 27.2 (Autumn 1999): 229–244.

Terminator 2: Judgment Day. Dir. James Cameron. Perf. Arnold Schwarzenegger, Linda Hamilton, Edward Furlong, Robert Patrick. Canal 1991.

Tess of Storm Country. Dir. John S. Robertson. Perf. Mary Pickford, Lloyd Hughes, Gloia Hope. Image Entertainment, 1922.

Thomson, Rosemarie Garland. *Extraordinary Bodies: Figuring Physical Disability in American Culture and Literature.* New York: Columbia UP, 1997.

Three of Hearts. Dir. Yurek Bogayevicz. Perf. Willian Baldwin, Kelly Lynch, Sherilyn Fenn. New Line, 1993.

Tilchen, Maida. "Ann Bannon: The Mystery Solved!" *Gay Community News.* 8 (January 1938): 8–12.

Times Square. Dir. Allan Moyle. Perf. Tim Curry, Trini Alvarado, Robin Johnson, Peter Coffield, Herbert Bergof, Miguel Pinero, Elizabeth Pena. Associated Films, 1980.

Toll, Robert C. *Blacking Up: The Minstrel Show in Nineteenth-Century America.* New York: Oxford UP, 1974.

"tom." *The Oxford English Dictionary.* 2nd ed. 1989.

"Tom." *The Oxford English Dictionary.* 2nd ed. 1989.

Tomboy. Dir. Herb Freed. Perf. Betsy Russell, Jerry Dinome, Eric Douglas. Crown International, 1980.

"tomboy." *The Oxford English Dictionary.* 2nd ed. 1989.

The Tomboy. Dir. Carl Harbaugh. Perf. Eileen Percy, Hal Cooley, Richard Cummins, Paul Kamp. Fox, 1921.

"tom cat." *The Oxford English Dictionary.* 2nd ed. 1989.

"tom'foolery." *The Oxford English Dictionary.* 2nd ed. 1989.

"Tommy." *The Oxford English Dictionary.* 2nd ed. 1989.

"tommy girl." *The Oxford English Dictionary.* 2nd ed. 1989.

Tompkins, Jane. *Sensational Designs: The Cultural Work of American Fiction, 1790–1860.* New York: Oxford UP, 1984.

"The Top Grossing Films of 1973." *Variety.* 8 May 1974: 69.

"Topsy." *The Oxford English Dictionary.* 2nd ed. 1989.

"topsy-turvy." *The Oxford English Dictionary.* 2nd ed. 1989.

Torgovnick, Marianna. *Gone Primitive: Savage Intellects, Modern Lives.* Chicago: U of Chicago P, 1990.

———. *Primitive Passions: Men, Women, and the Quest for Ecstasy.* New York: Alfred A. Knopf, 1997.

Torres, Tereska. *Women's Barracks.* New York: Fawcett Gold Medal, 1950.

"transsexual." *The Oxford English Dictionary.* 2nd ed. 1989.

Trask, Haunani-Kay. *From a Native Daughter: Colonialism and Sovereignty in Hawai'i.* Rev. ed. Honolulu: U of Hawai'i P, 1999.

Turner, Frederick Jackson. "The Significance of the Frontier in American History." *The Turner Thesis: Concerning the Role of the Frontier in American History.* 3rd ed. Ed. George Rogers Taylor. Lexington, MA: D. C. Heath and Company, 1972. 3–28.

Twain, Mark. "Hellfire Hotchkiss." wr. 1897. *Mark Twain's Satires and Burlesques.* Ed. Franklin R. Rogers. Berkeley: U of California P, 1967. 172–203.

"ukulele." *The Oxford English Dictionary.* 2nd ed. 1989.

United States Census Bureau. Index of Population. Fertility and Family Statistics Branch. *MS-1: National Status of the Population Over 15 Years Sex and Race 1950–Present.* June 2005. <http://www.census.gov/population/socdemo/hh-fam/ms1.pdf> (accessed 20 December 2005). .

Vallone, Lynne. *Disciplines of Virtue: Girls' Culture in the Eighteenth and Nineteenth Centuries.* New Haven, CT: Yale UP, 1995.

Van Nuys, Frank. *Americanizing the West: Race, Immigrants, and Citizenship, 1890–1930.* Lincoln: U of Nebraska P, 2002.

Van Vechten, Carl. *Nigger Heaven.* 1926. Urbana: U of Illinois Press, 2000.

Vaughan, Alden T. "From White Man to Redskin: Changing Anglo-American Perceptions of the American Indians." *American History Review.* 87 (1982): 917–954.

Vertinsky, Patricia. *The Eternally Wounded Woman: Women, Doctors and Exercise in the Late Nineteenth Century.* Urbana: U of Illinois P, 1989.

The Violent Years. 1956. Dir. William M. Morgan. Perf. Jean Moorhead, Barbara Weeks, Arthur Milan. Something Weird Video, 2001.

Voight, Cynthia. *Jackaroo.* New York: Scholastic, Inc., 1985.

Wade, Valerie. "As Tatum Turns Ten, Ryan's Daughter Is Ready for Her Body to Catch Up with Her Mind." *Rolling Stone.* 19 July 1973: 28–31.

Wagenknecht, Edward. *Willa Cather.* New York: Continuum, 1994.

Walk on the Wild Side. Dir. Edward Dmytryk. Perf. Laurence Harvey, Capucine, Jane Fonda, Barbara Stanwyck. Sony, 1962.

Walker, Lisa. *Looking Like What You Are: Sexual Style, Race, and Lesbian Identity.* New York: New York UP, 2001.

Walters, Ronald G. "Introduction." *A Black Woman's Odyssey through Russia and Jamaica: A Narrative of Nancy Prince.* By Nancy Prince. Princeton, NJ: Markus Wiener Publishers, 1990. ix–xxiii.

Walters, Suzanna Danuta. "As Her Hand Crept Slowly Up Her Thigh: Ann Bannon and the Politics of Pulp." *Social Text.* 23 (Fall-Winter 1989): 83–101.

Warde, Margaret. *Betty Wales, Sophomore: A Story for Girls*. Philadelphia: The Penn Publishing Co., 1909.

Warner, Susan. *The Wide, Wide World*. 1850. New York: The Feminist Press, 1987.

The Watermelon Woman. Dir. Cheryl Dunye. Perf. Cheryl Dunye, Guinevere Turner, Valarie Walker. Dancing Girl/First Run Features, 1996.

Weir, James B. "The Effect of Female Suffrage on Posterity." *American Naturalist*. (September 1895): 815–828.

Wells, Helen. *Cherry Ames, Army Nurse*. 1944. New York: Springer, 2006.

———. *Cherry Ames, Chief Nurse*. 1944. New York: Springer, 2006.

———. *Cherry Ames, Student Nurse*. 1943. New York: Springer, 2006.

Welter, Barbara. *Dimity Convictions: The American Woman in the Nineteenth Century*. Athens, OH: Ohio UP, 1976.

Westling, Louise. "Tomboys and Revolting Femininity." *Critical Essays on Carson McCullers*. Ed. Beverly Lyon Clark & Melvin J. Friedman. New York: G. K. Hall and Co., 1996. 155–165.

Wheeler, Edward. Deadwood Dick Series. New York: Beadle and Adams, 1877–1885.

When Night is Falling. Dir. Patricia Rozema. Perf. Pascale Bussières, Rachel Crawford, Henry Czerny. October Films, 1995.

"white." *The Oxford English Dictionary*. 2nd ed. 1989.

White, Barbara A. *Growing Up Female: Adolescent Girlhood in American Fiction*. Westport, CT: Greenwood, 1985.

White, Gwen. *European and American Dolls, and Their Marks and Patents*. London: B. T. Batsford Ltd., 1966.

Whiteman, Paul and His Orchestra. "It's Only a Paper Moon." Recorded September 11th, 1933. *Original Soundtrack Recordings from the Paramount Picture Paper Moon*. LP. Paramount, 1973.

Whitman, Walt. "Pioneers! O Pioneers!." *Walt Whitman: The Complete Poems*. Ed. Francis Murphy. New York: Penguin, 2005. 257–260.

Whitt, Jan. "What Happened to Celie and Idgie?: 'Apparitional Lesbians' in American Film." *Studies in Popular Culture*. 27.3 (April 2005): 43–57.

Wiggin, Kate Douglas. *Rebecca of Sunnybrook Farm*. 1903. New York: Penguin, 1985.

Wikholm, Andrew. *Gay American History*. 2000. <http://www.gayhistory.com/> (accessed 10 August 2005).

Wilder, Laura Ingalls. *By the Shores of Silver Lake*. 1939. New York: Harper Collins, 1971.

———. *Farmer Boy*. 1933. New York: Harper Collins, 1971.

———. *The First Four Years*. New York: Harper Collins, 1971.

———. *Little House in the Big Woods*. 1932. New York: Harper Collins, 1971.

———. *Little House on the Prairie*. 1935. New York: Harper Collins, 1971.

———. *Little Town on the Prairie*. 1941. New York: Harper Collins, 1971.

———. *The Long Winter*. 1940. New York: Harper Collins, 1971.

———. *On the Banks of Plum Creek*. 1937. New York: Harper Collins, 1971.

———. *These Happy Golden Years*. 1943. New York: Harper Trophy, 1971.

Williams, William Carlos. "Man Orchard." *Massachusetts Review*. (Winter 1973): 77–117.

Williamson, Joel. *The Crucible of Race: Black/White Relations in the American South Since Emancipation*. New York: Oxford UP, 1984.

———. *A Rage for Order: Black/White Relations in the American South Since Emancipation*. New York: Oxford UP, 1986.

Willsey, Alice. *Tomboy Ranch*. Washington, D.C.: Review and Herald Publishing Asn, 1981.

Wilson, Harriet. *Our Nig; or, Sketches from the Life of a Free Black*. 1859. New York: Vintage, 1983.

Wilson, Leanna. *His Tomboy Bride*. New York: Silhouette, 1998.

Without Love. Dir. Harold S. Bucquet. Perf. Katherine Hepburn, Spencer Tracy, Lucille Ball. MGM/UA, 1945.

Wolf, Naomi. "The Racism of Well-Meaning White People." *Skin Deep: Black Women and White Women Write About Race*. Ed. Marita Golden and Susan Richards Shreve. New York: Anchor, 1995. 37–46.

Woman of the Year. Dir. George Stevens. Perf. Spencer Tracy, Katharine Hepburn, Fay Bainter, Dan Tobin. Warner Brothers, 1942.

Wood, Ann Douglas. "'The Fashionable Diseases': Women's Complaints and Their Treatments in Nineteenth-Century America." *Clio's Consciousness Raised*. Ed. Mary Hartman and Lois W. Banner. New York: Harper, 1974.

Woodress, James. *Willa Cather: A Literary Life*. Lincoln: U of Nebraska P, 1987.

Work. Dir. Rachel Reichman. Perf. Geordie White, Heather Murphy, Cynthia Kaplan. 1996.

"World War I Armed Forces and Casualties by Country." *Facts About the 20ᵗʰ Century*. Eds. George Ochoa and Melinda Corey. New York: H. W. Wilson, 2001. 358.

Wray, Matt, and Annalee Newitz. *White Trash: Race and Class in America*. New York: Taylor and Francis, 1997.

Wyeth, Sharon Dennis. *Tomboy Trouble*. New York: Random House, 1998.

Wynn, Neil A. *The Afro-American and the Second World War*. Rev. ed. New York: Holmes and Meier, 1993.

Yamaguchi, Lynne, and Karen Barber. Introduction. *Tomboys!: Tales of Dyke Derring-Do*. Ed. Lynne Yamaguchi and Karen Barber. Los Angeles: Alyson, 1995. 9–14.

Young, Elizabeth. *Disarming the Nation: Women's Writing and the American Civil War*. Chicago: U of Chicago P, 1999.

Yusuba, Roberta. "Twilight Tales: Lesbian Pulps 1950–1960." *On Our Backs*. Summer, 1985.

Zagarell, Sandra A. "*Country*'s Portrayal of Community and Exclusion of Difference." *New Essays on The Country of the Pointed Firs*. Ed. June Howard. Cambridge: Cambridge UP, 1994. 39–60.

Zehr, Janet. "The Response of Nineteenth-Century Audiences to Louisa May Alcott's Fiction." *American Transcendental Quarterly*. 1.4 (1987): 323–342.

Zettsu, Tomoyuki. "Slavery, Song and the South: Cather's Reconfiguration of Stowe and Foster in *A Lost Lady*." *Arizona Quarterly: A Journal of American Literature, Culture, and Theory*. 52.2 (1996): 87–104.

Zevy, Lee. "Sexing the Tomboy." *Sissies and Tomboys: Gender Nonconformity and Homosexual Childhood*. Ed. Matthew Rottnek. New York: New York UP, 1999. 180–195.

Zitkala-Sa. "A Warrior's Daughter." *American Indian Stories*. 1921. Lincoln: U of Nebraska, 1985. 137–54.

Index